The Bauman Reader

BLACKWELL READERS

In a number of disciplines, across a number of decades, and in a number of languages, writers and texts have emerged which require the attention of students and scholars around the world. United only by a concern with radical ideas, Blackwell Readers collect and introduce the works of pre-eminent theorists. Often translating works for the first time (Levinas, Irigaray, Lyotard, Blanchot, Kristeva), or presenting material previously inaccessible (C.L.R. James, Fanon, Elias), each volume in the series introduces and represents work which is now fundamental to study in the humanities and social sciences.

The Lyotard Reader
Edited by Andrew Benjamin

The Irigaray Reader
Edited by Margaret Whitford

The Kristeva Reader
Edited by Toril Moi

The Levinas Reader
Edited by Sean Hand

The C.L.R. James Reader
Edited by Anna Grimshaw

The Wittgenstein Reader
Edited by Anthony Kenny

The Blanchot Reader
Edited by Michael Holland

The Elias Reader
Edited by Stephen Mennell

The Lukács Reader
Edited by Arpad Kardakay

The Cavell Reader
Edited by Stephen Mulhall

The Guattari Reader
Edited by Garry Genosko

The Bataille Reader
Edited by Fred Botting and Scott Wilson

The Eagleton Reader
Edited by Stephen Regan

The Castoriadis Reader
Edited by David Ames Curtis

The Goffman Reader
Edited by Charles Lemert and Ann Branaman

The Frege Reader
Edited by Michael Beaney

The Virilio Reader
Edited by James Der Derian

The Hegel Reader
Edited by Stephen Houlgate

The Norbert Elias Reader
Edited by Johan Goudsblom and Stephen Mennell

The Angela Y. Davis Reader
Edited by Joy James

The Stanley Fish Reader
Edited by H. Aram Veeser

The Žižek Reader
Edited by Elizabeth Wright and Edmond Wright

The Talcott Parsons Reader
Edited by Bryan S. Turner

The Certeau Reader
Edited by Graham Ward

The Adorno Reader
Edited by Brian O'Connor

The Jameson Reader
Edited by Michael Hardt and Kathi Weeks

The Bauman Reader
Edited by Peter Beilharz

The Bauman Reader

Edited by
Peter Beilharz

Copyright © Zygmunt Bauman 2001; editorial matter and organization copyright ©
Peter Beilharz 2001

First published 2001

2 4 6 8 10 9 7 5 3 1

Blackwell Publishers Inc.
350 Main Street
Malden, Massachusetts 02148
USA

Blackwell Publishers Ltd
108 Cowley Road
Oxford OX4 1JF
UK

Library of Congress Cataloging-in-Publication Data

The Bauman reader / edited by Peter Beilharz.
    p. cm.—(Blackwell readers)
    Includes bibliographical references and index.
    ISBN 0-631-21491-7 (alk. paper)—ISBN 0-631-21492-5 (pbk. : alk. paper)
    1. Postmodernism—Social aspects.   2. Bauman, Zygmunt. I. Beilharz,
Peter. II. Series.

   HM449.B38   2000
   301—dc21   00-022947

British Library Cataloguing in Publication Data
A CIP catalogue record for this book is available from the British Library.

Typeset in 10.5pt on 12pt Sabon-Roman
by Kolam Information Services Pvt Ltd, Pondicherry, India
Printed in Great Britain by TJ International Ltd, Padstow, Cornwall

This book is printed on acid-free paper.

Contents

Preface

Zygmunt Bauman has an almost ubiquitous presence in contemporary social theory – often textually in the margins, but substantively central to the currents and disputes that animate argument about modernity. The content of his work is both reactive and innovative. Its form varies; Bauman does not always make too many concessions to readers, for the point of his work is that we each must learn to think for ourselves, even if there are great riches already available to us, to help us along the way in the traditions we inhabit. So where to begin reading Bauman?

The purpose of this Reader is to offer a possible way in and to provide a survey of his contribution. Zygmunt Bauman said to me as I took on the task that my challenge was to put order into chaos. I do not think that his work is chaotic, though it is sometimes unpredictable; at other times it returns to older problems, for as Bauman says, we never really solve problems in social theory, we only become bored with them. If Bauman's work is less chaotic than nonsystematic, then my task in this book is less to order than to profile. To mash Bauman's work into bite-size chunks would be to do violence to his intention; for if Bauman does not bite, he does provoke. Consequently two major concerns have guided the choice of selections offered here. I have endeavored both to include selections which are indicative of the breadth and width of Bauman's thinking, while at the same time choosing especially those whose prose form best carries these arguments.

I have excluded his early Polish writing and his earlier English language work such as *Between Class and Elite*, *Towards a Critical Sociology* and *Culture as Praxis*, the latter just reprinted as a second edition by Sage. I have omitted more monographic, or purpose-specific books such as *Freedom* and *Thinking Sociologically*, and also important but more difficult and abstract recent work such as *Postmodern Ethics* and *Mortality, Immortality and Other Life-Strategies*.

Readers whose curiosities might take them to the library are welcome to pursue these titles; they are also discussed in my companion volume, *Zygmunt Bauman – Dialectic of Modernity*, published coterminously with this volume, by Sage. The selections here, then, are biased towards Bauman's incredible output into and after *Legislators and Interpreters* in 1987; but the volume also attempts to gesture back to Bauman's major contributions before then.

The materials in this Reader are grouped thematically as follows. The volume opens and closes with preparatory pieces, including two interviews with Bauman, the first published in English originally by *Telos* in 1992, the second conducted especially for this volume by me. The *Telos* interview is anticipated by a provisional editorial survey of Bauman's work. The thematic structure for the Readings that follow from chapter 3 to chapter 10 has emerged through the process of interpretation itself. Chapter 3 includes excerpts from Bauman's great 1976 study of utopia, as well as an essay on marxism from 1968 and his postmortem for communism, itself a symbolic marker in its own way of the end of modernity as marxism. Chapter 4 includes the prospectus for *Memories of Class*, which in many ways foreshadows the turn into postmarxism and the postmodern, and also includes some of the major claims of *Legislators and Interpreters*. Chapter 5, on Hermeneutics and Critical Theory, includes Bauman's introduction to *Hermeneutics and Social Science* and two beautifully condensed dictionary entries, one each on critical theory and on modernity; chapter 5 thus covers parallel theoretical lives. The sixth chapter offers Bauman's major statements on postmodern sociology or the sociology of postmodernity; also included is the lucid and powerfully written introduction to *Intimations of Postmodernity*, a piece which gets as close as Bauman might to a postmodern manifesto. Chapter 7, Figures of Modernity, brings together some vignettes of strangers, parvenus and pariahs; these illustrate the concern which Bauman takes on from Weber and more particularly from Simmel, with the question what kind of personalities modernity (or postmodernity) makes. Chapter 8, the Century of Camps, includes some basic introductory elements of *Modernity and the Holocaust*, as well as his critical review of *Dictatorship Over Needs* and his reflections on the Gulag and modernity. Chapter 9 profiles the basic arguments of *Modernity and Ambivalence* and anticipates the nature of the sociological concern with postmodern ethics. The final selections, in chapter 10, cover globalization and its exclusionary class consequences. The structure of the selections is therefore circular, but it also cross-references, in the sense that, for example, socialism occurs in chapters 3 and 8, or strangers figure in chapters 7 and 9; as Bauman says, the problems themselves do not go away, it is we who as interpreters become weary and shift on. Hopefully, then his readers here can step into the water at any point, returning, or visiting for the first time the thinking of the most significant sociologist writing in English today.

My thanks, in this process, go first to Zygmunt and Janina Bauman, whose friendship and inspiration I value; to Jill Landeryou, Susan Rabinowitz and Ken Provencher at Blackwell Publishers and to their readers, for enthusiasm and patience; to Anthony Grahame for fastidious help with preparing the manuscript for publication; to the participants in my 1997 Honours Seminar in Sociology at La Trobe, on Bauman's work, for clarification; to Fuyuki Kurasawa, for comments and for careful editorial assistance in assembling the volume; and to Bron, Merle and Elaine, for making scribble into words. As this is a personal road, too, this kind of self-imposed exile which Bauman describes as writing, my thanks to Dor, Nik and Rhea, who are always there to catch me when I fall.

Peter Beilharz
Harvard
December 1999

Acknowledgments

The publishers and editor wish to thank the following for permission to reprint copyright material in this book:

Zygmunt Bauman, "Modernity, Postmodernity and Ethics – An Interview with Zygmunt Bauman," *Telos* 93 (1992);

Zygmunt Bauman, "The Historical Location of Socialism," from *Socialism: The Active Utopia* (Allen & Unwin, 1976, reprinted courtesy of Routledge);

Zygmunt Bauman, "Modern Times, Modern Marxism," *Social Research* 34, 3 (1967);

Zygmunt Bauman, "Communism, A Postmortem," from *Intimations of Postmodernity* (Routledge, London, 1992);

Zygmunt Bauman, "Class: Before and After," from *Memories of Class: The Pre-History and After-Life of Class* (Routledge and Kegan Paul, London, 1982);

Zygmunt Bauman, "Gamekeepers Turned Gardeners," from *Legislators and Interpreters: On Modernity, Post-Modernity and Intellectuals* (Polity Press, Cambridge, 1987 and Cornell University Press, Copyright Clearance Center);

Zygmunt Bauman, "The Rise of the Interpreter," from *Legislators and Interpreters: On Modernity, Post-Modernity and Intellectuals* (Polity Press, Cambridge, 1987 and Cornell University Press, Copyright Clearance Center);

Zygmunt Bauman, "The Challenge of Hermeneutics," from *Hermeneutics and Social Science: Approaches to Understanding* (Hutchinson, London, 1978);

Zygmunt Bauman, "Critical Theory," from Henry Etzkowitz and Ronald M. Glassman (eds.), *The Renascence of Sociological Theory: Classical and Contemporary* (F. E. Peacock, Itasca, IL, 1991);

Zygmunt Bauman, "Modernity," from Joel Krieger (ed.), *The Oxford Companion to Politics of the World* (Oxford University Press,

Oxford and New York 1993. Copyright © 1993 by Oxford University Press, Inc. Used by permission of Oxford University Press, Inc.);

Zygmunt Bauman, "A Sociological Theory of Postmodernity," *Thesis Eleven* 29 (1991);

Zygmunt Bauman, "The Re-Enchantment of the World, or, How Can One Narrate Postmodernity," from *Intimations of Postmodernity* (Routledge and Kegan Paul, London, 1992);

Zygmunt Bauman, "Making and Unmaking of Strangers," *Thesis Eleven* 43 (1995);

Zygmunt Bauman, "Parvenu and Pariah: The Heroes and Victims of Modernity," from *Postmodernity and Its Discontents* (Polity Press, Cambridge, 1997);

Zygmunt Bauman, "Sociology After the Holocaust," from *Modernity and the Holocaust* (Polity Press, Cambridge, 1989 and Cornell University Press, Copyright Clearance Center);

Zygmunt Bauman, "Modernity, Racism, Extermination," from *Modernity and the Holocaust* (Polity Press, Cambridge, 1989 and Cornell University Press, Copyright Clearance Center);

Zygmunt Bauman, "Dictatorship Over Needs," *Telos* 60 (1984), reprinted by courtesy of Telos Press Limited;

Zygmunt Bauman, "A Century of Camps?," from *Life in Fragments: Essays in Postmodern Morality* (Blackwell Publishers, Oxford, 1995);

Zygmunt Bauman, "The Quest for Order," from *Modernity and Ambivalence* (Polity Press, Cambridge, 1991, Cornell University Press, Copyright Clearance Center);

Zygmunt Bauman, "The Social Construction of Ambivalence," from *Modernity and Ambivalence* (Polity Press, Cambridge, 1991, Cornell University Press, Copyright Clearance Center);

Zygmunt Bauman, "On Globalization: Or Globalization for Some, Localization for Some Others," *Thesis Eleven* 54 (1998);

Zygmunt Bauman, "From the Work Ethic to the Aesthetic of Consumption," from *Work, Consumerism and the New Poor* (Open University Press, Buckingham, 1998).

1

Introduction by Peter Beilharz: Reading Zygmunt Bauman

Who is Zygmunt Bauman? The greatest sociologist writing in English today lives in Leeds and watches Polish television by satellite. He travels widely and writes at a blistering pace. His works are in everybody's footnotes but, to use a characteristic term, the thinking is slippery, as difficult as it is powerful, puzzling, provocative. As a result, a figure as prominent as Tony Giddens can describe Bauman as the preeminent theorist of the postmodern, and yet there is very little by way of commentary or elucidation on Bauman's work. For as well as following the strategy of provocation, Bauman's sociology eschews the systemic; it pursues the fragment, and it resists the modular, have I got a theory for you mentality which is the key to publishing and academic success. So many readers and writers know about Bauman, yet the silence, and the awkwardness of it, are powerful. Ian Varcoe and Richard Kilminister have fired across it in their Festschrift, *Culture, Modernity and Revolution, Essays in Honour of Zygmunt Bauman* (Varcoe and Kilminister, 1996); but with due respect, the essays in that volume tend to tell us more about the interpreters than the interpreted; this is a collection which fails to generate critical foci, but spreads out, as does the canvas which Bauman works upon. Shaun Best, meantime, has exposed Bauman as a postmodern fraud, a modernist wolf in the sheep's clothing of postmodernism, which is quite an achievement. But he gets it wrong on both points (Best, 1998). Bauman's work is translated into an incredible array of languages; its influence is apparent in applied work like Brian Cheyette's, on the Jew, and Bülent Diken's, on Turks in Denmark (Cheyette, 1998; Diken, 1998). Other beginnings of recognition have been sighted across the Atlantic, where Bauman remains even more marginal, in Steven Seidman's book *Contested Knowledge* (Seidman, 1995). The

English presence is also evident in particular local responses such as Scott Lash's reply to Bauman's critique of communitarianism (Lash, 1996) or in David Torevell's essay on rationalism in *New Blackfriars* (Torevell, 1995), while Hans Joas and Dennis Smith have both written in appreciation of Bauman's work in *Theory Culture and Society*. Dennis Smith is working on an intellectual sociology of Bauman, which will indeed be welcome. I have myself recently finished a study entitled *Zygmunt Bauman: Dialectic of Modernity* (and see Beilharz, 1998a, 1998b). And the present *Reader* is also part of a growing program of publicity and recognition for Bauman's work.

Watching the Detectives

So why the fuss? What's the puzzle? For the average punter in social theory, I'd guess, there are perhaps two key signs of Bauman's contribution. The first is *Modernity and the Holocaust* (1989), one book by Bauman which has broken the silence even though with difficulty, for Bauman's message there inter alia is that the pertinence of the Holocaust for sociology is central, not a message most sociologists would care to hear. The second, I think, is to be located in Bauman's work on the postmodern. For Bauman is quite widely thought of as the postmodern sociologist, though as I shall suggest here, this is only half the story; the other half of the postmodern is the modern, and this is why it is ambivalence, rather than "the postmodern," which is the core value in Bauman's work. These, in any case, I suggest, are a recognizable signs people would readily associate with Bauman: Holocaust, and postmodern. Only given the centrality of hermeneutics to his way of thinking, each concept leads to another; Holocaust to sociology, modernity and ethics; postmodern to modern, and especially to Marxism and postmarxism, and so it goes on, freedom leading to dependence, proletarian to consumer, tourist to vagabond, interpreter to legislator, morality to ethics . . . Bauman insists on following the conversational image of interpretation and understanding, which is surely one reason his readers are both attracted and irritated, for he both pokes you in the eye and expects you to follow through, to stay awhile, and ponder, talk, and listen.

The purpose of critical sociology, indeed, is to poke you in the eye, not to massage. For in order to do sociology, we need both to feel sufficiently confident about our own places in the world, and sufficiently detached to view the familiar as though it were exotic, or at least contingent. We should never make peace with dogma, even though it is in our nature always to do so, to universalize the particular, to hypostasize the incidental. These kinds of problems are both more acute and more hilarious in the practice of sociology than elsewhere, as it is the claim of our discipline to be self-reflective, to include self-scrutiny as well as the critique of others. Bauman's voice is often friendly, but it is uncompromising in the demands that it makes upon the reader as reader and as ethical actor. For ultimately it is actors who are responsible for the human condition. This is one theme that stretches across Bauman's work.

The list of Bauman's achievements, when registered, is somewhat more sustained than the reader enthusiasm for the Holocaust or the postmodern might suggest. In English, and referring to books alone, the list reaches nineteen: *Between Class and Elite* (1972); *Culture as Praxis* (1973); *Socialism – The Active Utopia* (1976a), *Towards a Critical Sociology* (1976b), *Hermeneutics and Social Science* (1978), *Memories of Class* (1982), *Legislators and Interpreters* (1987), *Freedom* (1988), *Modernity and the Holocaust* (1989), *Thinking Sociologically* (1990), *Modernity and Ambivalence* (1991a), *Mortality, Immortality and Other Life Strategies* (1992a), *Intimations of Postmodernity* (1992b), *Postmodern Ethics* (1993), *Life in Fragments* (1995) and *Postmodernity and its Discontents* (1997). There are newer books on *Work, Consumerism and the New Poor*, and on globalization and glocalization, and on the search for politics; and then, of course, there are the essays, strewn widely across *Telos*, *Theory Culture and Society*, *Thesis Eleven* and elsewhere. We await a new title, *Liquid Modernity*, and there will be more to come, as though we will never catch up. Evidently Bauman's working strategy is to ingest whatever interests; this is a reactive project as well as an assertive one, so that most interesting topics come up sooner or later – eugenics, art, sexuality, criminology, capitalism, communism, the other. But this variety itself does not capture the lure of the thinking. For there are also other arcs which work through the writing, across certainty and order, marxism and the postmodern, socialism and sociology, the ambivalence which underlies all these.

The Plot Thickens

We all live, into the twentieth century and beyond, after Marx, and yet with Marx. Bauman's early Marxism was a rich cultural matrix, taking in Gramsci before his English-language invention as predecessor of the Birmingham School after 1968, but also linking Weber to Marx in that older tradition of critical theory for which Weber, Lukács, and Simmel are all equally fascinating. This latter attribute of Polish marxism meant that its substance was typically something like Weberian marxism, with a predominant critical curiosity directed to domination in general rather than class, alone, in particular. After all, the local ruling class in Poland and throughout central Europe were not capitalists: quite a puzzle, for orthodox marxists in English-speaking cultures. The critical presence of Marx, Weber, and Simmel can clearly be detected in an early essay like "Modern Times, Modern Marxism," published in *Social Research* in 1968. The critical tensions which this makes possible are intriguing. Thus the earlier English texts of Bauman such as *Socialism – The Active Utopia* can figure socialism as an other rather than as the mirror of production. Socialism is, as he puts it, the counterculture of modernity. Bauman knows Marxism as a rich combination of cultures, and this is one reason why he does not walk away from it after the fall of the Wall, or as he grows older; for if you leave it behind, it will follow you, like a shadow, or a stray. As I will argue later, the work of rethinking shifts on to the plane of the modern, so that Bauman's is the most interesting of postmodernisms available to us as postmarxisms. Bauman is uniquely well placed among postmoderns in that he does not begin conceptually from an economistic reduction of society or modernity. Culture is primary, even as marxism remains inevitable. Yet economy never disappears from his analysis either, and nor does suffering. Bauman's work thus evades the risk endemic to other approaches to the modern/postmodern divide, where either economy or culture is conceptually inflated at the expense of the other.

Some of Bauman's earlier writing in English now seems further away than other parts; its style is denser, and some of the authorities with whom he engages have disappeared into the dust of the libraries. Two clear hallmarks of his early work are socialism and culture; it only becomes more apparent later how these two are to be mediated, where culture leads into the discussion of the postmodern and socialism is historically relocated as a cultural moment within modernity which, in a sense, became its most aggressive proponent before Nazism showed us a secret of modernity that we still have difficulty facing up to (unless we choose perversely to celebrate the Holocaust as the truth of modernity, which leaves us with nothing at all to hope for or to aspire towards).

The turning point in Bauman's work here, I think, is to be located in the 1987 *Legislators and Interpreters*, but it is anticipated already in *Memories of Class* in 1982. The subtitle of *Memories of Class* already specifies its curiosities and basic themes: the pre-history and the afterlife of class. In this book Bauman extends his earliest interests in the configurations of British life and labor in the Industrial Revolution, developed in *Between Class and Elite*. *Memories of Class* works both axes, illustrating the way in which class talk is projected back by

Marxism upon formative, reactive struggles and forward, into the postwar period, when it is the outsiders rather than the proletariat who suffer exclusion from the corporatist political economy of Keynesian social democracy. The substance of Bauman's critique here concerns the economization of the world, the revaluing of all value in the image of the commodity-form and the insinuation of all in the consumption process. Memory, however, like utopia, points elsewhere. Socialism, in this context, is romantic rather than boosterist or modernizing; it remembers other ways, and different values (Bauman, 1982; Beilharz, 1992).

Memories of Class evokes the work of Edward Thompson and the social history revival of the seventies, but it is less the figure the forgotten stockinger than the elongated shadow of Michel Foucault which attracts attention here. Bauman aligns the historical sociology of Foucault à la *Discipline and Punish* with the work of Thompson et al. in order to draw attention to the corporeal regime of industrialism. Heidegger's critique of technology is in the margins of this book, as it is in Foucault's great work. Bentham, Marx, Foucault, and Thompson come together here in an argument about the political economy of capitalism, which is at the same time a new bodily and mental regime. Labor struggles were constructed against, rather than within, this regime in the beginning. Only by the twentieth century did labor celebrate its arrival as a systemic actor, prepared to heckle and barter over the spoils; and this, in turn, involves the slow transformation of a system of production into a system of consumption. The sociology of intellectuals also surfaces here, anticipating the development of the more substantial critique in *Legislators and Interpreters*. Who was it, that built this image of resistance to capitalism as incipient post-capitalism? Who was it, who cast the proletariat as stormers of heaven, and in whose interests? East European marxism had pioneered the critique of intellectuals as the new class, Milovan Djilas alongside Bruno Rizzi and James Burnham, and they refigured it via Konrad and Szelenyi's later work on *The Intellectuals on the Road to Class Power* (1979). The intellectuals had since Saint-Simon claimed to lead social development; the confirmation of technocracy and corporatism into the postwar period was in this sense nothing new. Marxism was part of the problem as well as part of the putative solution. The "problem," in turn, looked different, rather than the more of the same diagnosis of orthodox marxism. Yet Bauman's focus here was on the birth of factory, on modern or industrial culture rather than on the clinic or the school, and on its twentieth-century decline as the major site of social struggle or moral economy. All this was consistent with a Weberian Marxist sensibility that it was industrialism, rather than capitalism in the strict sense, which was the problem; only later was the argument to be further developed that consumption and desire would supplant production and the work ethic as dominant emerging social dynamics.

The Usual Suspects

Bauman did not cite him here, and indeed his major parallel work *Landscapes of Poverty* did not appear until 1985, but the resonances with the work of Jeremy Seabrook are powerful, and they were to emerge more fully in *Legislators and Interpreters*. Pauperization, on this view, is a modern perennial, but it is refigured historically, insiders and outsiders replacing bourgeoisie and proletariat as the working class became part of the system. Exclusion and domination thus remain the ethical concerns which hold up Bauman's sociology, alongside exploitation and consumerism, later, repression and seduction. In *Legislators and Interpreters* the emphasis shifts into the critique of Enlightenment, more explicitly of the Enlighteners; for the plotting of history as bourgeoisie versus proletariat in any case misses part of the action, and part of the problem of modernity. Modernity is a middle-class project, *par excellence*. And it is the intellectuals, or enlighteners, who manage to remain somehow invisible in the unfolding of this plot, given as they are to the representation of modernity's history as a populist battle between workers and bosses, managers and minions.

Modernity is a project, and not only a period, and it is, or was, a project of control, the rational mastery over nature, the planning, designing and plotting which led to planomania and technocracy (and, in a later phase of Bauman's work, to the Holocaust). Intellectuals *become* legislators, but in the process they forsake that part of their activity which is properly critical. The medium of the state is the field of this pretense and the site of its ambition. If modernity is the pursuit of a particular regime of order, however, then postmodernity involves pluralization. Modern intellectuals aspire to power, as legislators; postmodern intellectuals seek to live out, or to return? to their hermeneutical roles, as interpreters or translators across life-worlds or experiences. The suspects are close at hand. The problem, then, dear reader, is us. But more, the two modes mix, and necessarily so, for we are always ever animals of tradition. Thus modernity becomes a tradition, so that modernism, the desire to change the world, itself also becomes a habit, or at least a duty. The echoes here, among other things, are with the pragmatism of Richard Rorty, but without the complacency sometimes implied by that stance. Yet the critique of modernity emerging here remains more closely allied to Foucault and the issue of the power/knowledge syndrome, and Bauman extends the case by drawing on Ernest Gellner's work, for we are, in this view, gamekeepers turned gardeners, rapacious cultivators of the intellect and the world, developers all. Here the connection is to Freud, and to Elias, where civilization is the gain bought only through repression; civilization is also a loss. Habermas passes across this screen, diminishing in presence from the early writing to the late as his own work shifts from critique to construction, for it in turn to become part of the problem, as the hermeneutics of undistorted communication gives way in his work to the politics of system-building, so that second-generation critical theory is but one voice in Bauman's work. Indeed, the melancholy echo here is Adorno, or *Dialectic of Enlightenment,* alongside the middle-period Foucault, where much that moves is dangerous, for technology or instrumental reason reigns, and its intellectual advocates reign supreme. Yet Bauman ends his argument here with a conclusion entitled "Two Nations, Mark Two: The Repressed," per Disraeli, and per Seabrook, and he closes with two codas, one each modern and postmodern, to reiterate the sense that we are both, and both actually and potentially at that.

Legislators and Interpreters is the key text of transition in the project of transition which is Bauman's sociology. That project arrived, however, most visibly in *Modernity and the Holocaust,* doubtless Bauman's most influential book, and a symptomatic indication of the extent to which this postmodern theorist has profoundly modern identity crises. *Modernity and the Holocaust* is witness to Janina Bauman's inspiration of her husband, a story prosaically told with great power and beauty in her own books, *Winter in the Morning* (1986) and *A Dream of Belonging* (1988). Their work is symbiotic, as two essays copublished together in *Thesis Eleven* (1998) illustrate. Zygmunt Bauman's purpose in *Modernity and the Holocaust* is to confront sociologists, these proud bearers of the modern project, with the fact of the Holocaust as a consequence of modernity, not its dysfunction but its shocking result. Bauman explains here that having himself first viewed the Holocaust as the representation of a particular tragedy, he now came to view it as the frame of a view upon the world. The analytical consequence is profound, for the implication of this view is that the Holocaust expresses the particular path of German modernity, just as Fehér, Heller, and Markus argued in *Dictatorship Over Needs* (1982) that Stalinism was not a throwback or "residual," but a result of the project of an alternative, Soviet modernity. In other words, modernity is formed by the Holocaust, not just the other way around.

Modernity's Others

Bauman's analysis of the Holocaust is compelling, not least of all as it is suggestive of the later path into *Postmodern Ethics*, for one strong claim developed here concerns the substitution of morality (including Nazi morals) for ethical autonomy, which goes together with the substitution of scale and complexity for human proximity to the other, or others. The more general claim is that the Holocaust is neither a Jewish problem, nor an event in Jewish history alone; the Holocaust was born and executed in our modern, rational society and is therefore a problem of modernity itself. "The Holocaust was a characteristically modern phenomenon that cannot be understood out of the context of cultural tendencies and technical achievements of modernity" (1989: xiii), even though fascism itself is political and contingent. The contrast, say, with a popular controversial view like Daniel Goldhagen's in *Hitler's Willing Executioners* is apparent; Bauman, to simplify, sees nazism as a modern, rather than "German" accident waiting to happen.

For Bauman, the ethical worry is in and for all of us, not only Germans or Jews. We are all capable of this kind of monstrosity, increasingly so thanks to the wonders of technology and its enthusiastic servants. Sociology, in turn, also finds itself embarrassingly compromised in this, for it shares the zeal for social engineering with other scientific and social-scientific endeavors. Of course, modernity is not fascist, or totalitarian, but the Holocaust remains one possibility within it. Here, though, the argument again parallels *Dictatorship Over Needs*, for totalitarianism is viewed as a politically chosen imperative rather than as an economic logic or necessity. Before the Final Solution, there was Madagascar. Yet the politics of violence relies on a modern technological means of destruction, which in turn depends on scales of complexity that seem to deauthorize decision-making processes. The invisibility or social death of the Jews then becomes the prelude to elimination, as the Nazi model of modernity could simultaneously chase technological development and present elimination of the Jews as a synonym for the ideal rejection of modernism. Finally, the Nazis saw themselves as gardeners; their dreams were fuelled by traditionalistic fantasies of monocultural purity, so that modernity or a certain modernism became the main instrument of reactionary innovation.

Bauman's political purpose, however, is to get beyond Adorno's vision (or Goldhagen's) of a world divided into born proto-Nazis and their victims. Like Castoriadis, whose commitment to autonomy he shares, Bauman is interested in the dynamics which work between order-takers and order-givers and the gaps in between. How is geno-cide delivered, between the victims and the perpetrators, in a thou-sand smaller acts of compliance through the division of labor? How could so many people participate in evil? Here Bauman opens a vital issue, which then runs through to *Postmodern Ethics*. Why, and how, do individual actors comply with terror? Bauman deals, in passing, with the oversocialized conception of the subject associated in sociol-ogy with Durkheim. This part of his critique is especially devastating, given sociology's continued evasion of the question of the individual and individual responsibility. As Bauman argues, sociology's environ-mental kneejerk means that the problem of individual behavior is always referred somewhere else, to education, class, sex, culture, or whatever. The idea that individuals might choose, and that cons-equently evil is a choice rather than a "madness," is unavailable to them, to us. We have no ethics, only morals, no capacity to self-regulate, only road-drill rules to refer to.

It is on this theme that Bauman introduces into his work the pre-sence of Emmanuel Levinas and the image of recognition of the face of the other. I am uncertain as to what weight to give this presence in Bauman's work, especially now that Levinas has become the last refuge of theoretical redemption elsewhere. Certainly it could be observed that the influence, say, of Hans Jonas' ethics is ever-present in Bauman's work, and in general Bauman seems to use other thinkers as sources of stimulation rather than dependency. Heidegger's press-ence can certainly be felt in the arguments about framing, or the critique of technology, though the name appears less frequently per-haps in the texts than, say, Derrida's; but the project is not Derridean, either, as its echoes and sympathies are as various as its interests and ambivalences. Bauman uses Kafka, and Cioran, John Carroll and Baudrillard, Richard Sennett and Mary Douglas, Rorty and Gellner, Canetti and Attali, Bakhtin, Blanchot and Borges, de Certeau and Eco, Schopenhauer and Steiner, whatever sparks.

We could add to the list without thereby clarifying the issue. At times Bauman shows a deep affinity with the insights of Hannah Arendt, whether on the elision of the social and the political or on the ethical nature or presuppositions of totalitarianism. There are echoes of, and essays on, the work of Agnes Heller and Gillian Rose; there are signs of the mordant presence of Robert Musil, of Sartre and at the same time of Lévi-Strauss, whom Bauman employs as a cultural more than a structural anthropologist. Thinkers such as Castoriadis and Edgar Morin become lifesavers at particular moments. Bauman uses other peoples' ideas and his own life experience, ideas from Janina or from his architect-daughter Irena's experience in working with space, ideas from his newly reopened Polish boundaries on art or aesthetics. When I asked him once in conversation the inevitable, tedious academic question, what will you work on next? he said to me that he did not know; "I have not read anything interesting lately." Bauman's work is therefore more difficult to track, as it is less systematic than some other critical sociologists, certainly less predictable than Luhmann or Habermas. What is coming next? We do not know; for these are also postmodern times, when the desire to control intellectual creation is less manageable, or meaningful than before. Unpredictability rules; only this can be enabling as well as threatening.

Does Bauman then make a virtue of unpredictability, of chaos, of the wild, Dionysian alternative to Reason? This would be one possible logical conclusion open to us, if there were only one of two places to stand, with reason or with romanticism. The logic of Bauman's challenge to modernity, and to sociology, however is precisely to challenge these arbitrary choices and terms, which in itself of course is entirely reasonable; after all, the greatest romantics known to us, from Rousseau to Schiller to Marx, were advocates of reason as well. With the Viennese satirist Karl Kraus, Zygmunt Bauman would insist that if I have to be rationalist or romantic then I am neither. For like Kraus, Bauman is keen to pull our leg, to tease, to poke us in the eye, but not only in jest, or in some more predictable show of intellectual petulance; he wants also to remind us that these are words we have ourselves produced to control our senses of tradition, that they are as arbitrary and as exotic as any such binary categories that we might meet constructed by our pith-helmeted predecessors in colonial anthropology, or in any modernist museum.

Alles in Ordnung

Ambivalence, I indicated earlier, seems to be one key theme in Bauman's sociology. *Modernity and Ambivalence* is one of Bauman's toughest books, as *Modernity and the Holocaust* is perhaps the saddest. The critical impetus is continuous; but *Modernity and Ambivalence* goes at its object hard and direct. Modernity's core problem is located in its obsessive quest for order, neat, tidy, closed, A is A and not B, all anomalies forced into hegemonic systems of classification given godlike authority over us. When all is in order, *Alles in Ordnung*, however, all hell is set to break loose: wait for the trouble. Ambivalence, which makes us what we are, is the first victim of this maniacal urge to control. The direct point of connection to the themes of *Legislators and Interpreters* is the logic of classification, the rationalist claim of the Enlightenment project. Ambivalence or anomaly is effectively prohibited by classification, for ambivalence is the possibility of naming something multiply, of assigning an object or an event to more than one category. Ambivalence, on this account, is normal, through modernity (or modernism) constructs it as aberrant. Bauman's critical object is what Adorno called identity-thinking. The dominant system of classification involves symbolic violence, as it is based on patterns of compulsory inclusion or exclusion. Modernity, itself, is just one such linguistic referent. Bauman's worry about this kind of order is its brutality. "The other of order is not another order: chaos is its only alternative" (1991a: 7). Modernity is a regime fraught by traditionalism or fixity; why, otherwise, would alternative conceptions or habits of order be unavailable? The result, in any case, is that it is intolerance rather tolerance which becomes the modern norm (and as Bauman adds, while toleration is better than its opposite, it remains a weak rather than a strong value – it leads to assimilation rather than to the recognition of difference). The traditionalism of modernity means that it fails to live up to its radical claims.

The power of Bauman's argument lies in its sense that ambivalence is squeezed out of modernity; it is *"the waste of modernity"* (1991a: 15). Only, we could add, it is also the stuff of modernity, for ambivalence continues to happen, every day of our lives; modernity, perhaps, is rather a struggle between order and ambivalence. The height of the modern attack on ambivalence, again, can be witnessed in the Holocaust, less German than modern in its reliance upon the gardening–breeding–surgical ambitions of social engineering. The power of the social engineering imagination rests upon its claim to perfection, to stasis (1991a: 39); this why, to arc back to *Socialism: The Active Utopia*, utopia is a counterfactual rather than a state of affairs actually to be achieved. Claims to stasis or perfection smell of death, and in both cases, Stalinism and Nazism alike, posit a victim as the obstruction – a class, the Kulaks, in the first case, a race, the Jews, in the second. *Modernity and Ambivalence* follows this idea in a different direction, now plotting out the sociology of the stranger as a violation of order. For strangers are beyond classification. Strangers violate both sense of place and of time or origin. Plainly the core concern of Bauman's attack on gardening is in its critique of this kind of organicism; and this is one reason why Bauman's work cannot simply be assimilated into romanticism and rejected as such. Modernity, as he argues, is itself ambivalent, as it is also a rebellion against just this fixity, against fate and ascription. Modernity, in this way, remains fundamentally contradictory (1991a: 69); thus the later, more explicit sense that postmodernity is modernity without illusions (1993: 32). Bauman's enthusiasms vary between a weaker and a stronger postmodernity: weaker, in this sense of shift of mentality within modernity, stronger, in the sense that the postmodern pluralizes, opens, innovates (though these are also modernist attributes themselves). Postmodernity involves waking up from the modern, or modernist dream.

The arguments here concerning ambivalence then lead into others about the limits of assimilation, which in *Postmodernity and its Discontents* become linked to the idea that societies ingest or evacuate the others (1997: 18). Yet Bauman is also keen to argue that the stranger herself changes, as does his context; for we are all, now strangers. Luhmann and now Maffesoli are then recruited to extend these claims about what comes after belonging, differentiation, multiple identities and neo-tribalism, the desperate search for imagined community. Yet in all this the critical balance never wavers; Bauman does not fall for the easy conclusion, that we are also, all, homeless; for some are more so than others. *Modernity and Ambivalence* closes with the emergence of the new poor, and our indifference toward them. "It is only too easy for postmodern tolerance to degenerate into the selfishness of the rich and resourceful" (1991: 259). So this most devastating critique of modernity finishes with a reconsideration of socialism as "modernity's last stand," its counterculture, and with a cautious defense of the practice of social engineering; can it always do worse than the problems it sets out to solve? For all political positions have costs, and refraining from social engineering does not come free. Modernity – on this more minimal point Bauman remains in sympathy with Habermas – modernity is still a project, unfulfilled but just so, because unfulfillable (Beilharz, 1994, 1997).

Sociology and Weltverbesserung

Sociology, by extension, is the unfulfillable project of modernity; and so it is in this setting that Bauman takes on the issue that sets sociology and the postmodern apart. Do we now, in sociology, face a choice, between postmodern sociology and a sociology of the postmodern? (Bauman, in Beilharz, Robinson, Rundell, 1992). A postmodern sociology would embrace the postmodern moment; a sociology of postmodernity, in contrast, would view that phenomenon as what needs to be explained, not as the explanation. Yet in a broader sense, of course, sociology – modernity – is also exactly what needs to be explained, or interpreted, and postmodern forms will not simply replay the problems of modernity or modernism. The only position we can realistically take up, then, is ambivalence itself, towards the postmodern but especially towards modernity and – in this register – towards sociology. For Bauman postmodernizes, but does not reject, socialism or sociology, even though they disappoint our hopes so bitterly and worse, even though they become part of the juggernaut itself. We have no simple choice, contrary to the fashionable, combative option of modernity versus postmodernity.

Sociology itself is also animated by ambivalence. Sociology shifts historically between the attempt to explain and to change the world; sociology is certainly not identical with marxism, or even with socialism, but the two tend to run in tandem and are each in turn characterized by a deep ambivalence towards the state. Sociology, in particular, cannot finally decide whether it is better to work for the state in the cause of reform, or to keep a critical distance from the hand that normally feeds it. Part of this agenda is thus obviously beyond our control. There are moments when the push to reform takes up our energies, and others when sociology becomes part of the problem, and we have to speak out against its accommodation into managerial strategies of control. Consequently we find ourselves obliged to be ambivalent about sociology, and not only about modernity and postmodernity.

The situation is no different with marxism versus postmarxism. The oddity here is that the semantic slides have been enormous, especially those identifying modernity, structuralism and marxism, pitting them against the matching ghosts, postmodernity, poststructuralism, postmarxism. For marxism may have been an aggressive source of modernism (as well as of romanticism), but it is really Weber, rather than Marx, who is the sociologist of modernity as different spheres of value. Marx's theory of modernity is premodern, in the sense that it is singular in its logic: society is economy. This is a fundamental limit for Bauman, and not only because it is monological, but also because it elevates political economy over civil society as well. To identify marxism with modernity, or modernism, is to misunderstand all three. For marxism criticizes modernity qua economy, but there is also more to marxism than modernism (i.e. romanticism, etc.) and there is definitely more to modernisms into the twentieth century than marxism. And this is to say nothing about structuralism or what follows, but these are strictly speaking neither economy nor culture so much as intellectual trends, which only intellectuals could mistake for history.

Yet humans live through illusions, even though, as Bauman hopes, the postmodern attitude might be modernity without illusions;

perhaps only with less damaging, post-Faustian illusions. What unfolds subsequently, in *Postmodern Ethics*, is as much non-modern as postmodern. Modernity substitutes state or "society" for the sociable, morality and ultimately law for ethics. For Bauman, however, the points of return arc Jonas, Levinas and Løgstrup rather than Aristotle or Kant. What becomes more apparent here, as in *Life in Fragments*, is an existential arc which works back to Sartre and Camus in Bauman's earlier work, and runs parallel to Agnes Heller perhaps more than to Castoriadis. The difference between Bauman and Levinas is that in Bauman the social rests on the dyad but is not reducible to it; there is always a third, social and individual work together, as freedom, dependency and so that *Life in Fragments* turns back through all those other themes, the stranger, the intellectuals, racism, cruelty, the tribes... until finally (for the moment) the mood of *Postmodernity and its Discontents* becomes more conspicuously postmodern, celebrating postmodern developments in art at the same time as it disparages the meanness of postmodern political indifference to the fact of social exclusion. After *Postmodernity and its Discontents*, the postmodern seems more again like part of the problem. If the mood of this last book also differs, somehow, this may reflect Bauman's own return, full circle, to legitimacy in Warsaw; it referents are as often Polish as not, especially when it comes to the arts, and here the arts in particular seem to take on the vocation of critique as well as creation. To say "no" to postmodern art is to say no to ourselves; not that this ever stopped anybody. On the street, in any case, they still suffer. Glossy globalization is an illusion, much like emancipatory postmodernism.

Coda: Descending the Staircase

If, as humans, we live through illusions, we nevertheless do so with *nous* or ordinary intelligence. And this, too, is a constant undercurrent in Bauman's writing. These *Weltverbesserer*, the perennial lines of do-gooders who want to improve our lives for us whether we like it or not become difficult when they claim to legislate for us politically, or do so, by default, economically through their control of the resources of everyday life. Within all the constraints of our lives we nevertheless persist in going about our business. Bauman captures both the tenor and the content of this sense in the penultimate chapter of his brilliant introductory textbook, *Thinking Sociologically* (1990). The voice in this book is again conversational, linking back through the hermeneutic style, back through the negative lessons of modernity's history in

Legislators and Interpreters and the positive implications of *Hermeneutics and Social Science*. The chapter in point is called "Going About the Business of Life," and its story concerns the difficulties of ordinary autonomy, in this case trying to fix the recalcitrant electric switch in your home. Specialization impinges upon us all. "And it has been like this with everything else: sweeping the floor, mowing the lawn, cutting the hedge, cooking a meal or washing the dishes. In all these functions expertise, locked in technological implements and gadgets, took over, polished and sharpened the skills once in every one's possession" (Bauman, 1990: 199). We all know more and more about less and less, in sociology as in our domestic skills; overspecialization not only decreases human proximity, it makes idiots out of all of us, conferring upon us a second nature which we now also take for granted.

As the house guest of the Baumans, one morning in Leeds I descended the staircase to catch the sociologist sweeping up. He looked at me knowingly, and said it was like our situation: every day we sweep, everyday the dirt returns and we repeat the ritual, only now, in postmodern times, without illusion. If, as I have suggested above, there is an existential clue in Bauman's work, alongside all the others, then I detect that there also is an anthropological clue, a sense that values everyday life and its routines just as it also acknowledges its difficulty. This seems to me to suggest sociology at its best, both its most insightful and its most pedestrian. For Bauman's message, in this regard, is simple. It is less that we should embrace chaos, than that we need to make our own order, to create our own ethics using the ordinary materials of life that come to hand. We show our humanity not in claims to the sublime or the final, but in the care with which we attend to the routines of everyday life and to each other. In this way, we still have the prospect of making solidarity, or at least of behaving as though it is possible. The clues lie before us; but this is a journey without end. The oddity and the ongoing fascination of Bauman's work perhaps consists in this, that Bauman can tell us so many terrible stories and persist in expecting us to do better. We need to peer into the abyss of modernity, whether as Holocaust or as mortality, in order to sense the extent of our predicament, in order to glimpse what we are capable of, as example and as counterexample. Sociology in Bauman's work connects us as subjects, but does so through the pursuit of the smallest personal detail as well as the largest or most compelling of social issues. All that which seems so overwhelming in its bureaucratic permanence at the same time, via Bauman's sociology, is shown to exist because we make it so. It is precisely this combination of the cosmic and the individual and all that goes in between which opens the profound sense of ambivalence that we moderns contain, not only about the pasts we have shared but also about the future. Ambivalence is what holds all this together, for Bauman; and we are ambivalents all, even if our social arrangements have yet to catch up with us, or we with them. What looks like the permanence of our social institutions remains fragile; our capacity to create social solidarity and to seek out the good society remains open. Our responsibilities lie before us, as sociologists and as citizens, as do our possibilities as thinkers and actors.

References

Bauman, J. (1986) *Winter in the Morning*, London: Virago.

—— (1988) *A Dream of Belonging*, London: Virago.

—— (1998) "Demons of Other People's Fear: The Plight of the Gypsies," *Thesis Eleven*, 54.

Bauman, Z. (1968) "Modern Times, Modern Marxism," *Social Research*, 34.

—— (1972) *Between Class and Elite*, Manchester: Manchester University Press.

—— (1973) *Culture as Praxis*, London: Routledge.

—— (1976a) *Socialism: The Active Utopia*, London: Allen and Unwin.

—— (1976b) *Towards a Critical Sociology*, London: Routledge.

—— (1978) *Hermeneutics and Social Science*, London: Hutchinson.

—— (1982) *Memories of Class*, London: Routledge.

—— (1987) *Legislators and Interpreters*, Oxford: Polity.

—— (1988) *Freedom*, Milton Keynes: Open University Press.

—— (1989) *Modernity and the Holocaust*, Oxford: Polity.

—— (1990) *Thinking Sociologically*, Oxford: Blackwell.

—— (1991a) *Modernity and Ambivalence*, Oxford: Polity.

—— (1991b) *Mortality, Immortality and Other Life Strategies*, Oxford: Polity.

—— (1992a) "A Sociological Theory of Postmodernity," in Beilharz, Robinson, and Rundell (1992).

—— (1992b) *Intimations of Postmodernity*, London: Routledge.

—— (1993) *Postmodern Ethics*, Oxford: Polity.

—— (1995) *Life in Fragments*, Oxford: Polity.

—— (1997) *Postmodernity and its Discontents*, Oxford: Polity.

—— (1998) "On Glocalization: Or Globalization for Some, Localization for Some Others," *Thesis Eleven*, 54.

Beilharz, P. (1992) *Labour's Utopias – Bolshevism, Fabianism, Social Democracy*, London: Routledge.

—— (1994) *Postmodern Socialism – Romanticism, City and State*, Melbourne: Melbourne University Press.

—— (1998a) "Counting Memories? Revisiting Bauman, Reading Wright," *Political Theory Newsletter*, 9, 1.

—— (1998b) "McFascism? Reading Ritzer, Bauman and the Holocaust," in B. Smart, ed. *Resisting McDonaldization*, London: Sage.

—— Beilharz, P., G. Robinson, and J. Rundell, eds. (1992) *Between Totalitarianism and Postmodernity – A Thesis Eleven Reader*, Cambridge: MIT Press.

Best, S. (1998) "Zygmunt Bauman," *British Journal of Sociology*, 49, 2.

Cheyette, B. ed. (1998) *Modernity, Culture and "the Jew"*, Oxford: Polity.

Diken, B. (1998) *Strangers, Ambivalence and Social Theory*, Aldershot: Ashgate.

Fehér, F. A. Heller, and G. Markus (1982) *Dictatorship Over Needs*, Oxford: Blackwell.

Joas, H. (1998) "Bauman in Germany," *Theory, Culture and Society*, 15, 1.

Konrad, G. and I. Szelenyi (1979) *The Intellectuals on the Road to Class Power*, Brighton, Harvester.

Lash, S. (1996) "Postmodern Ethics – The Missing Ground," *Theory, Culture and Society* 13, 2.

Varcoe, I. and R. Kilminster, eds. (1996), *Culture, Modernity and Revolution, Essays in Honour of Zygmunt Bauman*, London: Routledge.

Seidman, S. (1995) *Contested Knowledge*, Oxford: Blackwell.

Smith, D. (1998) "Zygmunt Bauman: How to be a Successful Outsider," *Theory, Culture and Society*, 15, 1.

Torevell, D. (1995) "The Terrorism of Reason in the Thought of Zygmunt Bauman," *New Blackfriars* 76, 891, March.

2

The *Telos* Interview

Born in 1925 in Poland, Zygmunt Bauman has taught sociology in countries such as Israel, the US, the UK and Canada. Today he is professor emeritus after 20 years of service at the University of Leeds. His production dates from the 1950s and deals, among other things, with questions such as class, socialism and hermeneutics. While these works stimulated considerable interest, they cannot be compared to the influence of Bauman's writing since the late 1980s, when he started to analyze modernity and postmodernity.

In *Legislators and Interpreters* Bauman (1987) analyzes the role of intellectuals in the modern state. He emphasizes that, given their elitist notion of culture, intellectuals were the architects of the modern citizenry. They also served as the legitimators in the modern state's efforts to control and "civilize" its citizens. Under postmodern conditions, however, the intellectuals' role shifts to that of "interpreters," mediators between different cultures.

Bauman's *Freedom* (1988) is both a dense historical account of the Western notion of freedom and a sociological interpretation of the social function of freedom. He argues that freedom of consumption has become decisive for social integration as well as individual identity. This novel mechanism of integration is one of the phenomena Bauman describes as postmodern in the following interview.

Modernity and the Holocaust (1989), which won the European Amalfi prize for sociology and social theory, is Bauman's most celebrated book. It has had a wide impact beyond sociology. In it Bauman seeks to comprehend what the Holocaust can teach about modernity. One of his main conclusions is that genocide was not merely an irrational outburst of animality or a breaking down of civilization. On the contrary, this mass murder took place in a "civilized way," with the assistance of bureaucratic organization and instrumental rationality. Bauman's point is that it is a modern self-deception to identify modernity with civilization, understood as moral improvement. He claims that much of sociology is enmeshed in this modern self-legitimating myth, as it understands morality as being exclusively a product of social institutions. He points to Durkheim and Freud as two main figures who support the notion of people as *a priori* amoral beings who therefore need institutions (Durkheim) or culture (Freud) to make them social (moral). Inspired by Emmanuel Levinas' philosophy, Bauman argues in favor of understanding morality not as something that social institutions create, but as something they manipulate.

In *Modernity and Ambivalence* Bauman (1991) studies how modern politics, science, philosophy and culture have been obsessed with order. The problem with this is that it encourages intolerance because attempts to establish clear-cut order posit the ambiguous as something undesirable. Establishing order presupposes an exclusion and delegitimation of the other, i.e., the ambiguous that does not conform to the ordering categories. Faced with this problem, Bauman does not suggest an empty celebration of the chaotic. Rather, he considers to what extent postmodernity is a period when the fight against ambiguity is less intense, where people can accept ambivalence and thereby be more tolerant.

Intimations of Postmodernity (1992) is a collection of essays which closes with a theory concerning the contingent nature of postmodern social life. Crucial here is Bauman's attempt to formulate a sociological vocabulary for the postmodern experience. Such an effort requires liberation from conventional sociological concepts such as "society," "normative group," "socialization," etc.

In the context of other sociological interpretations, Bauman's analyses are particularly original when dealing with morality and ethics. Whereas most accounts of postmodernity emphasize aesthetics, Bauman argues that postmodernity implies a reconsideration of ethics. The following interview took place in Leeds, England, in June 1992. It is meant as a clarification of Bauman's account of modernity, postmodernity and related issues.

Modernity/Postmodernity

Cantell & Pedersen: What would you consider your core ideas of the relation between modernity and postmodernity?

Bauman: I would say today that postmodernity is modernity *für sich*, modernity which goes beyond its false consciousness and comes to understand what it actually was doing all along, i.e., producing ambivalence and pluralism, and also reconciles itself to the fact that the purposes which were originally set, e.g. rational order and absolute truth, will never be reached. Some social theorists suggest that we should talk about "late modernity," whereas I prefer the term postmodernity which provides more intellectual courage – you are not bound by certain articulations typical of modern times. You can try to put yourself aside and look in from outside at what is going on, and come forward with new concepts, new articulations and new models. It is simply a salutary decision to speak of postmodernity, rather than late modernity, without necessarily accepting every rubbish written in the name of postmodern theory. Otherwise, there is not much in this terminological discussion because the very term postmodernity is an acknowledgement of the fact that we are tied to modernity. It is not "post" anything, other than this particular kind of society.

C&P: Why is the discussion of postmodernity important?

ZB: Because it is a self-conscious stage in the development of modernity; we are damn sure about what we are doing. Thus, we know that ambivalence and contingency are here to stay. So the task is to learn how to live with them.

C&P: In order to grasp the postmodern condition you have suggested giving up classical sociological categories like society, normative group (class or community), socialization and control and replace them with "sociality," "habitat," "self-constitution" and "self-assembly." Why?

ZB: Once we are self-conscious, once we know that contingency and ambivalence are here to stay, then we can stop speaking about social system, society, and start speaking about processes like sociality, habitat, self-constitution. These categories are meant to capture the spatial and temporal flux of contemporary life. They acquire their meaning from the opposition to the orthodox vocabulary of "structure," "system," "constraints," "determinants" etc. organized around the "billiard ball" image of life. Today, less than ever before is "given" and even less is "forever." "Communities" of belonging are assembled and disassembled, and self-constituting activity is virtually synonymous with this process. We enter relations and create them by entering, we exit relations and dismantle them by exiting. Shifting interests, shifting attention, shifting foci of interaction and/or identification. Imagine drifting whirlpools: processing matter, yet retaining their "identity" only on condition of not holding it. We have been living like this for a long time, only we used to believe that somewhere around the corner there is an orderly, transparent, rational world, an end of history. Everything will come to a standstill once we have achieved the rationally organized, perfect world. Everywhere you have the same perspective, from Marx to Weber and Durkheim, not to mention the political ideologies which were set to replace the chaotic, disorderly world by some transparent reality.

The last great attempt to present the world as an orderly system was Talcott Parsons' theory – an attempt to impose on a disorganized world some sort of order, by selecting some aspects as normal and dismissing others as abnormal, deviations, pattern-breaking, etc. But every attempt to speak about "society" and present a consistent model is by necessity such an attempt to be selective, to arbitrarily proclaim certain ways of social life as the "norm" and by the same token to classify all other phenomena as abnormal: either the residue of a backward past, which eventually will outlive its purpose and disappear, or some alien intrusions which have to be exterminated or marginalized.

C&P: What characterizes postmodern forms of communities?

ZB: A very brief answer would be that the most characteristic form of this kind of community is fluidity, liquidity, changeability. What I argued in *Modernity and Ambivalence*, but also in *Intimations of Postmodernity*, is that postmodern communities are more like Immanuel Kant's aesthetic communities than Ferdinand Tönnies's *Gemeinschaften* which precede and determine member's choices. They have no other firm ground but the members' commitment to stand on, so communities live as long as the attention of the members is alive and emotional commitment is strong. Otherwise, they simply vanish.

C&P: The postmodern is often associated with the aesthetic. Thus Featherstone (1991) talks about the aesthetization of everyday life, and Harvey (1989) sees the postmodern as the hegemony of aesthetics over ethics. Though you also talk about aesthetics, your focus is on ethics. Postmodernity is the time when morality is more where it rightly belongs, i.e., with individual agents. Do you see this as opposed to theories of postmodernity which emphasize the aesthetic?

ZB: I am inclined to emphasize the ethical aspect of postmodernity. I agree with people who write about aesthetization; I just mentioned that postmodern communities are reminiscent of aesthetic communities. But ethical issues are more central to postmodernity because the modern way of dealing with ethical regulation of human intercourse is coming to a close. This modern way was twofold: on the one hand it was an attempt to take over moral responsibility from individuals by institutions, by organizations like the state or the church and, on the other hand, it was what I have called "adiaphorization." In the Middle Ages the church councils used to decide that certain questions were "adiaphoric," that means indifferent from the viewpoint of faith, so that the church did not have a position concerning them, they were neither sinful nor virtuous. I am using "adiaphorization" as an allegory: what has happened today is that a number of important human actions were declared morally adiaphoric, i.e., indifferent from the moral viewpoint. Most activities regulated by organizations are subject to adiaphorization: one performs one's duty not bearing moral responsibility for it.

Both forms of moral regulation are now in crisis; we do not trust large institutions to tell us what to do any more. The authority of churches, political parties, academic institutions and so on is clearly declining. The responsibility which was taken away from the individuals is coming back – you and I are very much left alone with our decisions. We do not have a moral code which has all the visibility of being absolute and universal. We confront moral problems again as if modernity had not happened: we are thrown back on individual responsibility. That is why I think sociological theories of morality which see society as the author and the guardian of morality have to be revised. This seems a crucial element in any attempt to understand the postmodern condition.

C&P: Do you see any similarities between premodern and postmodern times?

ZB: We sometimes call premodern societies "traditional." What we call the rule of "tradition" is, in fact, simply a reflection of a situation in which people live in a "I-watch-you-you-watch-me" situation, where everybody is under control, pulled down to a certain level of shared habits and customs. By and large, that was the premodern situation. It was replaced by the anonymity of modern life. Unlike premodern times, in modern times we live mostly among strangers who do not know each other. Thus the question is: how can one secure a certain predictability and order in human behaviour when there is no visual surveillance of neighbors, no pressure exerted by the neighborhood or by the local community? In modernity this was done by setting obligatory moral codes supported by oppression, which actually kept people in line, and by rendering much of human behaviour morally indifferent.

Now we are still in the company of strangers and from this viewpoint nothing has changed – we have not come back to Tönnies' local communities. Nevertheless, the grip of the "big code" is not holding as it used to, and therefore for the first time we have to negotiate our relation with our sexual partner, our spouse, our children, our parents, while bearing the burden of responsibility for the outcome.

C&P: Many people are uneasy with postmodernity, charging it with being a nihilistic relativism. But the category of nihilism is of little descriptive value and more a polemic category targeted against people not without but with other values. Why is this charge so common?

ZB: Well, I can only give you the answer you implied in your question, which is a commonsensical one. We are all dreaming about firm ground on which to walk. But postmodernity, which does not entail that "everything goes and do whatever you like," simply means that there are no hard and fast ways of separating the right and the wrong way, the right and the wrong culture, and so on. And this brings us back to the question of moral choice and responsibility – it makes you responsible and many people do not like it.

The deconstructionists show that every belief, definition and firm statement is just the crisscrossing of many different and arbitrary interpretations. And from there you can go to only another interpretation. Not from error to truth, but from one interpretation to another and that is what is disquieting, and that is why there are objections to this postmodern skepticism.

C&P: "Postmodernity is a chance of modernity. Tolerance is a chance of postmodernity. Solidarity is a chance of tolerance" you write in *Modernity and Ambivalence*. How do we get from tolerance to solidarity?

ZB: This is the most difficult question. My answer is simple: I do not know. I think that in the postmodern world we are constantly on crossroads, so we will never be sure that we have left crossroads behind, and there are always two kinds of tolerance. One leads to indifference or even some sort of heterophobia which is presently gathering in force all over Europe. The other theoretical possibility is, of course, solidarity, but I do not know how to get there. I am not in the business of prophecy. Social science does not have any credentials to make prophetic statements. Social scientists who use their authority to make predictions are false prophets. All we can do is to speculate about various possibilities.

C&P: Do you suggest embracing contingency as a way of cultivating a solidarian attitude?

ZB: Yes, but we are speaking about tolerance towards difference and that is an extremely tricky issue. It is not easy to say to what extent the anxiety felt in the presence of the other, the unknown, the stranger, is more solid than any kind of social arrangement. What is going on now in Europe is an extremeley rapid increase in migration. And with the growing unity of Europe there will be more and more of it, so presumably the populations will become more and more mixed and the presence of the other, the stranger, will be come a normal phenomenon. Such a situation does not cause any social trouble in times of prosperity when people feel economically secure. The present outburst of heterophobia, nationalism and hatred of immigrants and so on is connected with the present economic crisis and unemployment. How lasting this phenomenon is it is difficult to say.

C&P: You envisage a postmodern condition marked by variety, pluralism, ambivalence and contingency. What do you see as evidence for this?

ZB: That is a crucial question. Let me try to provide a few examples of this dissemination of ambivalence and pluralism. Do you remember the Aristotelian notion of catharsis, his theory of tragedy? The role of a drama was to offer the viewers catharsis. Catharsis meant "cleaning up." Drama showed people who in some fashion lost their way. They found themselves in an abnormal situation which created a lot of suffering. By the end of the drama, the abnormality was overcome and you returned to the normal: the moral rule had been restored. Contemporary art does not perform the role of catharsis for the very simple reason that contemporary artists do not assume that there is a "normal" as different from an abnormal human condition; that there is some general moral law or commandment to which you can return from the aberration. What we experience as a difficult situation, uncertainty, is not abnormality, but a permanent human condition. Everything is ambiguous, there is no authoritative solution in the end of the modern drama, novel and film. Instead, people are told that if they were seeking certainty and fool-proof answers, this search was in vain. In contemporary art the world is not presented as split into good people and villains. Spy thrillers, for example, are typically ambivalent, with heros committing awful crimes in the defense of their country.

Mikhail Bakhtin developed the concept of "carnival culture" in relation to Rabelais's *Gargantua and Pantagruel*. Carnival culture was the *temporal* reversal of ordinary life, the purpose of which, according to Bakhtin, was to bring into relief the *norm* as it *should* be in daily life, and make it more bearable. In contemporary culture carnival culture has moved from the margin to the center. In Britain the annual cycle consists of two parts. The one is people's saving for summer holidays, when they go to some mini-Disneyland in special areas reserved for holidays; the other is their preparation for Christmas festivities. Carnival elements dominate the year, giving meaning to the normal life. For Bakhtin carnival was just a brief exception to better underline the stern normality. Now the roles have been reversed. Worse yet: being "shown on TV" is the certificate of reality. Being a game is the condition of being real and that is why, when there are family events, to make sure that they are real you put them on video. Being seen on a screen is the contemporary definition of being "really real." What used to be a reflection of reality has become the standard of reality.

Another example of the spreading of ambivalence and contingency is that suspension of disbelief is no longer a temporary phenomenon, but a permanent condition. The difference between simulation and dissimulation has been eroded, and that is why Baudrillard speaks of simulacrum, neither simulation nor dissimulation. We no longer think that the distinction between pretense and reality is so tremendously important.

Freedom and Repression

C&P: In *Freedom* you argued that contemporary society is integrated through freedom (consumer freedom), not via the oppression of freedom. More recently, in *Modernity and Ambivalence*, you analyze how we freely become construed as "inherently non-self-sufficient entities" in our *privatized* dependency on expertise. There seem to be two different claims about freedom in your work. One is that the social sciences have underestimated the relative autonomy of human beings. The other is that in postmodernity freedom gains a historically exceptional role. Do you agree with this reading?

ZB: Yes, but it is not so much a question about the postmodern condition allowing more freedom for individuals than modernity. I do not know how to measure it, really. I think that any freedom is a social relation: the more freedom I have the less freedom somebody else has. Freedom means ability to act on your will, and if you are able to have it *your* way, that means somebody else must compromise and surrender. It has nothing to do with freedom towards nature, particularly, the freedom of the sculptor who cuts the stone and changes its shape; in his case the more skills he has the more free he is to implement his artistic ideals at nobody's expense but the stone's. But concerning freedom in society, the better you can implement your own wishes, the worse someone else may be able to implement theirs. That is why I do not know how to measure the "total amount of freedom in society."

What did happen in postmodernity is that freedom was accepted as our fate. We know that we are "condemned to be free" and that this is a situation of great risk. In his latest book Galbraith says that for the first time in the history of modernity the *majority* of people find the chances of freedom outweighing the risks. Through modernity there was always a minority of privileged people, members of the elite who wished less interference from society, but the majority of the population if allowed voted them down, preferring state redistribution of income. They felt that freedom worked against them. Only now we have in affluent countries a majority of people who are better off with all the risks which are involved in being free and standing on your own feet; better off not paying taxes and losing the state-guaranteed security. Galbraith concludes that people who can do little with their freedom as consumers will be systematically voted down. Today's poor are – culturally, by social and by self-definition – "flawed consumers," rather than "exploited producers." They are not the "carriers of emancipation," neither Parsifal nor Prometheus, not the harbinger of an alternative future, not politically "sexy." They are just people who cannot do what we do, but would be awfully glad to do it it they could.

With market choice moving simultaneously to the center of self-constitution, societal integration and systemic reproduction, market standards tend to dominate or replace moral responsibilities, and one of the consequences is dissipation of responsibility for the *distant stranger* – be it contemporary poor, or future generations. State concern with distributive justice is ever more difficult to legitimate – a recipe for electoral defeat. Market Standards also captured the imagination of the poor; vindications are all concerned with enhancing consumer power.

C&P: Do you think it possible for political and communal freedom to counter-balance consumer-oriented freedom?

ZB: The type of conflicts which the majority of the population faced in the 19th century led to the creation of mass political parties, mass trade unions, etc., because individually interests could not be satisfied – they required collective effort. But the way in which individual interests are satisfied today does not promote collectivization of interest. On the contrary, Western Europe is presently faced with the privatization of dissent. I have tried to explain this in *Intimations of Postmodernity.* Consequently, I do not think there is much chance for political freedom, i.e., freedom in the ancient Greek sense of *polis,* of congregating on the *agora* and making decisions.

C&P: What about an issue like the environment. Could it be an issue of collectivization of interest?

ZB: Single issues – but single issues are not the stuff of which politics is made. Single issues – groups exerting pressures on government – is probably the wave of the future. Traditional political parties were based on a situation where there was one major conflict which divided society into two parts. Today, however, there is no such single conflict overriding all others. There are many different conflicts and each one cuts society in different ways. How to put these conflicts together – that is the problem.

C&P: What kind of repressing mechanisms operate in contemporary society?

ZB: Briefly: dependency achieved through seduction. Tempting offers of advice from experts, offers of implements from traders, which will resolve all kinds of problems. Seductive proposals are welcomed by consumers; but once you accept them, you become dependent on experts and the market. Start relying on marriage counselors and you will be increasingly dependent on expert advice on how to make your marriage survive. It is a "velvet dependency," a dependency which people seek actively and choose willingly.

Freedom offers many wonderful things, but it does not offer one thing crucial to individual well-being, certainty – being sure that what you are doing is right, that what you have decided to do was not a mistake. To attain this certainty you need reassurance from an authority stronger than your self-confidence. Seeking such certainty leads people to sink ever deeper into dependency.

C&P: But is that repression?

ZB: It is a "velvet repression." Mind you, I am always speaking about free consumers. I am not speaking about people on welfare who are oppressed in a very traditional way – they are still dependent 24 hours a day on institutions, which either give or do not give them money, which can control what they do, which can invade their houses at any time. But today Foucault's panoptical power is applied to a minority. For the majority, it is a sort of do-it-yourself dependency; people gladly, willingly, joyfully enter the dependency relation with marketing companies, with experts, technological or scientific, psychologists, psychiatrists and so on.

C&P: But is that not too one-sided? Could one not see the use of expertise as a kind of personal empowerment as Giddens (1991) does?

ZB: Most recipients of the services of experts do not learn the skills. Instead, they define increasingly larger parts of their life as legitimate objects for experts. Look at the development of psychiatry. It consisted in defining more and more aspects of ordinary life as psychiatric cases until virtually everyone had become a potential object of psychiatric treatment.

I do not believe that it is "enabling." It may be only in a negative sense. We do not have any other skills, which would not involve specialist services. We are increasingly dependent on technology and the techno-logically-framed prescriptions for behavior, which we receive from coun-sellors. It is "velvet" repression because it does not feel like oppression. On the contrary, the usual response is: 'now I am wiser, now I am a better master of my fate.' But it is a restriction of freedom all the same. You are following somebody's recipes, you are not struggling with the problems anymore, you are just allowing other people to remove them from you. I am not saying that it is either good or bad. I am simply trying to under-stand how consumer freedom is so posited within individual and social life that it is no longer pitted against dependency. Freedom is not the opposite of dependency. Freedom is entangled with dependency: you become more free by purchasing more services from experts and becoming more dependent on them. So freedom is enhancing dependency.

Sociology Today

C&P: How do you see the current state of sociology?

ZB: Particularly in its dominant American form, sociology developed out of the false promise that it could help the managers of public, economic and political life. The two great bureaucracies in America – the Warfare and the Welfare bureaucracy – were behind the spectacular development of empirical sociology. This was an empirical sociology with practical aims, which promised to resolve social conflicts, prevent strikes, insur-gency and riots, i.e., helping people or institutions to realize their aims. Because of the end of the Cold War, the shift to an individualistic free market society and the collapse of the welfare state, both bureaucracies are now in deep crisis. Therefore, the traditional basis of sociology is slowly eroding or even in the process of disappearing.

Today, there is a tremendous anxiety among sociologists in America, because some departments of sociology have already been disbanded. I am not worried because my understanding of sociology is continental in the tradition of German and French sociology rather than American. I never believed that sociology could resolve any problems: we are not resolving problems, we are only becoming bored with them. However, sociology does play an important role, but a different one, which comes to full fruition precisely in the age of postmodernity. Sociology offers an informed, wise, enlightened commentary on current experience – a commentary which is fed back into this experience and therefore makes it richer while widening horizons.

The task of sociology today is to undermine certainties, because every certainty is cutting off options. I agree with Walter Benjamin, that history is the graveyard of possibilities. Every historical development means that several possibilities have been murdered and sociology is about keeping possibilities alive. It is showing that the grounds of every solution, every belief are not absolute or universal, and everything is open to discussion and should be negotiated. So, from this viewpoint, one should not be worried about the dismantling of American sociology departments, because they have been doing something completely different.

C&P: The role of the founders of sociology has traditionally been strong. If the postmodern turn undermines their importance, what is left for them to do?

ZB: In a sense we are coming back to the classics. Not that we are repeating what the classics said, but that we are doing the same kind of sociology again. What distinguished classical sociologists was that they dealt with the big problems of their time. That was the tradition of Durkheim, Weber and Simmel, who just tried to understand the plight of men and women thrown into an urban society. And that is what sociology, whatever is left of it, will be doing again. So there is a continuity, but there is also a discontinuity. While most classical sociologists believed that we are moving towards a rationally organized society, we no longer believe that. While they believed that history has a pointer, that there is progress, we no longer believe that either. We just believe that history is a succession of events without any pre-given directions.

The Problem of Globalization

C&P: How do you see the future of Europe and globalization?

ZB: First of all, I am not sure that postmodernity is fit for globalization. Postmodernity is a culture of the privileged part of the world and it depends on the high degree of consumption and affluence which is typical of this part of the world. It cannot simply be made into everybody's way of life. Normally, stimuli travel without the economic and social basis on which they grew, they acquire some sort of independence, they become stimuli elsewhere without conditions for their thriving having been met. But when stimuli travel alone, without the social-economic basis, they result in unpredictable consequences. I have argued that the fatal blow to communism was delivered by postmodernity. Communism could live happily ever after with the modern world, which was all about increasing production – more steel, more coal, building irrigation systems and so on. But it could not live with the world based on enjoyment, freedom, game, playfulness, variety, etc. That is what the communists could not produce. But does this mean that in Russia, the Ukraine or Bulgaria you will have a postmodern society? I do not think so. The stimulus was there and it has already triggered its consequences. The outcome will be some sort of a mixture which is very difficult to predict.

The most important phenomenon in Europe today is the slow withering away of the nation-state. The nation-state was a unique institution in history which united economic management, political authority and cultural hegemony. Today, economic management is moving away from the nation-state because of the globalization of the economy. The nation-state is no longer an economic system, self-contained or self-sufficient. As far as the cultural hegemony is concerned it moves downwards from the state. The movement is not upwards like the economy, but downwards towards social movements, communities, ethnic groups and so on. What is left in the nation-state is just pure political authority without it being supported by economic management and cultural hegemony. I wonder how long this fiction can survive without its two other pillars. At any rate, we are probably coming to the end of the nation-state. With what outcomes, it is difficult to say. We are witnessing both economic globalization and cultural tribalization as leading in opposite directions. This is something new, which we do not know how to handle since all sociology was used to a situation which enclosed all three aspects. Suddenly, each aspect has its own space and how they interact has yet to be established.

References

Bauman, Zygmunt (1987) *Legislators and Interpreters: On Modernity, Post-Modernity and Intellectuals.* Cambridge: Polity.
——(1988) *Freedom.* Milton Keynes: Open University Press.
——(1989) *Modernity and the Holocaust.* Cambridge: Polity.
——(1991) *Modernity and Ambivalence.* Cambridge: Polity.
——(1992) *Intimations of Postmodernity.* London: Routledge.
Featherstone, Mike (1991) *Consumer Culture and Postmodernity.* London: Sage.
Giddens, Anthony (1991) *Modernity and Self-Identity.* Oxford: Polity.
Harvey, David (1989) *The Condition of Postmodernity.* Oxford: Blackwell.

3

Socialism

3.1 The Historical Location of Socialism (1976)

Modernity is, admittedly, a multi-faceted phenomenon which valiantly resists clear-cut definitions. It has been widely accepted that the phenomenon is intimately related to the 'technological revolution', to the drastic thickening of the artificial intermediary sphere stretching *between* Man and Nature, often articulated as a dramatic strengthening of the human ascendancy *over* Nature. At the same time, however, it is agreed that the phenomenon is not reducible to the technological explosion. Modernity is also a social and psychological phenomenon; its advent means momentous changes in the social system as well as in the set of conditions in which human action takes place. One can only surmise that however the advent of modernity affects the dimensions and the content of yearnings and utopias, the impact is mediated by these latter phenomena more than by anything else. As a background and a source of inspiration for human ideals, modernity means, above all, a modern network of human relations.

In what is perhaps the best recent example of the Weberian ideal-type method in action, Reinhard Bendix went a long way toward elucidating major features of this network. Two processes, Bendix suggests, contributed more than anything else to the final shape which modern society has assumed: the first was the rising pre-eminence of 'impersonalism' as the paramount principle regulating the way in which individuals were pinioned into the network of socially defined roles and behavioural patterns; the second was the advent of 'plebiscitarianism', as – simultaneously – the authority's working rule and the keynote of its legitimation (Bendix, 1964).

"Impersonalism" comes to replace the paternalistic relationship between patron and client. To use Parsonian language, the latter may be described as subject to the patterns of universalism and specificity, in contradistinction to the particularism and diffuseness of the former. The non-modern patterns of human relations are thoroughly particularised and widely different from one pair of individuals to another; they are likewise diffuse, tending to embrace the totality of life-processes in which both individuals are entangled. Both attributes disappear with the advent of modernity, to be replaced by their opposites. Modernity begins, says Bendix, with the codification of rights and duties of a 'citizen', an individual *qua homo politicus*, i.e., as a member of the 'polis', the politically organised society. On the other hand, this 'individual' enters the society, or is of any interest to society, only in respect of those traits which have undergone this process of 'codification', have been standardised and subjected to a set of uniform rules. The individual, as defined and moulded by the modern network, is thereby charged with an irreducible paradox; his 'individuality' has been achieved at the expense of all and any of his idiosyncratic, purely personal and genuinely unique predicates, which constitute him as a separate, irreplaceable and unrepeatable being. This peculiar individuality is anonymous and faceless, pared to the bones of pure universality, swept clean of anything idiomatic and distinctive, of any personal faculty which may thwart his complete mapping into another 'individual'. This is not to say, to be sure, that the human denizens of the modern age are really like this; but it does mean that they are admitted into modernity in this capacity only. Modern society has, admittedly, no use for unstandardised human traits; these, classified as the realm of the subjective, are declared socially irrelevant in so far as they do not interfere with the codified domain. At the same time they delimit the sphere of individual freedom; the non-interference of society is ultimately founded on its programmatic indifference to anything which eludes the supraindividual ordering, or has been deliberately exempted from it.

The principle of impersonalism not only delimits the social essence of the individual; it is operative in generating a life-space congenial to and consonant with such delimited individuals. The realm enveloping the social existence of the individual likewise consists of averaged, impersonal, faceless and hence quantifiable individuals. It can be handled effectively, assessed and evaluated, in purely numerical terms; thanks to the prior qualitative reduction of its inhabitants, it is indeed quantifiable and therefore amenable to management ruled by the economics of rationality. Again, this does not mean that the human life-process in the modern milieu boils down to a series of rational calculations and choices; but it does mean that only this series is recognised as socially relevant, and thereby socially protected and attended to. The residue, however immense and subjectively important it may be, is left in what, from the social perspective, may as well remain forever the penumbra of 'the private'. Vast areas of human life – indeed, its most intimate, passionately lived and emotion-saturated areas – have been proclaimed 'off limits' for the sake of the regularity, and therefore certainty and predictability, of the societally processed nucleus.

A rather important remark is in order here. At least since the famous distinction made by Sir Henry Maine in the nineteenth century, the dichotomy of impersonalism-particularism tends to be analysed in 'either-or' terms, Bendix's study being no exception. This approach is entirely warranted in so far as we are interested solely in the texture of the social structure, the web of interhuman dependencies, which open, limit, and condition the individual's access to socially valued goods. But the social structure in this sense does not pre-empt the totality of the individual life-world. I wonder whether it would not be better to speak of a 'topping' of the traditional life-world, in modern times, with an impersonal structure of the greater society, rather than of the substitution of this structure for the old, particularised one. A very large part of the life-world still remains heavily 'particularised', densely packed with face-to-face, multi-faceted relations and apparently open to meaning-negotiating initiatives; it is still 'free' in the latter sense, its freedom having been given a new, deeper dimension and been made particularly conspicuous by contrast with the new domain of the thoroughly standardised, prefigured relations. The 'freedom' which prevails in this part of the life-world should be understood only in these comparative terms. Otherwise it becomes an illusion, since the sector of the life-world now under discussion, having been abandoned by the 'impersonal' control of the greater society, is still kept under tight control by the community (defined as the group able to hold its members under a face-to-face, immediate, and personal control). The activity of meaning-negotiating never takes off from a zero-point; in each case the cards have already been distributed and the hands are not even, while the rules of the game itself are hardly open to negotiation by the current players. The last decade showed what the consequences of this distorted perspective may be; the so-called 'youth revolt' tried in fact to shake off the constraints imposed on the community level, while being convinced that it fought the 'impersonal society'. Its success in subduing the power of community control was naturally proportionate to the widening of the sphere of impersonal regulation and interference (through new laws which introduced the 'greater society' into areas where it had traditionally been indifferent).

Plebiscitarianism – the second of Bendix's two parameters of modernity – consists in the inclusion of the masses in the political process. They now become 'citizens' of the state instead of subjects of a prince. Their collective will now becomes the seat of sovereignty and its supreme legitimation. Quantity is substituted for quality, numerical power for wisdom, interests for inalienable rights, accomplishment for properties. The substitution, to be sure, is perceived only too often as an improvement on the inductive definitions of old and immutable values, rather than as one value taking the place of another. Thus quantity is considered the best measure of quality, the number of supporters a true index of the wisdom of a decision, pursuit of interest the least alienable of human rights. From the vantage-point of their sociological content, however, the change in values is enormous and radical. The paramount novelty is the sheer notion of the masses as the 'flesh' of the body politic. The passage from the patrimonial ruler to the rule of the masses is not to be seen merely as a widening of the ruling group, as a substitution of the many for the few. The masses turned citizens do not take over the former rulers' faculty of entering the field of politics as socially identifiable persons. Only when they have undergone and completed the process of impersonalisation can the subjects of a patrimonial ruler re-emerge as the masses looming large in the modern idiom of authority. The masses are not a collection of specific, qualitatively distinct persons, complete with their multi-faceted qualities, needs, and interests. They are describable and intelligible in quantitative terms only, which is possible only on the assumption of their complete comparability and exchangeability in their role of citizens. It is thanks to this reduction, accomplished by the modern notion of citizenship, that public opinion can boil down to the computation of statistical distributions and democracy can be measured by a crudely arithmetical yardstick of numerical majority. The citizens are equal in so far as they are indistinguishable; whatever makes them different from each other is simply left outside the realm of politics and the interests of the body politic. So we see that, within the modern idiom, impersonalism and plebiscitarianism are not just parallel processes which happen to occur simultaneously; they complement, validate and support each other, and can be seen as two sides of the same coin. The impersonal equality of individuals as citizens can generate, or be squared with, only a plebiscitarian type of body politic; and plebiscitarianism cannot assure, or account for, any but an impersonal type of equality, i.e., equality contained in the citizen role.

However, this is not the end of the story. Plebiscitarianism does not only disregard the differentiation of citizens beyond the sphere of citizenship proper. It also works on the assumption that non-political inequality does not affect the role of the citizen; that citizens somehow shake off their non-political bonds at the threshold of the body politic. Having theoretically separated the sector of citizenship from the totality of the individual's status, the plebiscitarian legitimation conceives its conceptual feat as an operation on social reality; it is, indeed, founded on the belief that an individual can enjoy his equal political rights while remaining unequal in spheres other than the political.

It is true that the roots of inequality, in the modern society which has gradually emerged from the lasting victories and temporary setbacks of the French Revolution, were not political. They were dug deep into the network of economic dependencies and the web of communication which constituted the civil society of the era. But it is true as well that with these bases of self-perpetuating inequality left intact, the political equality of plebiscitarianism must have remained a purely formal legal category. It was precisely in this form that the ideal of equality had been adopted by the dominant, liberal culture of the capitalist brand of the modern society. And it was precisely in this form that the ideal of purely political equality had been challenged and rejected by its socialist counter-culture. The emphatic refusal to accept the notion of equality as limited to the political sphere alone, the insistence on the importance of the numerous links with other spheres which render political equality void if other inequalities are left intact, and the determined desire to extend the ideal of equality beyond the domain of *homo politicus* were to remain the only cultural postulates shared by all shades of the socialist counter-culture.

In this sense, the socialist counter-culture was a continuation of the liberal-capitalist culture as well as its rejection. Already in 1890, Bebel publicly acknowledged socialism's indebtness: no one had done more than the liberals to awaken the yearning for equality among the people. The liberal notion of political democracy was the first form in which the vision and the realism of equality had been brought to the mind of the common man and kindled his imagination. 'Patiently endured so long as it seemed beyond redress', wrote de Tocqueville, 'a grievance comes to appear intolerable once the possibility of removing it crosses men's minds' (Tocqueville, 1955, p. 176). In one fell swoop the capitalist cultural revolution disposed of the two pillars of the pre-modern belief system: that human inequality is beyond challenge and dispute; and that it is pre-ordained, and therefore cannot be changed by men. In this myth-destroying activity the liberal-capitalist culture soon reached the point of no return; from now on it was an unquestionable belief that inequality is unjust, man-made, and therefore subject to man's action. What remained to be done by the socialist counter-culture was to draw conclusions the liberal ideology could not, and did not wish to draw: that what had been done in politics could and should be repeated in the other spheres of human deprivation. As one of the delegates of the South German People's Party expressed it at a conference in 1868, 'Democracy must become social democracy if it honestly wants to be democracy' (quoted in Roth, 1963, p. 50).

Socialism may be seen, so to speak, as a radical but logical extension of capitalist liberalism. It was not, however, only an extension of the critical aspect of liberalism; it involved, simultaneously, an emphatic rejection of its positive side. Liberalism saw the equality of citizenship as the foundation and guarantee of the individual's freedom, i.e. his freedom to be unequal in other spheres than the political. Socialism, on the contrary, considered the establishment of political equality as a means and a first step to the incorporation of the totality of individual life into a community of equal men. In other words, liberalism saw the community as a major obstacle on the way to individual freedom and understood the body politic as the only desirable form of supra-individual integration on the new societal level, with citizenship as the only integrating link; while socialism aimed at the reconstruction of a community-type integration on the societal level.

Throughout the two centuries of socialist thought we find the two threads – the radical version of critical liberalism and the rejection of positive liberalism – closely knit together. The words which Jean Jacques Rousseau put into the mouth of Pliny speaking to Trajan, 'If we have a prince, it is in order that he keeps us from having a master', were to remain the leitmotiv of the socialist concept of the body-politic, but pushed well beyond the boundary of the liberal interpretation. This boundary was drawn by the idea that masters are born, as Morelly noted already in 1755, not of the usurpation of power, but of resources which precede all politics and whose usurpation alone can make men power-hungry. The legislators, Morelly was eager to make clear, support the masters rather than creating them; they do it by allowing for the usurpation of resources and defending the ensuing situation. The major disaster took place at the moment when the resources, which should belong in common to all humanity, had been usurped; the disaster consisted in breaking the primary link of sociability. Thus destruction of community and inequality became one; and the rebirth of community and the establishment of more than just political equality become one again.

It was left to Gracchus Babeuf to cross the t's and dot the i's. In the history of socialism the role of Babeuf is unique and perhaps decisive. It was he who finally brought together and blended two traditions which had previously developed independently of each other: the tradition of socialism as an abstract moral principle, as a verdict of reason, the heritage of Plato, More and Campanella, and the plebeian tradition of revolt against injustice, reaching back into antiquity to the brothers from whom Babeuf borrowed his assumed first name. In a sense, the role of Babeuf for socialism may be compared to the role of Galileo for science; it was Galileo who married the philosophers' rationalist tradition of logical truth with the plebeian tradition of craftsmen's empiricism and *techne*.

Babeuf articulated, as a separate and consistent system of ideas, the utopia of the sansculottes which strove, in the course of the French Revolution, to cut the umbilical cord tying it to bourgeois individualist egalitarianism. While the inchoate capitalist culture sought in political equality a bulwark to protect an unqualified and unchecked individualism, the sansculottes looked toward the state as an active power to be used for curbing and controlling the individual in the name of the community. Both currents could be accommodated in one river-bed until the river passed the point of the equality of political rights. Beyond this point, however, a bifurcation was inevitable.

In Babeuf's epoch-making statement in the *Manifesto of the Equals* (1796) the realisation of this inevitability was for the first time made explicit. The French Revolution was only a prelude to another revolution. The Declaration of the Rights of Man and the Citizen was a step in the right direction, but by no means the end of the process; in fact, merely its beginning. The equality which the Declaration proclaimed 'we must have in our midst, under the roof of our houses'. How to bring it there? By placing on the agenda a new revolutionary goal, on which the Declaration is mute, and which, in fact, flies in the face of the interpretation of equality which the Declaration took for granted: the goal of doing away with the terrible contrasts between rich and poor, masters and servants. Unless this goal is attained, equality will remain nothing but a fine and sterile fiction of the law.

Babeuf would elaborate further on these ideas a year later, when defending himself during the Vendôme trial. It was there that the concept of 'the welfare of men' was first brought to the fore, as Babeuf himself was apt to stress, as 'a new idea in Europe'. What followed was already a gigantic step beyond even the most generous promises of bourgeois equality: the existence of an unfortunate or a poor man in the state is not to be endured. 'The unfortunate are the powers of the earth; they have the right to speak as masters to the governments that neglect them.' The crucial point is that a state which, in the name of inalienable rights, refuses to intervene in the distribution of wealth and property, is by the same token a state which neglects the poor.

What the poor need is a state determined to trespass on the ground which the liberal utopia would gladly leave to the discretion of the individual; in other words, a state which is prepared to reach beyond *homo politicus*. Babeuf, indeed, epitomised practically the whole content of the ensuing century of socialist propaganda. 'It is necessary to bind together everyone's lot; to render the lot of each member of the association independent of chance, and of happy or unfavourable circumstance; to assure to every man and to his posterity, no matter how numerous it may be, as much as they need, but no more than they need.' The only means that can possibly lead to such a situation is a common administration: the political state ruled by the *demos*. What Babeuf wished to get rid of was precisely the loneliness of the isolated individual, which the bourgeois utopia eulogised and sacralised. Instead of guarding their dubious 'right to fight each other on equal terms', the state should take care of the personal and communal well-being of all individuals, so as to liberate them once and for all from the agonising uncertainty and fear of the future which competition inevitably brings about. Only such a state 'will put an end to the gnawing worm of perpetual inquietude, whether throughout society as a whole, or privately within each of us, about what tomorrow will bring, or at least what next year will bring, for our old age, for our children and for their children'. Babeuf's was the call for a welfare state, made on behalf of these who in the zero-sum game of competition expected to be the losers.

There is another idea in Babeuf's utopia which was to become a leitmotiv of socialist thought: the community should guarantee to each 'as much as they need, but no more than they need'. The idea is sometimes dismissed as a residue of the pre-industrial disbelief in the productive potential of mankind, as a sheer repetition of the defensive 'equality of poverty' in the style of More and Campanella. In fact, there is more to it; no less than an entire philosophy of human nature and its perversion. Its origin may be found in the austere scepticism of Seneca, but for Babeuf and his descendants it had probably been refurbished by Rousseau. The 'natural' needs of man are limited and one can satisfy them completely without transgressing the confines of modesty. It is not their needs which cause men to indulge in luxury and to revel in excess, but the pernicious influence of an artificially created human condition. 'The consuming ambition, the ardour to raise one's relative fortune', Rousseau wrote in his *Discourse on the Origin of Inequality among Man* (1755), 'is due less to a genuine need than to a desire to stand out from the others.' Needs are 'natural', human relations are artificial; as such they can be 'changed' and when changed appropriately they will remove the only motive for the human pursuit of wealth and thus return man to the 'natural' state of happiness founded on the satisfaction of his genuine needs.

The trouble with the emerging world of rampant individualism was that one could no longer derive satisfaction from the mere satisfaction of modest, unperverted needs, even if bent on resisting the splendours of affluence. A man, happy yesterday, becomes poor and so deprived today; he becomes poor 'without losing anything. Because as everything changed around him, he himself did not change at all'. For the sake of the happiness of these decent, modest men, one has to put some brakes upon change. Not necessarily in the sense of barring any further increase of the output of goods (though, not surprisingly, such an interpretation recurs time and again in the socialist literature), but in the sense of bringing some sort of constancy and stability into the network of human relations. Using a somewhat modernised terminology, one might say that a secured status would liberate man from anxieties generated by the efforts to retain it, as well as by yearnings to enhance it.

Here we come across a further and fateful departure of the socialist utopia from the liberal-bourgeois one. It was set out clearly by Saint-Amand Bazard, one of the most ardent Saint-Simonians, in his first lecture on his teacher's doctrine (delivered on 17 December 1828): what man needs more than anything else for his happiness is a 'regular social order', but such order has occurred only twice in human history – in ancient times and in the Middle Ages. The third return of the 'regular order' is still in the future. Obviously it won't be identical with the former two; but 'it will present striking analogies to them, with respect to order and unity'. Order, that is, certainty which can be furnished only by stability of the social pattern; and unity, which means freedom from the necessity to compete and to hazard one's status. Twelve years before, Robert Owen, addressing the inhabitants of his model socialist colony, stressed that permanence is the distinctive feature of that happiness which the wisely organised human community is expected to offer. Both Bazard and Owen were admittedly abstract schemers, dreaming of ready-to-wear social patterns designed in the atelier of Reason; but their concern was avowedly of an across-the-board type. Louis Auguste Blanqui, whom everybody without hesitation will place at the other end of the socialist spectrum, as the practitioner of revolutionary struggle rather than a self-appointed adviser to the Serene and the Powerful, saw precisely the 'constant uncertainty about tomorrow' as the supreme reason for a social revolution.

To sum up: the socialist utopia, in its starting-points and leitmotivs, may be justly described as 'the counter-culture of capitalism'. The notion of a 'counter-culture' contains a dialectical and conflict-ridden unity of continuity and rejection. To be a counter-culture, a system of beliefs and postulates must engage in a significant polemic with the dominant culture, must question it, so to speak, in its own words, and to do so must speak essentially the same language in order to make the dialogue comprehensible. These conditions were fully met by the socialist utopia in relation to the dominant liberal-bourgeois utopia. It accepted in full the bourgeois ideals of the reign of justice and law, supposedly safeguarded by the institution of political equality; but it emphatically denied the possibility of squaring this postulate with a free-trade economy, abandonment of the individual to his own solitude and a state which was indifferent to the anxieties of the abandoned individual. 'If you wish to enjoy political equality, abolish property', wrote Proudhon in the first chapter of his iconoclastic *What is Property?* in 1840; eight years later Louis Blanc wrote in his *Organization of Labour*: 'Freedom consists, not only in the *rights* that have been accorded, but also in the *power* given men to develop and exercise their faculties.... Are we for having the State intervene?... Most certainly.... Why? Because we want freedom'. To the ideal society envisaged in the ruling bourgeois utopia socialism offered a genuine alternative; but one which instead of dismissing casually the alleged virtues of the former, carried its guiding ideas much further than their original preachers intended.

It seems that the notorious convolutions of the political history of socialism were to a large extent contained already in this equivocal, dialectical relation between the bourgeois and the socialist utopias. The socialist utopia could present itself as a genuine substitute for the bourgeois way of dealing with the issues of modernity, or as a further stage into which the previous stages smoothly and imperceptibly merge.

References

Bendix, Reinhard (1964) *Nationbuilding and Citizenship*. Chichester: John Wiley & Sons.

Roth, Gunther (1963) *The Social Democrats in Imperial Germany*. Totowa: Bedminster Press.

Tocqueville, Alexis de (1955) *The Old Regime and the French Revolution*. New York: Doubleday.

3.2 Modern Times, Modern Marxism (1968)

I have chosen to write on Marxism, rather than on Marxist sociology. As a matter of fact the very attempt to differentiate Marxist methodology and Marxist *Weltanschauung* into separate domains within the established academic divisions is hardly a "Marxist" endeavor. If there is something specific and peculiar to the Marxist approach to the study of man, it is its stubborn effort to combine into a unified whole the multifarious and divergent images of man as seen from different points of observation. To use the modern technical terminology, we can say that Marxist social science aims at a "hologram" of man instead of a series of photographs. It is the basic methodological premise and, at the same time, the discriminating feature of the Marxist approach to social science, that "economic man," "social man," "cultural man," "political man" and similar products of scientific division of labor are nothing but model constructs, creations of a long process of abstraction maturing in institutionally separated micro-social settings. The only genuine reality, from which all these models depart and to which they refer, is man as such, pursuing the process of living through and by his social and cultural environment. If we perceive this process as an aggregate of relatively isolated functions set in fully autonomous frames of reference, it can be explained solely as a feed-back effect of cognitively fruitful, but also misleading, abstraction. To understand man we have to bring together all that we have discovered while penetrating the different aspects of his unified life-process ("unified" is not the proper word in this context; the word implies something which is brought together after having been divided; what we have in mind however is the kind of unity existing before any division took place).

One of the gravest misunderstandings among the current interpretations of Marxist social theory is the attempt to reduce it to a kind of "economic determinism." Not only is there nothing particularly Marxist about attempts at simplified, single-factor, genetic explanations of social phenomena, but there is involved a methodological habit most alien to the basic postulates put forward by Marx. What Marx meant by insisting on bringing the economic frame of reference into the analysis of social phenomena was something quite different from economic determinism and, for this reason, from any kind of single-factorial analysis; he demanded that in order to understand the social, cultural, or ideological aspects of human behavior one must look at it as an integral part of a whole, of a total structure embracing the economic dimension of the life-process as well as other dimensions. The notorious Marxist concern with the economic sphere of social life ought to be understood not on the genetic, but on the structuralistic plane. It is the entirely modern demand to understand-through-allocating-in-a-structure which is at stake, not the traditional search for *the* efficient cause.

These remarks may not seem promising as far as current prospects of Marxist thought are concerned. The totalistic ambitions of Marxism look very "unscientific" indeed in times when the realm of science is dominated by a trend toward "knowing all about nothing," that is, toward increasingly minute partition of concerns and competences. It seems as if the Marxian kind of reasoning about man and society has become outmoded by recent developments in the human sciences. It appears to be really old-fashioned to pursue a total image of society in times when precision and measurement are the most cherished scientific values even if achieved by picking up a single pair of variables from the Lazarsfeldian "universum of items." The Marxist research program stands in apparent opposition to the dominant trend of scientific development. Indeed, the norms of the scientific sub-culture are themselves values too important to be disposed of light-heartedly on behalf of a program which can substantiate itself only by referring to a century-long tradition.

But the Marxian program has something else to offer besides its conformity to time-honored tradition. Before specifying this "something else" we must however make some remarks on the social factors which are, at least in part, responsible for the present position of the human sciences.

Those of us who deal with the current history of the human sciences usually take at their face value the statements made by the proponents of "modern" and "scientific" sociology on the motivational premises of the strategy they have chosen. Judging from these statements the present positivistic trend in the human sciences is a result of a psychological impact of success achieved by the older and more honorable sciences like physics and chemistry. Quantification, atomization, limitation of hypotheses to the type immediately and experimentally verifiable, are generally pointed to as the main paths leading to both cognitive success and to the social appreciation and respectability of scholars. All the rest follows automatically, providing we have accepted the basic premise. Now, what people think about their own motives is not something to be neglected. It really is a powerful factor, which is responsible for these people being willing to do what they do. Still, there is another set of factors which helps us to understand why these people do what they do, or rather, why those who want to do it are selected to occupy the positions of the highest institutional influence.

In terms of institutions of societal integration our epoch is one of large-scale organizations. The main problem these organizations deal with is the manageability of their units, e.g., the human beings who perform the roles ascribed to them due to their positions in the organizational structure. The main instrumental values these organizations cherish are the set of manageable stimuli assuring the highest probability of achieving the expected response. The type of value determines the limits of variables which can contribute to the achievement of this task. That is, any large-scale organization is interested solely in those factors which are at the same time manageable (the necessary resources ought to be available to the organizational power center and be submitted to its decisions only) and evoke more or less uniform, repetitive, and therefore predictable responses. Organization itself is an attempt at limitation of the unbounded multiplicity of opportunities; an attempt at structuration of an amorphic, homogeneous universum. Organization is concerned with what is restricted, "realistic," relatively stable. Factors which fall outside this domain of interest and pragmatics are looked upon at best as being like the unmanageable "noise" in communication channels. Organizations are deeply interested in laws of "cause and effect," deterministic or at least of a high degree of probability. This interest, which is structurally and functionally determined, shapes in its turn the peculiarly organizational image of the human world. The interest and significance of human beings consist in their interest and significance for managerial purposes. Managers search for the correlative function tying the output indices of the organizational units to their respective input indicators. That is why the human units really are mechanisms with output indices which are predictable on the basis of input. The only thing which remains to be done, since this demand-image has molded the intellectual climate of the managerial world, is to ascertain how to order a manageable stimuli pattern so as to evoke the desirable distribution of behavioral responses. Managerial thinking is technical thinking. The type of human science managers stimulate intellectually and sponsor financially is technical science. It is, through its socio-cultural function, social engineering "by manipulation." It instructs how to manipulate human behavior by ordering the pattern of "objective," external situations; by restricting the possible range of "free" choice; by making the iron chain of necessity tight enough to assure a high degree of predictability and manageability of human behavior.

This is, in broad outline, the socio-cultural situation which feeds and fertilizes the type of human science which takes quantification, sober realism, etc., for heuristic principles. Inside the realm marked by signposts of this kind the postulate of increasing departmentalization is a sound one. It is just the reflection of the already accomplished partition of organizational spheres of interest, and of substituting clusters of roles for "total" personalities. A science which is really useful to managerial goals cannot be different. It is as it ought to be, and nobody can deny its functional adaptation to the role it has been called upon to play.

Managerial demand is the only demand organized and articulated, and combining lucid goal-formulation with adequate material resources. The alternative demand is, on the contrary, so diffuse and inarticulate that it can be easily overlooked and neglected. One can – as happens so often – doubt whether it exists at all. Its social basis is incomparably broader, but it is not sheer numbers which count in society, but the level of organization. And the social basis of this second type of demand is dispersed and atomized. It consists of the members of society in their role of no-role-performers, of personalities as yet undivided into roles, of just men and women whose fate appears to themselves as a unified and unique whole, undivided into departments ruled by specialized sets of variables. The problem any man as a pure and simple human being is confronted with is different from the kind of problems faced by men in their managerial function. According to the functional requisites of his role the manager is expected to deal with and to solve the problem of adapting the behavior of a human being to the structural demands of his institutional setting. It does not matter just what these demands and this setting are. As Abraham Maslow put it, providing that "you have attained a nice stabilization of forces and you *are* adjusted," it does not matter whether, perhaps, "adjustment and stabilization, while good because they cut your pain, are also bad because development toward a higher ideal ceases." It is only natural that the intellectual folklore, fed as always with crumbs which have fallen from the feast table of the masters' culture (this process being intensified to the utmost due to both mass media and mass production of cultural goods), shows currently an unmistakable tendency toward putting personal problems into managerial terms. How to adapt myself to the harsh demands of life? How to become a person such as people like me to be? How to adjust my dreams and cravings to the environment I can neither change nor even influence? These and the like are the dominant themes of the popular ideology, this diluted concoction of the managerial world-outlook, its inverse, parodistic brand. This is the modern form of the "false consciousness" (according to Marx's terminology) brought to life by the epoch of pragmatistic biotechnics which replaces the *Weltanschauung* and moral systems in their role of life guides. To be more precise, what is originally the product of the managerial, pragmatistic world-outlook becomes, when applied to personal experience, a set of purely pragmatic concerns and prescriptions. It is hard to imagine a more complete success of the dominant ideology. The ideal state in which "people want to do what they must" (Erich Fromm) is nearly achieved.

Still, though the individual is stunned and silenced, there exists another "functional requisite" of man in his anthropological frame of reference, prior to any kind of societal demand, which views the society itself as a better or worse means to adjust the natural and cultural environment to human needs. In view of this alternative requisite the terms "deviation" and "maladjustment" refer not to the personality but to the society. If numerous people experience "maladjustment" as their personal problem, what is really maladjusted is the society. From the moment we assume the anthropological point of view any "realistic" empirical feature of the current societal organization can no longer be taken for granted. The tacit assumption that "a partial individual, the bearer of the partial social action" should not or cannot be replaced by "an individual many-sidedly developed, to whom the different social functions are the alternative means of life-activity succeeding each other" (Karl Marx), ought to be proved before being accepted. What is of primary concern is how to adjust society to individual needs, not the reverse; how to extend the range of freedom of individual choice; how to provide room enough for individual initiative and non-conformity. To deal with these problems one needs knowledge of a different kind from that which one applies to solve the tasks faced by managers. What is needed is a kind of knowledge which shows how to "manipulate the human environment by enlarging the scope of information in human minds," instead of how to "manipulate human behavior by modifying the pattern of external situational pressures." Now, this kind of knowledge makes human behavior less, not more predictable. It functions in a manner exactly opposite to the knowledge created to suit the managerial world.

Marxist human science is as well fitted to the demands of this "anthropological" function as, let us say, multi-variable analysis of human behavior in terms of stimulus and response is fitted to the managerial function. This is not an evaluative statement insofar as both functions are firmly rooted in the structural-functional web of modern society. It is simply a theoretical assertion involving the act of choice of analytical categories to deal with the modern human sciences, though it is perfectly obvious that the two functions as well as the types of cognitive efforts stimulated by them are neither philosophically nor morally neutral.

What we have said above about Marxism may be looked at also as a definitional statement. The body of knowledge claiming the Marxist designation is far from being homogeneous. It is differentiated in its content as well as in the functions it fulfills. The shape of a human science depends – from the point of view of our analytical framework – on the type of functional demand it meets. That is why it is so difficult to imagine Marxian thought made to the measure of the managerial type of social problems. I believe this contradiction between the "anthropological" and "managerial" functions of social science helps us to understand more fully the intricate fate of Marxism during the lifespan of the last two generations.

Some additional comments are necessary to avoid misunderstanding and to make our distinction sufficiently clear.

First of all, the functional division we propose is not an attempt to classify types of facts investigated or methods applied. As far as research methods are concerned, their merits and shortcomings can be reasonably judged solely in light of the volume and competence of the information they lead to. The choice of cognitive methods always is, or should be, secondary to the choice of problems one thinks important enough to be investigated. As far as these problems are concerned, all kinds of ascertained facts can be used to the benefit of both functions. There is nothing "inside" the facts, inherent in their very nature, which makes them "managerial" or "anthropological." It is the human use of facts which makes them submitted to one or another function. I am rather inclined to the belief that facts of any kind are "by their nature" dysfunctional to managerial aims. Some kinds of facts are, it is true, useless for other than managerial purposes, since their application requires resources to which only managers have access. But other facts among those used to achieve managerial goals increase, if spread widely, the volume of "diffused" information, and thus act against restrictions the managerial activity aims at. This explains the constant managerial pressure towards maintaining secrecy in scientific investigations and simultaneously points to significant limitations, perhaps utopianism, in the managerial ideal of a perfectly manageable society. That is perhaps what Friedrich Engels meant when he spoke of truth as always serving to benefit the oppressed part of mankind.

From the "anthropological" point of view truth is a value in itself. Contrary to the managerial standpoint, the "anthropological" point of view denies the sense of dividing facts into "anthropologically" and "managerially" functional. The more facts are established and available to the public the stronger is the "anthropological" case. The real differentiation of the functional commitment begins much above the level of primary empirical data. It is the type of generalization one wishes to arrive at, the way of ordering data and making them comprehensible, which really count. (We are aware, of course, of the impact of both cognitive goal and assumed theoretical framework on the sort of facts produced; so we understand that different facts fit one or another function in different proportion. Still, the task of making our analytical categories operative on the level of protocol data meets almost unsurmountable difficulties).

What we have said above concerning human science which maintains an "anthropological" point of view refers even more precisely to its Marxian variety. "Non-Marxist" facts simply do not exist. That is, it is the way of ordering facts, of passing from "sensory" to "intelligible," which is Marxist or non-Marxist. The level of global theory of society, the level of world-outlook, determine the realm to which the terms "Marxist" and "non-Marxist" are applicable. On this level the peculiarity and uniqueness of Marxist thought is as clear and – what is more important – as fruitful and vital as it was one hundred years ago. It is vital because a very small portion of the problems tackled by Marx a century ago is so far resolved. It is vital because no major step has been taken so far toward the new type of – as Kolakowski put it – "expressive personality." Since almost nothing has been done to prevent fragmentation of human action and human personality, to prevent the restriction of the individual's liberty to the sphere of consumer choice, to prevent the limiting of his opportunities of expression to the selection of goods offered by the market, Marxist thought is of profound contemporary importance.

It does not happen very often that people approach the "global theory" level in order to solve managerial-type problems; the type of generalizations sought for by managers embraces rather the "middle-range" theories, connecting some presumably manipulable variables with "dependent" variables of human behavior. But it sometimes does happen, as in the case of Talcott Parsons, moved in his grand-theoretical endeavors, as C. Wright Mills pointed out, by the managerial type of curiosity to ask, just how is this society possible? Indeed, what Parsons has done in his theory of society is to mold a global world-image out of the everyday problems as seen by those in the managerial role, thus promoting the mundane efforts of those in the managerial position to the rank of a structural principle of social organization. Now, Marx has done the same thing with the everyday experience of those who are, by their structural allocation, put in the position of manipulable things. Marxist theory of society is an attempt at understanding "individual," "private," "unique" suffering as malfunctioning of the global society; at analyzing the case not in terms of personal adjustment, but in categories of societal transformation. That is why Marxian theory is so attentive to the problems of the social structure, viewed as something external, restrictive, alien, far distant from the image of a "structure" constructed from the universal consensus on mutually complementary norms and values.

This last point shifts our attention to another controversial issue in modern sociology. Grand methodological statements in the style of Thomas and Znaniecki are nowadays out of fashion, but the predispositions they stimulate can unconsciously as well as consciously determine the way of viewing the human world. As a result, the genuine subject-matter that many sociologists are concerned with is not the human condition as such, independent of what people think about it and whether people think about it at all, but the way people see and evaluate their situation. This methodological decision or unreflective practice is responsible for substantial impoverishment of the cognitive horizon. Conflict becomes a controversy between unreconciled opinions or discordant pieces of information; social structure becomes the intertwining of accepted cognitive, evaluative and cathexic norms; the behavioral situation itself becomes the pattern of the actor's goals and values. Some basic problems which for many centuries provided the sole reason why people were concerned with studying their own human world – such as "false" or "genuine" consciousness or "adequacy" or "discordance" between what culture suggests one should do and what society enables one to do – in this mental framework seem to be senseless and simply fall to the ground. Nowadays we are not philosophers, but it is not necessary to be a philosopher to adhere to the Hegelian identification of the "real" with "reasonable;" it takes even less philosophy to act as if all that is not "real" here and now is also "unreasonable" or at least "unscientific" forever. The fashionable ideas of natural science travel in most cases very rapidly to the realm of their social-science neighbors. It remains for the sociologists of knowledge to discover why this general rule does not apply as well to the fundamental premise of modern physics, that our world is one of many possible worlds. Indeed, if one judged according to most sociological writings, one would assume not only that our world is the only world possible, but also that what deserves the distinction of being "real," at least in the sense of being the proper field of scientific investigation, is the end product of the controversial socializing process and not the objective structure of the society which determines its shape. So far as this tacit assumption prevails in modern sociology, the Marxist approach to the study of human affairs retains its distinctive identity.

Thus we have arrived at the second dimension in which the question, what is and what is not Marxist human science in modern times, can be answered. But many other dimensions can be easily singled out. For example, the entire range of contrasts between the holistic approach and the pluralistic approach. The first is preoccupied with a system as a distinctive pattern of interconnected and interdependent parts – according to Koehler's famous saying, that "particular lungs have much more in common with the neighboring heart and liver than with other lungs." It views the system as a structure, that is, as a way of ordering the universum of events, a particular limitation imposed on the unlimited range of abstract possibilities by making some events more probable than otherwise and other events less. On the other hand, the semantic content of any particular event is ascertainable only if looked upon in its relation to the total structure, built up of pairs of binary oppositions. The notion of one particular class is meaningless unless it is related to some other class counterposed to the first; it is the binary relation, the opposition, which is both meaningful and logically as well as socially prior to the socially distinctive phenomena "consolidating" on its poles, whether they be cultural norms, behavioral habits, roles or social classes. Marxist human science shares this methodological approach as well as the other with certain other trends in the modern science of man, with, let us say, the structural anthropology of Claude Lévi-Strauss or the psychology of Jean Piaget. At the same time it is in opposition to the "pluralistic behaviorism" (to use Don Martindale's accurate term) type of sociology which knows no structure apart from statistical distribution and postulates the over-all reduction of the statements on wholes to the statistical statements on units. For pluralistic behaviorism to discover the "meaning" of an event or phenomenon is to trace its probable causes by ascertaining the statistically correlated variables. From the holistic-structuralistic point of view to discover the meaning is to determine the position occupied by a particular event or phenomenon in a structure of a higher level of which it is a part.

The other distinctive features of the Marxist approach to human science, which are closely related to the foregoing, may be enumerated briefly as follows:

(a) Intensive preoccupation with the structure of cognitive process; keen attention devoted to the continuous search for "conditions of obtaining truth" in social investigations (in the sense ascribed to this problem by the "sociology of knowledge" approach); importance ascribed to verifiability of sociological propositions and to its prerequisites.

(b) Significance attached to relationships between science and ideology, social science and social structure; to similarities and distinctions between social and natural sciences, the role of values, theoretical preconceptions and cultural biases in the cognitive process.

(c) The quite exceptional degree of sensitivity to the vocational self-designation; unceasing search for a lucid and unambiguous definition of the sociologist's role in society, for values and preconceptions not only introduced deliberately by external pressure, but also latent in the sociologist's individual research and theoretical constructs; careful scrutinizing of the social effects of the sociologist's research and educational activities.

(d) Continuing attempts at ordering the heterogeneous field of modern sociology, at discerning and classifying the notorious multitude of sociological schools and currents, at weighing, estimating and comparing their respective merits and shortcomings, at constructing an up-to-date, but always comprehensive, unified, all-embracing, though internally consistent body of knowledge aimed at understanding both diachronic and synchronic dimensions of the social structure and culture; deep concern with the cumulative nature of social facts and "theories of middle range" offered by representatives of different schools and attained by applying different methods, with comparability of measurements accomplished with different scales and supported by different theories; keen interest in the role of the scholar's personality and socio-cultural background in shaping the intellectual image of the human world.

(e) Predominance of macro-social problems and issues over partial, one-sided, and narrowly-framed research items; an outstandingly high proportion of research devoted to the general problems of social structure, culture, over-all trends of social and cultural mobility, multi-dimensionality of social stratification, integrative and disruptive factors in the societal system, etc.

(f) Emphasis on the ties connecting empirical "field research" with theory, and theory with empirical data; chronic maneuvering between the Scylla of abstract "grand theory" cut off from empirical data and the Charybdis of shallow and theoretically aimless collecting and counting of facts irrelevant to theory.

It requires no great effort to realize that every item the modern Marxists, at least in Poland, claim to be a distinctive feature of their own work is not its attribute only. Many are shared by representatives of trends of thought which hardly acknowledge their Marxist denomination; some others are simply a part of the present-day scientific folklore – if not shaping the scientist's behavior, being nevertheless the "must" object of everyday lipservice. One can hardly resist asking what is particularly Marxist in the foregoing list of heuristic principles and research preferences. There is indeed only one possible answer: what is Marxist in all postulates listed above is their integration, so that they constitute in common with the theoretical assumptions mentioned earlier a unified body of knowledge unique in its wholeness and entirety. Marxist human science can be understood properly, in my opinion, at least, as a pole on many different scales. Due to its placement on each individual scale, Marxist human science resembles closely many other trends in social sciences which are not and do not pretend to be Marxist. But on each scale it enjoys a different neighborhood and shares different company. The distinctively Marxist approach is, we may say, confined to the common sector of a multitude of trends differentiated on all scales we have listed above. It is still distinct and at the same time closely related to the main body of modern human science in all its vital attributes. That is why the very nature of Marxist theory makes it an open and developing system, existing only in permanent dialogue with the most modern of its scientific contemporaries. Cannon's or Piaget's understanding of homeostasis correctly defines the kind of active and dynamic, dialectic equilibrium which characterizes the way of being of the Marxist trend in human science.

Up to now we have spoken of Marxism as if, distinct as it is from non-Marxist currents in social thought, it were itself a unified and indivisible trend. This, of course, is not true, at least insofar as we accept as the defining indicator of Marxist theory the Marxist self-designation of the author. I do not have in mind the notorious differentiation of political ideologies each of which claims – to some extent justly – to be Marxist, sometimes "the only" Marxist political ideology. This dimension of internal Marxist division, however important politically, is not relevant to the present consideration. While introducing here the problem of the heterogeneity of modern Marxism I have in mind only its scientific aspect: Marxism as a trend within the realm universally accepted as the domain of human sciences. Still, even in this field modern Marxist thinking is far from being homogeneous. This applies not only to the images of Marxism to which self-designated Marxists adhere but also to those images held by the critics of Marx and Marxists.

As far as the critics are concerned, most of them assume "economic determinism" to be the "essence" of Marxism. Some of them even use this term to denote the doctrine they criticize. They cannot be accused of being at odds with facts, though one can reasonably expect from scientists that they distinguish between a portion and the whole. It is true that for a rather prolonged time the popular variety of Marxism, particularly that branch developing inside the mass movement, was dominated by "economic determinism," stressing obsessively the causal aspect of historical interpretation and neglecting almost completely its activistic nature. This variety evolved historically into an influential school with Plekhanov, Kautsky and Bukharin as the most famous representatives and spokesmen. We have no space for an elaborate analysis of the historical circumstances which nurtured this line of development, but I think it can be traced to functional prerequisites of a mass social movement: the necessity to bring the guiding philosophical doctrine closer to the natural cognitive set of the mass following, to make it digestible to those who are "spontaneously deterministic" and spontaneously convinced of the "material objectivity" of the universe. The other current within modern Marxism is its activistic interpretation which found its full expression and most sophisticated elaboration in the writings of Antonio Gramsci and Georg Lukács, with Rosa Luxemburg and Lenin (if we leave aside his *Materialism and Empirio-criticism*) as the closest adherents. This second current within Marxist human science is as far from any kind of "economic determinism" as one can imagine. With human historical action as its basic category, this current puts to the forefront the active, motivating role of mental structuralization of the human world. Instead of individual action, as dealt with by Znaniecki or Parsons, we have here the notion of "historical block" arising whenever the set of opportunities involved "objectively" in a historical situation finds the adequate ideology which in its turn is relevant enough to the private experience of the masses to gain their support and to stimulate their action. According to this interpretation of Marxist thought, ideas play the role of an historically active force. They do not reflect passively what is already inherent in the social reality. They have nothing in common with the famous "mirror image" persisting in many popular textbooks of a positivistic brand. The truth is understood here as a process, the very pronouncement of an idea being a powerful factor in making its content true through the praxis it initiates. It makes no sense to ask whether Marx predicted accurately the "absolute impoverishment" of the proletariat, or failed to foresee the actual course of historical events; as a matter of fact Marx caused the failure of his predictive statement and turned it into a "self-destroying prophecy" by mobilizing social forces adequate to counteract its fulfillment. It is equally nonsensical to ask whether Marx was able to "predict" the triumph of the Marxist revolution in Tsarist Russia, since he was one of its main causes, one part of the "historical block" which made the socialist upheaval really inevitable precisely in these "praxis-like" terms. This is, indeed, the only way one can make predictions in the realm of the social sciences; providing one does not keep them secret, one "ploughs in" predictions, thus making them a new and significant part of an historical situation, in which conscious human beings are the only actors.

Perhaps this assumption is mainly responsible for Marxist thinking being by its very nature so obstinately opposed to conformity to the norms of academic respectability. It can by no means stop being a revolutionary force, an ideology of non-conformists, without ceasing to be Marxist.

3.3   Communism: A Postmortem (1992)

The events of 1989 in the East-Central European belt of satellite communist regimes was a most fitting finale for the twentieth century, bound to be recorded in history as the age of revolutions. They changed the political map of the globe, affecting even parts ostensibly distant from the scene of the upheaval in ways which are still far from being fully grasped. They are also certain to be scrutinized for the updating they offer to our orthodox views of how revolutions come about and how are they conducted in a new sociocultural context.

Among *political* revolutions with which the modern era was fraught, genuinely *systemic* ones have been relatively rare. All political revolutions involved a change in the way in which the style of political rule affected the politically administered social system. Systemic revolutions, in addition, entailed a transformation of the system itself; a contrived, government-managed or at least government-initiated change of socio-economic structure, which took off at a moment when the political revolution has been completed. The two concepts are, of course, liminal; two opposite ends of a continuum along which the known revolutions – all or almost all of which have been 'mixed' cases – can be plotted.

Ideally-typically, revolution is 'merely political' (or, rather, non-systemic) in so far as it 'shakes off' a political regime dysfunctional in relation to a fully-fledged socio-economic system. Political revolution 'emancipates' the system from its political constraints. Recent revolutions in Portugal, Spain or Greece belong by and large to this category. They swept off oppressive dictatorial regimes, redundant from the point of view of fully developed bourgeois societies capable of self-sustained reproduction, already fully formed and capable of supporting a democratic order. Though it normally takes an organized, even conspiratorial minority, to overcome the coercive government of the day, such a minority may be justly seen in the traditional way: as an agent acting on behalf of certain well-established collective interests, an active and self-conscious vanguard of relatively integrated (economically and socially powerful, though politically disarmed) forces. One may say that the political revolutions of this kind simply remove an obstacle on the road already taken; or that they adjust the political dimension of the system to the other, economic and social, dimensions. This was, indeed, the original view of the revolution: having matured, like a butterfly inside the carapace of a pupa, society has to shatter the oppressive and gratuitous constraints that arrest its development. That imagery was a faithful reflection of the revolutions which accompanied the advance of the capitalist order: those revolutions were, so to speak, the instances of *bürgerliche Gesellschaften* shaking off the already obsolete frames of absolutist and despotic states within which they gestated.

The recent anti-communist revolutions come close to the other pole of the continuum. In this respect, paradoxically, they are akin to the bolshevik revolution of 1917 rather than to classic capitalist revolutions that brought the unduly archaic body politic into agreement with the needs of the socio-economic traits of the system. Recent anti-communist revolutions have been *systemic* revolutions: they face the task of *dismantling* the extant system and *constructing* one to replace it. True, they toppled old dictatorial or despotic political regimes, like the other revolutions did; but here the similarity ends. A society capable of sustaining and reproducing itself without the perpetual and ubiquitous wardenship and command of political rulers (this is precisely the meaning of *bürgerliche Gesellschaft*) has yet to be constructed there; and the political stage of the revolution is only the act of site-clearing and condition-setting for the system-building job – a project that will have to be implemented under a close political supervision and through state initiative.

A corollary of this is a contradiction that has yet to reveal the full scale of its impact on further political history of postcommunist Europe: the social forces which led to the downfall of the communist power (and so to the success of the political stage of the revolution) are not those that will eventually benefit from the construction of the new system. Forces whose interests will gain from the working of the new system will need to be brought into existence in the process of system-construction.

One of the reasons that even the most acute students of communist regimes were baffled and surprised by the sharply anti-communist direction of change prompted by the gathering social dissent, was the fact that before the series of revolutions started there were few, or no signs of organized social forces with interests pointing beyond the confines of the communist regime (as late as during the famous 'Round-Table Conference' in Poland there was no discussion of dismantling the planned economy or wholesale privatization of ownership; and none of the major participants indicated that they would put such matters on the political agenda, were the circumstances more favourable). Indeed, as the Polish sociologist Jadwiga Staniszkis observed, there were no 'transformative' interests among large classes of Polish society – none of the articulated groups raised the issue of private ownership or objected to the principle of the command economy (Staniszkis, 1988). In Aleksander Smolar's succinct summary of the situation barely a year before the end of the communist rule, 'the fundamental problem of a radical reform is the absence of any real social support' (Smolar, 1988, p. 22). Neither workers in the big industries who made up the core of the Solidarity movement, nor the state-protected individual farmers nor the few private entrepreneurs thriving on the inanities of clumsy central planning, wished a change that would go significantly beyond an essentially redistributive action (Bauman, 1989).

This was, let us emphasize, a *normal* picture for the state of social forces preceding any *systemic* revolution. Dissent the old system could not but generate tended to exceed the system's capacity for accommodation and thus pushed the crisis to breaking point; but this effect was precisely the result of couching demands in the language of the extant system (in the case of communist regimes – more planning, more centralized distribution, the reshuffling of resources within the order of administered justice, etc.) – and thus facing the system with output postulates it was unable to meet. It is a constant and the constitutive attribute, of systemic revolutions that the forces that destroy the *ancien régime* are not consciously interested in the kind of change which would eventually follow the destruction; before the old powers are removed, the design of a new system exists at the utmost as a vision held by a selected, narrow intellectual elite – not as a platform of any massive contest movement.

To put this in a different way: the systemic revolution is not a result of the mass mobilization of support for the blueprint of an alternative system. The first stage of the systemic revolution – the overthrow of the old rulers who hold to the past order of society – bears all the marks of the 'systemic crisis' (i.e., of the system failing to generate the resources, physical and moral, needed for its reproduction), but does not, by itself, determine the alternative to the system that failed. The link between the failure of the old system and the required traits of the new one is construed in a political struggle between competing *theories* conceived and preached by intellectual schools. The nature of social forces that brought about the downfall of the old regime is not a decisive factor in the choice between such theories. Neither does the enmity manifested by the contestant forces towards the old regime guarantee their support for the new one that would be eventually chosen. The toppling of the old rulers does not conjure up the 'transformative interests' missing in the old regime.

Because of this double non sequitur, the survival of the revolutionary alliance is the main issue any systemic revolution is likely to confront 'the morning after' its political victory. The original revolutionary alliance – one that overwhelms the resistance of the administrators of the *ancien régime* – is not normally a reflection of the unity of interests among forces of dissent. As a matter of fact, grievances which bring variegated groups into a political alliance united by its opposition to the government of the day, are highly differentiated as a rule – and more often than not mutually incompatible. It was – let us repeat – the persistent crisis of the old regime that condensed diffuse grievances into a united revolutionary force. Condensation (and unanimity in blaming the state for whatever the objected-to drawback or injustice may be) can follow the appearance of a large issue that seems to stand in the way of each and every demand (like the issue of continuing war in Russia of 1917). In a totalitarian system like the communist one, the tendency to condense the dispersed dissent into an integrated, frontal assault against the state is permanent. Aiming at the regulation of all aspects of social and economic activity, the state assumes willy-nilly explicit responsibility for each and every failing and suffering. All grievances are authoritatively interpreted as malfunctionings of the state and automatically politicized. But would the unity of opposing forces survive the fall of the communist state? And would such forces be similarly energized by the uncertain attractions of the future regime? Would they not rather oppose a change likely to invalidate the form of action and political purposes they learned to pursue?

Chances of Democracy in Systemic Revolutions

Systemic revolutions must yet create the social forces in the name of which they embark on the thorough systemic transformation. In this, let us emphasize once more, lies their deepest paradox – and also the dangers to the democracy they intend to install. As Jerzy Szacki, a leading Polish sociologist, observed in April 1990:

> the basis for the victory of Western liberalism was the spontaneous development of economic relations. Today's Polish liberalism still

remains a *doctrine* that is meant to provoke such a development in the first place – a doctrine the main inspiration for which has been the desire to exit from communism. In effect, today's Polish liberalism is strongly coloured by a 'constructivism' which the classical liberal thinkers most energetically fought against.   (Szacki, 1990, p. 491)

Unlike the purely political revolutions, the systemic ones do not end with the chasing away of the old rulers. The postrevolutionary state faces the awesome tasks of large-scale social engineering; of prompting the formation of a new social structure which – whatever gains it may promise 'in the long run' for everybody's interests – will certainly play havoc with the extant distribution of relative privileges and deprivations. It is likely, therefore, to give rise to discontents of its own and regroup the inherited political alliances. It is unlikely, on the other hand, to secure from the start a majority in support of the intended change. As it remains, however, an 'active state' to a degree not drastically different from that of its predecessor, the postrevolutionary state cannot count on that parcelling out and self-dispersion of social dissent which is so easily attained in the established, market-based democracies. It can be, on the contrary, pretty sure to turn against itself the discontent its actions cannot but generate. For quite a considerable time yet, it will continue to act as a 'dissent-condensing' factor, and hence find it difficult to push forward the systemic transformation while being guided by democratically generated support for its actions.

The consequences for various post-communist regimes differ. What differentiates them is the moment at which a given country joined the series of anti-communist revolutions, and their political and social characteristics at the moment of joining. The collapse of communism in East-Central Europe was indeed a serial process, and the 'state of the game so far' significantly modified the conditions under which the next step was taken and its sociological significance.

Jean Baudrillard wrote recently of 'un pouvoir s'effondrant presque sans violence, comme convaincu de son inexistence par le simple miroir des foules et de la rue' (Baudrillard, 1990, p. 69). This powerful picture of a power deemed invincible suddenly collapsing at the mere sight of the crowds refusing to leave the public square – 'as if persuaded of its own non-existence' – represents the endings of various communist states with varying precision. Certainly, for Czechoslovakia and Hungary and East Germany it is more correct than for Poland, which triggered off the series. For the few thousands in a carnival mood gathered at Vatzlavske Namesti or at the squares of Leipzig and Dresden to be so swiftly and so thoroughly successful (there was not even a need for the public squares of Budapest to be physically occupied), the 'non-existence' of the communist power had to be already convincingly demonstrated at the far end of the long and tortuous process of Polish permanent insurrection. People who filled the Vatzlavske Namesti, much as those who came with rifles to chase them away, knew already what the Poles had discovered by trial, error and a lot of suffering.

There were many factors that combined to make Poland first in the communism-dismantling process; it seems, however, that prominent among them was the protracted process of self-instruction in the self-management of society, culminating in the relatively early 'polonization' of the state–nation conflict in the aftermath of the military *coup d'état* of 1981. The process and the event meant to stop it put the relation between the state and the society, the role of the national state in the perpetuation of the oppressive regime as well as the extent of change attainable within the frame of the national state, in an entirely new perspective and triggered off ambitions that elsewhere looked more like idle utopias. Gorbachev's decision to abandon the European satellites to their own resources and fate found Poland in a state sociologically very different from the countries which had not accumulated similar experience: most importantly, Poland had a fully developed, articulated and self-sustained alternative political force in the shape of a politically seasoned, powerful workers' union.

Thorstein Veblen wrote once of the 'penalty for being in the lead'; indeed, the well entrenched, confident and politically skilled contestant labour movement gave Poland the lead it enjoyed in the sapping and in the end dismantling of the communist rule in the east of Europe. And yet the very assets which secured that advantage may turn into handicap when it comes to the construction of a stable liberal-democratic regime (and this on top of the sorry state of Polish, and other East European economies, particularly when emerging from the shelter of COMECON barter and forced to measure themselves by the competitive criteria of the world market). Dissident intellectuals of Hungary and Czechoslovakia, with the help of students and unsettled urban youth, shook off their respective communist rulers without a nationwide political mobilization and with minimum application of massive political forces of their own, taking advantage of the blows delivered to the confidence and will to resistance of their local rulers 'by proxy' – by the revelations made in the course of the Polish battles. Once in power, they may now proceed to further, evidently less popular and less enthusing, stages of the revolution without the powerful and politically alert, defiantly independent mass movement breathing down their neck and closely watching their hands. They may, indeed, count on the apathy and lack of political skills of the population at large to help them round the first, most awkward corners of economic and political transformation, so that no violation of democracy would be needed to pave the road towards stable liberal democracy of the future.

This chance seems to be denied to Poland. After all, the workers of the largest industrial enterprises, those most obsolete dinosaurs of the failed communist industrialization, least capable of entering the dream of Europe and marked for extinction – were exactly the force that brought communism down (and became such a force through being moved then, as they still are now, by essentially the 'non-transformative' interests of better wages, better work and living conditions, and better ways of defending both of them in the future); but they are now bound to be the first to bear the most severe hardships of the economic transformation – intensification of labour, sharpening of work discipline, loss of job security, unemployment and all.

The Hold of the Patronage State

The distinctive feature of the systemic revolutions now taking place in East-Central Europe is that the system they need to dismantle is one of state-administered patronage: that coercively imposed trade-off between freedom and security. Under the rule of the patronage state, freedom of individual choice in all its dimensions was to be permanently and severely curtailed, yet in exchange the less prepossessing aspects of freedom – like individual responsibility for personal survival, success and failure – were to be spared. To the strong, bold and determined, the patronage state feels like a most sinister rendition of the Weberian 'iron cage'; yet to many weak, shy and lacking in will it may also feel like a shelter. While the end of the oppressive supervision by the agencies of the state and the opening up of space for individual initiative is a change likely to be warmly greeted by all, the removal of the safety net and the burdening of the individual with responsibility previously claimed by the state may well arouse mixed feelings; it may also induce the past wards of state patronage to tune their antennae to populist promises of collective security, and make them into willing followers of any aspiring leader prepared to make such promises and lend his authority to popular suspicions about the dangers of unconstrained liberalism.

The tense period of the dismantling of the patronage state is ripe for complaints, Carlyle style, against the 'cash nexus' replacing much more fulsome, comradely, relations between masters and their men.

The patronage the passing of which Carlyle bewailed was, however, unlike that of the communist state, diffuse and unpolitical; the patronage engraved in popular habits and thought by communist rule is state-centred and thoroughly political. It militates against the self-reliant individual and against the order of liberal democracy cut to the measure of such an individual. This is why the individuals ready for self-reliant life oppose patronage. In the west, they tended to buy themselves off the welfare state services (admittedly a considerably milder, and certainly only a one-sided version of state patronage in the comprehensive, communist style) individually, until the camp of the get-aways reached the critical mass enabling them to take a stand, collectively, against the burden which the continuing existence of the welfare institutions put on them all. In the post-communist east, with its middle classes mortally wounded and unlikely to recover vigour without the active patronage of the state, the prospects of a similar 'buy-out' are rather remote. Looking towards the state for guarantees of security (in private and business life alike) could be a habit which the post-communist reconstruction may reinforce rather than uproot.

Political formulae articulated by the anti-communist intellectuals in the east differ between themselves in the way they balance individual freedom against state-administered distributional justice. One can explain the division by reference to the controversial prospects of the state-patronage heritage. But another factor seems to interfere, rooted not so much in the communist past, as in the present of the 'professional society' which, according to many contemporary commentators from Daniel Bell on, the capitalist society becomes in its modern stage. From his thorough study of the mechanics of the contemporary western type of professional society Harold Perkin concludes that 'the struggle between the public and private sector professions is the master conflict of professional society', and that 'ostensibly class-based political parties' are 'in reality large coalitions of diverse professional interests'. Perkin suggests that the rivalry between two groups of professionals (two sections of the knowledge class) is grounded in the rift between genuinely incompatible interests. The rivalry is about resources, or rather about the principle of their distribution. Each one of the two sections obviously prefers principles better geared to the kind of skills it possesses. Thus the

> ideology of free market appeals to the professional managers of great corporations and their allies because it protects them from the accusation they most fear, that they themselves are the major threat to competition and the freedom of the citizens.

Presenting themselves as the gallant knights of freedom expressed in market competition, they conceal the fact that all competition drives out competitors and tends toward monopoly – and thus hope to pass in the public eye as the guarantors of freedom of choice and even political liberty. The professionals of the public sector, on the other hand, prefer to argue

> in terms of social justice for every citizen, rather than self-interest of each profession; [as this argument is accepted] once a service becomes professionalized under public auspices, the professionals discover further needs to be met and problems to be solved and a host of reasons for extending their activities. Hence the self-generating expansion of the State in all the advanced countries. (Perkin, 1989, p. 37)

From Perkin's vantage point, the communist system could be seen as the domination of 'public sector professionals' pushed to the radical extreme and secured with the help of the coercive resources of the state. The collapse of the communist system brings the post-communist societies closer to the conditions prevalent in the professional societies of the west. The process of the dismantling of the patronage state will need to be performed under those conditions. It will not be guided, therefore, by its own logic alone. The moves explicable by reference to the leftovers of state patronage (or by reference to the opposition they arouse) will intertwine with political developments that can only be understood in terms of modern competition for resources between the *public* and the *private* sector professionals.

The patronage state offered poor services, yet it did cut down on both gains and losses that might have resulted from individual decisions. The overall result was the diminution of risk (except for the area in which initiative was strictly off limits, that is in the space defined by the state as belonging to politics, its monopolistic domain) and the development of economic skills and attitudes that provide little support in situations of contingency, where probabilities are even and outcomes of decisions uncertain. Behaviour proper to unrestrained market conditions has not been learned even among private entrepreneurs and farmers as long as they acted under the conditions of a planned economy. The climate of market competition may feel too inclement for their liking. There is no necessary connection between private business and enthusiasm for a *laissez-faire* style of economic setting; an absence which the charges repeatedly raised by the Polish Peasant Party (and various political spokesmen vying for the votes of urban businessmen) against the government 'that lacks economic policy' profusely demonstrate.

The Collapse of Communism and the Advent of Postmodernity

Communism was made to the measure of modern hopes and pro-mises. Socialism's younger, hotheaded and impatient brother, it wholeheartedly shared in the family trust in the wonderful promises and prospects of modernity, and was awe-struck by the breathtaking vistas of society doing away with historical and natural necessity and by the idea of the ultimate subordination of nature to human needs and desires. But unlike the elder brother, it did not trust history to find the way to the millennium. Neither was it prepared to wait till history proved this mistrust wrong. Its war cry was: 'Kingdom of Reason – now!'

Like socialism (and all other staunch believers in the modern values of technological progress, the transformation of nature and a society of plenty), communism was thoroughly modern in its passionate conviction that a good society can only be a carefully designed, rationally managed and thoroughly industrialized society. It was in the name of those shared modern values that socialism charged the capitalist administrators of modern progress with mismanagement, inefficiency and wastefulness. Communism accused socialism of fail-ing to draw conclusions from the charges: stopping at critique, denun-ciation, prodding – where an instant dismissal of inept and corrupt administrators was in order.

Lenin's redefining of the socialist revolution as a *substitution for,* instead of *continuation of,* the bourgeois revolution, was the founding act of communism. According to the new creed, capitalism was a cancerous growth on the healthy body of modern progress; no longer a necessary stage on the road to a society that will embody modern dreams. Capitalists could not be entrusted (as they once were by the founders of modern socialism, Marx and Engels) with even the pre-liminary job of site-clearing: 'melting the solids and profaning the sacred'. As a matter of fact, the site-clearing itself was neither a necessity, nor a job useful enough to justify the waste of time needed for its performance. As the principles of a rationally organized, good society (more factories, more machines, more control over nature) were well known and agreed upon, one could proceed directly to usher any society (and particularly a society without factories, with-out machines, without the capitalists eager to build them, without the workers oppressed and exploited in the process of building) into a state designed by those principles. There was no point in waiting till the good society arrived through the action of workers, fed up with the sufferings caused by capitalist mismanagement of progress. As one knew what the good society would be like, to delay or even slow down its construction was an unforgivable crime. The good society could be, had to be constructed right away, before the capitalists had a chance to mismanage and the workers to sample the outcomes of their mismanagement; or, rather, its designers should take over the management of society right away, without waiting for the consequences of mismanagement to show up. Capitalism was an unnecessary deflection from the path of Reason. Communism was a straight road to its Kingdom. Communism, Lenin would say, is Soviet power together with the 'electrification of the whole country': that is, modern technology and modern industry under a power conscious of its purpose in advance and leaving nothing to chance. Communism was modernity in its most determined mood and most decisive posture; modernity streamlined, purified of the last shred of the chaotic, the irrational, the spontaneous, the unpredictable.

To be fair to Lenin and other communist dreamers, we ought to recall that the good society of the nineteenth-century economists and politicians, disciples of Smith, Ricardo, James and John Stuart Mill, was not a society of *growth* (difficult as this is today to comprehend), but a society of *stability* and *equilibrium*; one of a steady, well-balanced economy, catering for all needs of the population – not an economy beefing up and pushing to new limits their consumptive needs and capacities. The goodness of society was to be measured by its productive performance, by the degree of gratification of needs (given, 'objective', finite), not by the growing richness and spectacularity of its consumptive display. Let us recall too that for the political theorists and practitioners of that century, disciples of Hegel, Comte or Bentham, the good society was one in which the individual conscience was well geared to the 'common interest', one in which the state acted as the supreme embodiment and the spokesman for the interests of all, while the members of the body politic were guided by awareness and loyalty to societal needs. The cravings and conscience of the individuals *mattered* to the state and to society as a whole. The well-being of society hung on the universal acceptance of its central values; to be effective, the body politic had to *legitimize* itself in terms of those shared values (which meant that the values shared had to be those defended and pursued by the leaders of society and organs of their leadership).

Let us also recall that long *after* the communist adventure started the memories of such a nineteenth-century vision found their most monumental codification in the theoretical system of Talcott Parsons, and that even at such a late date it was accepted at the time, on both sides of the capitalist/communist divide, as the crowning of modern sociology, the culmination of social-scientific wisdom, the long-awaited universal framework for analysis and comprehension of social, economic and political realities. That theoretical system viewed society from the vantage point of the managerial office (that is, posited society as first and foremost a managerial problem). It represented *equilibrium* as the supreme requisite and tendency of a social system, universal acceptance of *value-cluster* as the supreme means to that function's fulfilment, the *co-ordination* of individual and societal needs as the most conspicuous measure of a well-equilibrated society and the needs themselves (in tune with virtually all psychological teachings and the whole of the received humanistic wisdom) as unpleasant states of tension and anxiety which would cease to exist at the moment of needs-satisfaction.

Finally, let us recall that, well into the advanced stages of the communist experiment, the capitalist world watched its progress with bated breath, having little doubt that however wanting the emerging system might have been in other respects, it was a managerial and economic success. What counted for this overt or tacit admiration was that the productive capacity of that society quickly shortened the distance dividing it from the older and wealthier economies of the west. Giant steel mills (the more gigantic the better) and grandiose irrigation schemes (the vaster the better) were still accepted as a credible index of a well-managed society on the way to fulfilment of its mission: the satisfaction of the needs of its members. The communist state, in its own admittedly unprepossessing way, seemed to serve the same ideals of the modern era which even its capitalist haters readily recognized as their own.

In these now uncannily distant times the audacious communist project seemed to make a lot of sense and was taken quite seriously by its friends and foes alike. Communism promised (or threatened, depending on the eye of the beholder) to do what everyone else was doing, only faster (remember the alluring charm of convergence theories?). The real doubts appeared when the others stopped doing it, while communism went on chasing now abandoned targets; partly through inertia, but mostly because of the fact that – being communism in action – it could not do anything else.

In its practical implementation, communism was a system one-sidedly adapted to the task of mobilizing social and natural resources in the name of modernization: the nineteenth-century steam and iron ideal of modern plenty. It could – at least in its own conviction – compete with capitalists, but solely with capitalists engaged in the same pursuits. What it could not do and did not brace itself to do was to match the performance of the capitalist, market-centred society once that society abandoned its steel mills and coal mines and moved into the postmodern age (once it passed over, in Jean Baudrillard's apt aphorism, from *metallurgy* to *semiurgy*; stuck at its metallurgical stage, Soviet communism, as if to cast out devils, spent its energy on fighting wide trousers, long hair, rock music and any other manifestations of semiurgical initiative).

Heller, Feher and Markus defined communist society as *dictatorship over needs*; and this it was, though only in that later, 'postmodern', stage did the dictating of needs become an abomination *per se*, regardless of the degree to which the needs experienced by its objects had been provided for. This happened because the society that throughout its modern development viewed itself as a social arrangement aimed at production capable of matching *established* needs, in its capitalist version turned consciously, explicitly and joyously to the production of *new* needs. Once seen as a state of suffering demanding reprieve, needs now became something to be celebrated and enjoyed. Human happiness had been redefined as the expansion of one's consuming capacity and the cultivation of new, more capacious and ever more refined needs.

For the social system, this meant that the balanced economy would no longer do and constant growth was needed instead. For the individual, this meant *choice* as the foremost criterion of good life and personal success: choice of the kind of person one would like to become (ever new personality-assembling kits are offered in the shops), choice of pleasures one would like to enjoy, choice of the very needs one would like to seek, adopt and gratify. Choice has turned into a value in its own right; the supreme value, to be sure. What mattered now was that choice be allowed and made, not the things or states that are chosen. And it is precisely *choice* that communism, this dictatorship over needs, could not and would not ever provide – even if it could provide for the needs it itself dictated (which more often than not it spectacularly failed to do anyway).

Well fed and clad, educated and cosseted young East German professionals stampeding to the west did not pretend to be running away from a disliked political philosophy; when pressed by the journalists, they admitted that what they were after (and what they could not get in the country they abandoned) was a wider assortment of goods in the shops and a wider selection of holidays. On my recent visit to Sweden I was told by quite a few even better fed, clad and otherwise provided for intellectuals that – supremely efficient as it prides itself on being – the bureaucracy of the social-democratic state becomes ever more difficult to live with; and this is due to the limits it puts on individual choice. I asked my conversationalists whether, given choice, they would abandon the doctor currently assigned by the National Health, or seek another school for their children. No, was the answer: the doctor is excellent, and so is the school our children attend; why on earth should we go elsewhere? But, they told me in the next sentence, I missed the point. Quite obviously, the point was not the quality of doctor or school, but the gratifying feeling of self-assertion, expressed in the act of consumer choice. This is what no bureaucratic provision, however lavish, could offer.

Even if communism could hope (erroneously, as it turned out in the end) to out-modernize the modernizers, it has become apparent that it cannot seriously contemplate facing the challenge of the postmodern world: the world in which consumer choice is simultaneously the essential systemic requisite, the main factor of social integration and the channel through which individual life-concerns are vented and problems resolved – while the state, grounding its expectation of discipline in the seduction of consumers rather than the indoctrination and oppression of subjects, could (and had to) wash its hands of all matters ideological and thus make conscience a private affair.

Building a Capitalist Society in a Postmodern World

By common agreement, the passage from the state-administered to the market economy based on business initiative requires the accumulation of private capital as much as the presence of business motivations. What the latter are we know from Weber's unsurpassed analysis of the motives instrumental in the rise of the capitalist system. Greed and the pursuit of profit, Weber insisted, have little to do with capitalism; unless restrained by rational calculation, they can hardly lead to the capitalist transformation – and they hardly ever led there, though they were ubiquitously present in all known societies and reached the height of ruthlessness and intensity well before the advent of modernity. On the other hand, the ideologically induced trait of *this-worldly asceticism* had everything to do with the emergence of the capitalist order. It was that trait which made capitalist accumulation and the passage to rationally calculated business both possible and in fact inevitable (the original accumulation of capital was, according to Weber, an *unanticipated consequence* of religiously induced self-denial coupled with the pursuit of workmanship as the mundane reflection of divine grace). This-worldly asceticism means first and foremost the *delay of gratification*; a suppression, rather than letting loose the natural predisposition to quick gain and fast enjoyment, to self-indulgence and ostentatious consumption.

There are few puritans left in the world at the time when the post-communist societies embark on the 'primary capitalist accumulation'. In fact, what enraged the rebels against communist command economy and what eventually brought communism down was not the envious comparison with the productive success of capitalist neighbours, but the enticing and alluring spectacle of lavish consumption enjoyed under capitalist auspices. It was the postmodern, narcissistic culture of self-enhancement, self-enjoyment, instant gratification and life defined in terms of consumer styles that finally exposed the obsoleteness of the 'steel-per-head' philosophy stubbornly preached and practiced under communism. It was this culture that delivered the last blow to abortive communist hopes of competition with the capitalist rival. And it was the overwhelming desire to share (and to share immediately) in the delights of the postmodern world, not the wish to tread once more the tortuous nineteenth-century road of industrialization and modernization, that mobilized the massive dissent against communist oppression and inefficiency.

The postmodern challenge proved to be highly effective in speeding up the collapse of communism and assuring the triumph of anti-communist revolution in its supremely important, yet preliminary, political stage. This asset may however turn into a serious handicap at the stage of systemic transformation, on two accounts: first, the relative scarcity of puritan attitudes allegedly indispensable at the stage of primary capital accumulation; second, the possibility that the high hopes on which the anticipatory trust with which the post-communist governments have been credited has been based, will be frustrated – with adverse effects on the still barely rooted institutions of young democracy. Frustration may rebound in its usual sublimations, with scape-goating, witch-hunting and totalitarian intolerance most prominent and most vexing among them. The resulting socio-psychological climate may prove fertile for the growth of hybrid political formations with little resemblance to the liberal-democratic hopes of the intellectual leaders of the revolution.

East-Central European societies have victoriously accomplished their February revolution. The dangers of an October one are, as yet, far from being excluded. The revolutionary process has started, but its destination and the direction it will take in the foreseeable future is far from certain. One is reminded of Winston Churchill's view of the prospects of the war after the battle of El Alamein: 'This is not the end. This is not even the beginning of the end. This is only the end of the beginning.'

References

Baudrillard, Jean (1990) 'L'hystérésie du millenium.' *Le Débat* 60.
Bauman, Zygmunt (1989) 'Poland: On its Own.' *Telos* 79.
Perkin, Harold (1989) *The Rise of Professional Society: England since 1880.* London: Routledge.
Smolar, Aleksander (1988) 'Perspektywy Europy Srodkowo-Wschodniej.' *Aneks* 50.
Staniszkis, Jadwiga (1988) 'Stabilizacja bez uprawomocnienia,' in Andzej Rychard and Antoni Sulek (eds), *Legitimacja, Klasyczne Teorie i Polskie Doswiadczenia.* Warsaw: PTS Warszawa.
Szacki, Jerzy (1990) 'A Revival of Liberalism in Poland?' *Social Research* 57, 2.

4

Class and Power

4.1 Class: Before and After (1982)

Memory is the after-life of history. It is through memory that history continues to live in the hopes, the ends, and the expectations of men and women as they seek to make sense of the business of life, to find a pattern in chaos, to construe familiar solutions to unfamiliar worries. Remembered history is the stuff of which these hopes, objectives and insights are made; in turn, the latter are the repositories where images of the past are rescued from oblivion. Memory is history-in-action. Remembered history is the logic which the actors inject into their strivings and which they employ to invest credibility into their hopes. In its after-life, history reincarnates as a Utopia which guides, and is guided by, the struggles of the present.

Remembered history seldom agrees with the history of the historians. This does not mean that historians, great or small, are immune to the group practice which shapes historical memory; neither does this mean that the work of the historians exerts no influence on the way the memory of the group selects and transforms its objects. By and large, however, remembered history and the history (histories?) of the historians follow their own respective courses. They are propelled by different needs, guided by different logic, and subject to different validity tests. There is little point, therefore, in asking whether the beliefs in which remembered history may be verbalised are true or false, by the standards set by professional historical inquiry. The 'materiality' of remembered history, its effectivity, indeed, its historical potential – do not rest on its truth so understood.

For a sociologist trying to grasp the springs of group practices, remembered history (or historical memory) is not a competitive account of something which can be presented by another, perhaps better, narrative; it is not an object of critique, a text called upon to hold out its credentials, and dismissed once it fails to do so. Sociology is neither a rival, nor the judge of historical memory. The failure of the latter to pass the professional truth-test is therefore of no relevance to the question of its sociological importance.

The phenomenon of historical memory presents, however, problems more complex than this of the choice between the attitude of critique and the attitude of description and explanation. Before such a choice is made, remembered history must first be 'constructed'. Unlike the history of the historians, remembered history cannot be 'referentially defined' by pointing to so many books where its content has been duly and fully recorded. Worse still, it cannot always be gauged by extending inquiry to a new type of potentially objective evidence – say, the sales or library demand for some rather than other historical books, the intensity of the contemporary interest in or neglect of various types of historical literature, etc.; this latter method, if effective, is naturally limited to the 'historical memory' of the educated, the literate, the articulate. But not all historical actors belong to this category. In the case of those who do not (who neither write the books nor read them), one would search in vain for the direct or indirect articulations of history as they 'remembered' it. Also, the recently developing methods of 'oral history' would shed only oblique light on the issue; the problem with 'remembered history' of virtually all groups except the educated elite is not merely that it has not been recorded in writing, but that it rarely, if ever, surfaces to the level of verbal communication, written or oral. The historical memory of a group which has been ploughed into its collective actions, which finds its expression in the group's proclivities to some rather than other behavioural responses, is not necessarily recognised by the group as a particular concept of the past. The authority of the past, and the ensuing need to possess some clear knowledge of the past in order to select right patterns of present conduct, is a philosophers' issue, read into the collective actions by the interpreters, and not an organic factor of the action itself. The existential mode of historical memory is not unlike that of grammar. For the interpreter, the observed behaviour is incomprehensible unless its presence is assumed, and remains unexplained as long as its guiding rules remain inarticulate. But the actors themselves need not have the consciousness of the rules in order to follow them properly; and it is not they whom the interpreter would wish to interrogate in his search for the consistent formulation of the rules.

It is in this sense that the remembered history must be 'constructed'. The reconstruction is, essentially, the task of the interpreter, a task which is indispensable for the understanding of group action, though not for its accomplishment. In the process of construction, recorded opinions of the actors are not seen by the interpreter as accounts, complete or partial, of the living history which merely need to be assembled into a cohesive totality through hypothesising the possible forms of the missing links and employing analogy to postulate affinities: they are not treated as incomplete or imperfect theories of tradition which ought to be implemented and at times corrected. Such opinions, together with non-verbalised actions, are seen rather as elements of behaviour which is to be understood in its totality, by reference to the antecedent experiences of the group, and to the challenge the new situation of the group presents if perceived against this background. The interpreter's view of remembered, or living history emerges in the course of his effort to understand group reactions to the changing circumstances of life.

The procedure may be considered legitimate only if some assumptions are tacitly made. First, that – by and large – people prefer repetitive patterns of conduct, these being more economical and less unnerving than designing a response ad hoc, without being able to calculate the chance of success in advance. Second, that for this reason effective patterns practised in the past tend to be reinforced; the more they are habitualised, as it were, the more they are economical. Third, that it is precisely because of this propensity to learn that people experience a rapid change of circumstances as a threat; they resent the invalidation of the once trustworthy life wisdom. Fourth, when faced with such a change, people would be inclined either to refute the legitimacy of the new, or to try to force it into the familiar patterns; most often, they will attempt to do both things at the same time.

Projected upon our theme, these assumptions generate the notion of remembered history as a residue of historical learning, which 'makes sense' of the group reactions to the change in the circumstances in which their business of life is conducted. What the notion implies is that these reactions are best understood as backward-looking. Even when articulated in a vocabulary of future, as-yet-unachieved states, and however profound the alteration of social realities they bring about as a consequence, the group actions derive their meaning from tradition. Historical action – human existence as such, as it were – is, to borrow Heidegger's expression, a constant recapitulation of tradition: in other words, it is a process of constant negotiation between learned proclivities and new dependencies, marked by the resistance of the traditional language to resign its authority over perception of reality and the normative regulation of group behaviour. This account of the role of historical memory in historical action does not necessarily imply that a conservative bias is built into historical interpretation. What it does inevitably imply is the need for the interpreter to untangle the subtle dialectical interaction between the future orientation and the past determination, Utopia and tradition, the emergence of new structures of action and the language which had shaped, and was shaped by, the old.

To put it differently, the concept of historical memory does not imply the idea of well-formed, consciously appropriated and consulted visions of tradition, resilient to change and suggesting, by this very resilience, a 'natural preference' for traditionalism. Even less does the concept imply a version of the 'plus ça change, plus c'est la même chose' historiosophy. The concept refers simply to the fact that at the foundation of any historical transformation lies the growing inadequacy of the learned pattern of expectation and behaviour to the circumstances in which the business of life is conducted. The likely reaction to such inadequacy is initially an attempt to bring the circumstances back into accordance with the pattern of learned behaviour. If this fails (and it normally does), a situation of crisis follows, marked by a high degree of disorganisation and reflected, on the one hand, in the prophecies of imminent doom, and on the other in the proliferation of revolutionary Utopias. Apathy coupled with growing ineffectivity of social institutions, or radical vigour leading to political, social and cultural realignments are both possible outcomes. Neither is predetermined by the sheer configuration of inadequacy and guaranteed in advance. The choice between possible outcomes cannot be predicted; its mechanism can be only described retrospectively.

The two hypotheses followed [in this book] are concerned with the origins and the later crisis of a society articulated as a configuration of social classes characterised by opposed interests and preoccupied with rendering the distribution of social product to their advantage. According to the first hypothesis, the articulation of class society was an almost century-long process which culminated in the first part of the nineteenth century. It was an essentially unintended and unanticipated effect of a struggle to restore social institutions guaranteeing group status and individual security in a historical configuration which these institutions could not effectively serve: its mature product institutionalised the memory of this struggle as well as divisions and alliances which crystallised in its course. According to the second hypothesis, the current multifaceted crisis of class society (economic crisis: falling growth, falling rate of profit, growing unemployment; political crisis: 'blocked' corporatist state and a schizophrenic mixture of excessive expectations aimed at government with almost universal disapproval of the expansion of its activities; cultural crisis: the ever more evident ineffectuality of work-and-achievement ethics and the gradual substitution of the 'power of disruption' for the 'contribution to communal welfare' in the rhetoric of distributive struggle) is a symptom of the incapacity of the institutions of class society to guarantee group status and individual security in an essentially transformed social organisation. Either side can gain little, if anything at all, from the strategy of distributive class warfare. Nevertheless, it is the memorised class strategies which provide cognitive and normative patterns to deal with the crisis. In this sense, the present period rehashes the situation of the early nineteenth century: the rhetoric of restitution, restoration, defence of ancient rights and ancient justice actuated processes with effects which cannot be deduced from their conscious articulations, however strongly they depend on them.

The argument supporting the first hypothesis can be outlined in several points:

1 The factor mainly responsible for the crisis (an interruption in the gradual, accremental change when the extant institutions absorb new conditions, modifying in the process in a fashion not sudden enough to be perceived as revolutionary) in western Europe which was to lead eventually to the articulation of class society was the demographic explosion of the eighteenth century. A rapid growth in population is by itself merely a statistical phenomenon. Its sociological significance, and its role as a factor of historical change, cannot be deduced from the numbers (though many interpretations, skipping the whole area of socio-cultural mediations, try to do just this, from Malthus on); they derive instead from the inability of available institutions to assimilate the growing numbers of people and meet their status and security needs in keeping with the established standards. No population, however large, is supernumerary or superfluous because of its sheer numbers; 'superfluity' itself is a notion which cannot be defined with sense without reference to concrete socio-cultural patterns. The problem with the eighteenth-century demographic upsurge was that it exceeded the absorptive capacity of the then available social institutions. As Barrington Moore succinctly put it, 'it was surplus to that particular social order and that particular level of technical development at that specific stage of historical development. Later in the nineteenth century there was a much bigger increase in population without serious social strains' (Moore, 1978, p. 125).

For the overwhelming majority of the pre-modern population, the tasks of status definition and maintenance, as well as the provision of life security, were performed on the local level and grounded in local institutions – parishes, village and town councils, craft guilds. The parish and the guild were not specialised organisations, assigned clearly defined jobs; for most of the people they were total worlds, in which the expectation of work and insurance against poverty – indeed, the guarantee of the place in society – was naturally inscribed. It is not that the parish and the guild performed the task better than alternative institutions and were for this reason preferred; simply, there were no alternative institutions fit for the task. The failure of the parish or the guild to deliver according to the time-sanctioned expectations took the bottom out of the entire mode of life.

It is worth emphasising that England, where the modern class society, as well as the new industrial system which underlay it, were theoretically and institutionally articulated earlier than elsewhere in Europe, had had an intricate network of social relief, and the concomitant notion of the state responsibility for the subsistence of all its subjects, well entrenched for several centuries before the dramatic take-off of the late eighteenth century. In Harold Perkin's words, what made English history so different from that of continental Europe was the 'defeat of the peasants and their transformation into large commercial rent-paying farmers on the one hand and a larger body of landless labourers on the other', which, among other things, accounted 'for the unique English system of poor relief ... not needed in peasant societies where the holding supports everybody, or when famine comes they all starve together' (Perkin, 1981, p. 360). Writing in 1764, Richard Burn listed some twenty-five different legislative acts spelling out the duties of towns, villages, parishes in providing for the survival of 'impotent poor' and for the employment of the able-bodied. The equally profuse legislation which conceptualised the phenomenon of vagrancy and called for an exceptionally harsh treatment of 'unauthorised' beggars and vagabonds, tied the poor even more firmly to their native parishes, thus reinforcing the bond of the locally inscribed duties and rights. The centuries of such legally fortified structure bore heavily on the kind of historical memory which proved to be instrumental in the articulation of class society.

2 The demographic bulge of the late-eighteenth century, while providing the fuel for industrial take-off, stretched the locally based institutions of social security to the point of breakdown. The old system was slow to recognise its imminent bankruptcy, as testified by the abortive Speenhamland effort to maintain the old principles in the face of changed circumstances. But it had to declare its insolvency under the double pressure of the rapidly growing numbers of propertyless families and individuals, and the manufacturers keen to untie the local bonds which limited both the mobility and the pliancy of potential labourers. When the local network of the status and security

allocation finally gave way, the crucial 'second period' in the history of social services began, 'brief on the Continent, but more prolonged in England', when the state in Ernest Barker's words, had to take some responsibility for the 'mass of uprooted country-workers employed in the factories of the towns or in mining centres' (Barker, 1944, p. 69). With the benefit of hindsight, these times, marked by the despair, suffering, sometimes fury of the 'uprooted', appear as an intermediate stage between two successive systems through which society catered for status allocation and security needs; even as a period of 'site clearing' for the erection of the new, arguably more comprehensive and universal network of institutions. Obviously, this was not the way in which the contemporaries could perceive their turbulent times, when the old centre did not hold any more while the new could be at best conceived as a noble vision of social dreamers. The dearth of foresight was not the sole reason for alarm. The natural limits of historical imagination apart, the times were indeed institutionally under-provided, and the vanishing laws and ancient customs left a gaping hole where before (as historical memory suggested) spread the solid ground of secure existence.

No retrospective wisdom, however, can justify the dismissal of diagnoses and demands of the era as errors of historical judgment or product of sluggish imagination; still less can they be disposed of as retrograde, backward-looking ideas, slackening the pace of progress. If later history invalidated most of the diagnoses and took the steam off most of the demands, it did so precisely thanks to the shape these diagnoses and demands took, moulded as they were by historical memory. Far from being spokes in the wheel of history, these diagnoses and demands, and the 'living history' which gave them shape and vigour, set historical change in motion and pushed the vehicle of society to its qualitatively new mode of equilibrium.

3 What made the period in question an era of sharp conflicts, shifting alliances, consolidation of new divisions and, on the whole, an accelerating social change, was ultimately (to borrow Barrington Moore's cogent term) the sense of 'outraged justice' on the part of those who justly felt their status withdrawn and the grounds of their security undermined. Paradoxically, the most profound re-articulation of society in human history derived its momentum from the hostility to change which spurred the impaired and the threatened into defensive (to wit, subjectively conservative) action. The intensity of militancy did not reflect the absolute level of destitution, but the distance between expectations and reality. Penury correlated but feebly with social protest. The rebels were sometimes paupers – but more often than not they acted to stave off the spectre of indigence; invariably

they took to the warpath when the rung of the social ladder on which they stood just started to feel slippery. Habitual rights withdrawn accomplished what a habitualised privation never would have done.

In his recent survey of the seminal half century of European history, Olwen H. Hufton explored the consequences of the rapid increase of population for the insecurity of habitual ways and means of existence. The effect of the demographic upsurge of 1760s was in all parts of the West 'an uncomfortable imbalance between population and economic performance. Even in years of normal harvests the number of those unable to make their resources stretch without recourse to begging was rapidly growing.' The remarkable result of the widespread insecurity was, as Hufton documented country by country, that 'the poor themselves were not protesters but the same could not be said for those fighting to remain on the right side of the line marking sufficiency from destitution' (Hufton, 1980, p. 348). Insecurity as such made a miserable condition; but it was the withdrawal of security which kindled the fire of social protest.

The rapid erosion of protective institutions was a major (perhaps the major) immediate cause of discontent. The gradual disassembly of the legal foundation of state-enforced paternalism was particularly painfully felt by the groups which grew accustomed to the permanence of their, however humble, privileges of status. Since Brentano, historians have tended to underline the crucial role of certain parliamentary acts, like the repeal of the apprenticeship clause of the 1563 Statute of Artificers and Apprentices (5 Elizabeth) in 1814, as milestones in the re-alignment of social and political forces – as, indeed, crucial factors in the formation of labourers into a working class. In his seminal 'The Making of the English Working Class', E. P. Thompson profusely documented the role of the 'deep-rooted folk memory', which expressed itself not only in the natural longing for stable foundations of individual security, but also, more specifically, in the nostalgia for traditional patterns of work and leisure. Thompson's conclusion was that 'these years appear at times to display, not a revolutionary challenge, but a resistance movement, in which both the Romantics and the Radical craftsmen opposed the annunciation of Acquisitive Man' (Thompson, 1963, pp. 357, 830). The abolition of 5 Elizabeth meant not only the withdrawal of status for labourers used to expect, with reason, the custom-prescribed advancement in their trade position. It changed as well, and changed beyond recognition, the very character of apprenticeship as an initiation into a totality of patterned existence of the closely-knit trade community. The repeal of the limited access to apprenticeship meant in practice the denial of access to this community: the craftsmen's resistance against the withdrawal of legal protection of apprenticeship (the first protest movement of the disprivileged as producers, rather than consumers), was a struggle for the restoration of such a community. In John Rule's recent summary, 'the protest of the manufacturing poor was conservative in its appeal to custom, paternalistic legislation and in its seeking to reinforce traditional usage' (Rule, 1981, p. 212).

4 The dissipation of locally based paternalistic institutions giving way under the overwhelming pressure of demographic bulge resulted in a massive production of paupers and beggars. This was the aspect of change most easily sighted by both intellectual reformers and the governments worried with the anticipated threat to the public order; the end of the eighteenth century is the time of a most fervent, at times panic-stricken, legislative bustle aimed at the containment and confinement of vagrants and vagabonds and sweeping the beggars out of the streets and highways. It is, in Michel Foucault's apt summary, the 'age of the prison' – the time when legislatures, manufacturers, doctors and psychiatrists co-operated in using enclosure as a main method of separating order from disorder, the speakable from the unspeakable, the visible from the unseen. And yet, as Barrington Moore concludes in the wake of a scrupulous comparative research of the origins of the modern revolt against injustice, 'those who are the worst off are generally the last to organise and make their voices heard'. The voice of protest rises to its pitch just above the destitution line and fades off once the line is crossed. It was the guild masters of the suddenly overcrowded German towns of the early nineteenth century who stood fast: they wanted 'much greater power in the state, measures to preserve their social and moral role as well as the economic one – a harking back to the pre-capitalist situation with a certain amount of idealised window-dressing – and measures to restrict the number of apprentices and tighten up access to the guilds'. (Moore, 1978, pp. 143, 147).

The spectre of pauperisation undeniably added a sense of urgency to the defensive action, and subconscious fears to its passion. But the objectives of struggle were fixed by historical memory, and this was not the experience of poverty and lack of subsistence. The 'harking back' was towards the recollection of trade as property of the craftsman, as against the new-fangled idea, and practice, of labour (and, for all practical intents and purposes, the labourer himself) as commodity. Karl Polanyi, in his daringly synthetic 'Great Transformation', dwelt at length on the inconclusive, and in the end abortive, struggle of the expanding market system to absorb labour and dissolve it in the uniform mass of commodities dependent for their price on the free play of offer and demand: and on the intrinsic indivisible unity between economic and social facets of labour as the natural barrier between the reality of capitalist society and its idealised projection in the form of the perfect market. The barrier could be neither knocked down nor leapt over, however strong were the legally backed market pressures. Unlike other commodities, labour could not be separated from its former owner after the act of purchase; the way in which it was used or abused reflected back on the well-being of the owner, ineradicably present at the act of its consumption. The consumption of labour as commodity was in practice indistinguishable from the management of the condition of the labourer as a social being (looking from the market side of the coin, Ricardo was perhaps first to articulate this subsumption of the social category of labourers under the economic category of labour). Reduction of labour relations to a purely commodity transaction, the detachment of contract from all and any 'social strings' unrelated to the consumption of effort as an abstract value, could not but be experienced from the other side of the coin as an attack on the social standing of the labourer, an attempt to transform the labourer himself into a commodity. One can interpret in retrospect the resistance of the craftsmen against unhampered market play as, above all, the defence of labour as a property of those who labour; more generally and perhaps more abstractly than contemporary consciousness would have it – as the defence of the activity of labour as an integral part and parcel of social bonds, against its reduction to a merely economic transaction.

This interpretation goes some way towards the explanation of the remarkable loyalty to the customary privileges of the trade as a whole, and acceptance of the hierarchy of power within the trade, which throughout most of the epoch of the great transformation united masters and their apprentices against the landowner's interests, grain merchants, financiers, entrepreneurs, and the governments which lent their support to their destructive practices. The self-defence of labourers which left lasting sediment in the form of trade unions was originally seldom aimed at the masters; when it was, the intention was to bring the masters back into line with the custom-bound expectation of 'fairness'. As John Rule found out

> *within* a trade horizontal fissures arose because the component levels did not live up to reciprocal expectations. Thus *some* masters might be seen as acting in an *unmasterlike* manner, or at *some* time masters in general might forget their obligations sufficiently to act solely in their own interest. This would produce temporary conflict along horizontal lines implying perceived separation of interest. (Rule, 1981, p. 269)

The conflict, though, was to remain, for some time, temporary. The dominant tendency was the defence of the essential unity of the trade: more generally, the defence of the principle of labour as inscribed in the framework of inviolable social relations and thereby exempt from the heavy-handed, rough and callous 'justice' of the market.

It was ultimately the failure of this strategy of defence which led to the fateful re-alignment of solidarities and antagonisms known as the emergence of class society.

5 The conservative rebellion can be seen also in another way: as the last tremors of the long earthquake which shook the foundations of the old social power thus clearing the ground for the new one. The process took several centuries to accomplish, but its last stages made a particularly dramatic spectacle, as the process was compressed and accelerated with the advent of the factory system. The passage from the old to the new power was a corollary of the seminal change in the management of the surplus product. Up to the beginnings of the industrial society, this product was extracted from the producers mostly as an element of redistribution – as a levy, a tithe, a rent which the producer had to deduct from his output at the completion of his productive cycle. With the spread of hired labour, and in particular with the emergence of the factory system, the surplus product was extracted 'at the root'; it was now the right of the producer to a share of output which had become an outcome of redistribution.

The two distinct ways in which the surplus product was managed and divided could be only serviced by two entirely different types of social power. This first was a power which intervened in the life of the producer only on occasion; its sole function was to assure the periodical transfer of the product of labour – not the administration of labour itself. This power could therefore manifest its externality and operate, as its major resources, the twin terrors of physical punishment and spiritual damnation; but it had no concern with the administration of the producer's body, which was left largely to the logic of nature and habit. The second type of power, however, had to descend to the level with which the former type had no need to concern itself. Its task was to organise the productive process itself. It remained external only in the sense that the productive effort itself came to be external to the 'natural' logic of the producer's life. Otherwise it penetrated actions and functions left before to the discretion of the producer. The latter had to be forced now to subject himself to a daily and hourly rhythm which bore no evident relation to the logical order of his own life. The new power could not, therefore, limit its appearance to the annual tax collection and ceremonial reminders of its unchallengeable potency and super-human sanctions. It had to be a daily and an hourly power, permeating the totality of the producer's life and deploying constant surveillance and 'garrisons in conquered cities' (Freud's metaphor for the conscience sedimenting from repression) as its paramount weapon. Not the products of labour, but the producer himself, his body and thought, now had to become the objects of power. If not for the old power, the surplus product would not be split to maintain an unproductive elite; if not for the new power, the surplus would not be produced at all.

The new power was therefore directed at the bodies of producers, aspired to mould the totality of their life process, and displayed an unprecedented volume of repression. Large sections of ordinary behaviour were set aside as passion-ridden (in opposition to the ones classified as rational), bound to be confined and best of all suppressed altogether. The new power was mostly a disciplining force. It was set to reshape the behaviour of producers according to a pattern which, by definition almost, they would not choose if the matter was left to their discretion. Since the entire pattern of life was involved, the matter could not be solved by sheer compulsion or an occasional display of superior force. The new power had to be constant and ubiquitous. Through its numerous institutions it had to chart the entire territory of life. It had to come into the direct and permanent contact with the body of the producer.

It was in the factory system that the concerns and the ambitions of the new type of power attained their fullest and most vivid manifestation. For obvious reasons, factories were from the outset the first line of the power struggle. Labour bought by the factory owners could be brought to the machines only together with the labourers; and it could not be extracted otherwise than by forcing the labourers to apply their force and skill, continually and according to the pace set by machinery in motion. To prise their labour free, the labourers had to be, therefore, deprived of freedom. E. P. Thompson documented in a brilliant essay the tortuous process of drilling the factory workers into obedience to the clock (Thompson, 1974). The process was repeated everywhere and each time people brought up in a pre-industrial way of life had to be transformed into factory operatives.

The factory order, whatever its impact upon the standard of living measured by the quantity of commodities bought and consumed, had to appear to the producers as a superimposition of a coercive, other-controlled order on what seemed by contrast a self-regulated, autonomous existence. For this very reason the system had to arouse resentment, particularly among yesterday's craftsmen or cottage producers. When confronted with the new order, historical memory painted the picture of bliss and tranquillity destroyed by the 'satanic mills'. To the impersonal, enforced individuality of a factory hand, it juxtaposed the image of sociability and mutual esteem of independent producers. To the factory hands, the new order revealed itself first and foremost as the loss of freedom; its repressive impact arose mainly from its other-directedness. This order came supported by naked force but no meaning. In Weber's words:

> The Puritan wanted to work in a calling; we are forced to do so. . . . In Baxter's view the care for external goods should only lie on the shoulders of the 'saint like a light cloak, which can be thrown aside at any moment'. But fate decreed that the cloak should become an iron cage. (Weber, 1976, p. 181)

Factory hands were the first to experience this irony of fate. To them, the order which determined 'the lives of all the individuals who are born into this mechanism, not only those directly concerned with economic acquisition, with irresistible force', was an iron cage from the start. And, for a long time yet, its iron bars were not to be hidden behind the glittering prizes of the supermarkets.

6   In the pre-industrial order, the producer was forced to share his product with his social superiors. But until the moment the levy was collected, the product was his. The producer was in control of tools and materials which, when subject to the process of labour, resulted in the final product. Tools, work and the rights to the product of labour belonged 'naturally' together. Industrial society, on the other hand, 'requires that wealth be directly in the hands, not of its owners, but of those whose labour, by putting that wealth to work, enables the profit to be made from it' (Foucault, 1980, p. 41). The advent of industrial society brought, therefore, an ambiguous situation, poorly articulated by historical precedent. It made the re-definition of rights and duties inevitable, a matter of open contest and power struggle.

Never since the collapse of slave societies was such a formidable wealth entrusted to the care of people who had no stakes in its integrity. From the point of view of the owners, this situation meant taking enormous risk and called for constant vigilance; Bentham's 'Panopticon' encapsulated the dream of the all-penetrating supervisory gaze, of a surveillance unconstrained by walls of privacy and piercing through most sheltered niches of individual autonomy. The practice which 'Panopticon' idealised was one of the mixture of physical drill and moral preaching, aimed at the reversal of the traditional relation between things and their users. Through discipline and punishment the unity of capital, work and product was to be 'denaturalised' and dismembered. This could be achieved only by an uncompromising suppression of producers' autonomy; by transforming yesterday's subjects of rights into objects of control. From the point of view of the producers, however, the new situation presented an entirely different picture. It was seen as a sinister departure from the natural principle of the producer's control over the entirety of his work, including the tangible results of labour. Long before economists made their discovery of labour as the source of wealth, the intimate link between work and its product was too evident for the producer to call for reflection.

It seems strange, therefore, that most renderings of the origins of industrial conflict interpret the appearance of the demand of the 'whole product of labour' as the result of the socialist reading of Ricardo's economic vision. It has been accepted almost without further questioning that the idea of the right to the whole product was injected into inchoate associations of workers by their intellectual advisors and preachers, having been first distilled from abstract analysis of the structure of market economy. This idea is commonly seen, in other words, as the outcome of pushing the logic of market economy to its radical conclusions; or, alternatively, as the consequence of a value judgment applied to the structure of capitalist economy. In both cases, the producers' demand for the whole product of their labour is interpreted as a phenomenon born of the distinctive character of the capitalist society; sometimes – particularly within the Marxist tradition – it is presented as a fateful step beyond ('forward from') the capitalist organisation of the productive process. Most authors agree that the 'right to the whole product of labour' can and should be traced back to Ricardian socialists, who had the courage and the imagination to gaze beyond the confines of bourgeois self-interest which blinded Ricardo's vision, but who made their observation with both feet firmly put on the territory of bourgeois society, as charted by Ricardo's theory.

Contrary to the prevalent opinion, the 'right to the whole product of labour' seems much more at home in the historical memory of the individual producer, than in advanced Utopias of the forward-looking critics of the capitalist management of surplus value. Economic theory was hardly necessary for the producers to guard the remembered 'natural' link between labour and its product and – in the name of this memory of 'natural' order – resist the concentrated efforts of new industrial powers to break it. What had been articulated as the demand of the right to the whole product was, indeed, a call to restore the old order. Not that in past history the producers ever enjoyed and consumed the totality of their output without sharing it with the dominant and idle, or weak and impoverished groups; but the old order, when confronted with the factory system, did appear to place the producer in a position of control over the whole of his product and its later destination. In practice, therefore, the demand for the whole product of labour was a part of power struggle which the attack launched by the factory system against the self-management of the producer had set in motion. The images and the vocabulary dictated by 'remembered history' articulated the producers' defence against the new 'discipline power'.

This interpretation requires a qualification. It is meant to capture the meaning bestowed upon the demand by factory workers in the early power struggles of the new system. It was, at least obliquely, confirmed by the fact that for many decades, practically until the introduction of 'skilful', advanced technology in the later part of the nineteenth century, the factory owners failed to extend the unified pattern of factory discipline over skilled labour. Throughout most of the nineteenth century the skilled workers, organised for their self-defence in trade unions, retained considerable autonomy within the factory and to a large extent controlled their own part in the production process; it was the weak and unorganised labour, mainly women and children, to whom the discipline and surveillance of the new power were applied in full (it was the very inability of these groups, with no historical memory to fall back on, to resist the encroachment of the new power that made them the natural objects of the defensive legislation by the state). But in the intellectual debate of the era, and particularly in its socialist section, 'the right to the whole product of labour' tended to acquire a rather straightforward economic interpretation. There, it was translated into the language of the market discourse and decoded as the demand of the repayment of the full value of expended labour. In the classic version, later summed up by Anton Menger, this reading of the right to the whole product of labour founded it on self-interest (Menger, 1899, p. 28).

Menger's analysis, however, itself remained within the market discourse within which other analysed interpretations were enclosed. A longer view, embracing the historical context of the era when the intellectual debate on the right to the whole product was launched, reveals a somewhat different meaning of the economic readings of the 'right'. Rather than referring to the individual or group self-interest, the concept of 'the right to the whole product' appears to partake of the power discourse on global-societal level; it represents an alternative notion of the management of the socially produced surplus. Contrary to what Menger suggested ('under such a system every one works for himself alone, while under present conditions he works partly for himself and partly for another's unearned income'), the intellectual interpretations of the 'right' never implied the abolition of a social redistribution of surplus; hardly ever, even in case of most radically syndicalist solutions, did they intimate a possibility of the product being appropriated (not to mention consumed) in its entirety by its immediate producer. The emphasis in the economic interpretations of the right was always a negative one; in a sense, they attacked what the workers' concept of the right defended: the association of the right to dispose of the final product with the investment of factors which led to its creation. In the concrete circumstances of capitalist industry, these interpretations were aimed at the dissociation of the management of surplus from the ownership of capital, thereby allowing for a relatively narrow common ground on which the two (social and economic) interpretations of the right to the whole product could meet and even be mistakenly seen as identical. They met in so far as they pointed, for the time being, to the same adversary. Their tactical alliance could not, however, outlive the attainment of the right in either of the two versions. Realisation of any of the two versions was bound to reveal their long-run discordance. The economic version did not by necessity imply granting of the right postulated by the social one. The issues articulated in the social version could well retain all their topicality even with the postulates of the economic one met in full. On the other hand, were the demands of the social version ever fulfilled, this would not bring the redistribution of power implied by the economic version any nearer.

7 The social version of 'the right to the whole product of labour' derived its initial impetus from the producers' resentment of the discipline power represented by the factory system – resentment given shape by the 'memorised past' of the craftsman's workshop. It was at this stage a part of the power struggle for the control over the process of labour, a manifestation of the defiance of the externally imposed, alien order aspiring to a full control over the substance and the form of producers' actions. This power struggle was to be lost by the workers. The discipline power was, in the end, triumphant; its base extended far beyond the factory walls, and the factory floor was not a battlefield on which a successful war against the new type of power could be waged. With the advance made by the new order, the workers' version of 'the right to the whole product' did undergo a gradual, but seminal, change of meaning. It came closer to Menger's interpretation. As Offe and Wiesenthal recently commented:

> workers can neither fully submit to the logic of the market (first of all, because what they 'sell' on the market is not a 'genuine' commodity),

nor can they escape from the market (because they are forced to participate, for the sake of their subsistence).   (Offe and Wiesenthal, 1980, p. 104)

Once the defensive and delaying action failed to halt the advancement of the new power, the second aspect of the workers' situation, having become for all practical intents and purposes a necessity, began to generate a constant pressure, pushing labour to the never fully attainable 'commodity' pattern. Short of a drastic alteration of the 'discipline power' pattern, the only way of attending to their situation open to the workers was to behave as if labour was a commodity, while simultaneously exploiting the fact that it is not, and cannot be, a commodity tout court ('the capitalist cannot buy labour itself – a certain quantity of activity, as it were. Instead, he has to apply incentives, force, etc. to the *bearers* of labour power – that is, the workers – in order to get them to work and to keep them working') (Offe and Wiesenthal, 1980, p. 73). The liminal notion of the 'whole product of labour' turns, therefore, into a legitimating formula for bargaining in the name of increased incentives. The link between the practice of bargaining and the logic of its original legitimation tends to become, however, increasingly tenuous. Little is left of either the economic or social ambitions that the formula once implied. Contrary to what the economic view of labour-commodity would make us expect, the limits of bargaining power are weakly correlated with the value of the 'whole product'. They depend instead on the 'negative value' of distortion in the power pattern that a particular category of labourers may create through its refusal to expend its labour force. What really counts in the distribution of the 'whole product' is not 'how much do we contribute to the creation of the product', but 'how much harm we can cause by refusing to contribute'. This practice creates the visibility of a typically market-oriented behaviour, but only if all its highly specific contextual determinants and complex inner springs are ignored.

   Thus Menger's 'self-interest', allegedly underlying the demand of 'the whole product of labour', at no stage seems to give justice to the complexity of workers' behaviour. It could be used to construct working models of such behaviour only at a later stage; at the time when the vindication of the 'right to the whole product', which, according to Menger, it was meant to explain, has already receded into the background to be invoked, if at all, on rare, ceremonial occasions.

   At this later stage the chances of various categories of labour depend on their capacity to disrupt the production of surplus value – directly or indirectly (i.e., by undermining some of the 'meta-conditions' of such production). This means that the chances are unequal. It is then that the defence of the relative status of certain sectors of employed labour becomes in principle dissociated from the power struggle, aimed at the securing of existence of the non-capital-owners in general. The general notion of the 'labour versus capital' struggle is still held in the collective memory of the origins, but it now covers an essentially fragmented pursuit of gains. The fate of the two objectives is guided by two largely autonomous sets of factors. It becomes possible, therefore, that a success in one direction may have an adverse effect on the other.

It is time to recapitulate the argument.

The conflict between workers and the owners of capital is not similar to the immediately preceding conflict between producers of surplus and its non-producing consumers (inasmuch as the production of surplus in the industrial society is not similar to its production in the past). It arose from the struggle over the control over production of surplus, and not merely its distribution. The advent of industrial society meant that the external management of surplus, previously limited to its division, spread over its very production. This tendency meant not just depriving the producer of a part of his labour's product, but a total control over his body and soul; taking away the right to manage the application of his working capacity. The conflict between workers and the factory owners emerged as a resistance of the objects of such control against a new system of power which implied it. The organisation of workers into a class hostile to the rule of capital owners was an outcome of this resistance.

The odds in this defensive struggle were, and remain, decisively against the workers. One obvious disadvantage derived from the backing the other side received from the liquidity of 'dead labour' (their possession of tools, premises, raw materials) as against the incurable 'non-liquidity' of the live one; unlike the capitalists, workers depend for their livelihood on the other side's willingness to employ it; not being able to store their labour force or stock it for more propitious occasions, they are bound to lose it once they decide to opt out from the physical submission which selling it entails. Another disadvantage (as Offe and Wiesenthal recently indicated, often overlooked by political scientists who 'equate the unequal' and dissolve the uniqueness of workers' situation in the indiscriminating notion of 'interest groups') [Offe and Wiesenthal, 1980, pp. 71, 79] stems from the fact that the power of each and any capitalist is assured automatically by his legally guaranteed property rights; ultimately, the right of property means the right to control its use (and prevent its 'abuse', understood as such use as does not conform with the intention of the owner), which, in the case under discussion, amounts to the control over action, body and soul of the individuals employed to accomplish this 'use'. An individual worker, on the contrary, except for an unlikely case of possessing unique and irreplaceable skills indispensable for the use of a capitalist's possessions (the standardisation of machines renders such cases increasingly improbable), has no assets with which to counter and confine the capitalist's control; by himself he is not a 'source of uncertainty' which may confound the capitalist's calculation, and for this reason he is unambiguously an object of power, and not a side in the power game. In order to achieve what the capitalist attains as an individual, without surrendering virtually any of his personal autonomy, the worker has to associate with others: with other workers employed by the same capitalist, to make the replacement of his skills somewhat more costly; and, preferably, with all workers possessing the same skill or potentially employable by the same industry, in order to remove fully the power disadvantage arising from replaceability.

It is, in other words, the resistance to the new power's bid for the total control over body and soul of the producer which forces the workers to act in unison, to form associations, to surrender the individuality to the logic of group action – in short, to form a class rather than a loose aggregate of individuals of mostly statistical existence.

Regardless of their political persuasion, most economists and social scientists agree that the tendency of the workers to organise is best explicable in terms of the rational pursuit of gain. The science of economics, with relatively few exceptions, conceives of the worker (as, for this matter, of any other individual within the orbit of the market) as above all a 'maximising' entity; it is this inherent proclivity to maximise which bestows rationality upon joining of forces. Marxist sociologists and political scientists supplant a wider perspective and add the evaluation, but agree with the essence of the proposition: the workers unite to regain the possession of the surplus value expropriated by the capitalist. In both cases the interpreters view the class organisations of the workers as a form of adjustment to the logic of the market exchange, and particularly to the situation where labour itself is turned into a marketable commodity.

It is against this interpretation that our argument is aimed. The contention elaborated in this book is that the class of industrial workers came into existence in the course of the producers' resistance against the new system of power; this was a battle for control over body and soul of the producer, and not for the division of surplus value; much less for the right to manage the surplus. It was not the new form of surplus-management, as such, but its impact upon the autonomy of the producer, which generated the sense of outraged justice and led the producer to seek the restoration of the power balance through unification of their forces. The objective of a take-over of the surplus itself was never a factor in the formation of workers into a class (though, as will be seen later, it was imputed subsequently to the formed working class by sides participating in another power struggle).

It is a further contention of this book that the battle for control which sedimented and continues to sediment organised forms of resistance among its objects (consider the spreading of 'industrial action' to the work settings in which no surplus is produced, and hence no division of surplus may be disputed), if not exactly lost by the producers, was not won either. Instead it has led to a stalemate, within which both sides have the means and the willingness to draw and re-draw the limits to the other side's prerogatives or autonomy. It is within the framework of this tension-generating and tension-supported precarious balance of control that the wage-battle led by workers' unions is best understood. This battle is not just a manifestation of the alleged 'maximising tendency' of the market-oriented individuals. Still less is it an act of war against the current system of surplus-management. It is rather one of the few available ways in which the controlled may assert and manifest their not-yet-entirely-forlorn autonomy. It is not so much the ultimate monetary effects of the struggle which count, as the display of force which led to their attainment. This is, perhaps, the deepest reason of the workers' unions' resentment against all forms of wage control, and of their attachment to the principle of free collective bargaining. This attitude is unlikely to change even if it has been proved that the 'free bargaining' does not protect the real wages better than a well-administered and balanced incomes policy. It is unlikely to change precisely because the comparative virtues of the two forms of wage determination are measured not by their 'maximising' effects, but by their impact on the power relations built into the work situation.

If industrial society is above all about control reaching where other power systems did not reach and had no need of reaching, then the wider, unintended meaning of the wage battle as well as of other forms of asserting producers' autonomy is their continuous resentment of industrial society; it is not, contrary to what is frequently implied, a resentment against the specifically capitalist form of dividing surplus value in line with the property rights (not, in other words, the fight for the 'right to the whole product of labour' in the economic sense). This wider meaning applies to the management as such, rather than management legitimising its prerogatives by reference to legal ownership. Employees of nationalised, not privately owned, institutions go out of their way to establish the same principles of wage bargaining as in private industry, as if to manifest the irrelevance of the 'whole product' argument and the supreme importance of the issue of control. If, in consequence of the pressure exerted on wages, capitalist property rights are also affected and their exercise is limited, it happens because of the fact that these rights in their capitalist form cannot be deployed without a concomitant assault on the personal autonomy of producers. To put the issue still more sharply, the formation of workers into a class was a response to the advent of industrial society; only obliquely, because of the circumstances of the time and place, can this formation be portrayed as a reaction to the capitalist form of industrial society.

Manual workers were the first to be subjected to the new work discipline of industrial society; above all, they were first to be condemned to such a discipline for life – the first for whom the work regime was to become the total form of life. Other parts of the population were to enjoy for some time yet the status of economic independence. They remained connected with the rest of the society, including its dominant groups – through the traditional link of distribution, while retaining self-control in the sphere of production. For the time being, therefore, they found themselves among the beneficiaries of industrial society. This situation, however, was bound to end soon. By now the fully documented transformation of the 'middle classes' from self-employed and self-managing individuals into an army of employees reduced the manual workers to a constantly shrinking sector of those confronted with the same threat which the manual workers had faced from the outset of industrial society. The staging of the process, however, left manual workers for almost a century alone on the battlefield. This fact made it somewhat easier to depict their struggle as related to the issue conspicuously distinctive from the form of their productive activity: as related, in other words, to the control over the finished, tangible, product of labour, rather than over the bodies and souls of its producers.

The lapse of time between the beginning and the final stage of control expansion rendered such an interpretation plausible. But it can hardly be seen as its causal explanation.

The more likely cause of the interpretation was the natural tendency of the interpreters to view visible antagonisms of the society as manifestations of the conflict in which they themselves were engaged. This other conflict was indeed about the control over socially produced surplus. This conflict was not resolved by the ascent of industrialists. The many lurid intellectual pictures of the new society portraying the capitalist as in sole and full control of the surplus reflected the reality of industrial society at no stage of its history. They captured the true trends of development as much as they displayed, consciously or inadvertently, concerns and ambitions of the interpreters, more often than not they were sounds of alarm and declarations of continuing war over the control over surplus. In short, they are best understood as the texts of the ongoing struggle for power.

Many followers and readers of Marx were embarrassed or puzzled by the apparent incongruity of his list of historical contenders in the perpetual class struggle. Obviously, the landowners and the bourgeois were engaged in a different kind of war from slaves and slave-owners, or capitalists and proletarians. The blunder of comparing the incomparable, committed by an otherwise superbly logical mind, is somewhat less bewildering once it is seen against the overall tendency to collapse – indeed, to identify – the two separate strands of conflict intertwined in the dynamics of industrial society. Once the two strands have been twisted into a single continuous thread of class warfare, the struggle of the labourers to retain control over their labour could be presented as a further stage of the bourgeois struggle to acquire control over surplus; if the labourers were reluctant to conform to the logic of the latter struggle, they could be always charged with the sin, or the weakness, of false consciousness or opportunism.

In his critique of the capitalist society Marx was at pains to distinguish the phenomenon of expanding surplus labour, which the capitalist form of acquisition boosted, and the transformation of surplus labour into capitalist profit. The first advanced the productive potential of mankind and hence served the objective of human emancipation; the modern division of labour, with its careful planning of partial tasks, meticulous administration and supervision of productive functions, was to be seen in the long run as a powerful stride away from the realm of natural necessity. Like Adam Smith in his famous eulogy of the pin factory, Marx was deeply impressed by the possibility of well-nigh unlimited increase of surplus product which the factory system has created. To a large extent Marx shared an almost aesthetic admiration of the planned, rhythmical, co-ordinated effort brought about by industrial technology. Implicitly, he revealed it in the metaphor of the symphonic orchestra and its conductor who blends disparate sounds into a pleasing tune. The one point which Marx stressed over and over again throughout the three volumes of 'Capital' was that the quality of orchestral performance did not depend on the conductor being the

owner of the instruments. Indeed, all the ills of the capitalist society
Marx traced to this latter circumstance. There was nothing wrong with
the unprecedented increase of surplus product attained through the
new organisation of the productive process; everything, however, was
wrong with the acquisition of this surplus product as the profit of the
capital owner.

The ills of the capitalist form of the management of surplus product
which Marx (and other, both radical and not-so-radical critics) condemned, were two-fold. First, the personal union between management of productive process and profit-making resulted in the tendency
to a ruthless exploitation of labour force. Rationality of technology
was surrendered to the logic of gain. Hence the moral turpitude of the
capitalist-managed factory, which could be cured only by the breaking
of the unholy (and contingent) alliance between the administration of
the productive process and the ownership of the means of production.
Second, what appeared to the workers as a planned, tightly organised,
purposeful system, was in its higher regions an anarchy. The blending
of control and ownership enthroned the confusion of universal competition where the planned use of resources should rule, and thus
drowned the potential of organised production in the sea of massive
irrationality. Both evils of the capitalist system require, therefore, the
same medicine. One has to salvage the new form of production, which
capitalism pioneered, from the capitalist system of acquisition and
management of the surplus product. The surplus product ought to be
distributed as rationally as it is produced.

Marx was by no means alone in tracing the moral abomination of
industrial regime to the anarchy in the distribution of social product.
The two themes of critique and the intimate bond between them
remained a major characteristic of intellectual debate from the outset
of the new power. The general tendency of this debate was the
presentation of the issue of repression as subsidiary to the question
of the management of surplus. The need of discipline, management,
and organised control over the productive process (i.e., the producers)
was questioned by nobody but the anarcho-syndicalist margins who
were dismissed by dominant opinion, whether conservative, liberal, or
socialist, as Utopian or retrograde. What invited widely shared condemnation was the 'excess of repression', allegedly uncalled for by the
logic of production, and caused solely by the competitive pressure of a
disorderly market. By this reasoning, people who suffered most from
the repressive factory regime were naturally interested in changing the
rules according to which the surplus was appropriated and divided;
hence the tendency to present such a change of rules (depicted, with
varying degrees of radicalism, as state intervention, nationalisation, or

abolition of private property) as the ultimate horizon of working-class interests and the substance of its class consciousness.

This latter belief was most pronounced, of course, among radical participants of the debate. It appeared mostly as a hoped-for substitute for the missing, or inaccessible, levers of effective political action within the extant structure of power. Other participants of the debate, sufficiently close to the centres of authority, had less need of a messianic surrogate. They could instead bid realistically for a decisive influence on existing administrative agents. All participants, however, with minor exceptions only, shared in the condemnation of the irredeemable irrationality of the market anarchy. They demanded that the 'invisible hand' be guided by conscious advice of reason. J. S. Mill made the distinctiveness of the two themes explicit: production of commodities is subject to objective laws which ought to be learned and respected; distribution, however, is a matter of policy, dependent on man-made laws, and ought to be a matter of conscious care and well-informed choice.

It seems, in other words, that the intellectual critique of the capitalist market cannot be interpreted as a reflection of the same conflict which – as I suggested earlier – led to the formation of factory labour into the working class. In the intellectual critique, the focus of workers' concerns and discontents had been markedly displaced, as if moving under the force of gravity of another powerful conflict. As to the nature of this additional conflict the intellectual debate itself kept remarkably quiet, betraying its presence only obliquely, through its persistent concerns and steady shift of emphasis.

Marx's litany of 'historic classes', in which the conflict between capitalists and proletarians followed the conflict between feudal landlords and the bourgeois, ceases to puzzle once the actuality of the other conflict is admitted. Like the struggle waged by the bourgeois against the rights of land property, this new conflict is mainly about the administration of surplus product, to wit, about the ultimate foundation of political power. The question is, who, in this other conflict, represents the true adversary of the capitalist – or, more generally, of the right to the whole product attached to the ownership of capital.

The question is by no means new. It has been asked many times before, and a number of answers are already on offer, some backed by a tradition long enough to render the authorship forgotten or debatable. Some of the answers are fairly well-known and already receive their share of popularity and counter-argument.

The answer which stirred perhaps the widest, and probably the longest commotion was the one associated with James Burnham (though Burnham's originality has been seriously questioned by Daniel Bell, who defended the ownership rights to Burnham's ideas of writers publishing long before the spectacular bestseller success of the 'Managerial Revolution' – like Rizzi, Trotsky, or even Emil Lederer, who sensed the ascent of Privatangestellten as far back as 1912 [Bell, 1973]). This answer favours managers of privately and publicly owned firms as the next 'ruling class', eager to take over control over surplus from its titular owners. According to Burnham, the detachment of control from ownership was already well under way in the whole of the industrialised world and a virtual 'managerial revolution' was taking place, or was imminent, in a violent (Soviet or German) or quiet and hardly perceptible (American) form. Few authors adopted Burnham's historiosophic assertion in its shockingly radical version, but its milder variant – of the growing separation of control from ownership – had acquired enthusiastic supporters in quarters which Burnham perhaps did not expect to inspire. The thesis of the real power moving slowly but steadily into the laps of the hired managers acquired in the post-war decades wide popularity among economists and political scientists keen to disprove the persistence of the capitalist features of the current society and by so doing to prove that the charges once made by the critics incensed by the immorality of capitalist exploitation, had lost most of their force. The temporary popularity of the attenuated Burnham thesis was well geared to the brief, but exuberant period of managerial optimism – when it seemed to many that the zeal of the 'rationalisers' of the market economy would not be brought to a halt by entrenched powers inimical to the 'scientifically modelled' society. The popularity faded together with the hope.

The Burnhamian episode was both preceded and followed by another proposition, which never reached the heights of Burnhamian short-lived success, but which is likely to outlive the latter's memory thanks to the amazing survival-and-resurrection capacity it has demonstrated to date. According to this second proposition, the society ruled by competition and private appropriation is to be replaced by a society dominated and ruled by men of knowledge – variously described as intellectuals, scientists and technologists. The first formulation of this idea is sometimes ascribed to a Polish rebellious communist, Machajski (pen-name A. Wolski), who accused the intellectuals of exploiting the struggle of the workers to pave the way to their own rule and yet harsher repression of the proletariat. Even if Machajski did not succeed in originating an alternative, 'intellectual-free' proletarian movement, his indictment was to remain just below the level of consciousness of all left-wing movements claiming proletarian credentials, and surfaced time and again in spite of all exorcisms and the concentrated effort of repression. Quite recently the idea reappeared, with vengeance, this time at some distance from political battlefields, in the mainstream of sociological discourse. It immediately captured 'sociological imagination', thanks, at least in part, to the blunt, deliberately provocative way in which it was brought to public attention by its major proponents.

If I am not mistaken, the first major contribution to the recent renaissance came from the then doyen of American political science, Harold D. Lasswell (1965, pp. 86–7, 92). In direct reference to Machajski, Lasswell explored the developmental tendencies of the mature industrial society only to find out that they can be logically depicted as a 'permanent revolution of modernising intellectuals'. It was mostly the intellectuals themselves, wrote Lasswell, who failed to notice that they moved steadily towards the strategic positions of power; a curious case of the 'temporary "false consciousness" on the part of intellectuals who nevertheless served the power interests of the rising intellectual class. By deceiving themselves they were better able to deceive others'. Like most ruling classes, the intellectuals are pre-occupied with internecine squabbles to the point of overlooking a class unity which underlies all arguments and divisions. They are, in fact, a distinct entity, and one which already dominates the industrial world. The fact will decide the shape of the world to come:

> In characterising the outcomes and effects of an intellectually domin-ated world, it is possible to offer at least one major generalisation: the trend of policy will express a balance of power favourable to more and more intellectual activity, supported by more and more utilisation of social resources.

At the time Lasswell's study appeared the intellectuals were too neatly integrated in the mechanisms of power in both parts of the industrial world to need an exercise in self-consciousness. Lasswell's shot was fired before the ranks thought of a battle. Hence two books which did not significantly depart from Lasswell's main contention, but appeared a little more than a decade later, seem to have made from the start a much stronger impact. The first of the two, by George Konrad and Ivan Szelenyi (1979, pp. 14, 53, 224), set openly on the unmasking course. Lasswell's 'false consciousness' was replaced by a merciless pursuit of group interests:

> it has been the common aspiration of the intellectuals of every age to represent their particular interests in each context as the general

interests of mankind. The definition of universal, eternal, supreme (and hence immutable) knowledge displays a remarkable variability over the ages, but in every age the intellectuals define as such whatever knowledge best serves the particular interests connected with their social role.

Where Lasswell spoke of the late industrial society, Konrad and Szelenyi speak of 'every age'. Where Lasswell pondered the domination of the intellectuals as the outcome of technological transformation in modern society, Konrad and Szelenyi practically reverse the causal order of things: it was the perpetual thrust of intellectuals to class power which finally led to whatever technological, or any other, transformation is currently taking place. The present class ideal of the intellectuals, which (if realised) would finally place them at the helm, is one of 'rational redistribution'. Thus far, the ideal came closest to fulfilment in the communist states, where 'it is the rationality of the planning process, not the decisions of owners of capital, which redistributes the retained surplus product, whose size cannot be effectively regulated by the market'. 'Under rational redistribution it is above all technical knowledge, intellectual knowledge, which legitimises the right to dispose over the surplus product. That is what justifies the superior position of the redistributors and provides the ideological basis for the formation of the intelligentsia into a class.'

Almost simultaneously with the English translation of Konrad and Szelenyi's statement, Alvin Gouldner's book appeared which in its very first words proclaimed that

> in all countries that have in the twentieth century become part of the emerging world socio-economic order, a New Class composed of intellectuals and technical intelligentsia – not the same – enter into contention with the groups already in control of the society's economy, whether these are businessmen or party leaders.

It soon becomes clear that in Gouldner's view the New Class is best understood as a next link in the historical chain of dominant classes; its collective behaviour is to be interpreted in terms of a tendency, and an aspiration, to class domination in the historically established sense of the word: that of the control over surplus product, conducted in the controllers' own interest:

> The New Class is elitist and self-seeking and uses its special knowledge to advance its own interests and power, and to control its own work situation. Yet the New Class may also be the best card that history has presently given us to play. The power of the New Class is growing. It is

substantially more powerful and independent than Chomsky suggests, while still much less powerful than is suggested by Galbraith who seems to conflate present reality with future possibility. The power of this morally ambiguous New Class is on the ascendant and it holds a mortgage on at least *one* historical future.   (Gouldner, 1979, pp. 1–8)

Gouldner makes it explicit that he uses the term 'class' in its Marxist sense, constituted by the idea of 'certain communality' uniting members of a given group, particularly in regard to 'the same relationship to the means of production'. Even the type of means of production the New Class is related to, is analogous to the kind commanded by the preceding and currently rival dominant class: it is capital, though a distinct form of it, made to the measure of the ascending class power: 'cultural' or 'human' capital. It is the latter capital which becomes decisive for the effective possession of the mode of production, as distinct from its legal ownership.

The third answer to our question belongs to a somewhat different category. It has become, so to speak, a folklore of the thinking public brought up in the world conceptualised as a wrestling match between contradictory class interests. There is a constant feedback movement between this diffuse folklore and the articulated public or academic opinion; thanks, however, to its broad folkloristic base, the third answer does not require such a systematic theoretical elaboration as the other two. More often than not it is offered in the guise of the 'facts of life', a statistics which takes its meaningfulness for granted, a press report referring to the established community of meaning, academic propositions starting from 'as we know' – this sacramental incantation of paradigmatical consensus too universal to need legitimation.

Obviously, a belief which invokes folklore as its paramount authority must be lacking in precision. The third answer assumes, indeed, numerous verbalisations, which are not always easy to correlate. One reads of 'the government', 'the politicians', 'the bureaucrats' – various groups of rather unclear mutual relations, but always 'power greedy' and attempting with varying degree of success, to wrestle power, control and initiative from 'private industry'. The mental image behind these verbalisations, seldom articulated with the cohesion of a theoretical model, is of two integrated and powerful groups, pitted against each other in a continuing struggle for the control over economy. The image is of a zero-sum game; whatever 'politicians' or 'bureaucrats' manage to cream off from the profits made by 'private industry', detracts from the possessions, and the power, of the latter; the more freedom 'private industry' retains in the disposal of its product, the weaker 'the bureaucrats' become. For all practical intents and purposes, this is an image of class struggle, of an ongoing battle between two entrenched groups guided mostly by their respective interests, each aspiring to overpower and dominate the other.

The three apparently different answers have one crucial attribute in common. They are all determined by a tacit acceptance of the extant interpretative model, which identifies the task of explanation of socio-political processes with the need to locate a group which benefits from these processes; and which assumes that such a group could be imputed with an intuitive tendency, and in the long run also with a deliberate effort, to promote the said processes for this very reason. All three answers derive, therefore, their ultimate authority from common sense – this world image which projects on to the large screen of society the interpretative habits daily reinforced by micro-social individual experience. In unison with commonsensical predis-position, these answers anticipate a purposeful agent behind every event, self-interest behind every change or its prevention, an indi-vidual or collective culprit behind every guilt.

But this universal tendency of common sense, determined by the very structure of the life-world, has been given the currently specific shape by historical memory. It is in this form, mediated by 'living history', that common sense informs the three answers under discus-sion. To the constant, commonsensical search for a self-interested agent, historical memory contributed the belief that the point around which collective interests crystallise and integrate is the command over the 'whole product of labour', variously named 'control of economy', 'ownership of means of production', or 'right to profit' – depending on theoretical allegiance or political denomination. In other words, the historical memory which inspires and constrains all three answers is one of class conflict, but a class conflict interpreted in the course of the nineteenth century, in terms suggested by the idea-lisation of the capitalist market, as a conflict about the management of the surplus product, rather than about the regimentation of the body and the soul of its producer. It was this theoretical interpreta-tion, rendered plausible and steadily reinforced by the growing com-moditisation of life conditions, which has sedimented as the historical memory of our times. In this capacity, it supplies the chisels with which to carve the self-portrait of the era.

The way in which the problems are verbalised determines the range of possible solutions. All three answers are contained within the same set of assumptions. They all arise out of the search for the 'next dominant class'. No wonder all of them find one. Whatever class is found, it is defined in the same way: the way dictated by historical memory of a specific historical form of class domination. It is thus defined as a collection of people so situated in the network of social dependencies that they must, and often wish to, pursue a total control over social product and particularly over its distribution. Each answer locates the discovery in a different part of society; but each proclaims the discovery of the same thing.

All in all, the three answers, together with the orthodox Marxist view which insists that things have not changed since the 'Communist Manifesto', and that the labour versus capital struggle remains the main class conflict, are on the side of the *essential immutability* of the springs of historical *change*. They all in the end agree that now, as much as in the time of bourgeois revolution, the moving force of history is the thrust of a new class to take over the management of the social surplus which previous rulers are not able to administer properly. And much in the spirit of the bourgeois propaganda against the retrograde landed property, they describe the bid, and the chances of the challenger, in terms of efficiency and effectiveness of the management it is capable of providing.

The second of the two main hypotheses [of this book] contends that all the answers discussed thus far have little but historical memory to justify their claims; while historical memory, this pool of metaphors and analogies necessary to make sense of the present, fails in its task once the new realities refuse to be stretched or pressed so as to fit the moulds of historical tradition. If this happens, historical memory may well prevent the insight into the genuine levers of societal dynamics. It is the contention [of this book] that historical memory of class and class struggle plays at present such a 'holding back' role.

This second contention is argued along the following lines:

1 Late industrial society at its present stage is held together by systemic, rather than social, dependencies (thus, it is neither the 'segmental' nor the 'class' society of Durkheim's two-part division). Accordingly, the phenomena which tend to be identified as 'problems' of this society, or the dearth of available solutions to these problems, identified as its 'crisis', arise from endemic structural incongruities and contradictions of the system, rather than from structural location and ensuing policies of one particular class of people occupying a commanding position within the society. Though the consequences of each problem are distributed between various groups unevenly, they are in the end afflictions of the system as a whole and tend to accumulate and reinforce each other, so deepening the chasm between the volume of conflicts and the number of available solutions.

2 The management of surplus product (of its production as well as allocation) is now a function of the system; no single group, identified by a specific legal ownership status, or access to special sources of authority, or by any other unique property, can either do, or aspire to do, it alone. No group is free in a 'homo-oeconomicus' type tendency to the acquisition of surplus; no group's condition can be lastingly enhanced by pursuing the economic model of 'maximisation of goals'. The 'right to the whole product', allegedly the focus of crystallisation of the class-type conflict, is not, therefore, at issue. In a sense, the satisfaction of any group's interests depends on the systemic curb imposed on maximisation tendencies, in as far as these continue to be prompted by the market-mediated consumption.

3 Correspondingly, no single group can be identified as the 'historical class' of the late industrial society; i.e., as a class whose 'group interests' are identical with the 'interests of the society as a whole', and which for this reason cannot serve its own interests without simultaneously promoting social interests in general; or (according to the inspired vision of Marx) a class oppressed in such a way that the removal of its particular oppression would mean the end to social oppression in general. It was an integral belief of the class vision, and a major source of its intellectual attractiveness, that the passage to the next, improved form of the society is therefore assured, and in the long run inevitable, thanks to this structural identity of the particular and the universal. If this sociological concretisation of Hegel's dialectical law of reason ever approximated the realities of industrial society, it certainly does not apply to its late version. The intricate network of systemic interdependencies precludes the possibility of reducing the dynamics of the whole system to this of one of its sectors. The interests of no single group, however carefully scanned and veridically articulated, may be seen as representing the interests of 'the system as a whole'.

4 The other facet of the same is that no group pressure, or a group programme legitimising this pressure, is likely to provide a solution to the system's problems. Expectations, or promises, to the contrary, are ultimately based on an assumption that the system 'can be made to work', which is counter-factual. It seems rather that the difficulty of the system in coping with conflicting demands are endemic, and that promotion of no one of the contradictory interests will remove it, or even visibly alleviate it. The endemic nature of the system's problem has been traced by Jürgen Habermas to the impossibility of reproducing commodity relations without simultaneously weakening the motives and the predispositions (like work ethic or family privatism) which are indispensable for their effectivity (Habermas, 1976), by

James O'Connor, to the ineradicable tendency of the systemic outputs to outrace the inputs, and worse still, to deplete their sources (O'Connor, 1973); by Claus Offe, to the inherent proclivity of the state to neglect the weak or inarticulate parts of the system and hence to allow the gestation of problems beyond the capacity of systemic control (Offe, 1972). What follows from all these analyses is that, far from carrying the promise of a solution to systemic crisis, all group interests, demands, and pressures contribute to its aggravation. The crisis is not traceable to the interests of policies of any group in particular, but rather to the way in which these interests and policies relate to each other and influence each other's chances. In effect, the results of apparently purposeful, intentionally rational actions, have all the bearings of 'natural catastrophes'. Policy mistakes or groups' ill-will may perhaps account for the particular shape such catastrophes assume; certainly not, however, for their appearance and persistence.

5 One central feature of the system, which class vision on the whole relegated to a subsidiary role, is the function played in the production and distribution of social surplus by the state. In fact, the role of the state was from the outset of industrial society much larger than most political scientists or economists of the time were prepared to admit. If the economic significance of the state's defence of the internal and conquering of the external markets, protecting rights of ownership, and providing services which market interests were unwilling to support have been all universally acknowledged, one powerful factor in continuous expansion of the state, particularly in its earliest period, has been noticed on but a few occasions, namely, the function of the state consisting in 'legislating morals' (Lasswell, 1965, p. 80) – in guarding sexual ethics, teaching thrift, tutoring good manners, fighting display of passion in all possible forms, separating the public sphere from the private. However wary of an expanding and costly state, the bourgeois never objected to the state's tendency to redefine an ever-widening range of morally contentious behaviour as criminal activity, requiring intervention of state organs. The support for the new forms of control over body and spirit was perhaps the single most important factor of growth in the first stage of state expansion. More directly economic tasks joined later, when the tendency of the market to generate crises which it was ill-prepared to solve on its own became evident, and when growing costs of reproducing labour and controlling its carriers made it less and less possible for the capitalists to meet these costs in full from the surplus product they directly administered due to their ownership rights. The combined effect of all these needs (and many others) is a state occupying the position of the main 'throughput' of the system and best

understood as neither a 'parasite' feeding on the output of social production, nor source of authoritative command, but as a link within the communication network, without which no integrated existence of the system is further possible.

6 The unique location of the state within the totality of the system makes it, however, more socially visible than other units may be. This circumstance breeds the illusion of the centrality and the causal role of politics which the latter does not possess. Another illusion is the conscious character of political process, and in particular a causal connection between motives or purposes of the politicians and economic and social effects of the system. Perhaps the illusion most formidable in its consequences is that of the extensive power potential of the state. The form in which politics presents itself to public view suggests a rational nature of economic and social processes; one which can be, with due care, subordinated to the rules of argument and the test of truth. Hence the malfunctionings of the system appear as flaws in the rationality of state decisions, which can be rectified by the substitution of better policies. It is for this reason that most group demands and grievances assume a political form and tend to be articulated as postulates of changes in state policies, while systemic roots of problems tend to escape attention. As a result the state is chronically overloaded with demands, while simultaneously serving as a lightning rod absorbing tensions arising from systemically diffused agencies of power and control.

7 Under these circumstances, the state moves steadily into the focus of group divisions and alliances. The society, when seen as an aggregate of state subjects, is a pool of potential tensions which articulate into definite forces in response to the action (or the lack of action) on the part of the state. Groups integrate, enter alliances, set programmes in relation to the state. Their dimension, absorptive capacity, and possible scale of expansion are determined not so much by the attributes the group members possess individually or conjointly, as by the potential of common action defined by the state-originated issue. The boundaries of groups are, therefore, 'ad hoc' and shifting. Alterations of policy lead to successive re-alignments of divisions. Due partly to the varying degree of institutionalisation, some divisions are more lasting in comparison with others; one could plot the groupings along a scale ranging from such as are defined by more or less permanent organisations which determine the selection of issues and attitudes, up to one-issue, campaign-like, loosely integrated and short-lived movements. But no division seems to occupy an 'over-determining' position in relation to others; one to which all other divisions could be related as its manifestations or modifications.

Hence, as Alain Touraine repeatedly stated in a series of recent works (Touraine, 1973, 1978), political action becomes an ever more important, and all-powerful, determinant of group divisions. Action is ill-understood if interpreted as a reflection of underlying economic interests; it is, rather, the politically 'prompted' action which tends to articulate the identity of the group in the dominant vocabulary of economic gains or losses.

8 While it is true that groups and movements constitute themselves around demands addressed to the state, the impact of state policies does not only differentiate between groups; it has also an ambiguous effect on individual interests, further complicating the chart of the field of social forces. The widening scope of activity of the state as the principal agent of transfer, the growing proportion of social surplus directly administered by the state, favours some and harms some other aspects of individual interests, prompting truly schizophrenic attitudes towards the role of the state. Though the degree to which the expansion of social expenses of the state, or, alternatively, the confinement of its fiscal claims, is regarded as 'being in the group's interests', varies from one part of population to another – a proportion of both attitudes is present in each category. Moreover, the balance between the two is shifting in a nearly cyclical way, producing the notorious 'see-saw' movement of public mood. One can conclude that the 'through-put' role of the state in the social system does not split the society into opposing classes; it is not presently an object of class contention. More importantly still, the present location of the state within the system has passed the threshold line beyond which it acquires a self-perpetuating, and perhaps also a self-reinforcing, capacity. Under these conditions, even self-consciously anti-etatist demands and pressures lead in their practical consequences to the further enhancement of the strategic potency of the state and increase the dependency of the system on state activity. A good recent example is the monetarist adventure. As if to provide a textbook example of 'false consciousness', it led to the state reaching never yet attained commanding positions regarding economy, social and cultural life, while preaching the virtues of private initiative and the need to free the individual from bureaucratic control.

It is not the task [of these essays] to speculate about the possible scenarios of the future. Still less do they claim to articulate an unambiguous policy advice. The much more modest aim which I set for myself is to encourage a debate with 'ground-clearing' objectives only. They are, in the end, another contribution to the ongoing effort to discard the categories which do not help any more to understand the present crisis, and to construct a conceptual framework better fitted for its interpretation.

It is one of the suggestions promoted that such an interpretative framework should contain, as one of its major constructive blocks, the proper concept of social power able to replace the discipline power which once supported the spectacular success of industrial society, but which undergoes a crisis similar to this experienced by the sovereign power a couple of centuries ago, once industrial society is nearing its dead end, having succeeded in an almost complete translation of its control conflicts into conflicts over the share in the division of surplus. The economisation of social conflicts, which for many decades successfully defused the tensions arising from the bid to control the producers, led finally to the endemic excess of distributive demands over the productive potential, and hence becomes increasingly inadequate as a makeshift solution to the problem of social integration, and through it, of the reproduction of society. The present crisis can therefore hardly be resolved by another shuffle among the traditionally principal actors or a new, ingenious way of performing the old task of re-dividing the surplus in favour of the loudest and potentially most noxious claimant. All future attempts at its resolution can claim adequacy to the problem only to the degree to which they come to grips with the essential issue of 'discipline power' which serves as a constant source and boost of distributive pressures. They can hardly hope for success if they seek the impossible feat of meeting the ever higher targets of consumer satisfaction which the removal of the issue of control from the public agenda is bound to render ever less manageable.

In other words, it is one of the main arguments [of this book] that the mechanism of social reproduction which for a time assured the flourishing of industrial society is now near the exhaustion of its historic potential and that the crisis we experience is not 'more of the same' problems, but a qualitatively new stage in history which can be passed only with a change in the type of social power as seminal as the one which took place in the times preceding the advent of the industrial system.

References

Barker, Ernest (1944) *The Development of Public Services in Western Europe 1660–1930*. Oxford: Oxford University Press.
Bell, Daniel (1973) *The Coming of the Post-Industrial Society*. New York: Basic.

Burn, Richard (1973) [1764] *The History of the Poor Laws with Observations.* Clifton, NJ: A. M. Kelley.

Foucault, Michel (1980) *Power/Knowledge,* ed. Colin Gordon. Brighton: Harvester.

Gouldner, Alvin (1979) *The Future of Intellectuals and the Rise of the New Class.* London: Macmillan.

Habermas, Jürgen (1976) *Legitimation Crisis,* trans. Thomas McCarthy, London: Heinemann.

Hufton, Olwen H. (1980) *Europe: Privilege and Protest 1730–1789.* Brighton: Harvester.

Konrad, George and Szelenyi, Ivan (1979) *The Intellectuals on the Road to Class Power,* trans. Andrew Arato and Richard E. Allen. Brighton: Harvester.

Lasswell, H. D. (1965) 'The World Revolution of Our Time,' in H. D. Lasswell and Daniel Lerner (eds) *World Revolutionary Elites.* Cambridge, MA: MIT Press.

Menger, Anton (1899) *The Right to the Whole Product of Labour,* trans. M. E. Tanner. London: Macmillan.

Moore, Barrington (1978) *Injustice: The Social Basis of Obedience and Revolt.* London: Macmillan.

O'Connor, James (1973) *The Fiscal Crisis of the State.* New York: St. Martin's Press.

Offe, Claus (1972) 'Political Authority and Class Structures.' *International Journal of Sociology* 2.

Offe, Claus and Wiesenthal, Helmut (1980) 'Two Logics of Collective Action,' in I. M. Zeitlin (ed.), *Political Power and Society Theory,* vol. I. Greenwich, CT: JAI Press.

Perkin, Harold (1981) 'The Social Causes of the Industrial Revolution,' in *The Structured Crowd.* Brighton: Harvester.

Rule, John (1981) *The Experience of Labour in Eighteenth-Century Industry.* London: Croom Helm.

Touraine, Alain (1973) *Production de la société.* Paris: Seuil.

Touraine, Alain (1978) *La Voix et le regard.* Paris: Seuil.

Thompson, E. P. (1963) *The Making of the English Working Class.* London: Methuen.

Thompson, E. P. (1974) 'Time, Work-Discipline and Industrial Capitalism,' in M. W. Flint and T. C. Smout (eds), *Essays in Social History.* Oxford: Clarendon Press.

Weber, Max (1976) *The Protestant Ethic and the Spirit of Capitalism,* trans. Talcott Parsons. London: Allen & Unwin.

4.2   Gamekeepers Turned Gardeners (1987)

'Wild cultures', says Ernest Gellner, 'reproduce themselves from generation to generation without conscious design, supervision, surveillance or special nutrition.' 'Cultivated' or 'garden' cultures, on the contrary, can only be sustained by literary and specialized personnel (Gellner, 1983, p. 56). To reproduce, they need design and supervision; without them, garden cultures would be overwhelmed by wilderness. There is a sense of precarious artificiality in every garden; it needs the constant attention of the gardener, as a moment of neglect or mere absent-mindedness would return it to the state from which it had emerged (and which it had to destroy, evict or put under control to emerge). However well established, the garden design can never be relied upon to reproduce itself, and never can it be relied upon to reproduce itself by its own resources. The weeds – the uninvited, unplanned, self-controlled plants – are there to underline the fragility of the imposed order; they alert the gardener to the never-ending demand for supervision and surveillance.

The emergence of modernity was such a process of transformation of wild cultures into garden cultures. Or, rather, a process in the course of which the construction of garden cultures re-evaluated the past, and those areas that stretched behind the newly erected fences, and the obstacles encountered by the gardener inside his own cultivated plot, became the 'wilderness'. The seventeenth century was the time when the process acquired momentum; by the beginning of the nineteenth century it had by and large been completed in the Western tip of the European peninsula. Thanks to its success there, it also became the pattern to be coveted by, or to be forced upon, the rest of the world.

The passage from a wild to a garden culture is not only an operation performed on a plot of land; it is also, and perhaps more seminally, an appearance of a new role, oriented to previously unknown ends and calling for previously non-existing skills: the role of the gardener. The gardener now takes over the place of the gamekeeper. Gamekeepers do not feed the vegetation and the animals which inhabit the territory entrusted to their care; neither do they have any intention to transform the state of the territory to bring it closer to that of a contrived 'ideal state'. Rather, they try to assure that the plants and the animals self-reproduce undisturbed – the gamekeepers have confidence in their trustees' resourcefulness. They lack, on the other hand, the sort of self-confidence needed to interfere with the trustees' timeless habits; it does not occur to them, therefore, that a state of affairs different from the one sustained by such habits could be contemplated as a realistic alternative. What the gamekeepers are after, is something much simpler: to secure a share in the wealth of goods these timeless habits produce, to make sure that the share is collected, and to bar impostor gamekeepers (poachers, as the illegal gamekeepers are branded) from taking their cut.

The power presiding over modernity (the pastoral power of the state) is modelled on the role of the gardener. The pre-modern ruling class was, in a sense, a collective gamekeeper. The passage to modernity was the process in the course of which the first emerged and the second declined and was in the end displaced. This process was not a result of the invention of gardening; it had been set off by the growing incapacity of the wild culture to sustain its own balance and the annual reproductive cycle, by the disturbing disequilibrium between the volume of gamekeepers' demands and the productive capability of their trustees as long as the latter were guided by their own 'timeless habits', and finally by the inability of the gamekeepers to secure the yield they wanted while confining themselves to traditional game-keeper pastimes.

Gamekeepers are not great believers in the human (or their own) capacity to administer their own life. They are naturally, so to speak, religious people. Having practised no 'patterning', 'moulding' or 'shaping' of the wild culture they supervise, they lack the experience from which one can fashion the idea of the human origin of the human world, the self-sufficiency of man, the malleability of the human condition, etc. Their own lack of interference with the spontaneous working of the wild culture, which has constituted the virtual 'untouchability' of the latter, is reflected in their philosophy (if they need one) of the superhuman character of the world order. The wild culture itself cannot be perceived as a *culture*, to wit, an order imposed by humans – whether by design or by default. If it is at all reflected upon, it appears as something much stronger than a human – overt or tacit – agreement may call into being and sustain. It is seen as Nature, God's creation, as a design supported by superhuman sanctions and perpetuated by superhuman guardianship. Intellectually, the redefinition of social order as a product of human convention, as something not 'absolute' and beyond human control, was by far the most important milestone on the road to modernity. But for such a redefinition to happen, a revolution in the way social order was reproduced must have taken place. The gamekeeper stance of the ruling class must have revealed its ineffectiveness and yielded worries it was not prepared to cope with.

Hobbes's curt dismissal of the 'natural state' of mankind as a condition under which human life is 'nasty, brutish and short' is arguably the most quoted and best known of all ideas bequeathed to posterity by the seventeenth-century thinkers. It has received a great deal of attention and been widely accepted as the starting-point of modern social philosophy, political science and sociology. Talcott Parsons thought it possible to see the whole history of social science as the long and still inconclusive struggle with the problem that the Hobbesian metaphor put on the agenda: this problem provided the 'puzzle' around which the paradigm of modern social science could be organized. There is no denying the importance of Hobbes's proposition for the last three centuries of European intellectual history. What the profuse comments on Hobbes's idea have on the whole been silent about, is another puzzle: from where did Hobbes take his image of the 'natural state'? Did he simply conjure it up by the sheer strength of his imagination? Was it wholly an intellectual creation *ab nihilo*? Or, like most ideas, was it rather a response, perhaps exaggerated and unusually powerful, but still a response to some new experience which prodded Hobbes's imagination in the direction that his mind had taken?

Unless the contrary is proven, a plausible supposition is that the latter was the case. If so, then the question is: What was there, in the world of Hobbes's contemporaries, which could inspire the frightening image of the 'state of nature'?

It seems that Hobbes was the victim of an optical illusion of sorts: what he mistook for the living relics of the state of nature, were the artefacts of the advanced decomposition of a tight man-made system of social control. If anything, the worrying, alien bodies infesting his life-world were pointers to the future, an avant-garde of the society to come, the few scattered samples of what was to become the 'normal state' – a society composed of freely moving, gain-oriented individuals unbound by the now bankrupt community supervision. In a true wild culture such individuals were safety kept within the few supervised niches meant to cope with the inevitable failures of social control and their consequences; their numbers were steady, their status unambiguous, their conduct safely stereotyped and hence perceived as predictable and manageable. Now, for reasons discussed in the previous chapter, all these neutralizing factors were fast disappearing. In the cracks of the wild culture system of self-reproduction Hobbes could have thought he glimpsed the state of nature in its pristine purity.

The most significant of the eye-opening effects of the communal retreat was, however, the revelation of the essential brittleness of the principles on which human daily intercourse was based. To be sure, the very existence of such principles (not to mention their indispensability), was in itself a formidable discovery. Such principles could be hardly guessed, or construed, in relation to a society which reproduced itself 'without conscious design' and – let us add – without unpredictable side-effects of a scale too big for the policing system to tackle. Now, when the principles came to be broken too often to work properly, they became visible. Or, rather, once a society 'without design' started producing on a massive scale phenomena it did not anticipate and could not control, it was possible to ask about the real or ideal principles which had been breached, and any remedy proposed for the regrettable effects of such a break had to be in the nature of a *conscious* design. A 'social contract', a legislator or design-drawing despot were the only frames within which the problem of social order could be envisaged, once it became a problem rather than a manifestation of the nature of things.

The new perception of the relationship between (man-made) social order and nature – including the nature of man – found its expression in the notorious opposition between reason and passions. The latter was seen increasingly as the 'natural equipment' of men, something men acquire with their birth, with no effort on their part and no assistance from other men. The former, reason, comes with know-ledge, must be 'passed over' by other people, who know the difference between good and evil, truth and falsity. Thus the difference between reason and passion was from the very start more than a moral opposi-tion; it contained, implicitly but intrinsically, a theory of society, articulating the opposition between the 'natural', and also individual, roots of anti-social phenomena, and the social, organized, hierarch-ized mechanism of social order. It spelled out the indispensability of the supra-individual power (of the state) in securing and perpetuating an orderly relationship between men; and the morbid and disastrous effects of any loosening of the power grip, or of any reliance on the 'natural predispositions' of fellow men.

For the philosophers who thought in such terms the obvious contra-diction contained in the juxtaposition of passion-ridden individuals and the state promotion of reason must have been disturbing, as Albert O. Hirschman noted (Hirschman, 1977). Indeed, how could the precepts of reason possibly influence the conduct of men guided only by passions? As the concept of 'passions' stood for everything 'natural' in man, for everything 'wild' and not having its (artificial, designed) origin in man-made law, how could reason address itself to the 'man of passions' and find him listening and, more importantly, obeying? What Hirschman failed to note in his otherwise highly informative study, was the practical, not merely logical, character of this question. The answer was to be sought in political practice, not moral theory; the thinkers Hirschman quotes were busy developing a theory and pragmatics of social (state) power, not just debating the 'nature of man'.

The apprehensions widely shared by the participants of the debate were succinctly summarized by Spinoza: 'No affect can be restrained by the true knowledge of good and evil insofar as it is true, but only insofar as it is considered as an affect' (Spinoza, 1927, part 4, prop. 14). The message, if read out in terms of the pragmatics of social order, the main preoccupation of the time, is relatively clear: emotions, the anti-social drive which knows no distinction between right and wrong, cannot be dealt with by the *voice* of reason, by knowledge as the argument and dissemination of truth; or, rather, it can be dealt with in such a way only in cases where knowledge itself becomes an 'affect'. One would conclude that the latter case may have only limited application. It would only apply to those few men for whom knowledge itself is a passion – to philosophers, and perhaps also to those chosen few in whom the philosophers stir a similar devotion. As to the others, the problem is not so much how to channel their affects in the true direction, but how to restrain or neutralize their lusts. In Spinoza's view, devotion to God, the desire to be blessed and faith in the effectivity of the road to salvation as suggested by religion, could lead to the needed result.

Hirschman found *interest* one passion which the learned debate of the era treated with rising sympathy and hope. It is easy to explain away this choice as a 'prodromal symptom' of the capitalist future, thereby casting the philosophers of the seventeenth century in the role of prophets or at least heralds of a system which took a further century and a half to materialize. This would mean, however, imputing to the philosophers a conduct they seldom practised before or after. It makes more sense to assume that while promoting interest as one good passion to stifle all other, morbid, passions, they thought through the realities of their own time and proposed to deal with contemporary problems using contemporary means (including this 'contemporaneity' which had been construed with the help of historical memory). Indeed, only with some effort can the present reader squeeze the idea of interest as explicated in the seventeenth century, into the now familiar notion of profit-orientation. The kind of interests invoked by the seventeenth-century thinkers as a remedy against anti-social passions covered a much wider area. According to La Rochefoucault's *Maxims* (1666), the most frequent were interests in honour and glory; interest in welfare or wealth was just one of many, and in no way synonymous with interest as such. One would say rather that the idea of interest was meant to capture social motives rather than natural drives; it was something artificially added to the natural predispositions, something socially induced rather than deriving from human nature. The true opposition between interests and passions was, again, the difference between a socially designed order and the unprocessed, wild, natural state of man. The substance of interest mattered less than its artificiality, synonymous with its social orientation.

There was also another dimension to the opposition between interests and passions (again unnoticed by Hirschman): this was the class dimension, that between two types of men, rather than two sides of an individual's nature, or two types of conduct in which one and the same individual may indulge. *Un homme intéressé* could be the name given to a particular phase in an individual's life; but it could also stand, and it did, for a particular class of individuals, the motivated people, people who pursue socially oriented ends, instead of being pushed and pulled by their natural instincts. Using a later distinction, one can say that what set this class of 'interested men' apart from the rest was the dominant role played in their behaviour by 'in order to' motives – this epitomy of an instrumental–rational behaviour. The interest debate was just one of the many conceptual guises in which, at the age of disintegration of the old order, the theorizing of the new class bases of social order was conducted.

The more the interested behaviour was praised as socially beneficial, the more damaging and condemnable the passion-prodded, self-oriented conduct of the raw and crude people seemed. By setting their own goal-oriented action as a standard of socially useful and laudable life, the participants of the debate defined the contours of the new class divisions and the 'terms of reference' for the new mechanism of societal reproduction. However different the conceptual garb and semantic context of the debate, its social function did not depart significantly from the one perceptively described by Nietzsche in reference to the essential categories of the moral discourse:

> it was the 'good' themselves, that is to say the noble, mighty, highly placed, and high-minded who decreed themselves and their actions to be good, i.e. belonging to the highest rank, in contradistinction to all that was base, low-minded and plebeian. It was only this *pathos of distance* that authorised them to create values and name them...
>
> The basic concept is always *noble* in the hierarchical, class sense, and from this has developed, by historical necessity, the concept *good* embracing nobility of mind, spiritual distinction. This development is strictly parallel to that other which eventually converted the notions *common, plebian, base* into the notion *bad*. (Nietzsche, 1956, pp. 160–2)

This account of the origins of morality is of course mythological, much in the style of the *naturgeschichtliche* speculations fashionable in his time – but the power of sociological insight, with which the mechanism attaching positive signs to behavioural characteristics associated with social domination has been disclosed by Nietzsche, is remarkable. The enthronement of interest was no exception from the general rule; neither was the downgrading of the passions – which gradually came to mean, first and foremost, the base opposite of the praise worthy 'interested' conduct of the 'better men', the style of life that became fundamental to the orderly society.

The most important perlocutionary (in Austin's terms) effect of the reason vs. passions discourse was the recasting of the poor and lowly as the dangerous classes, which had to be guided and instructed to prevent them from destroying social order; and the recasting of the way of life of the poor and lowly as a product of human animal nature, inferior to, and at war with, the life of reason. Both effects amounted to the delegitimation of wild culture and rendering the carriers of the latter legitimate (and passive) objects for cultural gardeners. [...]

The scale and intensity of the political repression which swept seventeenth-century Europe, while masquerading as a cultural crusade, was truly unprecedented. For the popular masses, the reigns of Louis XIII and Louis XIV were – in Robert Muchembled's characterization – 'un siècle de fer'. 'Shackled bodies and subjected souls' had become the new mechanisms of power. Not that long ago, a century or two before, ordinary people 'were relatively free to use their bodies at their convenience; they did not have to refrain all the time from expressing their sexual and emotional impulses'. But it was all changed now. Under the rule of absolute monarchy, social conformity suffered a complete transformation:

> It was not now the question of respecting the norms of the group to which one belonged, but of submitting oneself to a general model, valid everywhere and for everyone. This implied cultural repression. The courtier society, men of letters, nobility, rich urbanites, in other words privileged minorities elaborated between themselves a new cultural model: one of *l'honnête homme* of the seventeenth century, or of *l'homme éclaire* of the eighteenth century. A model obviously inaccessible to the popular masses; but one they were called to imitate.   (Muchembled, 1978, pp. 226, 229, 230)

It is sensible to suppose an intimate link between the growing attachment felt by rulers for the uniform and universally binding cultural model, and the new, statistical-demographic, tenor of politics related to the techniques of absolutist power. Subjects, citizens, legal persons – all were essentially identical units of the state; their exemption from the local constraints (and thus their subjection to the supra-local power of the state) required their particularistic hues to be rubbed off and covered with the universal paint of citizenship. This political intention was well reflected in the idea of a universality of behavioural pattern that knew no limits for emulation. This pattern could tolerate alternatives, which claimed legitimacy by invoking localized traditions, no more than the absolute monarchy could tolerate local customs invoking ancient laws, written or unwritten, for their support. But this meant bulldozing the whole intricate structure of local cultures with the same determination and no less ferocity than that used in levelling down the solitary towers of communal autonomies and privileges. The political unification of the country had a cultural crusade as its accompaniment and the postulated universality of cultural values as its intellectual reflection-cum-legitimation. Let us borrow again from Muchembled, for the summary of the outcome:

> Popular culture, the rural as much as the urban, suffered an almost total collapse under the rule of the Sun King. Its internal coherence vanished definitely. It could not serve any more as a system of survival, or philosophy of existence. France of the Reason, and later France of *les lumières*, had room for only one conception of the world and of life: this of the court and of the urban elites, the carriers of the intellectual culture. The immense effort to reduce the diversity to a unity constituted the very base of the 'civilizing conquest' in France, as witnessed by the drive to subordinate spirits and the bodies, and by the merciless repression of the popular revolts, of deviant behaviour, heterodox beliefs and witchcraft... Toward the middle of the seventeenth century, the conditions had been put together for the birth of the 'mass' culture.   (Muchembled, 1978, pp. 341–2)

[...] Eileen and Stephen Yeo unmistakeably capture the sense of events investigated in the studies collected in their book: 'As well as being about their separate subject matter, the struggles mapped in the book were also about control over time and territory. They were about social initiative, and who was to have it.' The Yeos' own contribution is the study of the beginnings of modern amateur competitive sport in Britain. They quote the *Sporting Gazette* of 1872: 'Sports nominally open to gentlemen amateurs must be confined to those who have a real right to that title, and men of a class considerably lower must be given to understand that the facts of their being well conducted and civil and never having run for money are not sufficient to make a man a gentleman as well as an amateur.' And *The Times* of 1880: 'The outsiders, artisans, mechanics, and such like troublesome persons can have no place found for them. To keep them out is a thing desirable on every account.' The redeployment of power signalled by these quotations sowed the seeds of the pattern to come: 'administrators, teachers, and "social" scientists giving the people what they needed, as much as entrepreneurs like club entertainment secretaries...giving the people what they wanted' (Yeo, 1982, pp. 125, 134, 136).

This was indeed the most crucial of the consequences of the passage from the wild culture of pre-modern times to the garden culture of modernity; of the protracted, always ferocious, often vicious cultural crusade; of the redeployment of social power in the sense of the right to initiative and control over time and space; of the gradual establishment of a new structure of domination – the rule of the knowledgeable and knowledge as the ruling force. Traditional, self-managing and self-reproducing culture was laid in ruins. Deprived of authority, dispossessed of its territorial and institutional assets, lacking its own, now evicted or degraded, experts and managers, it rendered the poor and lowly incapable of self-preservation and dependent on the administrative initiatives of trained professionals. The destruction of pre-modern popular culture was the main factor responsible for the new demand for expert 'administrators, teachers, and "social" scientists' specializing in converting and cultivating human souls and bodies. The conditions had been created for culture to become conscious of itself and an object of its own practice.

References

Gellner, Ernest (1983) *Nations and Nationalism*. Oxford: Blackwell.

Hirschman, Albert O. (1977) *The Passions and the Interests*. Princeton: Princeton University Press.

Muchembled, Robert (1978) *Culture populaire et culture des élites dans la France moderne (XVe–XVIIIe siècles)*. Paris: Flammarion.

Nietzsche, Friedrich W. (1956) *The Genealogy of Morals*, trans. Francis Gotfrey. New York: Doubleday.

Spinoza, Baruch (1927) *Ethics*, trans. N. H. White. Oxford: Oxford University Press.

Yeo, Eileen and Stephen (1982) 'Ways of Seeing: Control and Leisure versus Class and Struggle,' in B. Waites, T. Bennett and J. Martin (eds), *Popular Culture: Past and Present*. London: Croom Helm.

4.3   The Rise of the Interpreter (1987)

Pluralism is not a recent experience. By itself, it cannot serve as a sufficient reason for the recent upsurge of the post-modernist intellectual climate in which pluralism of experience, values and criteria of truth stoutly refuses to be treated as a transitory feature of the yet incomplete reality, and a feature to be eliminated in the process of maturation. '[P]luralization of diverging universes of discourse', Jürgen Habermas remarked, 'belongs to specifically modern experience...We cannot now simply wish this experience away; we can only negate it' (Habermas, 1985, p. 192). Habermas here brings together two distinct kinds of pluralism, to be sure: one, deriving from the division of labour of sorts, the mutual separation of discourses concerned with truth, judgement and taste, which Habermas considers as the crucial feature of modernity as such, something the philosopher and social scientist have been living with for at least a couple of centuries; and another, pluralization of communally and traditionally contexted discourses, which reclaim the localization of truth, judgement and taste which modernity denied and set to overcome in practice. The second kind of plurality is not a recent development either; what is (so it seems) recent, is the recognition of the second type of pluralism as no less permanent and irrevocable than the first one. It is this recognition that is hard to reconcile with the spirit and the practice of modernity. By bringing the two kinds of pluralism together, Habermas, as it were, precludes the possibility of considering the present situation of the Western intellectual as essentially novel, and calls for rather far-reaching changes in the way the intellectual services have been traditionally dispensed.

Instead, Habermas can only perceive recent shifts in the intellectual world-view as a sort of aberration; a regrettable hardening of attitudes which in their more benign form were with us for a long, long time; an event engendered by a lapse of comprehension or theoretical errors; an ailment to be cured by better comprehension and a proper theory. What has indeed happened, according to Habermas, is the sharpening up of the time-honoured controversy between historicism (an attitude which admits historical plurality of truths, yet expects science to supply both the substance and the legitimacy of consensual knowledge) and transcendentalism (which aims at distilling the characteristics of *all* rational action which *must* be presupposed), into a barren polarization between relativism (which denies the possibility of agreement between truths) and absolutism (which seeks universal reason outside, and independently of, rational practice). The last two strategies are simultaneously mistaken; what is in fact the most mistaken aspect of them is that the gap they created between alternative philosophical strategies is so wide that one cannot expect any more the polarized strategies to mitigate mutually their respective extremisms.

There is no denying that both relativism and absolutism coexist as well-pronounced tendencies in contemporary discourse, the second being forced by the strides made by the first into obliquely confirming its presuppositions (the absolute cannot any more be sought in practice – either as an empirical generalization, or as logical premises). If the two hardened versions of the old controversy are indeed interdependent, it seems that the active role in their dialectic entanglement belongs to the view that all further search for supra-communal grounds of truth, judgement or taste is futile (if it has not been futile all along). Such a view, described as relativist, has been in recent years expressed with a force unprecedented for at least two centuries.

Lonnie D. Kliever's articulation of the novelty of the contemporary view of pluralism is as poignant as any one can find in recent writings:

> The dispersion of political power and the freedom of religious assembly within non-hierarchical societies represent differences and disagreements *within* a shared commitment to one nation and one God. Pluralism by contrast assumes no such overarching unity or loyalty. Pluralism is the existence of multiple frames of reference, each with its own scheme of understanding and criteria of rationality. Pluralism is the coexistence of comparable and competing positions which are not to be reconciled. Pluralism is the recognition that different persons and different groups quite literally dwell in irreducibly different worlds. (Kliever, 1982, p. 81)

Kliever goes on to emphasize that in a pluralistic world, there are no 'uncontested systems of reality definition'. All theoretical attempts to negotiate an agreed solution to the contest having failed in practice, we *must* admit, Kliever insists, that 'forms of life are logically and psychologically self-legitimating'. One can live with such admission nicely, Kliever thinks, providing, however, that this admission is as universal as the earlier agreement on the plausibility of the project of universal truth. What Kliever is afraid of, is the continuation, in a pluralist world, of the strategies and ensuing behaviour which derived their sense from the assumption of universal foundations of truth. What may prevent the danger is a sort of a self-inflicted modesty adopted and practised by all 'forms of life' coexisting in the pluralist world. Without such modesty, without reconciling oneself to the 'equality of limitation' between forms of life, old authoritarian habits would soon reassert themselves and the pluralist world would turn into one of 'multiple absolutism'. It is against this new threat, specific to the situation of pluralism establishing itself in the wake of the protracted rule of an authoritarian, monistic world-view, that Kliever wishes to mobilize the intellectuals. The new intellectual task, in his view, is to fight against partial, local absolutisms with the same energy with which their predecessors fought for an 'impartial', universal one. Relativism, far from being a problem, is for Kliever a solution to the pluralist world's problem; moreover, its promotion is, so to speak, a moral duty of contemporary intellectuals.

It is arguable whether the pluralism Kliever diagnoses is a turn in the structure of the world or in the intellectuals' perception of the world. There are valid arguments to support both possibilities. We have briefly scanned some of the arguments pointing to the first possibility. As to the other, the gradual abandoning of the pursuit of ultimate judgement by intellectuals overwhelmed by the incurable plurality of forms of life, the field of art supplies a most conspicuous example of the processes involved.

A pithy portrait of the state of arts at the age of post-modernity has been painted by Matei Calinescu:

> Generally, the increasing pace of change tends to diminish the relevance of any particular change. The new is no longer new. If modernity has presided over the formation of an 'aesthetics of surprise', this seems to be the moment of its total failure. Today the most diverse artistic products (covering the whole range from the esoterically sophisticated to sheer kitsch), wait side by side in the 'cultural supermarket' . . . for their respective consumers. Mutually exclusive aesthetics coexist in a sort of stalemate, no one being able to perform an actually leading role. Most of the analysts of contemporary art agree that ours is a pluralistic world in which everything is permitted on principle. The old avant-garde, destructive as it was, sometimes deluded itself into believing that there were actually new paths to break open, new realities to discover, new prospects to explore. But today, when the 'historical avant-garde' has been so successful as to become the 'chronic condition' of art, both the rhetoric of destruction and that of novelty have lost any trace of heroic appeal. We could say that the new, postmodernist avant-garde reflects at its own level the increasingly 'modular' structure of our mental world, in which the crisis of ideologies (manifesting itself by a strange, cancerous proliferation of micro-ideologies, while the great ideologies of modernity are losing their coherence) makes it more and more difficult to establish convincing hierarchies of values. (Calinescu, 1977, pp. 1, 146–7)

It is as if post-modern art has followed the advice offered in 1921 by Francis Picabia: 'if you want to have clean ideas, change them like shirts' (Picabia, 1971, p. 168) Or, rather, it has improved on the Dadaists' precept: if you do not have ideas, they surely will never get dirty. Post-modern art is conspicuous for its absence of style as a category of artwork; for its deliberately eclectic character, a strategy which can best be described as one of 'collage' and 'pastiche' (Jameson, 1983), both strategies aimed at defying the very idea of style, school, rule, purity of genre – all those things which underpinned critical judgement in the age of modernist art. The absence of clearly defined rules of the game renders all innovation impossible. There is no longer any development in art, perhaps only an undirected change, a succession of fashions, with no one form claiming credibly its superiority over its predecessors – which turn, by the same token, into its contemporaries. What follows is a sort of perpetual present, restlessness reminiscent more of a chaotic Brownian movement than of an ordered sequential change, not to mention a progressive development. It is the state that Meyer called 'stasis', a state in which everything is on the move, but nothing moves anywhere in particular. In the words of Peter Bürger:

> Through the avant-garde movements, the historical succession of techniques and styles has been transferred into a simultaneity of the radically disparate. The consequence is that no movement in the arts today can legitimately claim to be historically more advanced *as art* than any other... The historical avant-garde movements were unable to destroy art as an institution; but they did destroy the possibility that a given school can present itself with the claim to universal validity.

This means, in fact, 'the destruction of the possibility of positing aesthetic norms as valid ones' (Bürger, 1984, pp. 63, 87).

Post-modern art (which truly took off, according to most analysts, only in the 1970s) has gone a long way now from the iconoclastic gesture of Marcel Duchamp, who sent to an art exhibition a urinal dubbed 'Fountain' and signed 'Richard Mutt', with the explanation that '[w]hether Mr Mutt with his own hands made the fountain or not has no importance. He *chose* it. He took an ordinary article of life, placed it so that useful significance disappeared under the new title and point of view – created a new thought for the object' (Picabia, 1971, p. 43). In retrospect, Marcel Duchamp's scandalous act, which at the time was seen as flying in the face of virtually everything that Western aesthetics stood for, seems strikingly modern rather than postmodern; what Marcel Duchamp did was to present a new *definition* of art (something chosen by the artist), a new *theory* of artwork (cutting off an object from its ordinary context and viewing it from an unusual point of view; doing in fact what the Romantics had done a century before in making the familiar extraordinary), a new *method* of artistic work (creating a new thought for an object). By today's standards, Duchamp's gesture was not that iconoclastic at all. On the other hand, it could be seen as such just because at that time definitions, theories and methods still counted and were perceived as the necessary conditions and paramount criteria of artistic judgement.

There were dominant, agreed upon, universally accepted definitions, theories and methods which Duchamp could be radically opposed to and defy. In recent times, Duchamp's gestures came to be repeated and duplicated on an ever increasing scale and ostensible radicalism: Robert Rauschenberg would dispose even of the readymade and choose instead to present as a work of art the act of erasing a drawing; Yves Klein would invite three thousand sophisticated members of the art public to a private view of an empty gallery; Walter de Maria would fill a New York gallery with 220,000 pounds of earth, and dig a deep hole in the earth near Kassel, covering it later with a tight lid so it could not be seen (Gablik, 1984). The problem is, however, that the overall result of the collective efforts of the new avant-garde to remove the last thinkable and unthinkable limits of artistic work is the rapidly fading radicalism of any new, present or future, gesture; and the equally rapidly growing capacity of the art world to absorb, accommodate, legalize, market and make profit on, anything, however wild or unprecedented. All possibility of using artform as a protest, either against the art establishment, or – more ambitiously – against the society which isolated artistic work from all relation to other spheres of social life, has been effectively preempted. To quote Bürger again: '[i]f an artist today signs a stove pipe and exhibits it, that artist certainly does not denounce the art market but adapts to it ... Since now the protest of historical avant-garde against art as institution is accepted as *art*, the gesture of protest of the neo-avant-garde becomes inauthentic' (Bürger, 1984, pp. 52–3).

This is, indeed, a new situation, to which the philosophers, art historians and art critics were ill-prepared by three centuries of Western aesthetics. Post-modern art is indeed radically different from modernism. It is, from the perspective of this difference, only now, in the last decade or two, that the orderly nature of modernist art, its close kinship with an era which believed in science, in progress, in objective truth, in the ever rising control over technology and – through technology – over nature has become fully visible. Thanks to the post-modernist upheaval we can now see clearly the meaning of modernity, hidden as it was at the time under the panoply of rapidly changing schools and styles, often at open war with each other. This new perception has found cogent expression in Kim Lewin's famous essay of 1979:

> For those who stepped outside modernism, the successive styles of the modern period, which seemed so radically different from each other at the time, are beginning to merge together with shared characteristics – characteristics that now seem quaintly naive...

Modern art was scientific. It was based on faith in the technological future, on belief in progress and objective truth. It was experimental: the creation of new forms was its task. Ever since Impressionism ventured into optics, it shared the method and logic of science. There were the Einsteinian relativities of Cubist geometry, the technological visions of Constructivism and Futurism, de Stijl and Bauhaus, the Dadaists' diagrammatic machinery. Even Surrealist visualisations of Freudian dreamworlds and Abstract-Expressionist enactments of psychoanalytical processes were attempts to tame the irrational with rational techniques. For the modernist period believed in scientific objectivity, scientific invention: its art had the logic of structure, the logic of dreams, the logic of gesture or material. It longed for perfection and demanded purity, clarity, order. And it denied anything else, especially the past: idealist, ideological, and optimistic, modernism was predicated on the glorious future, the new and improved.

This family resemblance between the competing schools of the modernist era has been brought into relief and made well nigh evident by the radically different practice of post-modernist art, which in sharp contrast, is '[b]ased not on scientific reason and logic and the pretence of objectivity but on presence, subjective experience, behaviour, on a weird kind of therapeutic revelation in which it is not necessary to believe or understand – it is enough if it works' (Lewin, 1985, pp. 2, 7).

Rosalind E. Kraus saw the grid – an obsessively repeated motif of modern painting, particularly in its last phase – as a phenomenon which captured most fully the essential features of modernism in art; Kraus argued the representativeness of the grid, pointing to its virtual absence in pre-modern painting (a break with the past) and in real life (a break with society, a manifesto of the autonomy of art) (Kraus, 1985, p. 22). If there can be no objection to the first comment, the second seems to be based on a misunderstanding. Indeed, the grid in modern painting can be interpreted as the most radical and consistent attempt to capture and express, in an artistic medium, the essence of socially produced reality; it can be seen as a product of painstaking analysis of the essential features of the social world in the modern era. Levi-Strauss decoded the Nambiquara ornaments as subconscious expressions of the true shape of their authority structure, otherwise invisible behind the smoke-screen of mythology. In modern painting, arguably as the result of a fully conscious, scientific analysis, the grid decodes the work of modern authority manifesting itself in dividing, classifying, categorizing, filing, ordering, and relating. Obsessive about its autonomy and concentrating self-consciously on its own media and its own techniques as the crucial (or the only) subject-matter of its work and area of its responsibility, modern art seldom broke with the *Zeitgeist* of the modern era; it shared fully and whole-heartedly in this era's search for truth, its scientific methods of analysis, its conviction that reality can be – and should be – subjected to the control of Reason. The modernist artists broadcast on the same wavelength as their intellectual analysts and critics. They confronted their analysts and critics with tasks they could handle well, and were accustomed to handle by their professional training and inherited, institutionalized, aesthetics. The analysts and the critics could find many a development in modernist art a puzzle – but they knew that this puzzle had a solution, and they had the means to find it.

The puzzle presented by post-modernist art, on the other hand, is one which truly baffles its analysts. The feeling of bewilderment and being lost in the maze of new developments results from the absence of the comfortable conviction that the new is just more of the same, an unfamiliar form of the familiar, that it is only a matter of time for it to lose its strangeness, to be intellectually tamed, that the tools sufficient for the job are available and one knows how to apply them. In other words, the uneasiness results from the inability of the analysts to perform their traditional function; the very foundation of their social role now looks threatened. What this social role has been thus far, Howard S. Becker articulates with brevity and precision: 'Aestheticians do not simply intend to classify things into useful categories... but rather to separate the deserving from the undeserving, and to do it definitely... The logic of the enterprise – the bestowing of honorific titles – requires them to rule some things out, for there is no special honour in a title every conceivable object or activity is entitled to' (Becker, 1982, p. 137).

This is, indeed, the hub of the matter. Throughout the modern era, including the modernist period, aestheticians remained firmly in control of the area of taste and artistic judgement (or so it seems now, in retrospect, by comparison with the situation brought into being by the post-modernist developments). Being in control meant operating, without much challenge, the mechanisms transforming uncertainty into certainty; making decisions, pronouncing authoritative statements, segregating and classifying, imposing binding definitions upon reality. In other words – it meant exercising power over the field of art. In the case of aesthetics the power of intellectuals seemed particularly unchallenged, virtually monopolistic. In the West, at least, no other sites of power attempted to interfere with the verdicts proffered by those 'in the know'.

It is true that the power of the educated, sophisticated, sublimated, refined elite to proffer binding aesthetic judgement, to segregate the deserving from the non-deserving or non-art, was always expressed in acts of militancy aimed at judgements, or practices, whose authority was questioned. It could not be otherwise; the authority of the educated (and, indirectly but most importantly, the authority-bestowing capacity of education) could not be asserted in any other way but through construction of its opposite: pretentiousness without foundation, taste without legitimacy, choice without right. The elite ruling in the kingdom of art had always had its adversary against whom the rule was exercised and whose presence supplied the necessary legitimation of the rule: the vulgar. In Gombrich's words:

> [i]n the strict hierarchic society of the sixteenth and seventeenth centuries [we would rather say: under conditions of the disintegration of the old hierarchy in these centuries – Z.B.] the contrast between the 'vulgar' and the 'noble' becomes one of the principal preoccupations of the critics... Their belief was that certain forms of modes are 'really' vulgar, because they please the low, while others are inherently noble, because only a developed taste can appreciate them. (Gombrich, 1963, pp. 17–18)

At that early time, the point at issue was the need to redefine the old hierarchy, about to lose its traditional political and economic foundations, in terms better geared to the emerging structure of authority; but the distinction between the 'noble' and the 'vulgar' could still refer to relatively obvious and undisputed divisions. The matter did become more complicated later, once the intellectually comfortable binary opposition was blurred by the appearance of an expanding middle class, ever growing in numerical strength and purchasing power. Neither coarse nor fully refined, neither ignorant nor educated to the standards boasted by the elite, neither leaving art to its betters nor able to exercise its discretion in matters artistic – the middle class immediately turned into that 'slimy' element which threatened the very existence of the hierarchy of judgement and, with it, the authority of the aesthetically trained elite. No wonder it summoned all the most poisonous arrows of the latter.

'The vulgar' remained the term of abuse, but it changed its connotation; it now referred to the petty bourgeois, the philistine, the middle class daring to make aesthetic judgements in practice, by the act of selecting between cultural offers, but without, however, recognizing the authority of the aestheticians. The middle class juxtaposed to the power of intellect the power of money; left to its own discretion, it could conceivably make the power of intellect hollow and ineffective, without even bothering to challenge it on its own territory

– the theoretical judgement of taste. It was exactly this introduction of alternative criteria for *practical* cultural choices that was perceived by the intellectual elite as the threat to its power. In Bourdieu's words:

> what makes the petit-bourgeois relation to culture and its capacity to make 'middle-brow' whatever it touches, just as the legitimate gaze 'saves' whatever it lights upon, is not its 'nature', but the very position of the petit-bourgeois in social space ... It is, quite simply, the fact that legitimate culture is not made for him ... so that he is not made for it; and that it ceases to be what it is as soon as he appropriates it ... (Bourdieu, 1984, p. 327)

And this as long as the cultural consumer makes his own choices (it is for this reason that he has been dubbed 'vulgar', 'philistine', or, indeed, 'petty bourgeois'). It is the autonomy of artistic judgement – autonomy in regard to the judgement of the elite – that invites rage and condemnation.

Throughout most of the modern era, however, such rage and condemnation were effective; they did guard the superiority of elitist judgement in the face of real or construed inroads. They were effective because they were in the end interiorized by the victims of elitist attacks. Like Freud's conscience, the fear of 'vulgarity', of aesthetic incompetence, became 'garrisons in conquered cities' of the middle class 'artistic selves', and the most reliable safeguards of elitist rule. This process of interiorization was admirably captured by Wylie Sypher:

> [T]he nineteenth century produced a horde of parvenus who were obliged to discount the older rituals and who were a culturally discontented class like our prosperous 'workers'. The cultural malaise attending the rise of these shopkeepers, as Macaulay frankly called them [Macaulay's term of abuse, let us add, seems bland and innocuous when compared with 'ferocious and gross presumptiousness' which 'has freed the imbecile and the ignorant from their feelings of nullity' of Hippolite Taine, or 'the commonplace mind', who 'knowing itself to be commonplace, has the assurance to proclaim the rights of the commonplace and to impose them wherever it will' of Ortega y Gasset – Z. B.], is disclosed in the whole uneasy notion of vulgarity, which becomes a category in upper-middle-class values. The Victorian fear of being vulgar ... is a penalty for being successful. The successful men must be 'refined'. (Sypher, 1960, p. 104)

The elite's disdain and contempt for the vulgar parvenu remained unabated, the standards to measure 'refinement' were set at ever higher levels, so that yesterday's parvenu would find it ever more difficult to sigh with relief, 'I have arrived'. But the general structure of modern society, with its in-built cult of education, truth, science and reason (and respect for the authority of those who embodied such values) guaranteed a mechanism through which the potential threats to elitist judgement could be absorbed and thus neutralized. For all practical intents and purposes, superiority of sophisticated aesthetic judgement was never truly put in question, however often it was resented or disregarded. When insisting that '[e]verything that is beautiful and noble is the result of reason and thought' and that 'good is always the product of an art', Baudelaire, justly proclaimed a most profound thinker of modernity, was reflecting upon the firmly established authority of the aesthetic and its intellectual priests (Baudelaire, 1964, p. 104).

It is exactly this authority that is now in question; it has been brought into the focus of theory, as a problem instead of an assumption, precisely because it has been rendered ineffective in practice. It has suddenly become clear, that the validity of an aesthetic judgement depends on the 'site' from which it has been made and the authority ascribed to that site; that the authority in question is not an inalienable, 'natural' property of the site, but something fluctuating with the changing location of the site within a wider structure; and that the authority of the site traditionally reserved for the aestheticians – intellectual experts on art – is not any more to be taken for granted.

In the perception of artistic experts, the evident incapacity of aesthetic judgements articulated in the traditional way (that is, in reference to the established body of knowledge and established procedures, both embodied in the self-reproducing discourse and its privileged members) to function as self-authenticating descriptions rebounds as a state of chaos. Chaos is, after all, a state of affairs we cannot predict, change and control. In Hassan's words, while modernism 'created its own form of Authority' (that is, professional aestheticians were firmly in charge), post-modernism 'has tended towards Anarchy, with deeper complicity with things falling apart' (Calinescu, 1977, p. 142). It could be that the current uses of the term post-modernity retained some kinship ties with the original use of the concept, by Toynbee, as a synonym for irrationality, anarchy and threatening indeterminacy.

What appears to the philosophers of art as a state of anarchy, is above all the inherent 'impurity' of factors participating in the making of an X or a Y a 'work of art'; and the ensuing impossibility of separating art from non-art, or good art from bad art, by making statements referring only to phenomena fully and indivisibly under the control of the philosophers themselves. Impurity results, above all, from the rapidly expanding 'cultural consumption' that is met by philosophers with deep suspicion, as the creation of 'mass culture' – a debased, inferior culture, one where the vulgar and the philistine have got the upper hand – and its inevitable accompaniment, the art market, imposing its own criteria of practical judgement and bringing forth its own sites of authority. Philosophers naturally crave for a valid 'theory of reputation', that is, one that is obeyed and tends towards self-authentication, which, according to Howard S. Becker, should run along the following lines: '(1) specially gifted people (2) create works of exceptional beauty and depth which (3) express profound human emotions and cultural values. (4) The work's special qualities testify to its maker's special gifts, and the already known gifts of the maker testify to the special qualities of the work.' This scheme rotates, of course, around the concepts of 'beauty', 'depth', 'values', etc., all of which assume the monopolistic competence of the theorists; this kind of theory of reputation reaffirms and reproduces the authority of the latter. The trouble is that no theory of reputation built along these lines would hold today in practice. In fact, Becker comments, 'the reputation of artist, works, and the rest results from the collective activity of art worlds'. It has been like that all along, one could object. But even if this were the case, the role of the 'activity of art worlds' could remain invisible to the theorists as long as the art world which assigned reputations was confined, more or less strictly, to the theorists themselves. The role cannot remain invisible once the loss of control 'objectified', 'alienated' the products of the theorists' activity and made them into a *Vorhanden*, an object for scrutiny and reflection.

[. . .] I have dwelled for so long on the situation in the arts not only because it is to the 'aesthetic' branch of the intellectuals that we owe above all our sense of entering the post-modern era. Another reason for the lengthy digression is the fact that (not for the first time) it is in the domain of art and art criticism that a much wider redeployment of the intellectual world and its work seems to start. Let us repeat that in no other sphere of social life has the non-interference of the non-intellectual authorities been so traditionally low, and in consequence, the authority of the intellectuals so complete and indubitable. Rather than being the soft under-belly of the intellectual domain, the world of high culture was its inner and least vulnerable line of fortification – indeed, a shining though inimitable example to us all, engaged as we are with areas of social practice which come under the control of other earthly powers. The shock of the postmodern condition was therefore felt most profoundly where it brought about the most drastic change and exploded the most solidly entrenched myths. It therefore allows us to see more clearly the mechanisms rebounding throughout the intellectual world in a widespread feeling of unease and the urge to renegotiate the traditional strategy of intellectual work, captured (or, rather, concealed) by the idea of post-modern crisis.

References

Baudelaire, Charles (1964) *Baudelaire as a Literary Critic: Selected Essays*, trans. Lois Boe Hylsop and Francis E. Hylsop. University Park: Pennsylvania State University Press.

Becker, Howard S. (1982) *Art Worlds*. Berkeley: University of California Press.

Bourdieu, Pierre (1984) *Distinction: A Social Critique of the Judgment of Taste*, trans. Richard Nice. London: Routledge & Kegan Paul.

Bürger, Peter (1984) *Theory of the Avant-Garde*, trans. Michael Shaw. Manchester: Manchester University Press.

Calinescu, Matei (1977) *Faces of Modernity: Avant-Garde, Decadence, Kitsch*. Bloomington: Indiana University Press.

Gablik, Suzanne (1984) *Has Modernism Failed?* London: Thames & Hudson.

Gellner, Ernest (1983) *Nations and Nationalism*. Oxford: Blackwell.

Gellner, Ernest (1984) 'Tractatus Sociologico-Philosophicus,' in S. L. Brown (ed.) *Objectivity and Cultural Divergence*. Royal Institute of Philosophy Lecture Series 17.

Gombrich, E. (1963) *Meditations on the Hobby Horse*. London: Phaidon.

Habermas, Jürgen (1985) 'Questions and Counterquestions,' in Richard J. Bernstein (ed.) *Habermas and Modernity*. Oxford: Polity Press.

Jameson, Fredric (1983) 'Postmodernism and Consumer Society,' in Hal Foster (ed.) *The Anti-Aesthetic: Essays on Postmodern Culture*. Port Townsend: Bay Press.

Kliever, Connie D. (1982) 'Authority in a Pluralist World,' in Richard L. Rubenstein (ed.) *Modernisation: The Humanist Response to its Promise and Problems*. Washington, D.C.: Paragon House.

Kraus, Rosalind E. (1985) *The Originality of the Avant-Garde and Other Modernist Myths*. Cambridge, MA: MIT Press.

Lewin, Kim (1985) 'Farewell to Modernism,' in Richard Hertz (ed.) *Theories of Contemporary Art*. Englewood Cliffs: Prentice Hall.

Picabia, Francis (1971) *Dadas on Art*, ed. Lucy R. Lippard. Englewood Cliffs: Prentice Hall.

Sypher, Wylie (1960) *Rococo to Cubism in Art and Literature*. New York: Vintage.

5

Hermeneutics and Critical Theory

5.1 The Challenge of Hermeneutics (1978)

[...] Hermeneutics (from the Greek *hermēneutikós*, 'related to explaining'; 'explaining' is used here in the sense of 'clarifying', of rendering the obscure plain, the unclear clear) was for many centuries a sub-discipline of philology. Since most of the texts considered essential in the Christian world were available in contradictory versions, bearing traces of sloppiness and absent-mindedness in an endless chain of anonymous copyists, the question of authenticity, of the true version versus distorted ones – could not but turn into a major concern of scholars. Hermeneutics was originally developed to answer this question. Employing mostly philological methods, hermeneutics occupied itself with critical scrutiny of contending texts, with the re-possession of the authentic version – the 'true meaning' of the document – as its ultimate objective. At that stage, recovering the true meaning was seen as identical with demonstrating the authenticity of the text. For obvious reasons, historiography was the most keen and grateful client of hermeneutics.

It was in the sixteenth century that hermeneutics emerged from relative obscurity and swiftly moved into the very centre of scholarly argument. It owed its sudden eminence to the Catholic-Protestant debate regarding the authentic text of the Bible and what was understood as essentially the same problem, the true meaning of its message. The practical urgency of the matter, which had acquired much more than merely technical significance, propelled hermeneutics into a central position in the humanities. 'Philological critique' attracted the most brilliant and creative historians and philosophers. Its prestige was boosted by an impressive series of unquestionable accomplishments (going back to Lorenzo Valla) in exposing the falsity of documents whose authenticity had not been doubted for centuries.

Hermeneutics raised the critique of historical sources to the rank of methodical scholarship. In this capacity it became, and remained even when its initial motives lost much of their urgency, an indispensable branch of historiography. For different, but obvious reasons, its technical refinement has been also prompted by the jurists' concern with their interpretation of law.

It was not in this capacity, however, that hermeneutics became a challenge to the social sciences in general, sociology in particular. As long as the task of 'clarifying' which hermeneutics set for itself was seen as, above all, a search for the original, undistorted message of written sources, hermeneutics was rightly viewed simply as a tool, however powerful and indispensable. A tool helps to solve problems; it does not create them. By the end of the eighteenth century, however, a fateful shift took place. The philosophical reflection on the activity and results of hermeneutics moved beyond the mere critique of texts and began to ask difficult questions about the nature and the objectives of historical knowledge as such; indeed, of social knowledge in general.

Slowly, and at the beginning imperceptibly, the sense ascribed to the meaning sought by hermeneutical inquiry began to change. The texts dealt with by early hermeneutics were more often than not anonymous; even if the name of an author had been attached to them, they acquired enough weight of their own through the centuries to render them largely autonomous from their creators. The available knowledge of the lives of the genuine or putative authors was on the whole still less reliable than the extant texts themselves; it could hardly contribute to their clarification. An almost total concentration on the text itself, as the only guide to its meaning, was the most obvious response. Philology, rather than psychology, was the obvious framework for the quest for authenticity.

Perhaps more important still was the essential harmony of the task so defined with the cognitive predisposition of the era. The perception of the author as the legitimate 'owner' of his ideas was only beginning to capture the imagination. Artists were still regarded as craftsmen guided by the anonymous rules of the guild rather than by thoroughly individual and 'private' feelings and visions. The middle of the eighteenth century saw a genuine revival of classical aesthetics – with its emphasis on the work of art itself, its form and structure, its harmony, its inherent logic – and utter lack of interest in author's intentions. To Winckelmann, by far the most influential theorist of the time, beauty – this innermost meaning of the work of art – was a matter of the inner proportions of the artistic product; the product could communicate no information beside that contained in its finished form. This aesthetics had no room for the personality of the author; it considered bad any art which bore too visible an imprint of its author's individuality. Winckelmann's theory of art, and indeed the enlightened opinion of his time, saw eye to eye with the credulous and over-confident pre-Kantian view of knowledge in general – as a skilful, but essentially unproblematic reflection of the world 'as it is'.

Kant's discovery of the crucial role of the subject in the process of all cognition (which itself came in the wake of the socio-political establishment of the individual as the sole lawful owner of everything pertaining to his social identity) was soon followed by the discovery of the artist behind every work of art, a thinking and feeling personality behind each creation. To find the meaning of a work of art, wrote W. H. Wackenroder in 1797, one has to contemplate the artist rather than his products, to the point of 'embracing all his characteristic individuality'. Not much later, Novalis spoke confidently of the 'inner universe' of the artist whose representation of the work of art is. In the words of Shelley, the artist turns into the 'legislator of the world'. With personal freedom fast becoming the inviolable canon of the new aesthetics (as, indeed, of the dominant world-view of the new era), there was little point in searching for meaning in the text while neglecting the author. With authors repossessing their texts, readers were denied the authority of their judgement.

The new image of the artist and his work (as, indeed, of all human creation) was recorded in the intellectual history of the western world under the name of Romanticism. Though the artistic theories of Romanticism hardly outlived the intense poetic and visual-artistic movements they accompanied, they had lasting effects on the later developments of the social sciences. In particular, they were instrumental in the fateful transformation of the subject-matter and strategy of hermeneutics.

It was a Romantic discovery that the work of art (like human creation in general) was, above all, a purposive system. The text, the painting, the sculpture came to be seen as visible embodiments of ideas which, though represented in the result, were not exhausted by it. They were fully at home only within the artist's experience, and it was there they could be discovered, if they could be discovered at all. The work of art seemed suddenly less important as a reflection of reality 'out there' than as a reflection of a design of the author, his thoughts and emotions. It became evident that the genuine meaning of the text could not be found by immanent analysis. One had to go beyond the text. Lest the true meaning of the text should elude him, the reader must plumb the impenetrable depth of the author's spiritual experience. In this effort the reader could not be guided by hard and fast rules. There are few laws of uniformity in the act of creation; the work of art acquires its value from the individuality, uniqueness, irregularity of the experience from which it is born. Unless the reader was capable of similar experience, the meaning of art would forever remain for him a closed book. To grasp the meaning, the reader had to employ his imagination, and be sure that his imagination is rich and flexible enough to be truly commensurate with that of the artist.

To remain true to its task, hermeneutics had now to extend its concerns beyond the faithful description and structural analysis of the text. It had to interpret, to advance hypotheses regarding the hidden meaning of the text. The text itself could only advise the reader as to the plausibility of his interpretation; it could not offer conclusive proof that the choice had been right. Indeed, one could establish whether descriptions were true or false; but one could at best speak of the 'plausibility' or 'implausibility' of interpretations. The methods of philology, so helpful in the test of authenticity, could not suffice when the real meaning was perceived to be located somewhere 'beneath' the text proper, of an entirely different nature from the text itself. Philological critique remained an integral part of hermeneutics, though of an auxiliary status. The main attention of hermeneutics shifted to the truly 'frontier' area, the interpretation of meaning. There the methodological questions arose which presented difficulties never confronted before, and which threatened to undermine the very foundation of social science.

Social science developed, throughout the nineteenth and well into the twentieth century, 'in the shadow of the triumphs of natural science' (Giddens, 1976, p. 12). These triumphs were spectacular and convincing. In the dazzling splendour of technological accomplishment for which natural science rightly claimed credit and from which it drew ever-renewed supplies of confidence, shadowy corners of doubt were barely discernible. The preachers of the new social science, cut to the measure of the new self-reliant age, dreamt of emulating, in social knowledge, 'the same kind of sensational illumination and explanatory power already yielded up by the sciences of nature' (Giddens, 1976, p. 13).

The visible achievements of natural science were too headstrong and intoxicating for their enthusiasts to waste time in hole-picking – or, indeed, in reflecting upon the suitability of the natural scientists' approach for the study of social life. Neither was the time propitious (at any rate at the beginning) for meditating on the exact nature and intrinsic limits of the 'scientific method' as such; philosophers of science came nowhere near the level of subtlety and self-awareness reached much later by philosophers of science like Bachelard or

Popper. This was an age of exuberance, and the optimistic self-image which befits such an age did not allow for obstacles to human mastery over the world other than those temporarily erected by the sinful sluggishness of human inventiveness and ingenuity.

One feature revealed by even the most superficial look at the natural-scientific success story was the spectacular absence in the scientific accounts of the category of 'purpose'. Natural science gradually developed a language in which exhaustive accounts could be given without any reference to 'will', 'purpose', 'intention'. This new quality of scientific language had been expressed by Comte as the supercession of the 'theological' or 'metaphysical' by the 'positive'; the many who were unaware of Comte's terminology would speak of the triumph of secular sobriety over religious illusion. Not that the natural scientist had to be an agnostic in order to produce scientific results; but his results were scientific in so far as they talked about 'what had to happen' and left no room for an essentially voluntaristic 'divine purpose' which, in principle, could deprive phenomena of their observed and recorded regularity. Natural science could be defined almost by the absence of miracles and, indeed, of anything bizarre and extraordinary, suggestive of a conscious, deliberative, scheming and intending subject. In this approach the 'understanding' of phenomena collapsed into 'explaining'. Without 'meaning' in the sense of purpose, 'understanding', i.e. the intellectual grasp of the logic of phenomena, was one with their 'explanation', i.e. the demonstration of the general rules and specific conditions which made the occurrence of given phenomena inevitable. Only this kind of 'understanding' seemed compatible with a science of society aspiring to emulate the magnificent accomplishments of the science of nature.

To this emerging concept of a 'natural science of the social', hermeneutics, inspired by the Romantic vision of creation, presented a serious challenge. Indeed, it questioned the very possibility that we could cleanse our knowledge of the social by taking away the consideration of purpose. True, we ought to stop the vain search for 'design' and 'objective' in nature; if there was such a design and such an objective, it would not be ours, human, in the first place – and thus it was futile to hope that we would ever be able to grasp it. This, however, does not apply to human affairs. Here the presence of design and objectives is unquestionable. Men and women do what they do on purpose. Social phenomena, since they are ultimately acts of men and women, demand to be understood in a different way than by mere explaining. Understanding them must contain an element missing from the explaining of natural phenomena: the retrieval of purpose, of intention, of the unique configuration of thoughts and feelings which preceded a social phenomenon and found its only manifestation, imperfect and incomplete, in the observable consequences of action. To understand a human act, therefore, was to grasp the meaning with which the actor's intention invested it; a task, as could be easily seen, essentially different from that of natural science.

Whoever agreed with this suggestion of hermeneutics was immediately confronted with a number of fundamental difficulties. The most haunting was the legitimate doubt that the study of the social could ever rise to the level of precision and exactitude, the 'explanatory power', which had come to be associated with science. The Romantic image of the work of art served as a pattern for the model of social action in general; the acts of writing and of reading, of acting and of interpreting action, seemed to belong to the same family and to bear a strong family resemblance. To understand the work of art was to recover the artist's design, a labour of art in itself; to interpret any human act was to re-create the actor's web of motives and intentions. Both cases required above all the forging of affinity into shared experience, a sort of sympathetic self-identification with another human being. Like the essentially voluntaristic, design-oriented act which was to be understood, the imaginative sympathy which was to bring about such an understanding could not be reduced to a set of rules which eliminated the role played by subjective purpose and purpose-subordinated decisions. Thus understanding was an art, rather than a science.

The artistic rather than scientific nature of understanding was a natural obstacle to the consensus of interpretations, a first essential step in the construction of a communal activity called science. Even during the periods of rift and dissent which punctuate the history of every science, its practitioners can derive comfort and confidence from the belief that there are, or can be found, some specific rules of conduct which will command communal agreement and thereby secure a communal consensus for the result. The notion of such rules does not square well with the image of artistic creation. Faced with the necessity to choose between several competing interpretations, practitioners of hermeneutics could not easily refer to impersonal rules which could govern thoroughly a personal act of sympathetic insight and self identification. The constitution of the consensus of interpretation appeared to present complications unheard of in the science of nature.

This difficulty, considerable in itself, was a relatively minor irritant compared with the complexity of the question of truth. The nineteenth-century image of science went beyond the aim of reaching a consensus that specific results were valid 'beyond reasonable doubt'. It was an integral part of the image, and an important reason for the prestige natural science enjoyed, that the validity of results had a foundation more solid and lasting than the consensus of science's current practitioners; that, in other words, the rules which found a consensus here and now can as well support a reasonable hope that the results are conclusive, final. The results of natural science were seen, in principle, not just as universally accepted, but as true, that is, likely to be accepted forever. This belief was based on the laboriously observed impersonality of the operations which led, in communally controllable fashion, to the formulation of results. However important the role of individual genius, insight, lucky accident or flash of inspiration in *articulating* the new idea, there must be a set of universal rules (which specifically did not hinge on unique, personal factors) employed in *validating* the claim of the idea to the status of truth. Science was seen as an utterly legal-rational, therefore impersonal and democratic, activity. Discovery was a matter of genius or talent, but validation was founded on rules which could be applied by everybody who mastered the publicly accessible skills, and which therefore avoided the differences arising from the personalities of scientists. Validation was, therefore, thoroughly impersonal; as personal factors did not intervene in its process, there were no obvious reasons to doubt that whatever had been validated would remain valid for successive generations of scholars.

It was obvious, however, that the validation of the interpretations of meaning could not easily be raised to the level of impersonality or, indeed, the hoped-for a-temporality, achieved by natural-scientific findings. Hermeneutics saw 'understanding' as residing in a sort of 'spiritual unification' of the writer and the reader, the actor and his interpreter. Unification, whether achievable or not, was bound to start from a specific, always to an extent unique, historical and biographical position. Even if interpreters could find the means to neutralize the personal differences between them, they would still remain 'historically enclosed' by the volume and type of experience made available to them by tradition. Consensus, therefore, would not guarantee truth. The resources used in validating their interpretations could, at best, be impersonal only within the given stage of history. Impersonality was not, in this case, equivalent to a temporality. On the contrary, the impersonality of the act of interpretation (and, consequently, the chance of a consensus between interpreters) could only be conceived as resting on the shared participation of interpreters in the same historical tradition; on their drawing resources from the same pool of shared historical experience. It seemed that the consensus could only be temporary, tradition bound, and therefore organically incapable of meeting the standards of truth. The very foundation of its attainment and validation, as consensus, precluded its treatment as a-temporal and conclusive.

In short, the challenge of hermeneutics to the idea that social sciences should measure up to the standards of cogency and authority of the natural sciences consisted of two problems: that of consensus and that of truth. Accordingly, social science, in asserting its scientific status, was bound to prove that its rules of consensus and its standards of truth for the interpretation of meaning could attain a cogency comparable to that achieved in the study of nature. [This book] is dedicated to a discussion of the most eminent attempts to offer such a proof.

To be sure, the continuous efforts to parry the challenge of hermeneutics do not exhaust the history of sociology. A powerful current within social science (dominant in the nineteenth century, and by no means marginal in the twentieth) is either oblivious to the challenge or stubbornly belittles its seriousness. This current derives its confidence from the assumption that no significant difference exists between the situations in which the natural and social sciences operate. The assumption is defended on one of two grounds: that 'subjective meanings', intentions, motives and similar 'internal' experiences are not accessible to observation and therefore ought to be left out of scientific study, whose only legitimate object is observable behaviour; or that subjective factors present no methodological problem of their own, since they can be fully reduced to external phenomena, amenable to normal scientific treatment. The right to deny the challenge of hermeneutics is justified by the view that the subjective aspect of social life either presents no special problem to scientific study, or – in asmuch as it does – ought to be left where it belongs, in the domain of poetry or philosophy. It is not the task of this book to deal with the school of sociology which stems from this attitude. Only such standpoints have been selected for analysis which admit that the subjective aspect of social, as distinct from natural, phenomena does present a problem of unusual complexity but which, however, hope to find a solution which will either neutralize its impact or will reconcile social science to its inescapable fate: the necessity to remain tradition-bound and to proclaim admittedly relative and temporal assertions. These standpoints consider relativity of knowledge as a problem particularly acute in the study of the social.

The unintended effect of my criteria of selection is that [this book] favours ideas developed within the predominantly German intellectual tradition, while paying relatively less attention to the French. The

French fathers of modern social science took little notice of the pecularity of social reality as conditioned by the subjective character of social action, and were largely unconcerned with the resulting complexity of research strategy. They remained strikingly unimpressed by the soul-searching analyses of philosophical hermeneutics; indeed, one can follow the development of French sociology from Saint-Simon to Durkheim, Halbwachs or even Mauss while neglecting the presence, across the Rhine, of concerns which the hermeneutical tradition forced social scientists to regard as their own. Neither Comte nor Durkheim, nor the most eminent among their heirs, were seriously worried by the danger of relativity in the study of the social; still less were they inclined to suspect that relativity might be a chronic affliction resistant to all known medicine. Believing that social facts are 'things' like all others, i.e. that they exist in their own right as real entities 'out there', outside the realm of individual experience, they naturally concluded, first, that one can study social realities without necessarily looking at the processes of their social production and, second, that whoever does this study with proper method and diligence will certainly arrive at the same results. This is, after all, how the activity of the natural sciences was seen in the nineteenth century. Faithful to the unbroken French rationalist tradition, they regarded true knowledge as, above all (if not solely), the question of method and of its systematic application. The cognizing reason and the object of its scrutiny were not made of the same stuff nor subject to the same laws. Autonomous and attentive only to the rules of logic, reason (including its sociological brand) was viewed as immune by and large to the historical or other constraints (indeed, historical concreteness) typical of its object. Reason, in short, was not a part of the social reality it was bent on studying.

This was, exactly, the assumption challenged by the German intellectual tradition, in which reflections upon hermeneutic activity and problems played a dominant part. There, the interpretation of social reality came to be revealed as a conversation between one historical era and another, or between one communally founded tradition and another; even an 'inside', immanent study of one's own social reality was accordingly regarded as a particular case of the tradition-bound activity of understanding. To anyone concerned with reaching an objectively valid knowledge of the social, relativism was a real danger, which could not be staved off simply by discarding wrong methods, or by being sceptical towards uncontrolled assumptions and 'evidencies'. Both partners of the conversation called 'understanding' or 'interpretation' were historically specific and tradition-bound, and the study of the social could only be seen as an endless process of re-evaluation and recapitulation, rather than a bold step from ignorance to truth. In an excellent characterization by Isaiah Berlin, Germany during the Romantic era held that human forms of life 'could be felt, or intuited, or understood by a species of direct acquaintance; they could not be taken to pieces and reassembled, even in thought, like a mechanism compounded of isolable parts, obedient to universal and unaltering causal laws'. Due to contingencies of their own history, going back at least to the Reformation, German thinkers of the era 'were acutely aware of the differences between their world and the universalism and scientific rationalism deeply embedded in the outlook of the civilisations west of the Rhine' (Berlin, 1972, ix–x).

It can be shown that the heretofore technical discipline of hermeneutics had been given its new philosophical depth and theoretical relevance mainly by the powerful vision of Hegel's philosophy. No philosophical system before Hegel was nearly as successful in condensing reason and its object, knowledge and history, into a monolithic unity; and in presenting their separation and opposition as merely a moment of development, to be transcended when history runs its course. In Hegel's philosophy, consciousness of each historical era is a stage in the progress of reason coming to know itself and gradually discovering itself as the only 'essence' of being: 'The whole process of History... is directed to rendering this unconscious impulse a conscious one.' Through the historical activities of peoples, Reason 'completes itself into a self-comprehending totality'. The effort aimed at self-comprehension is, simultaneously, the consummation of Reason (Hegel, 1956, pp. 25, 78, 456–7). History and its understanding become essentially the same process; the understanding of the past, the effort to penetrate and to capture the meaning of human deeds is itself history. Acting as an agent of this understanding, the historian is subject to the logic of history. He has no transcendental ground from which to contemplate the process of which he is irretrievably a part. He can see as much as can be seen from his position in the process.

This realization has been reflected in philosophical hermeneutics in the notion of 'hermeneutic circle'. Understanding means going in circles: rather than a unilinear progress towards better and less vulnerable knowledge, it consists of an endless recapitulation and reassessment of collective memories – ever more voluminous, but always selective. It is difficult to see how any of the successive recapitulations can claim to be final and conclusive; still more difficult would be to substantiate this claim. The plight came to be seen as specific to the study of the social, presenting the 'understanding' sciences with problems unknown to the science bent on mere 'explaining'.

The development of hermeneutical ideas through the nineteenth century reached its culmination in the work of Wilhelm Dilthey, where they found their most profound and – in a sense – extreme expression. A brilliant philosopher and a masterly historian, Dilthey arrived, it seemed, as far as one could go with the notion of the historical, and tradition-bound nature of understanding. As the most thorough exploration of the activity of understanding led Dilthey to abandon his initial hope of providing history with a finite set of stern methodological, truth-generating rules – the inherent 'inconclusiveness' of understanding seemed to be conclusively demonstrated. This challenge had to be faced, or else social science would have to surrender its claim to scientific results. [This book] is concerned with the major strategies employed by those who agreed that the question of valid knowledge of the social cannot be resolved without facing the queries raised by hermeneutical reflection.

We shall start from the discussion of strategies developed by Marx, Weber, and Mannheim. All the conspicuous differences between them notwithstanding, the three great sociologists share one prominent feature: they all worked, by and large, within the Hegelian theme of 'history coming to understand itself'; or, more simply, history bringing to pass conditions in which not just an interpretation of its diverse manifestations but the *true* interpretation becomes possible, or inescapable. They all agreed that these conditions did not exist in the past; but all three looked hopefully to the present, or to the immediate future, for a cognitive situation qualitatively different, and sharply better than all past vantage points of interpretation. All three found their conviction, that a true knowledge of the social is accessible, in the already accomplished, or imminent transformations of the fabric of society: they viewed the merger of understanding and science as an end to which both cognition and its object must move.

Karl Marx translated the Hegelian theory of history and knowledge from the philosophical language to the language of sociology. This had been done already before Dilthey drew full methodological conclusions from Hegelian theory enclosed in the philosophical discourse alone. Though preceding Dilthey chronologically, Marx was, therefore, ahead of Dilthey in realizing that the problem of true understanding of a history which is itself historical can be resolved, if at all, as a sociological problem: as such it is a transformation of human community which renders it both amenable to, and capable of, objective understanding. Max Weber, unlike Karl Marx, was confronted with the work of Dilthey in which the historicality of understanding had been explored to the full and presented as, in fact, the perpetual predicament of humanities. Weber had, therefore, to engage directly the question of the scientific nature of social study as dependent on the plausibility of an objective understanding of an essentially subjective reality. While facing a relatively new adversary and a novel task, Weber could however draw from the findings of Marx and his 'sociological translation'. It was Weber who brought Marx's socio-logical theory, shaped in the argument with Hegel's historicism, into a direct relevance to hermeneutical debate.

A major proposition Dilthey firmly established in the methodology of humanities was that essential 'commensurability' of the two tradi-tions who meet in the act of understanding is a necessary condition of the validity of interpretation. Accordingly, Weber's task consisted of the demonstration that our society (in its tendency, if not yet in its actuality) makes the fulfilment of this condition highly plausible. For the first time in history the subject and the object of understanding meet on the ground of rationality – this most prominent feature of the truth-seeking activity which we call science. Objective knowledge is rational knowledge; one can, therefore, objectively understand human actions as they are, and in as far as they can be viewed as, rational actions. But rational action does become the dominant mode of con-duct in the modern society.

This last proposition, however, has been denied by Karl Mannheim. In his own analysis of the structural conditions of knowledge in modern society rationality did not emerge as a mode of thinking on the way to dominance and universality. On the contrary, having traced the divergence of meanings back to its source – to the very fact of social structure, the positional differentiation of society – Mannheim concluded that partiality, distortion and contention are and will remain a universal feature of social knowledge and stand in the way of understanding between various groups of society. History has brought nearer the chance of a truth-based consensus not because the conduct of society at large is becoming more rational, but because within the structure of the society a unique group, the intellectuals, has been brought into being which is determined by its structural location to think and act rationally. It is this group which can (or, rather, is bound to) merge the understanding into science. The intel-lectuals are to act as a sort of collective messiah, bringing the truth into human understanding.

The same role, albeit without reference to changing social structure or, indeed, to history – has been assigned by Edmund Husserl to the activity of philosophical analysis. Husserl sought to solve the problem of true understanding within the context of human knowledge as such, rather than as a question peculiar to the knowledge of the social. Husserl tended to merge science into the universal activity of understanding, rather than the other way round. Instead of showing how the understanding of human action can reach the precision of scientific knowledge, he demonstrated that all knowledge, science included, is ultimately founded on the activity of understanding, where its validity is, or ought to be, grounded.

In Husserl, hermeneutical discourse incorporates the French–Cartesian legacy of rationalism. The encounter has far-reaching consequences: the hope that meanings can be adequately grasped is now seen to reside in the possibility of freeing the meaning from its tradition-bound context, instead of meeting it there, in its 'natural' habitat. Historically and structurally determined tradition can only produce understanding inherently protean and contingent. Meanings can be grasped in their apodictic, absolute truth only outside that tradition, where they can be rooted in soil on which history and structural divisions have no impact. Husserl postulates 'transcendental subjectivity' as such a soil, as a sort of extra-historical 'community of meanings' which generates and sustains phenomena in the only relevant mode of existence – in the mode of 'being known'. True meanings can be glimpsed only if one gets access to this 'transcendental subjectivity'. This can be done by a phenomenological contemplation of 'pure meanings', as disclosed by the experience of phenomena laid bare of their historical–structural guise.

[...] The sociology of Talcott Parsons is an attempt, by applying Husserl's precepts, to reach an understanding of human action which will be largely independent of the historical-structural contexts of meaning. Starting from the phenomenon of social action in its given state of 'being known', Parsons proceeds to disclose the action's transcendental, apodictically predicated features, which include the presence of society and a cultural system. With all its intrinsic meaning fully revealed and articulated, social action acquires an 'immanent' framework in which its meaning is founded and in which it can be objectively grasped. While admitting that human action is a meaningful entity which ought to be understood, one can now proceed to study it objectively – as it must be, rather than as it happens to be in this or that tradition-bound context.

Some of Husserl's major tenets, however, have been objected to and revised by Heidegger. Above all, the fundamental supposition that meanings, understanding and interpretation can be founded in a universe other than 'life-world', the world of existence, has been put in doubt. Meanings are constituted, and understanding is called for and accomplished, not in the act of pure, a-historical contemplation, which is always an activity within a tradition, and an activity which consists in recapitulating this tradition. Truth, though by no means dissolved in a mere communal consensus, becomes now a feature of existence-disclosing-itself, rather than a relation between existence and something (like a proposition turned out by a detached work of reason) which stands out outside existence. The demon of relativism is deprived of much of its terror by showing that the notion of truth cannot be sensibly grounded outside the tradition-bound context; therefore, the failure so to ground it should no longer haunt the conscience of men of science.

Schutz and ethnomethodology are discussed [in this book] as examples of the hermeneutically conscious sociology which operates within the Heideggerian framework of life-world as the ultimate foundation, and the only habitat, of meanings and of the activity of understanding. Here the community of interacting members is shown as a universe powerful enough, and the only universe able, to establish, to sustain in life, and to warrant interpretation of meanings. In a sense, the search for an adequate response to the challenge of hermeneutics has come full circle; ethnomethodology brings us back to square one, to the realization that all meaning and understanding is essential 'inside'.

The search did not stop with the advent of ethnomethodology and is not likely to stop. Our story is inconclusive, as no solution to the challenge of hermeneutics has yet succeeded in eliciting a consensus and escaped criticism of its own peculiar limitations.

References

Berlin, Isaiah (1972) 'Foreword.' In Friedrich Meinecke, *Historicism*. London: Routledge & Kegan Paul.

Giddens, Anthony (1976) *New Rules of Sociological Method*. London: Hutchinson.

Hegel, Georg Wilhelm Friedrich (1956) *The Philosophy of History*, trans. J. Sibree. New York: Dover.

5.2   Critical Theory (1991)

The Project

Critical theory is not, strictly speaking, an alternative sociological theory. It is, rather, a mode of theorizing. Critical theory is not constituted by its opposition to some other body of theoretical assertions, which for the sake of brevity can be given a collective name of *traditional, normal,* or simply *non-critical* theory. It is constituted, rather, by bringing theory into the focus of analysis, by refusing to accept its authority without proof, by demanding that the grounds on which this authority is claimed be revealed, and, eventually, by questioning these grounds. Critical theory, in other words, is not a theory in the ordinary sense, but a theory of the foundation and validation of theory. Critical theory is a name of the activity through which the building site is cleared, not the name of any particular building. It may (and should) be considered as relevant to the search of alternative sociological theories only insofar as, once its task has been accomplished, a substantive sociological theory may be constructed, conscious of its foundations and resting its self-confidence on its constant readiness to examine them.

The term *critical theory* stands, therefore, for an activity rather than a body of knowledge. For this reason the name is potentially misleading, as it may suggest that critical theory is something it is not, and cannot strive to be without violating its own identity and betraying its own principles: a model of the world negating other models, and by the same token sharing their substantive concerns. Critical theory is not in opposition to any theory of the world in particular; it is in opposition to the refusal by any substantive theory to examine its grounds. For this reason it opposes, indirectly, all theory which renders its own validity claim dependent on the concealment of its grounds.

There are several tacit assumptions of knowledge which critical theory forces into the open and articulates as topics of analysis, suspending the acceptance of any theory based on them until these assumptions are discursively redeemed.

First and foremost, it is a set of assumptions related to the status of theory in general, and its relation to its object in particular. More precisely, the beams of critique are first cast upon the very separation of theory and its object. It is assumed that knowledge is knowledge *of* facts; that, in other words, there is a sphere of tough, irreducible facts which the theory tries to penetrate in order to grasp them, capture them, handle them, learn their shape, color, and smell, and reconstitute them later in a verbal account. "Let us first get the facts straight." Theory is a stranger, a visitor in the world of facts – an observer whose wisdom consists in respecting local habits, dissolving his own distinctiveness, trimming whatever is out of place in his behavior. Theory will fulfill its calling only if it respects the facts. It has, after all, little choice: in the encounter between theorizing reason and the facts, only the first is impressionable, vulnerable, and also flexible. As to the facts, they are hardly affected at all by the visit of the stranger; even less likely are they to be impressed by the judgment the visitor might wish to pronounce. In this view, the building of knowledge occurs in the encounter between inquisitive reason and facts oblivious to its presence. Facts go about their daily business unaware of Peeping Tom's curiosity. Wary of disturbing their natural conduct, reason expends its energy on keeping its active impetus in check. The activity specific to reason consists in its achieved passivity; the measure of its success is the faithfulness with which it records the facts *as they are* in order later to reflect, emulate, and reproduce them in theory.

The naïveté of this image of mind as a surface covered with a pliable stuff in which objects leave their exact imprint so that their verbal replicas may be later cast, was first exposed two centuries ago. Immanuel Kant, a German philosopher of the late eighteenth century often described as the first critical theorist, represented cognition as a creative work of reason. In the encounter between reason and reality, facts are not found or discovered, but produced. More precisely, what is produced are facts of knowledge, as distinct from the facts of reality. The latter can be only guessed. For all practical intents and purposes, their presence is merely postulated; we will never approach them directly, and so never satisfy ourselves fully of their existence. What we can be sure of is what we know; but what we know is our knowledge. What is evident to us with a high degree of certainty is what has been already processed by the activity of cognition: that is, facts of knowledge. It follows that in the emergence of knowledge the role of the mind is far from passive. It is, on the contrary, active and crucial. Whatever the reality may be in itself, as an object of theory it is constituted by the work of reason. Our knowledge is therefore a combined product of the object and the subject, of the world and the reason, of things out there and the organizing, ordering, interpreting activity of mind.

Kant's critique of the naive model of passive reason, of which we have presented above only its essential imagery, originated a long chain of philosophical research in the role of reason in the production of knowledge. Kant's imagery determined the theme and set the boundary of the research. It has been directed at the exact nature and degree of the influence exerted by reason upon the process and the results of cognition. It has been accepted that the facts do not exist by themselves; if they do, or insofar as they do, they are not accessible to knowledge; the facts which are so accessible are not given at the outset of the inquiry, performed in advance; they are products, not the raw materials of theory. In the post-Kantian model of knowledge, the facts have been shifted from input to the output of cognition. The attention of philosophical research has been accordingly focused on the *through-put*, on what is done to the part of the world, subject to the process of cognition, by the cognizing mind. Epistemology – the theory of cognition – has been set apart from ontology – the theory of the world. It has become now mainly an exploration of the activity of the subject. Various aspects of this activity have been singled out as decisive for the shape of knowledge. It has been pointed out that the subject's cognitive interests are selective, that any cognitive effort consists in a differential allocation of relevance to various elements of studied reality, in sharpening the perception of some elements while blinding the observer to some others. It has been pointed out that the previous training of the subject results in a cognitive framework which prearranges the data of experience; their arrangement, therefore, is not derivable from the data themselves, but without a framework no arrangement whatsoever (and, therefore, no cognition resulting in knowledge) would be possible. It has been pointed out, more generally, that unless related by theory to other data, and tied with them into an orderly totality, experience has no meaning – an alternative way of saying that no order can be perceived in the givens of experience unless supplied by theory.

Even when, in loyalty to Kant, the intervening role of the subject was conceived as indispensable and irremovable, it was, more implicitly than overtly, felt as an irritant. The persistent uneasiness found its most spectacular expression in these variants of the sociology of knowledge which thematized the cognitive framework as the pernicious, distorting impact of prejudice, bias, or ideology, and set about exploring the conditions of their elimination. In philosophy proper the dream of finding the way back *to the things themselves* survived all successive refinements of Kantian critique. As a return to pre-Kantian naive sensualism was no more a realistic option, the hope, as in Edmund Husserl's phenomenology, was now attached to the *other side of critique*: perhaps the things themselves may be retrieved from the inside of the subject, if only one suspends all worry about the world outside consciousness and takes the things for what they realistically are: intentional meanings generated by the activity of the *transcendental subject*. The unconvinced rightly indicated that Husserl dodged the issue instead of solving it.

Whether the role of theory is seen as neutral, technical, or partisan and substantive, the post-Kantian critique shares with the naive image of the world embossed in the soft tissue of mind the essential imagery of cognition as a process in which the subject *captures* its object; and the view that the problem of perfecting the cognition is confined to a strategy of making the *grasp* sure, and what is grasped trustworthy. In this sense critical theory steps beyond the Kantian critique of reason.

Critical theory is not, essentially, in quarrel with what the post-Kantian critique of cognition says; its reservations are aimed at what the critique of cognition does *not* say, what it fails to notice or what it voluntarily declares as being out of its concern. The post-Kantian critique was concerned exclusively with such distortion, or formative action, as may be, or must be, accomplished inside the act of cognition by the cognizing subject, moved solely by his or her urge to grasp the object which he or she conceives as complete in itself, as something which has acquired its identity *before* it comes into the focus of his or her cognition. But the post-Kantian critique has by and large assumed that epistemology, the theory of cognition, should not concern itself with this before. That whatever might have happened during this before bears no relevance to whatever epistemology wishes to propose; that, in other words, the problem of the relationship between reason and the world may be translated into the problem of the subject-object relation in the act of cognition. Accordingly, the degree of adequacy, rationality, truth, etc., of knowledge may be fully measured by the analysis of the cognitive act. It is to this self-limitation, to the reduction of the idea of knowledge-production to the cognitive process, that critical theory objects.

In a crude approximation we could say that if critical theory sides with the post-Kantian critique in underlining the active role of the cognizing subject in producing the facts of knowledge in the course of its encounter with the world, it insists also that the world itself, assumed complete at the outset of cognition, has come into being with the active participation of reason. Therefore, the analysis of theory-object relation should go beyond the act in which the theory tries to recapture the world in whose production it took part. Adequacy, rationality, truth, etc., of the theory would depend not just on the success of recapturing effort; it will depend also, and perhaps to a yet higher degree, on the way in which the recaptured objects have been first constructed. A theory which adequately grasps or reflects a poorly constructed world will be still a poor theory. Whatever happened *before* the act of cognition is not, therefore, another matter as far as epistemology is concerned. On the contrary, it must be its part and parcel. It organically and irretrievably belongs with any analysis aiming at the conditions and productive rules of adequate knowledge.

The problem of the relation between reason and the world is, in consequence, translated by critical theory not as a question of subject and object cognition, but as the question of *theory* and *practice*. Theory and practice meet in the act of cognition, when theory strives to explain and to interpret practice, to make sense of it; but they meet as well in the process of labor, when the practice as it comes later within the sight of cognizing subject is brought into being and made into a potential object of cognition. In other words theory both produces and (intellectually) reproduces practices. Before theory can err in the act of reproduction, it might have already been charged with a still more serious weakness: with producing wrong practice. No set of exquisite cognitive tools will then repair the results.

Critical theory shifts the epistemological emphasis from the cognitive act to the social production of the cognized world. It allows for the possibility that the world itself, not only its reflection in theory, may be untrue. This may happen when a wrong theory is applied to its construction. A theory which insists that its test should be confined to the framework of cognition may therefore, contrary to its intention, perpetuate and aggravate the error. It may do so simply by elevating the world as it is to the status of ultimate authority to which all knowledge should submit, and which theory has no tools to evaluate. The world, like nature, would be then neither true nor false, neither right nor wrong, neither good nor evil.

If the world which theory strives to recapture is recognized, however, as practice, untenability of the latter stance becomes easy to expose, and the way to the theoretical critique of the world is re-opened. It can be seen then that any form the world-practice takes on in its history bears a cumulative imprint of previous practices guided by past theories. These practices and theories, like all practices and theories, were selective; they actualized some possibilities while leaving behind, and often repressing, others. They produced in the result a onesided, mutilated world in which alternative options are not easily visible. It is a world which hides as much as it reveals. It is a living memorial to a limited historical practice, inheriting in full all its wrongs. It has already forged human potential. To take it as the ultimate criterion of truth would be like accepting counterfeit coins as the currency standard.

Unlike other theories, critical theory will not be, therefore, satisfied with the optimally faithful reproduction of the world "as it is." It will insist on asking, "How has this world come about?" It will demand that its history be studied, and that in the course of this historical study the forgotten hopes and lost chances of the past be retrieved. [...]

Basic Concepts

Critical theory is prominent for its tendency to culturalize the interpretation of the human world. It makes a point of not taking nature's hold for granted. To paraphrase the famous legal principle, for critical theory an aspect of human existence is cultural unless proved natural. Cultural theory accepts as its constant working hypothesis that even most obstinate necessities may well be artifacts of historically made cultural choices that can be challenged. If the hypothesis is true, then the exposure of the cultural essence of ostensibly natural facets of the human predicament is an important and urgent task, as the imposition of the natural mode may be itself a crucial factor in concealing and suppressing possibilities of a better society.

Indeed, between the natural mode of cognition and the naturelike social situation, there is a looplike, dialectical interaction. Application of the natural mode is painless and uncontroversial as long as its object's conduct manifests repetitiveness and regularity. In the case of human objects, such a regularity can be only achieved by an effective repression of a great number of alternatives. This, in turn, more often than not includes the application of coercion – physical or mental. It takes a lot of pain to smother the intrinsically refractory propensity of human activity. As Barrington Moore put it with remarkable cogency:

> [T]he assumption of inertia, that cultural and social continuity do not require explanation, obliterates the fact that both have to be recreated anew in each generation, often with great pain and suffering. To maintain and transmit a value system, human beings are punched, bullied, sent to jail, thrown into concentration camps, cajoled, bribed, made into heroes, encouraged to read newspapers, stood up against a wall and shot, and sometimes even taught sociology.

As a rule of thumb, we can say that with the growth in the volume or efficiency of coercion the plausibility of the natural mode also grows. Routine monotony of behavior is always enforced. It requires a forceful and continuous repression of alternative responses to repetitive situational settings. As long as the repression remains effective, the conduct of its objects is indeed amazingly regular and as such can be calculated and predicted with a negligible margin of error. It is strikingly like the conduct of nonhuman nature. Its interpretation *modo naturae* retains, therefore, its credibility. We have few reasons to doubt, for instance, that effectively tamed slaves are more animal than human, driven as they are by outside pressures and reacting to them in a boringly predictable manner. We easily believe that the indigent confined to poorhouses are moved solely by laws of nature, and thus could – and should – be goaded into the right demeanor by the sheer manipulation of external conditions. We can believe, at least for a time, that the frightened, disoriented migrant workers clinging convulsively to their fragile chance of survival are fully creatures of nature, reacting in a dull, machinelike fashion to the visual and acoustic stimuli cleverly arranged by their supervisors. We can believe, as long as women docilely consent to their confinement to the cozy little world of kitchen and bedroom, that they are somehow closer to nature and less artificial, that their animal self is closer to the surface and harder to domesticate or conceal.

The credibility of nature-mode interpretations is, therefore, an outcome of successful oppression. But once established and gotten hold of human imagination, these interpretations turn into powerful factors of reproducing and perpetuating the oppression which made them credible. More precisely, they become a major obstacle standing in the way of exposing the empirically observed regularity as oppression. As long as these interpretations remain in force, the sheer repetitiveness of the oppressed objects' conduct effectively hides the oppressive determinants of reality instead of indicating their presence. The validity of nature-mode interpretations must, therefore, be challenged and called to prove its case against the humanity of its objects *before* the oppression which is simultaneously its cause and effect can be sapped. It must be challenged, in consequence, *before* the empirical sources of its legitimation dry out.

The successful challenge of the nature-mode interpretation is a necessary condition of success in fighting the oppression which lies at its foundation. The practical opening up of repressed human potential depends, therefore, on the intellectual redemption of the cultural roots of the human condition. Theory, therefore, is a serious matter. It reveals just how serious it is once it refuses to follow slavishly the petrified product of its own past activity. That is to say, when it reclaims its own priority over practice – its ability to dissolve the ostensibly tough and indomitable bone structure which consigned the limits of practical freedom. Theory becomes such a powerful solvent of naturelike constraints once it builds its strategy on the assumption that, unless proved false, the hypothesis that the human condition is culturally made and can be culturally unmade must be believed to be true.

The validity of such a cultural mode of interpretation can be confirmed only if it is demonstrated that the part of human reality which is its object owes its *materiality*, its apparently necessary character, to the forceful suppression of discursive challenge. Practically, this can be confirmed only negatively; i.e., if the discourse of the normative foundations of reality is initiated and if it eventually succeeds in changing the shape of reality. All reality, whatever its foundations, is perceived as *reality* insofar as it is experienced as constraint. People call reality whatever is revealed as an obstacle to their will. Discovery of reality is unthinkable unless people first set purposes for their action and then act to attain them, as the German philosopher Arthur Schopenhauer pointed out a century and a half ago: by defining themselves as I *wish*, human beings discover the *objective world* – a term they coin to denote resistance to their will. Without first wishing, the constraining impact of the world can well pass unnoticed and successfully evade challenge. If wishing is suppressed, reality becomes invisible. The call to realism – the call to set human sights low, not to fight difficult or uncertain battles, not to dream of never-never (thus far) lands – is in its practical consequences, even if not in its intentions, a defense of the current constraints by *deproblematizing* them and preventing them from turning into topics of discussion. The hold of reality is inversely related to its visibility. The less visible these constraints are, the more potent, lasting, immutable, and real do they become.

To release the grip of constraints requires, therefore, a two-step strategy. First, the hopes once discredited by defeat and subsequently cast into disdain as utopias must be redeemed and awarded at least a provisional credit. When fed into human practices, they bring the actors into a confrontation with the resistance of the world and expose the exact nature of the world as constraint. Second, once this happens, the continuing resistance of the world must not be interpreted as a clinching proof that its present state cannot be transformed. The task still remains of testing whether the failure to overcome constraints derives from invariant features of human action that are not given to discursive renegotiation, or whether it has been temporarily effected by the persisting relations of power and dominance, hiding behind the yet unproblematized forms of oppression. The failure is, therefore, an invitation to further testing and the extension of analysis into the regions heretofore glossed over.

This is, in rough outlines, the stance taken by critical theory. Its strategy is often condensed into the postulate of *self-reflection*. Indeed, self-reflection is an indispensable and crucial factor in the revelation of structures owing their power to the concealment of their presence, and in the ensuing *pulverization* of allegedly solid realities. When reduced to self-reflection, critical theory is, however, insufficiently articulated. It is then indistinguishable from a host of mostly philosophical theories which also put their stake on self-reflection as a powerful solvent of alleged realities.

In particular, critical theory must be distinguished from phenomenological and existentialist currents in modern philosophy, with which it shares a number of propositions and strategies and for this reason is frequently confused. Phenomenology sees in self-reflection the royal road to the purification of truth from sedimentations of mystifying practices. It advocates a chain of *transcendental reductions*, consisting in *bracketing* or *suspending* commonsensical assumptions about the existence of things, of historically and culturally contingent *oughts*, and of all other extrinsic bodies contaminating the subjective world of a real, empirical person. Phenomenology hopes that by so doing the empirical person can dig through into the usually hidden realm of *transcendental subjectivity* – subjectivity which is nobody's in particular subjectivity, which is truly universal and immune to the vagaries of history or cultural whims. The phenomenological version of self-reflection is, therefore, a program of self-transcendence attainable through philosophical analysis. In the last account, it is a recipe for individual rumination. It does not include stipulation of any other activity except for the activity of cogitation. On the contrary, it calls for a decisive disengagement from the world. The emancipation it offers is a liberation *from* the world, rather than *of* it. Critical theory doubts whether the two tasks can be separated; whether one can be accomplished in disregard of the other. However deeply humans may descend in their effort to reach the pure essences suspended in the aseptic void of transcendental subjectivity, they will find always in the end their *socially* produced selves. Beyond the social, there is only nothingness; with the social *thought away*, there is no thought. The emancipatory effort must, therefore, engage the social essence of human existence, and this means coming to grips with the network of human interaction in which truth or untruth are communicatively produced and reproduced. Recovery of truth means undermining the social grounds of the repression of human potential – and this requires theory as well as practice, the work directed to restructuring the condition of interhuman communication. The road to truth leads not through further suppression, but through untying people's active interest in their life-world.

The emancipatory project offered by existentialist philosophy goes perhaps further still toward articulating freedom as the matter of individual self-redemption. It boils down, by and large, to the transformation of *in itself* (an objectified existence, defined for me from outside, an existence into which I have been cast, in which I am acted upon, looked at, told what to do, and judged) into the *for itself* (the subjectivity restored, my life is again controlled by me, subordinated to the project I have pondered and chosen). In the writings of the most prominent representatives of the existentialist current in philosophy, Martin Heidegger and Jean Paul Sartre, this transformation is presented as a single-handed job. In fact, it can be only performed single-handedly or not at all. One can hardly think of external, social conditions which would be particularly propitious to the task. Indeed, the success of self-redemption is measured by the degree to which any external, social conditions have been rendered irrelevant. Because success does not depend on the structure of the external world, it does not matter what the content of the emancipating project is. Any project will do, providing it is freely chosen and uncompromisingly adhered to. The critical edge of existentialism is turned inward; its moral message is reduced to the intense preoccupation with its own autonomy combined with disbelief in the chance of designing a world that offers more congenial conditions for autonomous persons. Existentialism, in the last resort, cedes the world *out there* to the natural mode, confining the cultural mode to an intellectual operation which, in the middle of an essentially strange world, the ego should commit upon itself. Again, critical theory doubts the viability of the existentialist program and rejects its defeatist withdrawal into the self. Critical theory points out that it is the matter of socioculturally produced conditions whether individual autonomy is identified as the emancipatory topic; it is the matter of such conditions whether the emancipation, however defined, is easier or more difficult to achieve. We would expect that the image of the *good life* providing a blueprint for improvement rarely takes account of the totality of human possibilities. More often than not this image is imposed as, simultaneously, the result and a factor of domination and repression. The model of improvement can outgrow its normally maimed, truncated form only if the repressive situation is transcended. This, in turn, as we remember, depends on the progress made by the discursive redemption of the repressed aspect of human potentiality – a social, interactive process by definition. The social character of the process assures the substantive character of the emancipatory model which will eventually emerge. It is the very disregard for the validating power of interaction which left existentialism with no choice but a purely formal moral injunction.

The self-reflection of critical theory differs, therefore, from similar concepts developed by phenomenology and existentialism in that it designates a collective, interactive, and communicative practice. It grounds its hope in the effectivity of self-reflection, not on the intellectual prowess of the individual, but on the reality-producing ability of a self-conscious collective practice. This ability turns into a moral force once this practice reaches the degree of self-awareness which gives it complete mastery over the situation, the possibilities it contains, and the decisions taken on the basis of their examination. Critical theory sees itself as an important constituent of such self-awareness of emancipatory practice. As one of the founders of critical theory, Max Horkheimer, declared in his famous comparison of traditional and critical theories, "The object with which the scientific specialist deals is not affected at all by his own theory. Subject and object are kept strictly apart. . . . A consciously critical attitude, however, is part of the development of society". Critical attitude is such a part since it penetrates areas normally guarded by the protective fence of silence. It questions the grounds of habitual recognition of necessities and impossibilities and, by transforming usually tacit and uncontrolled assumptions into the topic of discourse, it opens new, previously unconsidered, alternatives. This multiplying of possibilities has emancipatory significance. Its effect is the enhancement of freedom. The fuller clarification of the genuine meaning of tradition, the resurrection of its hopes, and keeping its promises alive, all these make the future perhaps less certain, but more hospitable for freedom. The exposure of the relations of dominance which hide behind the *naturalness* of social reality and praise for adjustment to the necessary are in themselves a powerful step toward the realization of a self-conscious history.

Critical theory is not just another moral indictment of an oppressive reality. After all, the remarkable resilience of any social reality does not rest on moral self-glorification. People submit to domination because primarily they believe in the uncontrollable and unassailable power of *facts* and because they strive to be *rational* and aim at *realistic* targets – not because they necessarily accept the superiority and higher intellectual or moral virtues of their superiors. This has been particularly true during the long period of market capitalism, in which the outcomes of human labor solidified into a network of seemingly *natural* economic necessities, able to impose the needed pattern of behavior without recourse to ideological legitimation, by the sheer pressure of a reality which offered survival only in exchange for submission to the rules of the game. Under these conditions emancipation is not a matter of a moral battle or of a struggle between ideologies. It is, rather, a matter of the thorough study of the process normally exempt from examination: the process through which the respect-claiming reality is produced and reproduced. By the same token, the otherwise unconscious process becomes a potential object of conscious control. Critical theory, to quote Horkheimer again, "considers the overall framework which is conditioned by the blind interaction of individual activities . . . to be a fiction which originates in human action and therefore is a possible object of planful decision and rational determination of goals." Critical theory is not an ethical system, an ideology, a philosophy of human nature, or a platform for political action. Instead, it is a program of serious study of society. It does not intend to offer advice as to the substance of decisions the actors of history ought to take – apart from its belief that unhampered depth study of the grounds of the situation in which historical action takes place may render all historical decisions more conscious than before.

> Clarification of the intellectual and situational grounds of historical action, making these grounds a topic of study and debate rather than taking them for granted or repressing them into silence, is a necessary condition of self-conscious history.

It is not, however, its sufficient condition. Can we reasonably expect that the sheer availability of such a clarification will increase people's control over their own history? Set them on the road to what they decide is akin to their idea of the good life? Can we hope, following the eighteenth-century philosophers of the Enlightenment, that the power of reason and argument will prove stronger than the entrenched powers resting on the control of the means of survival and life fulfillment? Once asked, these questions immediately expose the vulnerable points of the critical theory project. Questions of this kind can be addressed to any theory which offers an interpretation of the human condition, but while other theories may disregard them and continue with their business unperturbed, critical theory must take them seriously, since it knows of no criterion of its own validity except the practical transformation of the historical process.

Most writers within the orbit of critical theory sensed, and made this explicit, that physical and economic oppression are not the only powerful forces standing in the way of emancipation. Perhaps still more vexing is the likelihood that people who are to gain most from the advance of critical theory will be reluctant to accept its findings. Critical theory, as it were, relativizes what seems to be absolute, pulverizes the solid contours of reality, transforms certainties into a mere game of chance, strips external pressures of their authority and brings them into the reach of human control. This has three consequences, each likely to cause resentment and none experienced as psychologically pleasant and satisfying. First, as Theodor W. Adorno and Max Horkheimer indicated in their study of the *Dialectic of Enlightenment*, the western European cultural tradition which gained dominance in the eighteenth century instilled in the psychic makeup of Western people a constant fear of the unknown: Adorno and Horkheimer described the Enlightenment as "mythic fear turned radical," this fear emanating from "the mere idea of outsidedness." Just as pre-Enlightenment myths tended to compound the inanimate with the animate, the Enlightenment attempted, with success, the reverse. The result was a culture of the *universal taboo*, in which everything which resists *naturalization*, which cannot be easily routinized, schematized, and modeled as a mechanism, is repressed in practice and banned in theory. Its possibility is not admitted. The obstinate manifestations of its presence, as always in the case of tabooed phenomena, have a terrifying effect. *Horror vacui* is the psychological defense of the Enlightenment project. Fear and panic having been the learned reactions to the project's failure, most people would experience the mechanized world as a protective shield as much as an oppression. Far from resenting it, people will run to its defense. Its defeat they will perceive as a personal disaster. Second, the life process in the world we know consists of an incessant, always difficult, and sometimes heroic effort of adaptation – of designing a bearable, possibly gratifying *modus vivendi*. Most people like what they have won in a hard, uphill struggle. They come to cherish it and they would not be happy for its loss. What they would resent more than anything else is the devaluation of their life achievement of which they are proud and from which they draw their self-dignity. To learn that the task as they set it for themselves, the task to which they dedicated their life and by which they measured their life's success, was a result of self-deception and, therefore, misdirected, would be indeed a high price to pay for the offer of liberation. We would therefore expect the would-be beneficiaries of critical theory to develop vested interests in perpetuating the fiction of a mechanized, naturelike, extrinsic world composed of unchallengeable necessities and irrefutable facts. Third, the exposure of an essentially pliable, artificial nature of the world and the widening of the perceived range of human choice makes life a moral responsibility. It is less easy then to lay the blame for our action on indomitable external necessities. The self-absolving excuse, "I had to do it," is not available, and if resorted to, sounds hollow. Life history is redefined as a series of personal choices, and the only allegedly indestructible constraints limiting the next choice are consequences of previous choices. This vision of life puts the responsibility fairly and squarely on the actor's shoulders. It calls for an unfading vigilance, a continuous self-scrutiny, a never relenting effort of self-correction, a constant urge to transcend the horizons already reached and to challenge the ever new ultimate frontiers of yesterday. Intense ethicality, unabated by the tranquilizing drug of divine will, natural law, or historical inevitability, makes life a heroic task. Again it is unlikely that the demand for this kind of life will be massive and enthusiastic.

Unlike the eighteenth-century philosophers, critical theorists do not believe, therefore, that the insights of reason will be embraced and followed automatically. They do not believe, either, that history by its own relentless logic will conquer the world for the rule of reason. They are skeptical about Marx's hope that the unique position of the proletariat, the class of the deprived, the universal sufferer most painfully experiencing the incongruities of an oppressive world, will make it keen to absorb the truth and defy the falsified reality. They doubt the wisdom of Max Weber's expectation of an increasingly rational world, warning against the confusion of the rationalization of mastery and domination with the rational self-designing of life. With economic and political domination safely entrenched behind the protective walls of physical inertia, the prospects of emancipation are bleak. The call to liberty may fall on deaf ears. The chance of emancipation may be seen as a threat. Critics may be cast at best as troublemakers, at worst as insane.

Reflecting on radical critics of the past, Adorno and Horkheimer noted that they might have spoken the truth, but that they were "not in step with the course of social life," and because of this they were forced into the role of madmen. This was partly for the original intention to keep their ideas pure and uncompromising, partly because of the banishment from the orderly society they wished, or had to wish, for in order to break all links with normal life. The most radical among them, like St. John the Baptist, or the Cynics among the Greek philosophers, refused to marry, bear children, and own property, as all this required involvement in the world and, therefore, entailed a seed of future compromise and surrender. This made their ideas indeed pure, but also powerless. Their successors (St. Paul, the founder of the Church, and the Stoic philosophers, the founders of the Academy) set about winning for the ideas a worldly success. They knew that "the price of survival is practical involvement, the transformation of ideas into domination." But then, are the ideas that have conquered the world and attained the dreamed-of domination the same ideas that once challenged the old reality? The odds are that they were compromised and truncated in the process. While criticism turned into administrative action, critique turned into religion, doctrine, or dogma. From a weapon of liberating change, the ideas became instruments of an oppressive stability.

This reflection made some among the most prominent representatives of critical theory wary of any apostolic, proselytizing activity. Any attempt to turn critical analysis into communal practice will necessarily impoverish the message, blunt its cutting edge, be, in other words, self-defeating. Such a conclusion had two significant consequences. On the one hand, compassion for the deplorable plight of the oppressed has been now mixed with disdain for their cowardly diffidence to part with the piteous comforts of the oppressed life. People unwilling to lift their eyes above the level of perhaps ungratifying, but known and secure, existence, are referred to as the *herd*; they are victims of *cultural barbarity*, but they have come to enjoy their incarceration and are willing actually to defend it. On the other hand, some theorists criticized all classes and their particular forms of self-ishness and longing, and hoped for the preservation of critical thought with groups "in which an established psychic make-up does not play the decisive role and in which knowledge itself has become a vital force." (This was the view of Max Horkheimer in *Authority and the Family.*) The work of criticism came to be seen, in other words, as a task inescapably confined to a highly selective intellectual elite. This elite should never relent in its effort to reduce the tension between its critical insights and the oppressed humanity these insights are supposed to serve, but should be conscious at the same time that the tension will never vanish completely. Critical theory is, so to speak, the only practice it can hope for. Critical practice, so to speak, has been collapsed into theory. It has been fully confined to reflection, detached analysis, and the critical spirit.

Such a conclusion has, in turn, two truly devastating consequences for critical theory. First, it defeats the original legitimation of the project. If the *denaturalization* of the world is reduced to an operation accomplished on the intellect of the thinkers endowed with a critical spirit, if it does not change a thing in the state of the world, if it leaves the world counterfeit as it was before, then the claim of critical theory that there is nothing necessary about the *naturalness* of the world and that it can be restored to its cultural character, is belied.

> If, for example, one confines oneself to the discovery that the inequality of human life chances and individuals' shares in socially available goods depends on man-made legal and economic institutions, rather than on inviolable features of social existence, these institutions will continue unperturbed to act with the indomitable power of natural forces and the hypothesis of their artificial nature remains in doubt.

There is nothing left to distinguish critical ruminations from self-centered projects of personal salvation offered by, say, existentialism, and ostensibly opposed by critical theory. There is nothing critical theory could offer sociology. It becomes instead a variant of personal philosophy. Second, and still more important, the above conclusion makes the insights of critical theory untestable. With its anchor in historical activity severed, critical theory is reduced to a set of more or less ingenuous, inventive, or appealing ideas which can be, however, neither proved nor refuted. Their claim to verity must remain forever inconclusive; their authority, a never attainable horizon. This, of course, makes critical theory a body of ideas which science (which, in a critical theory view, rests on the very assumptions this theory is set to undermine) has neither duty nor compulsion to treat seriously. A sociology which would wish to follow critical theory inspiration would limit itself to the generation of, in principle, untestable hypotheses and, therefore, would have to satisfy itself with the status of art or philosophy.

Because of these two consequences, the conclusion offering intellectual self-contentment as the only reason to accept critical theory must be seen by many an attentive reader of its analyses as unsatisfactory. It is likely to be rejected not just because of its lack of coherence with the rejectors' particular ambitions or purposes, but because it is intrinsically unfit to provide a basis for any communal practice. Whatever its own merits, it does not belong with the historically established tradition of scholarship, distinguished by its standing invitation to communal participation and its determination to make its propositions, at least in principle, open to test.

The second generation of critical theorists (among which the names of Jürgen Habermas and Karl-Otto Apel are the most prominent) has been preoccupied with the task of rebuilding the bridge linking critical theory with this tradition – a bridge which the disenchanted older generation all too carelessly discarded. The twin pillars on which the bridge can be erected are, first, a reason why the emancipatory propositions could and should find their way from intellectual ruminations to historical practice, and second, a method of testing the truth of such propositions.

To start with the first pillar, the link between critical theory and critical practice can be elucidated through exploring the general relationship between knowledge and human interests. This topic has been neglected by ordinary science. Science is an attempt to prove something about its object; it neither intends nor is able to prove anything about itself. It is a commonplace that science, which purports to be a codification of rational thought and rational action, cannot rationally prove why it should be selected as a commendable approach to the world in preference to other attitudes. The choice of science over other types of knowledge is ultimately a value judgment, and as such it escapes the strict criteria of choice that science developed for its own propositions. Assertions about the virtues of science are not themselves scientific assertions. This circumstance detracts nothing from the coherence and consistency of science, as the theoretical cohesion and practical usefulness of its propositions can be established without reference to the reason which justifies concerns leading to their pursuit. The set of scientific propositions is complete and self-supporting without the propositions articulating the reasons of their generation. This lack of concern of science with its own pragmatic grounds derives, as it were, from the nature of its rules, which cannot be applied to questions of preference among ultimate ends. This lack of concern is, however, a minor irritant, or not an irritant at all, since in spite of the suspicious and vigilant stance science takes toward commonsensical beliefs, the normative structure of science is not divorced from the tacit but ubiquitous concerns of common sense. To the contrary, there is remarkable continuity between the two, with science pursuing in a systematic and self-conscious way the interests which on the commonsensical level are already followed, though in a somewhat diffuse and usually unself-conscious fashion. Science may afford the neglect of its own normative groundings precisely because it is so permanently and securely rooted in ordinary life. As Horkheimer states:

> After all, it helps to perform better, more efficiently, at a lesser cost what people in their daily life must do anyway. It supplies instrumental knowledge of how to make people's shelters warmer, how to get to wherever they need quicker, how to construct more reliable bridges spanning the shores of a river; and a more general knowledge which helps to solve such tasks. Through telling us why things happen the way they do (this function makes it explanatory), it tells us as well how to anticipate, or even correlate their appearance (this makes it predictive). On the other hand, science offers us means to facilitate our mutual communication and agreement, by clarifying for us the meaning of linguistic and other signs providing the right orientation of behavior, and making plain the message contained in strange cultural lores or our own historical tradition.

It is in everyday life that we first encounter the two practical tasks which require knowledge already embedded in daily routine action, but later raised to a higher level of sophistication and exactitude by organized science. The two tasks are mastery and cooperation. Mastery applies to the elements of experience which are constituted as movable objects; bodies which, by application of right action, can be set in motion required or moved into desirable places. What we need to know about such bodies is "what makes them move"; once we know it, we can manipulate them, or at least know what sort of force we should muster in order to do so. The kind of knowledge which

serves mastery consists, therefore, of explanatory/predictive propositions – propositions which simultaneously tell us about the external
forces responsible for the movements which occurred and the movements which a given external force would without fail evoke. Cooperation, on the other hand, applies to these elements of experience
which in all circumstances cannot be grasped as, simply, movable
objects: objects which cannot be seen as set in motion by just application of external force; objects which, in other words, are constituted
as self-activating entities – as sources rather than objects of action.
These elements of experience are acting and speaking individuals.
They are "acting," not "moving," since in order to make sense of
their behavior, we need to visualize the motives they set for themselves, rather than pressures exerted upon them by other agents. The
information about these motives, and therefore the indispensable link
in our "making sense" activity, is contained in the utterances they
generate, and cannot be drawn simply from the nonverbalized observations. Accommodation to their presence in our experience calls for
cooperation, a mutual adjustment of motives, achievable in the course
of communication, consisting in the exchange of utterances. Knowledge required for this purpose is not, as in the case of mastery,
explanatory/predictive. It is instead interpretive knowledge, consisting
of the "hermeneutical" (concerned with understanding) rules of the
passage from symbols to meanings, from collectively available utterances to the autonomous world of motives.

To sum up, the interest in mastery calls for instrumental action
served by explanatory/predictive knowledge; the interest in cooperation demands interaction, made possible by hermeneutical (interpretive) knowledge. Without these two types of knowledge, no daily life
is possible. For this reason Jürgen Habermas described the interests
which underlie the two categories of knowledge as *species-transcen-
dental*. They are transcendental, as no social life is possible without
them; they are, so to speak, universal preconditions of all forms of
human existence. They are, however, *species*-transcendental, as their
ubiquity may be traced to the characteristic form which the human
species attained in the course of evolution; hand and tongue, labor
and language – all have evolved as the principal instruments of this
species survival and perfectibility.

Being ubiquitously present in the specifically human way of life,
interests in mastery (technical interest) and in cooperation (practical
interest) determine the way in which human experience is collectively
perceived, categorized, and typified. The aspects of experience are
selected according to their relevance to the two fundamental interests.
This is what we all, singly and communally, do all the time. Recent

ethnomethodological studies have shown how elaborate and sophisticated are the commonsensical rules which guide this activity. In spite of all its revisionist attitude toward common sense, science is indeed an extension of this activity. It rests ultimately on the same silently accepted assumptions as common sense. It derives its legitimation from the same interests which sustain everyday life activity. This is why its wisdom might be questioned, but its purpose never is. Science has to prove that it goes rightly about reaching its end. It need not legitimate the end itself. Having been excused from this onerous requirement, it can concentrate fully on the instrumental task of sharpening its cognitive tools. It can, therefore, legitimately claim rationality without being unduly worried about the ultimate grounds of its action.

The status of emancipatory knowledge is a different matter. Emancipatory interests are not a transcendental condition of human survival. Human life is inconceivable without the pursuit of technical and practical interests, but it is fully imaginable and logically noncontradictory without any interest in emancipation. Experience of subjects capable of speech and action cannot be "objectified," reacted to, coped with, unless appropriate instrumental and hermeneutical skills have been developed. But it can, in principle, be adequately handled, up to the standards required by the continuation of species life without emancipatory knowledge. At least it may be the case for long stretches of human history. We can conclude that if technical and practical interests are suprahistorical (they explain history, rather than requiring a historical explanation), emancipatory interest has its historical origins. If at any time a claim is made that it is as compellingly necessary as the other two interests are, it must be justified by reference to specific historical circumstances. The necessity of emancipation can be only historical; it appears under particular, not species-universal, conditions.

Being deprived of prescientific, indeed precognitive, roots, cognitive knowledge cannot leave its activating/legitimizing interest outside its focus of attention. Hence, it cannot limit itself to the realm of fact leaving value behind. No knowledge, as we have seen, is truly disinterested; but emancipatory knowledge is the only one which cannot pretend being such. It must consciously and overtly articulate not only its instrumental procedure but its ends as well; and it must bear responsibility for the legitimation of both, without right to appeal for commonsensical support.

The general strategy of historical legitimation consists in demonstrating that, under specific conditions, emancipatory knowledge and corresponding practice do become prerequisites of survival; that emancipatory interest becomes a compelling necessity (i.e., if it is not followed, no continuation of social life is feasible). Necessity of emancipation is, as we have seen, an outcome of a historically specific situation. The acquisition by the emancipatory interest of pressure power sufficient for its satisfaction is not, therefore, precognitively assured. The necessity of emancipatory action must be argumentatively vindicated. Thus this interest must be consciously incorporated into the main body of emancipatory theory. Without such an incorporation this theory is incomplete and inconclusive. To try to construct a case for the desirability of technical or practical interests would be equivalent to the attempt to force open a gate permanently ajar; it is, however, a matter of theoretical argument, and a difficult one, that survival may require going beyond the horizons drawn by technical and practical interests together.

Emancipatory knowledge is in effect distinguished by a double function in relation to the practice it serves. Like other types of knowledge, it is capable of *instrumentalizing, rationalizing*, smoothing, and facilitating the ensuing action. But in addition, it also creates conditions for the action to be willingly undertaken. Without it, the action not only would be less effective; it would be hardly attempted. Technical and practical interests may be well met without people being conscious of their imperatives. This does not apply to emancipatory interest. It may exist only in the conscious form; it becomes reality once it has been identified, recognized, and admitted. In this sense it may be said that emancipatory knowledge generates not only assertions about reality but the very reality of which assertions are made; emancipatory theory is itself an element of emancipation, as it relativizes reality which the other two interests could only further solidify in its objectivity.

Habermas has chosen Marx's theory of capitalist society and Freud's theory of the civilized personality as examples of emancipatory theories. Marx showed that social reality as determined by capitalist practices creates a necessity of its own transcendence; that emancipation from the apparently compelling realities objectified by capitalist practices has become an indispensable condition of the continuation of social life able to pass the criteria established by civilizing history. The alternative to emancipation, as Rosa Luxemburg later summarized, would be (by the same criteria) barbarism. It is the recognition of this alternative which, according to Marx, was needed for the emancipatory interest to be realized in practice. The reality of interest was, therefore, mediated by theory. Historical situation preceded theoretical reflection; but theoretical reflection, in turn, was prior to the reality of interest and to the historical action which such an interest, having become a historical reality, was likely to trigger off. A similar strategy was followed by Freud in substantiating the claims of his metapsychological theory. The reality of civilized existence, unless elucidated by emancipatory interest, often leads to psychological disturbance. Ill health is caused by the repression of needs, by barring important constituents of personality from becoming conscious. Almost by definition, without the intervention of a theory armed with a knowingly postulated ideal of healthy existence, ill health can be only vaguely experienced as discomfort, but it cannot be identified as a case of normative distortion. Definitions generated within already distorted reality serve to conceal, not to articulate, the trouble. Hence the hidden needs must first be drawn to the surface of consciousness to regain their action-motivating potency. Not only liberated conduct but the very recognition of the emancipatory interest depends, therefore, on the availability of theory which saps the seemingly overwhelming power of distorted reality.

To sum up, the peculiar difficulty encountered by critical theory in establishing its link with practical action is traceable back to the historical, rather than transcendental, character of emancipatory interest. The practical consequence of this historicalness is the need of critical theory to perform tasks which other theories are ill prepared to fulfill but can legitimately dispense with. In addition to the normal tasks routinely performed by other sciences, critical theory must first accomplish the job which for other sciences is normally done by common sense: it must justify its own validity, prove that its undertaking is significant and its possible consequences are relevant to social survival. Critical theory is the one discourse which openly topicalizes its own grounds.

This brings us to the second of the two pillars: can critical theory subject itself to a test of truth? If so, in what way? Obviously not in a way legitimized by the long practice of other sciences. Other sciences confront phenomena already objectified, congested into "things," by the incessant, tacit work of commonsensical practices. They, therefore, can, in principle, measure their own assertions against objects *out there*. They can accept without further discussion that the objects are independent from, and unaffected by, statements made about them. This is not the situation of critical theory, however. As we have already seen, critical theory constitutes its own object and neither can nor intends to hide its active role in reality production. In the case of critical theory, this production is an organic element of the theory itself. It has to account for its own development as a process of interaction between the subject and the object of knowledge.

Emphatically rejecting the authority of a commonsensically established social reality, critical theory shifts its testing ground into the yet
unaccomplished future – this territory of, simultaneously, freedom
and uncertainty. Moreover, critical theory is itself a factor in bringing
this hypothesized future to pass. The unique position of critical theory
does not consist merely in the delay of a test. It is not related just to the
impossibility of testing its hypotheses here and now, by measuring
them against an already available existence. If this were so, the
distinction of critical theory from traditional theories would be only
the question of a time lag. Unlike traditional theories, critical theory
would have to wait and see whether its hypotheses come true, much
like, say, daily weather forecasts. But this is not the case. The gist of
critical theory is, as we have seen, the *culturalization of nature*, the
discovery of historical contingency and choice behind the ostensibly
natural necessities. In critical theory's view, the illusion of necessity
has been achieved above all by the repression of cultural alternatives.
The illusionary character of natural necessities can be proved only if
the repression is overcome, and repressed alternatives are redeemed.
This would not happen if alternatives were not first theoretically
postulated and efforts were made to implement them practically.
Critical theory, therefore, not only generates theory to be tested. It
participates in producing conditions of the test.

Sociological Applications

It has been said that the truth of critical theory is a "truth in the
making." The articulation of hypotheses is a crucial part in the production of social reality which corresponds to the hypothetical anticipation. We can express this differently: hypotheses of critical theory
are not truth-tested, but actualized. They can find their confirmation
only in the changed social conditions they themselves help to bring
about. The question of truth testing in the case of critical theory turns,
therefore, into the problem of bringing about the conditions of its
actualization. This problem, in turn, splits into two. First, we must
ask what features a conditions must possess which can be seen as
offering the adequate testing ground for social theory. Second, we
have to explore the mechanism by which such a testing ground may,
and is likely to, be created.

To start with the first question, we must recall that the authority of
truth is in all cases related to the rationality of discourse in which the
truth was argued and vindicated. A rational discourse is, of course, an
ideal rarely reached in practical circumstances. Most discussions

depart from the ideal. But thanks to an agreement on what the ideal conditions would be like, participants in empirical discussions can criticize the achieved results as inconclusive (because attained in imperfect conditions), and strive to improve them. In Jürgen Habermas's precise description, a genuinely rational discussion would mean that:

> validity claims of assertions, recommendations, or warnings are the exclusive object of discussion; that participants, themes and contributions are not restricted except with reference to the goal of testing the validity claims in question; that no force except that of the better argument is exercised; and that, as a result, all motives except that of the cooperative search for truth are excluded.

The idea of rational discourse as the only acceptable ground of credible and trustworthy opinion has been long established in the European tradition. In *On Liberty* John Stuart Mill was already appealing to general agreement when he concluded that "the beliefs which we have most warrant for, have no safeguard to rest on, but a standing invitation to the whole world to prove them unfounded." The ideal of rational discourse, or the authority granted to it, is not an invention of critical theory. What critical theory has contributed to the time-honored intellectual tradition is a sharpened understanding of socially produced conditions under which the ideal of rational discourse cannot be actualized – under which, moreover, it tends to be systematically and continually distorted. Critical theory shows that a "standing invitation to the whole world" is not a sufficient guarantee that the whole world will indeed try to prove the established beliefs unfounded. It is enough to spell out the requirements which must be met in order to enable the whole world to make such an effort, to see how far the real society departs from the ideal:

> Since all those affected have, in principle, at least the chance to participate in the practical deliberation, the "rationality" of the discursively formed will consists in the fact that the reciprocal behavioural expectations raised to normative status accord validity to a *common* interest ascertained *without* deception. The interest is common because the constraint-free consensus permits only what *all* can want; it is free of deception because even the interpretations of needs in which *each individual* must be able to recognise what he wants become the object of discursive will-formation. The discursively formed will may be called "rational" because the formal properties of discourse and of the deliberative situation sufficiently guarantee that a consensus can arise only through appropriately interpreted, *generalisable* interests, by which I mean needs that can be *communicatively shared*.

In these words of Jürgen Habermas, universality, equality of participants, no prohibitions or other restrictions imposed on the selection of topics of discourse, and lack of deception are all named as conditions under which a discourse can be described as rational. None of these conditions are met in the real world. Hence, the consensus reached in this imperfect condition cannot be awarded authority, which can be granted only by rational discourse. A commonsensical verdict of the utopianism or irrealism of alternative situations cannot be accepted as conclusive for the same reason. But critical theory does not only refuse to comply with the verdict. It also explains why the authority of the verdict cannot be admitted. It does so by developing a sociology of communication. In particular, it studies the social structures of domination which are responsible for systematic distortion of public communication. The study shows that a large part of society is in practice excluded from the public discourse in which decisions concerning their fate are formed; that vital elements of the decisions themselves, and of their true reasons, are systematically excluded from public discourse; that the concealment of vital information, the structure of secrecy, and the formalization of procedures generate a systematic deception; and that the summary result of all these departures from the ideal of rational discourse is the situation in which the stipulation of the equality of participants cannot be met.

It is hoped that by bringing these facts into relief while invoking the tradition-rooted, universal commitment to the principles of rational discourse, critical theory can both invalidate the allegedly empirically confirmed reality of public authority institutions and expose the repression involved. Critical theory hopefully can show that forces capable of exploding the existing network of repressions are organically present and perpetuated within the structure of dominance itself; that, in other words, this structure breeds conditions of its own supercession and, so to speak, cannot help it.

We can now return to the point from which our analysis of critical theory started. We said at the beginning that critical theory is not, strictly speaking, an alternative sociology; that it is, rather, a mode of theorizing. Now we can summarize the conclusions to which the analysis starting from these assumptions has brought us. The consequence of the mode of theorizing which critical theory practices is the demand to extend the realm of sociology to include areas normally ceded to philosophical study. The mode of theorizing practiced by critical theory leads us to conclude that the question of truth grounding, of the validity of beliefs, is not a matter for epistemology – a philosophical theory of cognition – to decide for the empirical sciences in general, and for sociology in particular. Epistemology should be *resociologized*, as the problem of truth is ultimately the sociological question of the historically shaped conditions under which normative beliefs are founded. Critical theory is not, therefore, an alternative sociology. But it may be internally coherent only if it substantiates a drastic expansion of the sociological project.

5.3 Modernity (1993)

The word *modern* entered the center of West European intellectual debate in the seventeenth century (although it had been sporadically used as far back as the fifth century); ostensibly, it meant no more than "current" or "of recent origin." And yet the context of its appearance and fast-growing popularity suggest a deeper than merely technical meaning: the quality of "being of recent origin," being newly created, had suddenly become a matter of acute interest, apparently acquiring a thoroughly novel significance. That significance derived from changing values, which now, unlike in previous centuries, favored the new over the old, denied authority to the past, and approved of irreverence to tradition and readiness to innovate, to "go where no man dared to go before." From the moment of its triumphant entry into public discourse, the idea of the modern tended to recast the old as antiquated, obsolete, out of date, about to be (deservedly) sunk into oblivion and replaced.

The idea of the modern reappeared in the seventeenth century as a militant concept, as the focus of contention in the so-called "Quarrel of Ancients and Moderns" that lasted in France and England for almost a century. Arts and literature served as the initial battleground: after the spectacular achievements of scientists like Newton and Descartes, with the Royal Society in England and more diffuse but no less influential *sociétés de pensée* in France valiantly promoting the unprecedented excellence of new science and philosophy, the question had to be asked sooner or later whether this upward movement was the lot of science alone or of all human endeavours – particularly of creations like painting and poetry. The Ancients (like Nicolas Boileau and Jean de La Fontaine in France, Sir William Temple and Jonathan Swift in Britain) defended the long-standing conviction that the peak of human achievement had been reached in Greek and Roman antiquity and that the inevitably inferior products of later generations could attempt no more than to struggle in vain to approximate its perfection. Earlier, such propositions were voiced routinely, seen as trivially true, and aroused no dissent. Now, however, inspired by the astonishing discoveries of the new science, opposing views began to spread and gain in popularity. The holders of the traditional views were redubbed Ancients – a concept, for the Moderns, tinged with contempt and derision. Charles Perrault and Bernard de Fontenelle were among the most pugnacious and vociferous advocates of the modern, daring attitude, which would draw its confidence from the belief that, as in science, so in all other fields of spiritual creation, the new may be better (truer, more useful, more right, more beautiful) than the old; that the potency of human reason and skill is unlimited; and that therefore human history has been and will forever remain a relentless march upward and forward.

The Quarrel was never conclusively resolved to everybody's satisfaction (a century later the Romantic movement resuscitated the ideas that the Moderns strove to put to rest once for all); it just fizzled out, as the philosophical edge of the issue was blunted by the rapid pace of practical cultural change. In retrospect, however, the Quarrel may be better appreciated as the condensed expression of a revolution taking place in the European mentality; of the new feeling of self-reliance and self-assurance, readiness to seek and try unorthodox solutions to any current trouble and worry, belief in the ascending tendency of human history and growing trust in the capacity of human reason. In the nineteenth century, the emergent mentality itself came to be described as modern, and the dominance of such mentality came to be seen as one of the crucial symptoms of the new age of modernity.

Modernity may be best described as the age marked by constant change – but an age aware of being so marked; an age that views its own legal forms, its material and spiritual creations, its knowledge and convictions as temporary, to be held "until further notice" and eventually disqualified and replaced by new and better ones. In other words, modernity is an era conscious of its historicity. Human institutions are viewed as self-created and amenable to improvement; they can be retained only if they justify themselves in the face of the stringent demands of reason – and if they fail the test, they are bound to be scrapped. The substitution of new designs for old will be a progressive move, a new step up the ascending line of human development.

Progress is, essentially, a human accomplishment. It consists in applying human reason (rationalizing) to the task of making the world better geared to serve human needs. Whatever is seen as a human need, as a condition of agreeable life, is accorded unqualified priority over all other considerations: the nonhuman part of the world (nature) is of itself meaningless, and any meaning it may be given can derive only from the human uses to which it is put. Designing an artificial, rational order of the human habitat is not an arbitrary choice; it is a necessity, an unavoidable human condition, for to be habitable the world must be made fit for the satisfaction of human needs through science-assisted technology. Science and its technological applications are therefore the principal sources and instruments of political, social, cultural, and moral progress. They are both the expression and the vehicle of human ascendancy over nature.

To modern Europe, conscious of its own historicity, styles of life and institutions that differed from those it currently approved were merely steps leading to its own, superior condition – survivals of its own past. Other cultures were seen as forms temporarily arrested in their development, and in this "frozen" state retarded. This belief gave modern Europe its characteristic self-confidence as a carrier of historical destiny, a collective missionary with the duty to spread the gospel of reason and to convert the rest of the world to its own faith and form of life. In case of resistance, the objects of prospective conversion could only be viewed as primitive, as victims of superstition and ignorance, whose authority (and particularly the ability to decide what was best for them) reason denied in advance. The modern period in European history (and the history of countries that underwent early the process of Europeanization) was therefore an age of proselytism, one marked by colonization of the non-European world and by repeated cultural crusades aimed at the regional, ethnic, or class-bound traditions within European societies themselves.

The modern state was invested with functions never contemplated by premodern rulers. It had to impose a unified order on vast territories heretofore regulated by a variety of local traditions; by the same token, it had to make the creation and maintenance of social order a matter of deliberation, conscious design, monitoring, and daily management, rather than limit itself to the observance of traditional customs and privileges. (It had, one might say, to assume a gardener's, rather than a gamekeeper's, stance toward the society.) The new tasks involved standardization of law and legal institutions across the state; unification, and often direct administration, of the process of popular education; and securing the priority of unified legal discipline over all other, particularistic loyalties. It is for this reason that modern states engaged in the process of nation building, having assumed the form of nation-states rather than dynastic realms. They promoted national unity over ethnic differentiation, deployed nationalism in the service of state authority, and adopted the promotion of national interests as the criterion and purpose of state policies. It is for the same reason that the modern state rejects and devalues traditional entitlements to rule (such as the longevity of rights) and charismatic rule (which is grounded on peculiar – and superior – personal qualities of a given ruler), demanding discipline to its own commands solely on formal, legal grounds: that is, referring to the fact that the commands have been issued by duly appointed incumbents of offices entitled to make rulings related to the given area.

By all historical standards, modernity (often referred to as "modern civilization," to locate it as a distinct type of social organization and culture among other civilizations, ancient, medieval, or contemporary) has been a remarkable success. It has come closer than any other known civilization to the status of genuine universality. It seems to be on the way to becoming the first global civilization in history. The states of the modern world may be politically and ideologically divided and even locked in mutual conflict, but they all agree on the superiority of the modern way of running human affairs and use modern methods and implements to assert themselves and pursue their ends. The modern form of life seems to have no serious competitors left among the forms it displaced; it has succeeded, moreover, in confronting its own difficulties and "developmental problems" in a way that strengthens the ascendancy of the worldview and pragmatic stance that are its own most characteristic traits. Thus modernity is usually described as the ultimate form of historical development. Inherently dynamic, modern civilization yet retains its own identity. It is capable of continuous creativity rather than, like other civilizations, ossifying and losing the capacity of creative adjustment to new challenges. With its arrival, the world has been split into a modern part and the rest, confronted with the challenge of modernization.

Most theoretical models of modernity select inner dynamism and the capacity for change and self-improvement as the central characteristics and the ultimate sources of modernity's worldwide ascendancy and attractiveness. They also agree that to explain that dynamism is the most important task – and duty – of any theory of modernity. Beginning with the early nineteenth century, most analysts sought the secret of modern dynamism in the emancipation of human action from the shackles of custom, tradition, and communal obligations and in its subjection solely to the critieria of efficient task performance. In Karl Marx's picturesque expression, "everything solid melts into air, everything sacred is profaned": once the authority of tradition has been sapped and denied, nothing can prevent human courage from setting ever more ambitious tasks and designing ever more effective ways of performing them. It is the match between means and ends that now decides which course of action is to be chosen. As the U.S. social theorist Talcott Parsons put it (elaborating on the ideas of the nineteenth-century German sociologist Ferdinand

Tönnies), in modern times the traditional ways of assessing actors and their actions have been reversed. Action is now judged "out of context," independently of the sociocultural setting in which it takes place and the social standing of its human objects – solely according to the universal rules of adequacy and efficiency. By contrast, actors are judged by their specific performances relevant to the task at hand, not by their general qualities. What truly counts is what is being done and how, not by whom and why. Selection of action is freed from all criteria – personal loyalties, political commitments, and moral norms, for example – that are irrelevant to the pursuit of the task at hand.

Division and separation are indeed constant themes in the theoretical discourse of modernity. The German sociologist Max Weber proposed that the separation of business from household was the constitutive act of modern economy. Thanks to that separation, business decisions were emancipated from the pressure of moral obligations and personal commitments that guide family life. In still more general terms, the significance of separation was elaborated on by Immanuel Kant. In reference to his division between pure reason, practical reason, and judgment, many theorists of modernity (notably Jürgen Habermas in Germany and Ernest Gellner in Britain) consider the separation and mutual autonomy of the discourses of truth, moral norms, and aesthetic judgment (setting apart the spheres of science, ethics, and arts) as the most distinctive and decisive feature of modern mentality and practice. Beginning with Adam Smith, division of labor and splitting of complex functions into smaller and more manageable tasks has been seen as the most conspicuous factor of modern efficiency and productivity. Emile Durkheim, a French sociologist of the early 1900s, saw in the progressive, ever more minute division of labor the substance and the motive force of all aspects of historical development. The more complex is the division of labor, the simpler and more straightforward are separated functions; therefore they may be better mastered and more efficiently performed by specialists, who can now concentrate fully on effective means of "problem resolution." Expertise becomes a trademark of modern economy, science, art, and politics alike.

All fields of modern life, as Weber insisted, tend to become progressively rationalized. Action is rational (in the instrumental sense) insofar as it is oriented toward a clearly conceived and well-defined end, and thereafter based on the calculation of relative efficiency of alternative means to achieve it. Rational action is guided by motives and purposes, amenable in principle to conscious scrutiny and correction, and not determined by forces of which the actor is unaware or over which he or she has no control. Rational action splits the context of performance into ends and means and is guided solely by the effort to match the second against the first. Action is rational (again, in the instrumental sense) insofar as it consists in such decision-making and choice, even if a specific choice made by a given actor here and now is not the best conceivable or is even downright mistaken. Indeed, most choices stop short of the ideal. Means may be miscalculated because of inadequate or erroneous knowledge. Moreover, task-oriented activity is seldom free from interference by "impure" factors, irrational insofar as they are irrelevant to the task at hand – like the actor's uncontrolled habits and traditional loyalities, affections that get in the way, or commitment to values that interfere with the efficient performance of the given task. Rationality is therefore a tendency rather than the accomplished reality of modernity; a continuous, though by and large inconclusive, trend discernible in all fields of social life. For instance, according to Weber, the rule-governed, task-subordinated, impersonally acting organization, subjected to a meticulous division of functions, strict hierarchy of command, and scrupulous matching of personal skills of incumbents to the objective requirements of office, is the specifically modern, rational form of government.

The other side of rationalism is, of course, the taming or suppression of everything irrational – everything that interferes with the work of reason and detracts from the pragmatic effectivity of action. This irrational element in human behavior is called passion, which has been construed as the major obstacle on the road to the rule of reason. Modern civilization is prominent as much for its suppression of passions as for its promotion of the rationality of human conduct. More than in any other sphere, rational organization of society consists in controlling, defusing, incapacitating, or channeling away human instinctual drives and predispositions. A thorough analysis of this other, dramatic face of modernity is associated first and foremost with the work of Sigmund Freud. According to Freud, modern civilization substitutes the "reality principle" for the "pleasure principle" – the first being the necessary condition of peaceful, secure coexistence, the second being a natural predisposition of humans that clashes with the first. In practical terms, this substitution means constraint: pursuit of happiness is trimmed and limited by the consideration of what it is possible to achieve without paying costs too excessive to conceive of the effort as worthwhile. Partial security is obtained in exchange for at least part of the individual's freedom. Adequately civilized behavior is marked by self-constraint; society, so to speak, "leaves a garrison in a conquered city" in the form of the socially trained individual conscience that prompts the individual to suppress such urges as may fall in conflict with the socially approved norms.

In his study of the modern condition – entitled *Civilization and Its Discontents* – Freud theorizes that modern civilization inevitably breeds discontent and resistance, and that its perpetuation thus involves an element of mental or physical coercion. The picture of modernity that emerges from Freud's analysis is far from peaceful and benign. The rule of reason has psychologically traumatic consequences. From the individual's point of view, it cannot be an unambiguous blessing, as it leaves quite a considerable part of human needs downgraded, unattended, or starved. This is why reason's rule is continuously resented and can never be complete; it will go on prompting rebellion against itself. Again and again, people pressed to abide by the cool and unemotional rules of calculation of costs and effects will rally instead to the defense of suppressed affections, natural urges, and the immediacy of human contact.

Another rendition of the inner contradiction and ambiguous impact of civilization (and modern civilization in particular) can be found in Friedrich Nietzsche's concept of a spontaneous and instinctual "Dionysian" rebellion as a constant, only barely tamed threat, ever again boosted by the "Apollonian" effort to construct a logical, rational, and harmonious world order. This theme, in its Freudian-Nietzschean rendition, is directly or implicitly present in virtually all of the numerous critiques of modernity as an ambitious, but in many respects abortive, project aimed at overall rationalization of social organization and individual human behavior. Two types of critique are particularly prominent. One (undertaken by the "mass politics" theoreticians inspired, in somewhat different ways, by the "elite" theory of Vilfredo Pareto, the concept of the "revolt of the masses" popularized by José Ortega y Gasset, and the "iron law of oligarchy" articulated by Robert Michels) points out that, contrary to rationalistic rhetoric, modern conditions promote a blatantly irrational, heavily aestheticized mass politics that hinders rather than promotes rational choice. Another (mainly associated with the Frankfurt School tradition of critical theory, established by the work of Theodor Adorno and Max Horkheimer, but going back for many of its ideas to the early twentieth-century German sociologist Georg Simmel) uncovers the irreparable conflict between the drive to rationalize supra-individual institutional structures and the promise to render individual decisions amenable to free rational choice.

All in all, resistance to rationalization has been as prominent a mark of modernity as has rationalization itself. The history of modernity is punctuated by criticisms of its excesses or even of the vanity or evil of its motives and historic ambitions. For every intellectual expression of enthusiasm for the breathtaking vistas opened by modern science, technological expertise, and political expediency, there has been a protest against the "drying up" of individuality and genuinely human affectivity. Against the modern promise of a human species empowered in its struggle to make the world more hospitable, critics have hastened to point out that even if the species as a whole gains in freedom, its individual members do not; they are denied true choice, having been "functionalized" and transformed into "cogs in the machine." Against the utility of reason-guided problem solving, the critics have defended the values of individuality, the indivisible whole, and the all-too-human right to be different, erratic, and altogether irrational. Beginning with the Romantic poetry of the early nineteenth century, through decadence, the militantly "modernistic" avant-garde of the early twentieth century, dadaism, surrealism, and up to present-day postmodern culture (which proclaims normlessness the only cultural norm and calls for resistance to all authority, declining even to supply a foundation for its own practice) – the modern rationalization drive has been accompanied by a stridently oppositional culture bent on the defense of individual freedom and emotional experience. Cultural rebellion against the reality of society, a virtually constant antagonism between social and political practices and advanced cultural creation, whether in philosophy, art, or literature, has been thus far a most astonishing – and apparently permanent – feature of modernity.

An explanation of this paradox is sought in the specifically modern structure of daily life and individual experience. The most salient attribute of the latter is its fragmentariness; cast into the densely packed urban environment and bound to spend most of his or her life among strangers, the individual finds it difficult, perhaps impossible, to integrate experience into a meaningful whole. Within the horizon drawn by individual experience, time seems to split into unconnected events and space into unrelated spots. If there is a bond of mutual dependence that unites them into a cohesive totality – such a link eludes the individual observer, facing but brief and spatially limited episodes of the drama. Modern experience, it was first pointed out by the French poet and critic Charles Baudelaire, is a sighting of a fleeting moment. To be in tune with modern experience, art ought to represent the world as fragmentary and transitory – as a collection of "fleeting moments."

As Georg Simmel indicated, the characteristic feature of modern experience is the lack of coordination and communication between civilization as total cultural product and the snippets of cultural achievement that individuals are capable of assimilating and using as the building material in constructing their own identities. The sum total of cultural products far exceeds individual absorptive capacity. This fact, on the one hand, frees cultural creation from its bonds with daily life and permits thereby an infinite specialization and infinite expansion within each specialized field (hence the logarithmic acceleration in the growth of science, technology, and the arts, which exacerbates still further the original conflict); on the other hand, however, it leaves to individuals the awesome task of patching together "meaningful lives" out of the subjectively meaningless splinters of other, unknown or invisible totalities. While performing this task, individuals must be able to compare the incomparable and combine elements that apparently do not belong together; for this they need a strategy that, so to speak, "imposes" comparability between wildly discrepant experiences, and thus allows them to make choices while neglecting the qualitative differences between the objects of choice. Hence the intellect (capacity for abstract, formal thinking) and money are simultaneously inevitably products and indispensable instruments of life under modern conditions. Both address themselves solely to the quantitative aspects of experienced phenomena, and downplay their qualitative characteristics.

These and related characteristics of human habitat have persisted throughout the modern era, constantly gathering force. They continue to mark present-day Western and Westernized societies and continue to spread into areas of the globe until recently seen as "traditional" or "premodern." Nonetheless, some observers suggest that modernity in its classic form has run its course and has been replaced, or is about to be replaced, by another sociocultural formation, which they call postmodernity. Descriptions of this allegedly new formation (meant to demonstrate its novelty and qualitative distinction from modernity) do not differ on the whole from the above description of the modern condition. There is, however, one significant difference on which the assertions about the "end of modernity" and the advent of postmodernity tend to found their credibility: if throughout the modern era the "messiness," ambivalence, spontaneity, and uncertainty inherent in social and individual life were seen as temporary irritants, to be eventually overcome by the rationalizing tendency, they are now seen as unavoidable and ineradicable – and not necessarily irritants. It now has been accepted that historical processes have no specific end or direction; that pluralism of values and forms of life is here to stay; and that the centers of political power, most notably state governments, have lost both the resources and the ambitions that characterize the "gardening stance." The all-inclusive designs of "rational society" and global social-engineering schemes and cultural crusades that backed them seem to have fallen into disrepute and have been all but abandoned. The recent collapse of the communist command economies and all-regulating states has provided a most spectacular display of this tendency.

6

Sociology and the Postmodern

6.1 A Sociological Theory of Postmodernity (1991)

I propose that:

1. The term *postmodernity* renders accurately the defining traits of the social condition that emerged throughout the affluent countries of Europe and of European descent in the course of the 20th century, and took its present shape in the second half of that century. The term is accurate as it draws attention to the continuity and discontinuity as two faces of the intricate relationship between the present social condition and the formation that preceded and gestated it. It brings into relief the intimate, genetic bond that ties the new, postmodern social condition to *modernity* – the social formation that emerged in the same part of the world in the course of the 18th century, and took its final shape, later to be sedimented in the sociological models of modern society (or models of society created by modern sociology), during the 19th; while at the same time indicating the passing of a certain crucial characteristic in whose absence one cannot anymore adequately describe the social condition as modern in the sense given to the concept by orthodox (modern) social theory.

2. Postmodernity may be interpreted as the fully developed modernity; as modernity that acknowledged the effects it was producing throughout its history, yet producing inadvertently, by default rather than design, as *unanticipated consequences*, by-products often perceived as waste; as modernity conscious of its true nature – *modernity for itself*. The most conspicuous features of the postmodern condition: institutionalized pluralism, variety, contingency and ambivalence – have been all turned out by the modern society in ever increasing volumes; yet they were produced, so to speak, "by the way", at a time when the institutions of modernity, faithfully replicated by modern

mentality, struggled for *universality, homogeneity, monotony* and *clarity*. The post-modern condition can be therefore described, on the one hand, as modernity emancipated from false consciousness; on the other, as a new type of social condition marked by the overt institutionalization of the characteristics which modernity – in its designs and managerial practices – set about to eliminate and, failing that, tried to conceal.

3. The twin differences that set the postmodern condition apart from modern society are profound and seminal enough to justify (indeed, to call for) a separate sociological theory of postmodernity that would break decisively with the concepts and metaphors of the models of modernity and lift itself out of the mental frame in which they had been conceived. This need arises from the fact that (their notorious disagreements notwithstanding) the extant models of modernity articulated a shared vision of modern history as a *movement with a direction* – and differed solely in the selection of the ultimate destination or the organizing principle of the process, be it universalization, rationalization, or systemization. None of those principles can be upheld (at least not in the radical form typical of the orthodox social theory) in the light of the postmodern experience. Neither can be sustained the very master-metaphor that underlies them: one of the process with a pointer.

4. Postmodernity is not a flawed variant of modernity; neither is it a diseased state of modernity, a temporary ailing yet to be rectified, a case of "modernity in crisis". It is, instead, an essentially viable, pragmatically self-sustainable and logically self-contained social condition defined by *distinctive features of its own*. A theory of postmodernity cannot be therefore a modified theory of modernity, a theory of modernity with a set of negative markers. An adequate theory of postmodernity may be only constructed in a cognitive space organized by a different ensemble of assumptions and needs its own vocabulary. The degree of emancipation from the concepts and issues spawned by the discourse of modernity will be the measure of its adequacy.

Conditions of Theoretical Emancipation

What the theory of postmodernity must discard in the first place is the assumption of a *systemic character* of the social condition it purports to model: the vision of a system (a) with a degree of cohesiveness, (b) equilibrated or marked by an overwhelming tendency to equilibration, (c) defining its elements in terms of the function they perform in that process of equilibration or the reproduction of the equilibrated state. It must assume instead that the social condition it intends to model is essentially and perpetually *unequilibrated*: composed of elements with a degree of autonomy large enough to justify the view of totality as a kaleidoscopic – momentary and contingent – outcome of interaction. The orderly, structured nature of totality cannot be taken for granted; nor can its pseudo-representational construction be seen as the purpose of theoretical activity. Randomness of the global outcome of uncoordinated activities cannot be treated as a departure from the pattern which the totality strives to maintain; any pattern that may temporarily emerge out of the random movements of autonomous agents is as haphazard and unmotivated as the one that could emerge in its place or the one bound to replace it, if also for a time only. All order that can be found is a local, emergent and transitory phenomenon; its nature can be best grasped by a metaphor of a whirlpool appearing in the flow of a river, retaining its shape only for a relatively brief period and only at the expense of incessant metabolism and constant renewal of content.

The theory of postmodernity must be free of the last vestiges of the metaphor of progress that informed all competing theories of modern society. With the totality dissipated into a series of randomly emerging, shifting and evanescent islands of order, its temporal record cannot be linearly represented. Perpetual local transformations do not add up so as to prompt (much less to assure) in effect an increased homogeneity, rationality or organic systemness of the whole. Postmodern condition is a site of constant mobility and change, but no clear direction of development. The image of Brownian movement offers an apt metaphor for this aspect of postmodernity: each momentary state is neither a necessary effect of the preceding state nor the sufficient cause of the next one. Postmodern condition is both *undetermined* and *undetermining*. It "unbinds" time; weakens the constraining impact of the past and effectively prevents colonization of the future.

Similarly, the theory of postmodernity would do well if it disposed of concepts like *system* (or, for this matter, *society*), suggestive of a sovereign totality whose welfare or perpetuation all smaller (and, by definition, subordinate) units serve – and thus a totality entitled to define, and capable of defining, the meanings of individual actions and agencies that compose it. A sociology geared to the conditions of postmodernity ought to replace the category of *society* with that of *sociality*; a category that tries to convey the processual modality of social reality, the dialectical play of randomness and pattern (or, from the agent's point of view, of freedom and dependence); and a category that refuses to take the structured character of the process for granted – which treats instead all found structures as emergent accomplishments.

With their field of vision organized around the focal point of system-like, resourceful and meaning-bestowing totality, sociological theories of modernity (which conceived of themselves as sociological theories *tout court*) concentrated on the vehicles of homogenization and conflict-resolution in a relentless search for a solution to the "Hobbesian problem". This cognitive perspective (shared with the one realistic referent of the concept of "society" – the national state, the only totality in history able to seriously entertain the ambition of contrived, artificially sustained and managed monotony and homogeneity) a priori disqualified all "uncertified" agency; unpatterned and unregulated spontaneity of the autonomous agent was pre-defined as a de-stabilizing and, indeed, anti-social factor marked for taming and extinction in the continuous struggle for societal survival. By the same token, prime importance was assigned to the mechanisms and weapons of order-promotion and pattern-maintenance – the state and the legitimation of its authority, power, socialization, culture, ideology etc. – all selected for the role they played in the promotion of pattern, monotony, predictability and thus also manageability of conduct.

The sociological theory of postmodernity is bound to reverse the structure of the cognitive field. Focus must be now on agency; more correctly, on the *habitat* in which agency operates and which it produces in the course of operation. As it offers the agency the sum-total of resources for all possible action as well as the field inside which the action-orienting and action-oriented relevancies may be plotted, the habitat is the territory inside which both freedom and dependency of the agency are constituted (and, indeed, perceived as such). Unlike system-like totalities of modern social theory, habitat neither determines the conduct of the agents nor defines its meaning; it is no more (but no less either) than the setting in which both action and meaning-assignment are *possible*. Its own identity is as under-determined and motile, as emergent and transitory, as those of the actions and their meanings that form it.

There is one crucial area, though, in which the habitat performs a determining (systematizing, patterning) role: it sets the agenda for the "business of life" through supplying the inventory of ends and the pool of means. The way in which the ends and means are supplied determines as well the meaning of the "business of life": the nature of the tasks all agencies confront and have to take up in one form or another. In as far as the ends are offered as potentially alluring rather than obligatory, and rely for their choice on their own seductiveness rather than supporting power of coercion, the "business of life" splits into a series of choices. The series is not pre-structured, or is pre-structured only feebly and above all inconclusively. For this reason the choices through which the life of the agents is construed and sustained are best seen (as it tends to be seen by the agents themselves) as adding up to the process of *self-constitution*. To underline the graduated and ultimately inconclusive nature of the process, self-constitution is best viewed as *self-assembly*.

I propose that sociality, habitat, self-constitution and self-assembly should occupy in the sociological theory of postmodernity the central place that the orthodoxy of modern social theory had reserved for the categories of society, normative group (like class or community), socialization and control.

Main Tenets of the Theory of Postmodernity

1. Under postmodern condition, habitat is a *complex system*. According to contemporary mathematics, complex systems differ from mechanical systems (those assumed by the orthodox, modern theory of society) in two crucial respects. First, they are unpredictable; second, they are not controlled by statistically significant factors (the circumstance demonstrated by the mathematical proof of the famous "butterfly effect"). The consequences of these two distinctive features of complex systems are truly revolutionary in relation to the received wisdom of sociology. The "systemness" of the postmodern habitat does not lend itself anymore to the organismic metaphor, which means that agencies active within the habitat cannot be assessed in terms of functionality or dysfunctionality. The successive states of the habitat appear to be unmotivated and free from constraints of deterministic logic. And the most formidable research strategy modern sociology had developed – statistical analysis – is of no use in exploring the dynamics of social phenomena and evaluating the probabilities of their future development. Significance and numbers have parted ways. Statistically insignificant phenomena may prove to be decisive, and their decisive role cannot be grasped in advance.

2. Postmodern habitat is a complex (non-mechanical) system for two closely related reasons. First, there is no "goal setting" agency with overall managing and coordinating capacities or ambitions – one whose presence would provide a vantage point from which the aggregate of effective agents appears as a "totality" with a determined structure of relevances; a totality which one can think of as an

organization. Second – the habitat is populated by a great number of agencies, most of them single-purpose, some of them small, some big, but none large enough to subsume or otherwise determine behaviour of the others. Focusing on a single purpose considerably enhances the effectivity of each agency in the field of its own operation, but prevents each area of the habitat from being controlled from a single source, as the field of operation of any agency never exhausts the whole area the action is affecting. Operating in different fields yet zeroing in on shared areas, agencies are *partly* dependent on each other, but the lines of dependence cannot be fixed and thus their actions (and consequences) remain staunchly under-determined, that is autonomous.

3. Autonomy means that agents are only partly, if at all, constrained in their pursuit of whatever they have institutionalized as their purpose. To a large extent, they are free to pursue the purpose to the best of their mastery over resources and managerial capacity. They are free (and tend) to view the rest of the habitat shared with other agents as a collection of opportunities and "problems" to be resolved or removed. Opportunity is what increases the output in the pursuit of purpose; a problem is what threatens the decrease or a halt of production. In ideal circumstances (maximization of opportunities and minimization of problems) each agent would tend to go in the pursuit of purpose as far as the resources allow; the availability of resources is the only reason for action they need and thus the sufficient guarantee of the action's reasonability. The possible impact on other agents' opportunities is not automatically reforged into the limitation of the agent's own output. The many products of purpose-pursuing activities of numerous partly interdependent but relatively autonomous agents must yet find, *ex post facto*, their relevance, utility and demand-securing attractiveness. The products are bound to be created in volumes exceeding the pre-existing demand motivated by already articulated problems. They are still to seek their place and meaning as well as the problems that they may claim to be able to resolve.

4. For every agency, the habitat in which its action is inscribed appears therefore strikingly different from the confined space of its own automatic, purpose-subordinated pursuits. It appears as a space of chaos and chronic *indeterminacy*, a territory subjected to rival and contradictory meaning-bestowing claims and hence perpetually *ambivalent*. All states the habitat may assume appear equally *contingent* (that is, they have no overwhelming reasons for being what they are, and they could be different if any of the participating agencies behave differently). Heuristics of pragmatically useful "next moves"

displaces therefore the search for algorithmic, certain knowledge of deterministic chains. The succession of states assumed by the relevant areas of the habitat no agency can interpret without including its own actions in the explanation; agencies cannot meaningfully scan the situation "objectively", that is in such ways as allow to eliminate, or bracket away, their own activity.

5. The existential modality of the agents is therefore one of insufficient determination, inconclusiveness, motility and rootlessness. Identity of the agent is neither given nor authoritatively confirmed. It has to be construed, yet no design for the construction can be taken as prescribed or foolproof. It lacks a benchmark against which its progress could be measured, and so it cannot be meaningfully described as "progressing". It is now the incessant (and non-linear) activity of *self-constitution* that makes the identity of the agent. In other words, the self-organization of the agents in terms of a "life-project" (a concept that assumes a long-term stability; a lasting identity of the habitat, in its direction transcending, or at least commensurate with, the longevity of human life) is displaced by the process of self-constitution. Unlike the "life-project", self-constitution has no destination point in reference to which it could be evaluated and monitored. It has no visible end; not even a stable direction. It is conducted inside a shifting (and, as we have seen before, unpredictable) constellation of mutually autonomous points of reference, and thus purposes guiding the self-constitution at one stage may soon lose their current authoritatively confirmed validity. Hence the self-assembly of the agency is not a cumulative process; self-constitution entails disassembling alongside the assembling, adoption of new elements as much as shedding of others, learning together with forgetting. The identity of the agency, much as it remains in a state of permanent change, cannot be therefore described as "developing". In the self-constitution of the agencies, the "Brownian movement"-type spatial nature of the habitat is projected onto the time axis.

6. The only visibility of continuity and cumulative effects of the self-constitution efforts is offered by the human body – seen as the only constant factor among the protean and fickle identities. Hence the centrality of *body-cultivation* among the self-assembly concerns, and the acute attention devoted to everything "taken internally" (food, air, drugs, etc.), and everything coming in touch with the skin – that interface between the agent and the rest of the habitat and the hotly contested frontier of agents' autonomously managed identity. In the postmodern habitat, DIY operations (jogging, dieting, slimming etc.) replace and to a large extent displace the panoptical drill of modern factory, school or the barracks; unlike their predecessors,

however, they are not perceived as externally imposed, cumbersome and resented necessities, but as manifestoes of the agent's freedom. Their heteronomy, once blatant through coercion, now hides behind seduction.

7. The process of self-constitution is devoid of the advance design and thus generates an acute demand for a substitute: orientation points that may guide successive moves. It is the other agencies (real or imagined) of the habitat who serve as such orientation points. Their impact on the process of self-constitution differs from that exercised by normative groups in that on the whole they neither monitor nor knowingly administer the acts of allegiance and the actions that follow it. From the vantage point of self-constituting agents, other agents can be metaphorically visualized as a randomly scattered set of free-standing and unguarded totemic poles which one can approach or abandon without applying for permission to enter or leave. The self-proclaimed allegiance to the selected agent (the act of selection itself) is accomplished through the adoption of *symbolic tokens* of belonging, and the freedom of choice is limitedly solely by the availability and accessibility of such tokens.

8. *Availability* of tokens for potential self-assembly depends on their *visibility*, much as it does on their material presence. Visibility in its turn depends on the perceived *utility* of symbolic tokens for the satisfactory outcome of self-construction; that is, on their ability to reassure the agent that the current results of self-assembly are indeed satisfactory. This reassurance is the substitute for the absent certainty, much as the orientation points with the attached symbolic tokens are collectively a substitute for pre-determined patterns for life-projects. The reassuring capacity of symbolic tokens rests on borrowed (ceded) authority: of *expertise*, or of *mass following*. Symbolic tokens are actively sought and adopted if their relevance is vouched for by the trusted authority of the expert, or by their previous or concurrent appropriation by a great number of other agents. These two variants of authority are in their turn fed by the insatiable thirst of the self-constituting agents for reassurance. Thus *freedom* of choice and *dependence* on external agents reinforce each other, and arise and grow together as products of the same process of self-assembly and of the constant demand for reliable orientation points which it cannot but generate.

9. *Accessibility* of tokens for self-assembly varies from agent to agent, depending mostly on the resources that a given agent commands. Increasingly the most strategic role among the resources is played by knowledge; the growth of individually appropriated knowledge widens the range of assembly patterns which can be realistically

chosen. Freedom of the agent, measured by the range of realistic choices, turns under postmodern condition into the main dimension of inequality and thus becomes the main stake of the *re-distributional* type of conflict that tends to arise from the dichotomy of privilege and deprivation; by the same token, access to knowledge – being the key to an extended freedom – turns into the major index of social standing. This circumstance lifts the attractiveness of *information* among the symbolic tokens sought after for their reassuring potential. It also further enhances the authority of experts, trusted to be the repositories and sources of valid knowledge. Information becomes a major resource, and experts the crucial brokers of all self-advancement.

Postmodern Politics

Modern social theory could afford to separate theory from policy. Indeed, it made a virtue out of that historically circumscribed plausibility. Keeping the separation watertight has turned into a most distinctive mark of modern theory of society. A theory of postmodernity cannot follow the pattern. Once the essential contingency and the absence of supra- or pre-agentic foundations of sociality and of the structured forms it sediments have been acknowledged, it becomes clear that the politics of agents lies at the core of the habitat's existence; indeed, it can be said to be its existential modality. All description of the postmodern habitat must include politics from the beginning. Politics cannot be kept outside the basic theoretical model as an epiphenomenon, a superstructural reflection or belatedly formed, intellectually processed derivative.

It could be argued (though the argument cannot be spelled out here) that the separation of theory and policy in modern *theory* could be sustained as long as there was, unchallenged or effectively immunized against challenge, *practical* division between theoretical and political practice. The latter separation had its foundation in the activity of the modern national state, arguably the only social formation in history with pretensions and ambitions of the administration of a global order, and of a total monopoly, and the procedure of its formulation had to be made separate and independent from the procedure legitimizing an acceptable theory and, more generally, intellectual work modelled after the latter procedure. The gradual, yet relentless erosion of the national state's monopoly (undermined simultaneously from above and from below, by trans-national and sub-national agencies, and weakened by the fissures in the historical marriage between nationalism and the state, none needing the other very strongly in their mature form) ended the plausibility of theoretical segregation.

With the state's resourcefulness and ambitions shrinking, responsibility (real or just claimed) for policy shifts away from the state or is actively shed on the state's own initiative. It is not taken over by another agent, though. It dissipates; it splits into a plethora of localized or partial policies pursued by localized or partial (mostly one issue) agencies. With that vanishes the modern state's tendency to precipitate and draw upon itself almost all social protest arising from unsatisfied redistributional demands and expectations – a quality that further enhanced the exclusive role of the state among societal agencies, at the same time rendering it vulnerable and exposed to frequent political crises (as conflicts fast turned into political protests). Under the postmodern condition grievances which in the past would cumulate into a collective political process and address themselves to the state, stay diffuse and translate into self-reflexivity of the agents, stimulating further dissipation of policies and the autonomy of postmodern agencies (if they do cumulate for a time in the form of a one-issue pressure group, they bring together agents too heterogeneous in other respects to prevent the dissolution of the formation once the desired progress in the issue in question has been achieved; and even before that final outcome, the formation is unable to override the diversity of its supporters' interests and thus claim and secure their *total* allegiance and identification). One can speak, allegorically, of the "functionality of dissatisfaction" in a postmodern habitat.

Not all politics in postmodernity is unambiguously postmodern. Throughout the modern era, politics of *inequality* and hence of *redistribution* was by far the most dominant type of political conflict and conflict-management. With the advent of postmodernity it has lost its dominant role, but remains (and in all probability will remain) a constant feature of the postmodern habitat. Even such an eminently modern type of politics acquires in many cases a postmodern tinge, though. Redistributional vindications of our time are aimed more often than not at the winning of *human rights* (a code name for the agent's autonomy, for that freedom of choice that constitutes the agency in the postmodern habitat) by categories of population heretofore denied them (this is the case of the emancipatory movements of oppressed ethnic minorities, of the black movement, of one important aspect of the feminist movement), rather than at the express re-distribution of wealth, income and other consumable values by the society at large.

Alongside the survivals of the modern form of politics, however, specifically postmodern forms appear and gradually colonize the centrefield of the postmodern political process. Some of them are new; some others owe their new, distinctly postmodern quality to their recent expansion and greatly increased impact. The following are the most prominent among them (the named forms are not necessarily mutually exclusive; and some act at cross-purposes):

1. *Tribal politics.* This is a generic name for practices aimed at collectivization (supra-agentic conformation) of the agents' self-constructing efforts. Tribal politics entails the creation of tribes as *imagined communities.* Unlike the pre-modern communities the modern powers set about to uproot, postmodern tribes exist in no other form but the symbolically manifested commitment of their members. They can rely on neither executive powers able to coerce their constituency into submission to the tribal rules (seldom do they have clearly codified rules to which the submission could be demanded), nor on the strength of neighbourly bonds or intensity of reciprocal exchange (most tribes are de-territorialized, and communication between their members is hardly at any time more intense than the intercourse between members and non-members of the tribe). Postmodern tribes are, therefore, constantly in *statu nascendi* rather than *essendi,* brought over again into being by repetitive symbolic rituals of the members but persisting no longer than these rituals' power of attraction (in which sense they are akin to Kant's *aesthetic communities* or Schmalenbach's *communions*). Allegiance is composed of the ritually manifested support for positive tribal tokens or equally symbolically demonstrated animosity to negative (anti-tribal) tokens. As the persistence of tribes relies solely on the deployment of the affective allegiance, one would expect an unprecedented condensation and intensity of emotive behaviour and a tendency to render the rituals as spectacular as possible – mainly through inflating their shocking power. Tribal rituals, as it were, compete for the scarce resource of public attention as the major (perhaps sole) resource of survival.

2. *Politics of desire.* This entails actions aimed at establishing the relevance of certain types of conduct (tribal tokens) for the self-constitution of the agents. If the relevance is established, the promoted conduct grows in attractiveness, its declared purposes acquire *seductive* power, and the probability of their choice and active pursuit increases: promoted purposes turn into agents' needs. In the field of the politics of desire, agencies vie with each other for the scarce resource of individual and collective dreams of the good life. The

overall effect of the politics of desire is heteronomy of choice supported by, and in its turn sustaining, the autonomy of the choosing agents.

3. *Politics of fear.* This is, in a sense, a supplement (simultaneously a complement and a counterweight) of the politics of desire, aimed at drawing boundaries to heteronomy and staving off its potentially harmful effects. If the typical modern fears were related to the threat of totalitarianism perpetually ensconced in the project of rationalized and state-managed society (Orwell's "boot eternally trampling a human face", Weber's "cog in the machine" and "iron cage" etc.), postmodern fears arise from uncertainty as to the soundness and reliability of advice offered through the politics of desire. More often than not, diffuse fears crystallize in the form of a suspicion that the agencies promoting desire are (for the sake of self-interest) oblivious or negligent of the damaging effects of their proposals. In view of the centrality of body-cultivation in the activity of self-constitution, the damage most feared is one that can result in poisoning or maiming the body through penetration or contact with the skin (the most massive panics have focused recently on incidents like mad cow's disease, listeria in eggs, shrimps fed on poisonous algae, dumping of toxic waste – with the intensity of fear correlated to the importance of the body among the self-constituting concerns, rather than to the statistical significance of the event and extent of the damage). Politics of fear strengthens the position of experts in the processes of self-constitution, while ostensibly questioning their competence. Each successive instance of the suspension of trust articulates a new area of the habitat as problematic and thus leads to a call for more experts and more expertise.

4. *Politics of certainty.* This entails the vehement search for social confirmation of choice, in the face of the irredeemable pluralism of the patterns on offer and acute awareness that each formula of self-constitution, however carefully selected and tightly embraced, is ultimately one of the many, and always "until further notice". Production and distribution of certainty is the defining function and the source of power of the experts. As the pronouncements of the experts can seldom be put to the test by the recipients of their services, for most agents the certainty about the soundness of their choices can be plausibly entertained only in the form of *trust*. Politics of certainty consists therefore mainly in the production and manipulation of trust; conversely, "lying", "letting down", betrayal of trust, abuse of privileged information emerge as the major threat to the already precarious and vulnerable self-identity of postmodern agents. Trustworthiness, credibility and perceived sincerity become major criteria by which

merchants of certainty – experts, politicians, sellers of self-assembly identity kits – are judged, approved or rejected.

Postmodern Ethics

Similarly to politics, ethics is an indispensable part of sociological theory of postmodernity pretending to any degree of completeness. Description of modern society could leave ethical problems aside or ascribe to them but a marginal place, in view of the fact that moral regulation of conduct was to a large extent subsumed under legislative and law-enforcing activity of global societal institutions, while whatever remained unregulated in such a way was "privatized" or perceived (and treated) as residual and marked for extinction in the course of full modernization. This condition does not hold anymore, ethical discourse is not institutionally preempted and hence its conduct and resolution (or irresolution) must be an organic part of any theoretical model of postmodernity.

Again, not all ethical issues found in a postmodern habitat are new. Most importantly, the possibly extemporal issues of the orthodox ethics – the rules binding short-distance, face-to-face intercourse between moral agents under conditions of physical and moral proximity – remain presently as much alive and poignant as ever before. In no way are they postmodern; as a matter of fact, they are not modern either. (On the whole, modernity contributed little, if anything, to the enrichment of moral problematics. Its role boiled down to the substitution of legal for moral regulation and the exemption of wide and growing sectors of human actions from moral evaluation.)

The distinctly postmodern ethical problematic arises primarily from two crucial features of the postmodern condition: *pluralism* of authority, and the centrality of *choice* in the self-constitution of postmodern agents.

1. Pluralism of authority, or rather the absence of an authority with globalizing ambitions, has a twofold effect. First, it rules out the setting of binding norms each agency must (or could be reasonably expected to) obey. Agencies may be guided by their own purposes, paying in principle as little attention to other factors (also to the interests of other agencies) as they can afford, given their resources and degree of independence. "Non-contractual bases of contract", devoid of institutional power support, are thereby considerably weakened. If unmotivated by the limits of the agency's own resources, any

constraint upon the agency's action has to be negotiated afresh. Rules emerge mostly as reactions to strife and consequences of ensuing negotiations; still, the already negotiated rules remain by and large precarious and under-determined, while the needs of new rules – to regulate previously unanticipated contentious issues – keep proliferating. This is why the *problem* of rules stays in the focus of public agenda and is unlikely to be conclusively resolved. In the absence of "principle coordination" the negotiating of rules assumes a distinctly *ethical* character: at stake are the principles of non-utilitarian self-constraint of autonomous agencies – and both non-utility and autonomy define *moral* action as distinct from either self-interested or legally prescribed conduct. Second, pluralism of authorities is conducive to the resumption by the agents of moral responsibility that tended to be neutralized, rescinded or ceded away as long as the agencies remained subordinated to a unified, quasi-monopolistic legislating authority. On the one hand, the agents face now point-blank the consequences of their actions. On the other, they face the evident ambiguity and controversiality of the purposes to which actions were to serve, and thus the need to justify argumentatively the values that inform their activity. Purposes can be no more substantiated *monologically*; having become perforce subjects of a *dialogue*, they must now refer to principles wide enough to command authority of the sort that belongs solely to ethical values.

2. The enhanced autonomy of the agent has similarly a twofold ethical consequence. First – in as far as the centre of gravity shifts decisively from heteronomous control to self-determination, and autonomy turns into the defining trait of postmodern agents – self-monitoring, self-reflection and self-evaluation become principal activities of the agents, indeed the mechanisms synonymous with their self-constitution. In the absence of a universal model for self-improvement, or of a clear-cut hierarchy of models, the most excruciating choices agents face are between life-purposes and values, not between the means serving the already set, uncontroversial ends. Supra-individual criteria of propriety in the form of technical precepts of instrumental rationality do not suffice. This circumstance, again, is potentially propitious to the sharpening up of moral self-awareness: only ethical principles may offer such criteria of value-assessment and value-choice as are at the same time supra-individual (carry on authority admittedly superior to that of individual self-preservation), and fit to be used without surrendering the agent's autonomy. Hence the typically postmodern heightened interest in ethical debate and increased attractiveness of the agencies claiming expertise in moral values (e.g. the revival of religious and quasi-religious movements).

Second, with the autonomy of all and any agents accepted as a principle and institutionalized in the life-process composed of an unending series of choices, the limits of the agent whose autonomy is to be observed and preserved turn into a most closely guarded and hotly contested frontier. Along this borderline new issues arise which can be settled only through an ethical debate. Is the flow and the outcome of self-constitution to be tested before the agent's right to autonomy is confirmed? If so, what are the standards by which success or failure are to be judged (what about the autonomy of young and still younger children, of the indigent, of parents raising their children in unusual ways, of people choosing bizarre life-styles, of people indulging in abnormal means of intoxication, people engaging in idiosyncratic sexual activities, individuals pronounced mentally handicapped)? And – how far do the autonomous powers of the agent extend and at which point is their limit is to be drawn (remember the notoriously inconclusive contest between "life" and "choice" principles in the abortion debate)?

All in all, in the postmodern context agents are constantly faced with moral issues and obliged to choose between equally well founded (or equally unfounded) ethical precepts. The choice always means the assumption of responsibility, and for this reason bears the character of a moral act. Under postmodern condition, the agent is perforce not just an actor and decision-maker, but a *moral subject*. The performance of life-functions demands also that the agent be a morally *competent* subject.

Sociology in the Postmodern Context

Strategies of any systematic study are bound to be resonant with the conception of its object. The orthodox sociology was resonant with the theoretical model of modern society. It was for that reason that the proper accounting for the self-reflexive propensities of human actors proved to be so spectacularly difficult. Deliberately or against its declared wishes, sociology tended to marginalize or explain away self-reflexivity as rule-following, function-performing or at best sedimentation of institutionalized learning; in each case, as epiphenomenon of social totality, understood ultimately as "legitimate authority" capable of "principally coordinating" social space. As long as the self-reflexivity of actors remained reduced to the subjective perception of obedience to impersonal rules, it did not need to be treated seriously; it rarely came under scrutiny as an independent variable, much less as a principal condition of all sociality and its institutionalized sedimentations.

Never flawless, this strategy becomes singularly inadequate under the postmodern condition. Postmodern habitat is indeed an incessant flow of reflexivity; sociality responsible for all its structured yet fugitive forms, their interaction and their succession, is a discursive activity, activity of interpretation and re-interpretation, of interpretation fed back into the interpreted condition only to trigger off further interpretative efforts. To be effectively and consequentially present in a postmodern habitat sociology must conceive of itself as a participant (perhaps better informed, more systematic, more rule-conscious, yet nevertheless a participant) in this never ending, self-reflexive process of reinterpretation – and devise its strategy accordingly. In practice, this will mean in all probability replacing the ambitions of the judge of "common beliefs", healer of prejudices and umpire of truth with those of a clarifier of interpretative rules and facilitator of communication; this will amount to the replacement of the dream of the legislator with the practice of an interpreter.

6.2   The Re-Enchantment of the World, or, How Can One Narrate Postmodernity? (1992)

Postmodernity means many different things to many different people. It may mean a building that arrogantly flaunts the 'orders' prescribing what fits what and what should be kept strictly out to preserve the functional logic of steel, glass and concrete. It means a work of imagination that defies the difference between painting and sculpture, styles and genres, gallery and the street, art and everything else. It means a life that looks suspiciously like a TV serial, and a docudrama that ignores your worry about setting apart fantasy from what 'really happened'. It means licence to do whatever one may fancy and advice not to take anything you or the others do too seriously. It means the speed with which things change and the pace with which moods succeed each other so that they have no time to ossify into things. It means attention drawn in all directions at once so that it cannot stop on anything for long and nothing gets a really close look. It means a shopping mall overflowing with goods whose major use is the joy of purchasing them; and existence that feels like a life-long confinement to the shopping mall. It means the exhilarating freedom to pursue anything and the mind-boggling uncertainty as to what is worth pursuing and in the name of what one should pursue it.

Postmodernity is all these things and many others. But it is also – perhaps more than anything else – a *state of mind*. More precisely – a state of those minds who have the habit (or is it a compulsion?) to reflect upon themselves, to search their own contents and report what they found: the state of mind of philosophers, social thinkers, artists – all those people on whom we rely when we are in a pensive mood or just pause for a moment to find out whence we are moving or being moved.

This is a state of mind marked above all by its all-deriding, all-eroding, all-dissolving *destructiveness*. It seems sometimes that post-modern mind is a critique caught at the moment of its ultimate triumph: a critique that finds it ever more difficult to go on being critical just because it has destroyed everything it used to be critical about; with it, off went the very urgency of being critical. There is nothing left to be opposed to. The world and the life in the world have become themselves nothing but an unstoppable and obsessive self-criticism – or so it seems. Just as modernist art, bent on censoring modern reality, ended up in taking apart the very subject-matter of its critique (painting ended up in a clean canvas, writing in an empty page, music in silence: in the desperate attempt to purify the work of the artist, Walter de Maria dug a deep hole near Kassel, Yves Klein invited the art connoisseurs to a private view of blank gallery walls, Robert Barry transmitted his art ideas telepathically to bypass the polluting blight of word and paint, and Rauschenberg put up for sale erased drawings of his artistic friends), so critical theory confronts an object that seems to offer no more resistance; an object that has softened, melted and liquidized to the point that the sharp edge of critique goes through with nothing to stop it. Past tragedies mock themselves in a no-smile-raising grotesque. How ridiculous it seems to try to change the direction of history when no powers give an inkling that they wish to give history direction. How empty seems the effort to show that what passes for truth is false when nothing has the courage and the stamina to declare itself as truth for everybody and for all time. How farcical it seems to fight for genuine art when one can no more drop anything incidentally without the dropped object being proclaimed art. How quixotic to debunk the distortion in the representation of reality once no reality claims to be more real than its representation. How idle it seems to exhort people to go there rather than somewhere else in a world in which everything goes.

The postmodern state of mind is the radical (though certainly unexpected and in all probability undesired) victory of modern (that is, inherently critical, restless, unsatisfied, insatiable) culture over the modern society it aimed to improve through throwing it wide open to its own potential. Many little victorious battles added up to a victorious war. One after another, hurdles have been taken apart, ramparts crushed and locks broken in the incessant, stubborn work of emancipation. At each moment a particular constraint, an especially painful prohibition was under attack. In the end, a *universal dismantling of power-supported structures* has been the result. No new and improved order has emerged, however, from beneath the debris of the old and unwanted one. Postmodernity (and in this it differs from modernist culture of which it is the rightful issue and legatee) does not seek to substitute one truth for another, one standard of beauty for another, one life ideal for another. Instead, it splits the truth, the standards and the ideal into already deconstructed and about to be deconstructed. It denies in advance the right of all and any revelation to slip into the place vacated by the deconstructed/discredited rules. It braces itself for a life without truths, standards and ideals. It is often blamed for not being positive enough, for not being positive at all, for not wishing to be positive and for pooh-poohing positivity as such, for sensing a knife of unfreedom under any cloak of saintly righteousness or just placid self-confidence. The postmodern mind seems to condemn everything, propose nothing. Demolition is the only job the postmodern mind seems to be good at. Destruction is the only construction it recognizes. Demolition of coercive constraints and mental blocks is for it the ultimate purpose and the end of emancipatory effort; truth and goodness, says Rorty, will take care of themselves once we have taken proper care of freedom.

When it happens to be in a self-reflective, philosophical cast, the postmodern mind would point out, against its critics, that despite appearances to the contrary it is not a 'destructive destruction', but a *constructive* one, in which it has been engaged all along. Its job has been a sort of a site-clearing operation. While renouncing what merely passes for the truth, dismantling its past, present and future putative, ossified versions, it uncovers the truth in its pristine form which modern pretensions had maimed and distorted beyond recognition. More than that: the demolition uncovers *the truth of the truth*, truth as residing in the being itself and not in the violent acts performed upon it; truth that has been belied under the domination of legislative reason. The real truth is already there before its laborious construction has started; it is re-posited in the ground on which the elaborate artifices have been erected: ostensibly to display it, in fact to hide and stifle it.

Of this demolition of false pretences the postmodern mind claims to be performing, the 'second Copernican revolution' of Heidegger is often seen as the archetype and trend-setter. As Paul Ricoeur explains, since *Sein und Zeit* appeared in 1927, understanding began to be recognized as the 'mode of being before defining the mode of knowing. It consists essentially in the capacity of *Dasein* to project its most proper possibilities inside the fundamental situation of being in the world'. Heidegger's seminal insight has been taken up and put to manifold uses by his followers – for instance by Gadamer, who took it upon himself to re-examine Dilthey's worried question through Heideggerian spectacles. That question has been subjected to the test in three areas:

> that of the arts, in which our hold of aesthetic reality precedes the distanced judgment of taste; that of history, where the consciousness of being exposed to the labours of history precedes the objectifications of documentary historiography; that of language, where the universally linguistic character of human experience precedes all linguistic, semiotic and semantic methodology. (Ricoeur, 1990, pp. 173–4)

All in all, postmodernity can be seen as restoring to the world what modernity, presumptuously, had taken away; as a *re-enchantment* of the world that modernity tried hard to *dis-enchant*. It is the modern artifice that has been dismantled; the modern conceit of meaning-legislating reason that has been exposed, condemned and put to shame. It is that artifice and that reason, the reason of the artifice, that stands accused in the court of postmodernity.

The war against mystery and magic was for modernity the war of liberation leading to the declaration of reason's independence. It was the declaration of hostilities that made the unprocessed, pristine world into the enemy. As is the case with all genocide, the world of nature (as distinct from the house of culture modernity set out to build) had to be beheaded and thus deprived of autonomous will and power of resistance. At stake in the war was the right to initiative and the authorship of action, the right to pronounce on meanings, to construe narratives. To win the stakes, to win all of them and to win them for good, the world had to be *de-spiritualized*, de-animated: denied the capacity of the *subject*.

The dis-enchantment of the world was the ideology of its subordination; simultaneously a declaration of intent to make the world docile to those who would have won the right to will, and a legitimation of practices guided solely by that will as the uncontested standard of propriety. In this ideology and in the practice it reflected and legitimized, spirit was all on one side and matter all on the other. The world was an *object* of *willed action*: a raw material in the work guided and given form by human designs. Meanings and designs became one. Left to itself, the world had no meaning. It was solely the human design that injected it with sense and purpose. So the earth became a repository of ores and other 'natural resources', wood turned into timber and water – depending on circumstances – into an energy source, waterway or the solvent of waste. The link that may be spotted between earth, forest and water was difficult to perceive between ores, timber and waste disposal; in their new incarnations they were parcelled out between distinct and distant functions and purposes and all their once pristine links were now subject solely to the logic of the latter. And as nature became progressively 'de-animated', humans grew increasingly 'naturalized' so that their subjectivity, the primeval 'givenness' of their existence could be denied and they themselves could be made hospitable for instrumental meanings; they came to be like timber and waterways rather than like forests and lakes. Their dis-enchantment, like that of the world as a whole, stemmed from the encounter between the designing posture and the strategy of instrumental rationality. The achievement of that encounter was the world split between wilful subject and will-less object; between the privileged actor whose will counted and the rest of the world whose will did not count – having been denied or disregarded. It is against such a disenchanted world that the postmodern re-enchantment is aimed.

Modernity, or Desperately Seeking Structure

The kind of society that, retrospectively, came to be called modern, emerged out of the discovery that human order is vulnerable, contingent and devoid of reliable foundations. That discovery was shocking. The response to the shock was a dream and an effort to make order solid, obligatory and reliably founded. This response problematized contingency as an enemy and order as a task. It devalued and demonized the 'raw' human condition. It prompted an incessant drive to eliminate the haphazard and annihilate the spontaneous. As a matter of fact, it was the sought-after order that in advance construed everything for which it had no room or time as contingent and hence lacking foundation. The dream of order and the practice of ordering constitute the world – their object – as chaos. And, of course, as a challenge – as a compulsive reason to act.

   Discovery of contingency was not a feat of reason. One does not see the given-to-hand, much less does one think of it, until it goes bust and lets one down. One does not conceive of regularity unless one is buffeted by the unexpected, one does not notice monotonousness until the fashion in which things behaved yesterday stops being a reliable guide to their conduct tomorrow. Contingency was discovered *together* with the realization that if one wants things and events to be regular, repeatable and predictable, one needs to do something about it; they won't be such on their own. Awareness of the world's contingency and the idea of order as the goal and the outcome of the *practice of ordering* were born together, as twins; perhaps even Siamese twins.

The dissipation of socially supervised routine (theorized as the preordained order of being) could have been an exhilarating experience. But it also kindled a heretofore unknown fear. The weakening of routine was the blessing of freedom for the strong and bold; it was the curse of insecurity for the weak and diffident. The marriage between freedom and insecurity was prearranged and consummated on the wedding night; all subsequent attempts at separation proved vain, and the wedlock remained in force ever since.

The Renaissance celebrated the collapse of the preordained (and thus visible only in its collapse) order as liberation. The withdrawal of God meant a triumphant entry of Man. In Pico della Mirandola's rendering, the Divine Creator said to Adam: 'thou shouldst be thy own free moulder and overcomer; thou canst degenerate to animal, and through thyself be reborn to godlike existence.... Thou alone hast power to develop and grow according to free will' (quoted in Rank, 1932, p. 24). This sort of freedom, if contemplated at all, was previously thought of as a Divine attribute. Now it was human; but as it was human by Divine order (the *only* briefing given by God to man), it was also man's duty. Freedom was a chance pregnant with obligation. It was now up to man to 'be reborn to godlike existence'. This was a life-long task, brandishing no hope of respite. Nothing was to be satisfactory if short of the ultimate, and the ultimate was no less than *perfection*, described by Leon Battista Alberti as a harmony of all the parts fitted together in such a way that nothing could be added, diminished or altered, but for the worse. Human freedom of creation and self-creation meant that no imperfection, ugliness or suffering could now claim the right to exist, let alone claim legitimacy. It was the contingency of the imperfect that spurred the anxiety about reaching perfection. And perfection could be reached only through action: it was the outcome of laborious 'fitting together'. Once a matter of providence and revelation, life had turned into the object of *techne*. The urge to re-make the world was planted in the primary experience of liberation. It was forced into buoyant growth by the fear of the chaos that would overwhelm the world were the search for perfection to be abandoned or even slackened in a moment of inattention.

A pure, unclouded celebration was therefore short; just a brief interlude between the Divine and the man-made orders, between

being what one was and *making oneself what one should be.* From
Erasmus, Mirandola, Rabelais or Montaigne to Descartes or Hobbes
there was but the distance of a generation. And the celebration was
confined to those lucky few who could concentrate on 'moulding
themselves' thanks to the concentration of ample resources, not yet
questioned as a right, and therefore enjoyable without the attendant
worry about foundations. (The celebrations did not go on for long,
however, and could not be universal, as the foundations were bound
to prove shaky or altogether absent, the resources to dry up, and thus
the effort to secure their unhampered flow to clash with the right to
enjoy one's contingency.)

It was in that brief interlude, and among those who could savour
the sweet fruits of the sudden collapse of power-assisted certainties,
that diversity was not merely accepted as the human fate, but lovingly
embraced and hailed as the sign and condition of true humanity.
Openness, readiness to refrain from condemnation of the other and
to argue with, rather than to fight the antagonist, cognitive and
cathexic modesty, settling for the credible instead of chasing the
absolute – were all conspicuous marks of the humanist culture (later,
from the heights of modern ambitions, to be redubbed as the 'Pyr-
rhonian crisis', a moment of weakness before the resurgence of
strength) that for all practical intents and purposes was to be shortly
shelved in dust-gathering libraries for the centuries to come. Harsh
realities of politics in the aftermath of religious wars and the final
collapse of the feudal order made the diversity of lives and relativity of
truths much less attractive, and certainly not at all laudable. Enlightened and not-so-enlightened rulers set out to build anew, wilfully and
by design, the order of things which the anointed monarchs of the
past had stupidly allowed to crumble. When seen from the watch-
towers of new ambitious powers, diversity looked more like chaos,
scepticism like ineptitude, tolerance like subversion. Certainty, orderliness, homogeneity became the orders of the day.

What followed was a long (roughly three centuries long) age of
Cosmopolis (to borrow the apt term recently coined by Stephen
Toulmin [1990]). In the Cosmopolis, the vision of visionaries joined
hands with the practice of practitioners: the intellectual model of an
orderly universe blended with the ordering bustle of the politicians.
The vision was of a hierarchial harmony reflected, as in a mirror, in
the uncontested and uncontestable pronouncements of reason. The
practice was about making the pronouncements, adorned with the
badges of reason, uncontested and uncontestable. As St Augustine's
City of Man reflected the glory of the *City of God*, so the modern,
obsessively legislating, defining, structuring, segregating, classifying,

recording and universalizing state reflected the splendour of universal and absolute standards of truth. Whoever questioned St Augustine's wedlock between the mundane and the divine could only speak in the name of evil and devil; whoever questioned the modern wedlock between absolute truth and absolute power could only speak in the name of unreason and chaos. Dissent had been discredited and delegitimized even before it was spoken – by the very absoluteness of the dominant syndrome, the universalism of its proclaimed ambitions and the completeness of its domination. The new certainty had defined scepticism as ignorance or ill will, and difference as fossilized backwardness, or as a rudiment of bygone ignominy living on borrowed time. In an apt expression of Harry Redner, 'just as in the language of faith God cannot be denied or even seriously questioned, so too in the languages of Progress it is Progress itself that has that status' (Redner, 1982, p. 30).

The different – the idiosyncratic and the insouciant – have been thereby dishonourably discharged from the army of order and progress (as Comte put it, of orderly progress and progressive order). The degradation was unequivocal, complete and irrevocable. There was really no good reason to tolerate the Other who, by definition, rebelled against the truth. As Spinoza justly pointed out – if I know the truth and you are ignorant, to make you change your thoughts and ways is my moral duty; refraining from doing so would be cruel and selfish. 'Modernity was not merely the Western Man's thrust for power; it was also his *mission*, proof of moral righteousness and cause of pride'. From the point of view of reason-founded human order, tolerance is incongruous and immoral.

The new, modern order took off as a desperate search for structure in a world suddenly denuded of structure. Utopias that served as beacons for the long march to the rule of reason visualized a world without margins, leftovers, the unaccounted for – without dissidents and rebels; a world in which, as in the world just left behind, everyone will have a job to do and everyone will be keen to do the job he has to: the *I will* and *I must* will merge. The visualized world differed from the lost one by putting assignment where blind fate once ruled. The jobs to be done were now gleaned from an overall plan, drafted by the spokesmen of reason; in the world to come, design preceded order. People were not born into their places: they had to be trained, drilled or goaded into finding the place that fitted them and which they fitted. No wonder utopias chose architecture and urban planning as both the vehicle and the master-metaphor of the perfect world that would know of no misfits and hence of no disorder; however much they differed in detail, they all lovingly detailed the carefully segregated

and strictly functional urban quarters, the straight, unpolluted geometry of streets and public squares, the hierarchy of spaces and
buildings which, in their prescribed volumes and austerity of adorn-
ment, mirrored the stately sovereignty of the social order. In the city of
reason, there were to be no winding roads, no cul-de-sacs and no
unattended sites left to chance – and thus no vagabonds, vagrants or
nomads.

In this reason-drafted city with no mean streets, dark spots and no-
go areas order *was to be made*; there was to be *no other order*. Hence
the urge, the desperation: there would be as much order in the world
as we manage to put into it. The practice stemming from a conviction
that order can be only man-made, that it is bound to remain an
artificial imposition on the unruly natural state of things and humans,
that for this reason it will forever remain vulnerable and in need of
constant supervision and policing, is the main (and, indeed, unique)
distinguishing mark of modernity. From now on, there would be no
moment of respite, no relaxing of vigilance. The ordering impulse
would be fed ever again by the fear of chaos never to be allayed.
The lid of order would never seem tight and heavy enough. Escape
from the wilderness, once embarked on, will never end.

In a recent study, Stephen L. Collins put the spotlight on the
'Hobbesian problem' as the epitome of this modern spirit:

> Hobbes understood that a world in flux was natural and that order
> must be created to restrain what was natural.... Society is no longer a
> transcendentally articulated reflection of something predefined, ex-
> ternal, and beyond itself which orders existence hierarchically. It is
> now a nominal entity ordered by the sovereign state which is its own
> articulated representative... [Forty years after Elizabeth's death] order
> was coming to be understood not as natural, but as artificial, created by
> man, and manifestly political and social.... Order must be designed to
> restrain what appeared ubiquitous (that is, flux).... Order became a
> matter of power, and power a matter of will, force and calculation....
> Fundamental to the entire reconceptualization of the idea of society
> was the belief that the commonwealth, as was order, was a human
> creation.   (Collins, 1989, pp. 28–9)

To create order means neither to cultivate nor to extirpate the differences. It means *licensing* them. And it means a *licensing authority*.
Obversely, it means also de-legalizing unlicensed differences. Order
can be only an all-inclusive category. It must also remain forever a
belligerent camp, surrounded by enemies and waging wars on all its
frontiers. The unlicensed difference is the main enemy: it is also an
enemy to be eventually conquered – a temporary enemy, a testimony

to inadequacy of zeal and/or resource of the fighting order (for early modern thinkers – one may repeat after Peter de Bolla – 'the heterogenous experiences of the real indicate a number of differences which must be brought to similarity, which must be homogenized into a unitary subject through comparison and combination' [de Bolla, 1989, p. 285]). The subversive power of *unlicensed* difference resides precisely in its *spontaneity*, that is in its indeterminacy *vis-à-vis* the decreed order, that is in its unpredictability, that is in its uncontrollability. In the shape of the unlicensed difference, modernity fought the real enemy: the grey area of ambivalence, indeterminacy and undecidability.

One can hardly imagine a social group more strictly differentiated, segregated and hierarchic than the population of the Panopticon – Jeremy Bentham's grand metaphor of an orderly, reason-led society. Yet *all* residents of the Panopticon – the Overseer, the supervisors and lowliest of the inmates alike – are *happy*. They are happy because they live in a carefully controlled environment, and thus know exactly what to do. Not for them the sorrows of frustration and the pain of failure. The gap between the will and duty has been bridged (Bauman, 1988). Bridging of this gap was, indeed, the *focus imaginarius* of the modern struggle for rationally designed order. It was left for Bentham's genius to perceive that by no other arrangement is the purpose better served and secured than by prison. Or, rather, that the main task of the day overtakes and dwarfs the 'merely functional' distinctions between prisons, houses of detention, houses of correction, workhouses, poorhouses, hospitals, lunatic asylums, schools, military barracks, dormitories and factories. Modernity was a long march to prison. It never arrived there (though in some places, like Stalin's Russia, Hitler's Germany or Mao's China, it came quite close), albeit not for the lack of trying.

Postmodernity, or Hiding from Fear

We have been brought up in the shadow of the sinister warning of Dostoyevsky: if there is no God, everything is permissible. If we happen to be professional social scientists, we have been also trained to share the no less sinister premonition of Durkheim: if the normative grip of society slackens, the moral order will collapse. For whatever reason, we tend to believe that men and women can only be goaded or cajoled, by superior force or superior rhetoric, into peaceful coexistence. So we are naturally inclined to view the prospect of levelling up of hierarchies with horror: only universal mayhem can follow the disappearance of universality-claiming truths. (This is, probably, the main reason why many a philosopher and politician, and that part of each of us where a philosopher or a politician resides, militates against facing contingency as inescapable fate; let alone embracing it as a welcome destiny.) I propose that it is precisely in that horror and this resentment that the most dangerous potential of the postmodern condition lay in ambush.

The threats related to *postmodernity* are highly familiar: they are, one may say, thoroughly *modern* in nature. Now, as before, they stem from that *horror vacui* that modernity made into the principle of social organization and personality formation. Modernity was a continuous and uncompromising effort to fill or to cover up the void; the modern mentality held a stern belief that the job can be done – if not today then tomorrow. The sin of postmodernity is to abandon the effort and to deny the belief; this double act appears to be indeed a sin, once one remembers that abandoning effort and denying belief does not, by itself, neutralize the awesome propelling force of the *fear of void*; and postmodernity has done next to nothing to support its defiance of past pretence with a new practical antidote for old poison.

And thus men and women have been left alone with their fears; they are told by philosophers that the void is here to stay, and by politicians that coping with it is their own duty and worry. Postmodernity has not allayed the fears which modernity injected into humanity once it left it to its own resources; postmodernity only *privatized* these fears. This may be good news: after all, in its collectivized form the struggle against the void all too often ended up in the missions of classes, nations or races – a far cry from the philosophers' dream of eternal peace brought about by the universality of human reason. The privatization of fears may not bring peace of mind, but it just may take away some of the reasons for the wars of classes, nations or races. And yet, the news is not unambiguously good. With fears privatized, the temptation to run for cover remains as potent as ever. But there is no hope left that human reason, and its earthly agents, will make the race a guided tour, certain to end up in a secure and agreeable shelter.

References

Bauman, Zygmunt (1988) *Freedom*. Milton Keynes: Open University Press.
Collins, Stephen (1989) *From Divine Cosmos to Sovereign State: An Intellectual History of Consciousness and the Idea of order in Renaissance England*. Oxford: Oxford University Press.

de Bolla, Peter (1989) *The Discourse of the Sublime: Readings in History, Aesthetics and the Subject*. Oxford: Blackwell.

Rank, Otto (1932) *Art and Artist: Creative Urge and Personality Development*, trans. Charles Francis Atkinson. New York: Knopf.

Redner, Harry (1982) *In the Beginning was the Deed: Reflections on the Passage of Faust*. Berkeley: University of California Press.

Ricoeur, Paul (1990) *Au Jardin des malentendus*, ed. Jacques Leenhardt and Robert Picht. Paris: Actes Sud.

Toulmin, Stephen (1990) *Cosmopolis: The Hidden Agenda of Modernity*. New York: Free Press.

7

Figures of Modernity

7.1 Making and Unmaking of Strangers (1995)

All societies produce strangers; but each kind of society produces its own kind of strangers, and produces them in its own inimitable way. If strangers are the people who do not fit the cognitive, moral, or aesthetic map of the world – one of these maps, two or all three; if they, therefore, by their sheer presence, make obscure what ought to be transparent, confuse what ought to be a straightforward recipe for action, and/or prevent the satisfaction from being fully satisfying, pollute the joy with anxiety while making the forbidden fruit alluring; if, in other words, they befog and eclipse the boundary lines which ought to be clearly seen; if, having done all this, they gestate uncertainty, which in its turn breeds discomfort of feeling lost – then each society produces such strangers, while drawing its borders and charting its cognitive, aesthetic and moral map. It cannot but gestate people who conceal borderlines deemed crucial to its orderly and/or meaningful life and are thus charged with causing the discomfort experienced as the most painful and least bearable.

The most oppressive of nightmares that haunted our century notorious for its fears, gory deeds and dreary premonitions, was best captured in George Orwell's memorable image of a jackboot trampling the human face. No face was secure – as everyone was prone to be charged with the crime of trespassing or transgressing. And since humanity bears ill all confinement while the humans who transgress the boundaries turn into strangers – everyone had reasons to fear the jackboot made to trample the strangers in the dust, squeeze the strange out of the human and keep those not-yet-trampled-but-about-to-be-trampled away from the mischief of boundary ignoring.

Jackboots are parts of uniforms. Elias Canetti wrote of "murderous uniforms". At some point in our century it became common knowledge that men in uniforms are to be feared most. Uniforms were the insignia of the servants of the state, that source of all power, and, above all, coercive power. Wearing uniforms, men become that power in action; wearing jackboots they trample, and trample on the behest and in the name of the state. The state which dressed men in uniforms so that they be allowed and instructed to trample was also the state which saw itself as the fount, the guardian and the sole guarantee of orderly life, a dam protecting order from chaos. It was the state that knew what the order should look like, and that had enough strength and arrogance not only to proclaim all other states of affairs to be disorder and chaos, but also force them to live down to such a condition. This was, in other words, the modern state – that which legislated order into existence and defined order as the clarity of binding divisions, classifications, allocations and boundaries.

The typical modern strangers were the waste of the state's ordering zeal. What the modern strangers did not fit was the vision of order. When you draw dividing lines and set apart the so divided, everything that blurs the lines and spans the divisions undermines the work and mangles its products. The semantic under- and/or over-determination of the strangers corrupted neat divisions and marred the signposts. Their mere being around interfered with the work which the state swore to accomplish, and undid its efforts to accomplish it. The strangers exhaled uncertainty where certainty and clarity should have ruled. In the harmonious, rational order about to be built there was no room – there could be no room – for neither-nors, for the sitting astride, for the cognitively ambivalent. The order-building was a war of attrition waged against the strangers and the strange.

In this war (to borrow Levi-Strauss's concepts) two alternative, but also complementary strategies were intermittently deployed. One was *anthropophagic*: annihilating the strangers by *devouring* them and then metabolically transforming them into a tissue indistinguishable from one's own. This was the strategy of assimilation – making the different similar: the smothering of cultural or linguistic distinctions, forbidding all traditions and loyalties except those meant to feed the conformity of the new and all embracing order, promoting and enforcing one and only measure of conformity. The other strategy was *anthropoemic*: *vomiting* the strangers, banishing them from the limits of the orderly world and barring them from all communication with those inside. This was the strategy of exclusion – confining the strangers within the visible walls of the ghettos or behind the invisible, yet no less tangible prohibitions of *commensality, connubium*, and *commercium*, expelling the strangers beyond the frontiers of the managed and manageable territory; or, when neither of the two measures was feasible – destroying the strangers physically.

The most common expression of the two strategies was the notorious clash between the liberal and the nationalist/racist versions of the modern project. People are different, implied the liberal project, but they are different because of the diversity of local, particularistic traditions in which they grew and matured. They are products of education, creatures of culture, and hence pliable and amenable to re-shaping. The progressive universalization of the human condition – which means nothing else but the uprooting of all parochiality and the powers bent on preserving it, and consequently setting human development free of the stultifying impact of the accident of birth – meant that it was believed pre-determined, stronger-than-human-choice, diversity would fade away. Not so, objected the nationalist/racist project. Cultural remaking has limits which no human effort could transcend. Certain people will never be converted into something other than they are. They are, so to speak, beyond repair. One cannot rid them of their faults; one can only get rid of them, complete with their oddities and evils.

Cultural and/or physical annihilation of strangers and of the strange was therefore, in modern society and under the aegis of the modern state, a *creative* destruction; demolishing, but building at the same time; mutilating, but also straightening up. It was part and parcel of the ongoing order building effort, its indispensable condition and accompaniment. And obversely whenever building-order-by-design is on the agenda, certain inhabitants of the territory to be made orderly in the new way turn into strangers that need to be eliminated. Under the pressure of the modern order-building urge, the strangers lived, so to speak, in a state of suspended extinction. The strangers were, by definition, an anomaly to be rectified. Their presence was defined a priori as temporary, much as the current stage in the prehistory of the order yet to come. A permanent coexistence with the stranger and the strange, and the pragmatics of living with strangers, did not need to be faced point blank as a serious prospect. And it would not need to be as long as modern life remained a life-towards-a-project, as long as that project remained collectivized into a vision of a new and comprehensive order, and as long as the construction of such an order remained in the hands of a state ambitious and resourceful enough to pursue the task. None of these conditions seem to be holding today, though – a time which Anthony Giddens calls "late modernity", Ulrich Beck "reflexive modernity", George Balandier "surmodernity", and I, together with many others, have chosen to call postmodern: the time we live in now, in our part of the world.

Disembedding into Setting Afloat

In its order-building pursuits, the modern state set about discrediting, disavowing and uprooting the intermediary powers of communities and traditions. If accomplished, the task would "disembed" (Giddens) or "disencumber" (MacIntyre) the individuals, give them the benefit of an absolute beginning, set them free to choose the kind of life they wish to live and to monitor and manage its living in the framework of legal rules spelled out by the sole legitimate legislating powers – those of the state. The modern project promised to free the individual from inherited identity. Yet it did not take a stand against identity as such, against having identity, against having a solid, resilent and immutable identity. It only transformed the identity from the matter of ascription into achievement, thus making it an individual task and the individual's responsibility.

Much like that global order which collectively underwrote individual life-efforts, the orderly (comprehensive, cohesive, consistent, and continuous) identity of the individual was cast as a *project, the life project* (as Jean-Paul Sartre, with already retrospective wisdom, articulated it). Identity was to be erected systematically, floor by floor and brick by brick, following a blueprint completed before the work started. The construction called for a clear vision of the final shape, for careful calculation of the steps leading towards it, for long-term planning and seeing through the consequences of every move. Thus there was a tight and irrevocable bond between social order as a project and individual life as a project; the latter was unthinkable without the first. Were it not for the collective efforts to secure a reliable setting for individual actions and choices, constructing a lasting and stable identity and living one's life towards such an identity would be all but impossible.

Settings appear reliable (1) if their life-expectancy is by and large commensurate with the duration of the individual identity-building process; and (2) if their shape seems immune to the vagaries of fads and foibles promoted singly or severally (in sociological jargon – if the "macro-level" is relatively independent of what goes on at the "micro-level"), so that individual projects can be sensibly inscribed in a trustworthy, unyielding eternal frame. This was the case, by and large, through most of modern history, the notorious modern acceleration of change notwithstanding. "Structures" (from physical neighborhoods to currencies) appeared to be endowed with enough resilence and solidity to withstand all inroads of individual endeavours and survive all individual choice, so that the individual could measure itself up against the tough and finite set of opportunities, convinced that choices can be, in principle, rationally calculated and objectively evaluated. When compared to the biologically limited span of individual life, the institutions embodying collective life (and the nation-state first of all) appeared truly immortal. Professions, occupations and related skills did not age faster than their carriers. Neither did the principles of success; delaying gratifications paid up in the long run, and the savings book epitomized the rationality of long-term planning. In modern society which engaged its members primarily in the role of producers/soldiers (Bauman, 1995), adjustment and adaptation pointed one way only: it was fickle individual choice which needed to take stock as well as notice of the "functional" prerequisities of the whole, in more than one sense, to use Durkheim's apt phrase, "greater than itself".

If these are indeed the conditions of the reliability of settings, or of the appearance of the settings as reliable, the context of postmodern life does not pass the test. Individual life-projects find no stable ground to cast the anchor, and individual identity-building efforts cannot rectify the consequences of "disembedding" and arrest the floating and drifting self. Some authors (notably Giddens) point to the widely fashionable efforts of "re-embedding"; being however postulated, rather than pre-given, and sustained solely by the notoriously erratic supplies of emotional energy, the sites of the sought "re-embedment" are plagued with the same unsteadiness and eccentricity which prompts the disembedded selves to seek them in the first place. The image of the world generated by life concerns is now devoid of genuine or assumed solidity and continuity which used to be the trademark of modern structures. The dominant sentiment is the feeling of uncertainty – as to the future shape of the world, as to the right way of living in it, and of the criteria by which to judge the rights and wrongs of the way of living. Uncertainty is not exactly a newcomer in a world with the modern past. What is new, though, is that it is no longer seen as a mere temporary nuisance, which with due effort may be either mollified or altogether overcome. The postmodern world is bracing itself for life under a condition of uncertainty which is permanent and irreducible.

Dimensions of the Present Uncertainty

Many a feature of contemporary living contributes to the overwhelming feeling of uncertainty: to the view of the future as essentially undecidable, uncontrollable and hence frightening, and of the gnawing doubt whether the present contextual constants of action will remain constant long enough to enable reasonable calculation of its effects. We live today, to borrow the felicitous expression coined by Marcus Doel and David Clarke in the atmosphere of *ambient fear*. Let me name just a few of the factors responsible.

1. The new world disorder. After half a century of clear-cut divisions, obvious stakes and evident political purposes and strategies, came the new world devoid of visible structure, and any – however sinister – logic. The power-bloc politics dominated a world frightened by the awesomeness of its possibilities; and whatever came to replace it was frightened by its lack of consistency and direction – and so by the boundlessness of possibilities it forebodes. Hans Magnus Enzensberger fears the impending era of the Civil War (he has counted about forty such wars being waged today from Bosnia through Afghanistan to Bougainville). In France, Alain Minc writes of the coming of New Dark Ages. In Britain, Norman Stone asks whether we are not back in the mediaeval world of beggars, plagues, conflagrations and superstitions. Whether this is or is not the tendency of our time remains, of course, an open question which only the future will answer – but what truly matters now is that auguries like these can be publicly made from the most prestigious sites of contemporary intellectual life, listened to, pondered and debated.

The "Second World" is no more; its former member countries woke up, to use Claus Offe's felicitous phrase, to the "tunnel at the end of the light". But with the demise of the Second World, the "Third World", constituting itself in opposition to power blocks, as the third force in the Bandung era and proving to be such a force through playing up the fears and inanities of the two power-greedy world empires, quit the world political stage. Today twenty or so wealthy, but anxious and unself-assured countries confront the rest of the world which is no longer inclined to look up to their definitions of progress and happiness yet grows by the day ever more dependent on them in preserving whatever happiness or "secondary barbarization" best sums up the overall impact of the modern metropolis on the world periphery.

2. Universal deregulation, the unquestionable and unqualified priority awarded to the irrationality and moral blindness of the competitive market, the unbounded freedom granted to capital and finance at the expense of all other freedoms, the tearing up of the socially woven and societally maintained safety nets, and the disavowal of all but economic reasons gave a new push to the relentless process of polarization, once halted by the legal frameworks of the welfare

state, trade union bargaining rights, labour legislation, and – on a global scale, though in this case much less convincingly – by the initial effects of world agencies charged with redistribution of capital. Inequality, inter-continental, inter-state, and inner-societal (regardless of the level of the GNP boasted or bewailed by the particular country) reaches once again proportions which the world once confident of its ability to self-regulate and self-correct seemed to have left behind once for all. By cautious and, if anything, conservative calculations, rich Europe counts among its citizens about three million homeless, twenty million evicted from the labour market, thirty million living below the poverty line. The switch from the project of community, as the guardian of the universal right to a decent and dignified life, to the promotion of the market, as the sufficient guarantee of the universal chance of self-improvement, adds further to the suffering of the new poor, glossing poverty with humiliation and with denial of consumer freedom, now identified with humanity.

The psychological effects, though, reach far beyond the swelling ranks of the dispossessed and the redundant. Only the few powerful enough to blackmail the other powerfuls into the obligation of a golden handshake can be sure that their home, however prosperous and imposing it may seem today, is not haunted by the spectre of tomorrow's downfall. No jobs are guaranteed, no positions are foolproof, no skills are of lasting utility, experience and know-how turn into liability as soon as they become assets, seductive careers all-too-often prove to be suicide tracks. In their present rendering, human rights do not entail the acquisition of the right to jobs however well performed, or – more generally – the right to care and consideration for the sake of the past merits. Livelihood, social position, acknowledgement of usefulness and the entitlement to self-dignity may all vanish together, overnight and without notice.

3. The other safety nets, self-woven and self-maintained, second lines of trenches, once offered by the neighborhood or the family where one could withdraw to heal the bruises acquired in the market-place, if now not fallen apart, then at least have been considerably weakened. The changing pragmatics of interpersonal relations (the new style of "life politics" described with great conviction by Giddens) are now permeated by the ruling spirit of consumerism and thus cast the other as the potential source of pleasurable experience, and partly to blame: whatever else it is good at, it cannot generate lasting bonds, and most certainly not the bonds which are presumed as lasting and treated as such. The bonds which it does generate have an in-built until-further-notice and withdrawal-at-will clauses and promise neither the granting nor the acquisition of rights and obligations. The slow yet

relentless dissipation and induced forgetting of social skills bears another part of the blame. What used to be put together and kept together by personal skills and with the use of indigenous resources, tends to be mediated now by technologically produced tools purchasable at the market. In the absence of such tools partnerships and groups disintegrate, if they emerge in the first place. Not only the satisfaction of individual needs, but the presence and resilience of collectivities as well, become market-dependent, and so duly reflect the capriciousness and erraticism of the marketplace.

4. As David Bennett recently observed "radical uncertainty about the material and social worlds we inhabit and our modes of political agency within them . . . is what the image-industry offers us" (Bennett, 1994, p. 30). Indeed, the message conveyed today with great power of persuasion by the most ubiquitously effective cultural media (and, let us add, easily read by the recipients against the background of their own experience, aided and abetted by the logic of consumer freedom) is a message of the essential indeterminacy and malleability of the world: in this world, everything may happen and everything can be done, once and for all – and whatever happens, comes unannounced and goes away without notice. In this world, bonds are dissolved into successive encounters, identities into successively worn masks, life-history into series of episodes whose sole lasting importance is their equally ephemeral memory. Nothing can be known for sure, and anything which is known can be known in a different way – one way of knowing being as good, or as bad (and certainly as volatile and precarious) as any other. Betting is now the rule where certainty was once sought and taking risks replaces the stubborn pursuit of goals. Thus there is little in the world which one could consider solid and reliable, nothing reminiscent of a tough canvas in which one could weave one's own life itinerary. Like everything else, the self-image splits into a collection of snapshots, each one having to conjure up, carry and express its own meaning, more often than not without reference to other snapshots. Instead of constructing one's identity, gradually and patiently, like one builds a house, through the slow accretion of floors, rooms, connecting passages, we encounter a series of "new beginnings", experimenting with instantly assembled yet easily dismantled shapes, painted one over the other; a *palimpsest identity*. This is the kind of identity which fits the world in which the art of forgetting is an asset, no less if no more important than the art of memorizing, in which forgetting rather than learning is the condition of continuous fitness, in which ever new things and people enter and exit the field of vision of the stationary camera of attention, without rhyme or reason and where memory itself is like video-tape, always ready to be wiped clean in order to admit new

images, and boasting a life-long guarantee thanks to the wondrous ability of endless self-effacing.

These are some, certainly not all, of the dimensions of post-modern uncertainty. Living under conditions of overwhelming and self-perpetuating uncertainty is an experience altogether different from life subordinated to the task of identity-building and lived in a world bent on the construction of order. The oppositions, which in that other experience underlay and endorsed the meaning of the world and of the life lived in it, lose much of their meaning and most of their heuristic and pragmatic potency in the new experience. Baudrillard has written profusely about this implosion of the sense-giving oppositions. Yet alongside the collapse of the opposition between reality and its simulation, truth and its representation, comes the blurring and the watering down of the difference between the normal and the abnormal, the expected and the unexpected, the ordinary and the bizarre, the domesticated and the wild – the familiar and the strange, us and the stranger. The strangers are no more authoritatively pre-selected, defined and set apart, as they used to be in times of the state-managed, consistent and durable programmes of order-building. They are now as unsteady and protean as one's own identity; as poorly founded, as erratic and volatile. *L'ipséité*, that difference which sets the self apart from the non-self, and "us" apart from "them", is no more given by the pre-ordained shape of the world nor by command from on high. It needs to be constructed, and re-constructed, and constructed once more, and re-constructed again, on both sides at the same time, neither of the sides boasting more durability, or just "giveness", than the other. Today's strangers are by-products, but also the means of production, in the incessant, never conclusive, process of identity building.

Freedom, Uncertainty, and Freedom from Uncertainty

What makes certain people "strangers" and therefore vexing, unner-ving, off-putting and otherwise a "problem", is their capacity to befog and eclipse the boundary lines which ought to be clearly seen. At different times and in different social situations, different boundaries ought to be seen more clearly than others. In our postmodern times, for reasons spelled out above, the boundaries which tend to be simul-taneously most strongly desired and most acutely missed are those of *identity*: of a rightful and secure position in the society, of a space unquestionably one's own, where one can plan one's life with the minimum of interference, play one's role in a game in which the rules do not change overnight and without notice, act reasonably and hope for the better. As we have seen, it is the characteristic of contemporary men and women in our society that they live perpetually with the "identity problem" unresolved. They suffer, one might say, from a chronic absence of resources with which they could build a truly solid and lasting identity, anchor it and stop it from drifting. Or one can go still further and point out a still more incapacitating feature of their life situation, a genuine double-bind which defies most ardent efforts to make identity clear-cut and reliable: while *making* oneself an identity is a strongly felt need and an activity eloquently encouraged by all authoritative cultural media, *having* an identity solidly founded and resistant to cross-waves, having it "for life", proves for many who do not sufficiently control the circumstances of their life, a handicap, rather than an asset; a burden that constrains the movement, a ballast which they must throw out in order to stay afloat. This, we can say, is a universal feature of our times. Hence the anxiety related to the problems of identity and the disposition to be concerned with everything "strange", on which anxiety may be focused and by being focused made sense of, is potentially universal. But the specific gravity of that feature is not the same for everybody; the feature affects different people to a different degree and brings consequences with varying importance to their life-pursuits.

In her illuminating study *Purity and Danger*, Mary Douglas taught us that what we perceive as uncleanness or dirt and busy ourselves scrubbing and wiping out is that anomaly or ambiguity "which must not be included if the pattern is to be maintained" (Douglas, 1970, p. 53). She added a sociological perspective to Jean Paul Sartre's brilliant and memorable analysis of *le visqueux*, "the slimy" in *Being and Nothingness*. The slimy, says Sartre, is docile – or so it seems to be.

> Only at the very moment when I believe that I possess it, behold by a curious reversal, it possesses me...If an object which I hold in my hands is solid, I can let go when I please; its inertia symbolizes for me my total power... Yet here is the slimy reversing the terms: [my self] is suddenly *compromised*, I open my hands, I want to let go of the slimy and it sticks to me, it draws me, it sucks at me... I am no longer the master... The slime is like a liquid seen in a nightmare, where all its properties are animated by a sort of life and turn back against me...If I dive into the water, if I plunge into it, if I let myself sink in it, I experience no discomfort, for I do not have any fear whatsoever that I may dissolve in it, I remain a solid in its liquidity. If I sink in the slimy, I feel that I am going to be lost in it... To touch the slimy is to risk being dissolved in sliminess. (Sartre, 1969, pp. 608–10)

Feeling the difference of the water in which I swim (if know how to swim, that is, and if the current is not too strong for my skills and muscles) is not only free of fear, it is pleasurable. The joy obtained from an uncommon or rare sensuous experience is unclouded by apprehension that something important to me and more lasting than pleasure may result. If anything, immersing myself in the lake or the sea reasserts my power to keep my shape intact, my control over my body, my freedom and mastery: at any time I may come back if I wish, dry myself, not for a moment dreading the compromise, the discreditation of my being myself, being what I think/want myself to be. But imagine taking a bath in a barrelful of resin, tar, honey or treacle. Unlike water, the substance sticks, holds to my skin, will not let go. Rather than invading unpunished a foreign, novel element, I feel invaded and conquered by an element from which there is no escape. I am no longer in control, no more a master of myself. I have lost my freedom.

Thus the slimy stands for the loss of freedom, or for the fear that freedom is under threat and may be lost. But, let us note, freedom is a *relation* – a power relation. I am free if I can act according to my will and reach the results I intend to reach; this means, though, that some other people will be inevitably restricted in their choices by the actions I have taken, and that they will fail to reach the results they wished. In fact, I cannot measure my own freedom in absolute terms, I can measure it only *relatively*, comparing with other people's ability to obtain it. Thus, ultimately, freedom depends on who is stronger – on the distribution of the skills and material resources which the effective action requires. What follows is that the "sliminess" (stickiness, stubbornness, resilience, compromising potency, transforming possession into being possessed, mastery into dependency) of another substance (and this includes, more than anything else, other people) is a function of my own skills and resources. What seems slimy to some, may be fresh, pleasant, exhilarating to others. And the purest of waters may act in the "slimy style" against a person ignorant of the art of swimming, but also a person too weak to defy the powerful element, to withstand the torrent, to steer safely through the rapids, to stay on course among the eddies and the tidal waves. One is tempted to say that much as beauty is in the eye of the beholder, the sliminess of the slimy is in the strength (or in the wallet) of the actor.

The stranger is hateful and feared as is the slimy, and for the same reasons (not everywhere, to be sure, and not at all times). As Max Frisch caustically observed in his essay *Foreignization*, dedicated to our feelings about foreigners coming to stay in our cities: "there are just too many of them – not at the construction sites and not in the factories and not in the stable and not in the kitchen, but during after-hours. Especially on Sunday there are suddenly too many of them." If this is so, then the same relativity principle which rules the constitution of sliminess regulates the constitution of resented strangers, strangers as people to be resented: the acuity of strangerhood, and the intensity of its resentment, grow up with relative powerlessness and diminish with the growth of relative freedom. One can expect that the less people control and can control their lives and their life-founding identities, the more they will be perceived by others as slimy, and the more frantically they will try to disentangle and detach themselves from the strangers they experience as an enveloping, suf-focating, sucking in, formless substance. In the postmodern city, the strangers mean one thing to those for whom "no go areas" (the "mean streets", the "rough district") means "no go in", and those to whom "no go" means "no go out".

For some residents of the modern city, secure in their burglar-proof homes in the leafy suburbs, fortified offices in the heavily policed business centres, and cars bespattered with security gadgets to take them from homes to offices and back, the "stranger" is as pleasurable as the surfing beach, and not at all slimy. The strangers run restaurants promising unusual, exciting experience to the taste buds, sell curious and mysterious objects fit to be talking points at the next party, offer services other people would not stoop or deign to offer, dangle morsels of wisdom refreshingly different from the routine and boring. The strangers are people whom you pay for their offers and for the right to terminate their services once they no longer bring pleasure. At no point do the strangers compromise the freedom of the consumer of their services. As the tourist, the patron, the client, the consumer of services is always in charge: s/he demands, sets the rules, and above all decides when the encounter starts and when it ends. Unambiguously, the strangers are purveyors of pleasures. Their presence is a break in the tedium. One should thank God that they are here. So what is all that uproar and outcry for?

The uproar and the outcry comes, let there be no mistake, from other areas of the city, which the pleasure-seeking consumers never visit, let alone live. Those areas are populated by people not able to choose whom they meet and for how long and to pay for having their choices respected; powerless people, experiencing the world as a trap, not an adventure park, incarcerated in a territory from which there is no exit for them, but which the others may enter at will. Since the only tokens for securing freedom of choice which are legal tender in the consumer society are in short supply or are denied them altogether, they need to resort to the only resources they possess in a quantity large enough to make an impression; they defend the territory under siege, to use Dick Hebdidge's pithy description in *Hiding in the Light*, through "rituals, dressing strangely, striking bizarre attitudes, breaking rules, breaking bottles, windows, heads, issuing rhetorical challenges to the law" (Hebdidge, 1988, p. 18). They react in a wild, rabid, distraught and flustered fashion, as one reacts to the incapacitating pulling/dissolving power of the slimy. The sliminess of strangers, let us repeat, is the reflection of their own powerlessness. It is their own lack of power that crystallizes in their eyes as the awesome might of the strangers. The weak meets and confronts the weak; but both feel like Davids fighting Goliaths. They are both "slimy" to each other, but each fights the sliminess of the other in the name of the purity of one's own.

Ideas, as well as the words that convey them, change their meaning the further they travel, and travelling between the homes of the satisfied consumers and the dwellings of the powerless is a long-distance voyage. If the contented and the secure wax lyrical about the beauty of nationhood, New Jerusalem, glorify the heritage and dignity of tradition, the insecure and hounded bewail the defilement and humiliation of the race. If the first rejoice in a variety of guests and pride themselves on open minds and open doors, the second gnash their teeth at the thought of lost purity. The benign patriotism of the first rebounds as the racism of the second.

Nothing spurs into action as frenzied, licentious and disorderly as the fear of the dissolution of order, embodied in the figure of the slimy. But there is much energy boiling in this chaos; with a degree of skill and cunning it can be gathered and re-deployed to give the unruliness a direction. The fear of the slimy, precipitated by powerlessness, is always a tempting weapon to be added to the armory of the power-greedy. Some of the latter come from the ranks of the frightened. They may try to use the accumulated fear and anger to climb out of the besieged ghetto; or, as Erving Goffman wittily suggested, to make the crutch into a golf club. They may try to condense the diffuse resentment of the weak into an assault against equally weak strangers, thus kneading it into the foundation of their own power, as tyrannical and intolerant as power can be, while all the time claiming to defend the weak against their oppressors. But many other power-seekers are attracted. One needs, after all, only to take a bus to refill the empty tank of nationalism with racist fuel. Not much navigating skill is needed to make the nationalist sails gather the wind blowing from racist hatred; to enlist, by the same token, the powerless in the service of the power-greedy. What one needs is but a reminder of the sliminess of strangers.

Theorizing The Difference: or the Twisted Road to Shared Humanity

The essential difference between the socially-produced modality of modern and postmodern strangers is that while modern strangers were earmarked for annihilation and served as bordermarks for the advancing boundary of the order-under-construction, the postmodern ones are by common consent or resignation, whether joyful or grudging, here to stay. To paraphrase Voltaire's comment on God: if they did not exist, they would have to be invented. And they are indeed invented, zealously and with gusto, patched together with salient or minute and unobtrusive distinction marks. They are useful precisely in their capacity of stranger; their strangerhood is to be protected and caringly preserved. They are indispensable signposts in the life itinerary without plan and direction. They must be as many and as protean as the successive and parallel incarnations of identity in the never ending search for itself.

In an important respect, and with important reasons, ours is a *heterophilic* age. For the sensation-gatherers or experience-collectors that we are, concerned (or, forced to be concerned) with flexibility and openness, rather than with fixity and self-closure, difference comes at a premium. There is a resonance and a harmony between the way we go about our identity problems and the plurality and differentiation of the world in which the identity problems are dealt with, or which we conjure up in the process of that dealing. It is not just that we need the strangers around because, due to the way we are culturally shaped, we would miss precious life-enhancing values in a uniform, monotonous and homogenous world; more than that – such a world without difference could not, by any stretch of the imagination, evolve out of the way in which our lives are shaped and carried on. In our postmodern part of the world the age of *anthropophagic* and *anthropoemic* strategies is over. The question is no longer how to get rid of the strangers and the strange, but how to live with them, daily and permanently. Whatever realistic strategy of coping with the unknown, the uncertain and the confusing can be thought of, it needs to start from recognizing this fact.

And indeed, all intellectually conceived strategies still in competition today seem to accept this. One may say: a new theoretical/ ideological consensus is emerging, to replace another, more than a century old. If the left and right, the progressivists and the reactionaries of the modern period agreed that strangerhood is abnormal and regrettable, and that the superior (because homogenous) order of the future would have no room for the strangers, postmodern times are marked by an almost universal agreement that difference is not merely unavoidable, but good, precious, and in need of protection and cultivation. In the words of that towering figure of the postmodern intellectual right, Alain de Benoist, "we see reasons for hope only in the affirmation of collective singularities, the spiritual reappropriation of heritages, the clear awareness of roots and specific cultures" (1977, p. 9). The spiritual guide of the Italian neo-fascist movement, Julius Evola, is even more blunt: "The racists recognize difference and want difference" (1985, p. 98). Pierre-André Taguieff sums up the process of the postmodern re-articulation of racist discourse, coining the term of "differentialist racism".

Note that these self-admittedly right-wing, even fascist, professions of faith no longer propose, unlike their precursors, that differences between people are immune to cultural interference and that it is beyond human power to make someone into somebody else. Yes, they say, the differences – our differences as much as the differences of the others – are all human products, culturally produced. But, they say, different cultures make their members in different shapes and colours – and *this is good*. Thou shalt not tie together what culture, in its wisdom, has set apart. Let us, rather, help culture, any culture, to go its own separate, and better still inimitable way. The world will be so much richer then. The striking thing, of course, is that a reader unaware that the author of the first quotation was Benoist, could be forgiven for mistaking it for a left programmatic statement; and that Evola's sentence would lose none of its conviction were the word racist replaced by "progressive", "liberal", or for that matter, socialist. Are we not all *bona fide* differentialists today? Multiculturalists? Pluralists?

So it happens that both right and left agree today that the preferable mode of living with strangers is to keep apart. Though perhaps for different reasons, both resent and publicly denigrate the universalist/imperialist/assimilationist ambitions of the modern state, now debunked as innately proto-totalitarian. Disenchanted or repelled by the idea of legislated uniformity, the left, which – being left – cannot live without hope, turns its eyes towards "community", hailed and eulogized as the long lost now rediscovered home of humanity. To be a born again communitarian is widely considered today as a sign of critical standpoint, leftism and progress. Come back community, from the exile to which the modern state confined you; all is forgiven and forgotten – the oppressiveness of parochiality, the genocidal propensity of collective narcissism, the tyranny of communal pressures and the pugnacity and despotism of communal discipline. It is, of course, a nuisance, that one finds some unwelcome and thoroughly repulsive fellows in this bed. How to keep the bed to oneself, how to prove that the unwelcome fellows have no right to be in it – this seems to be the question.

I propose that the racist bedfellows in the bed of communitarianism are perhaps a nuisance for its new occupants, but not at all a surprise. They were there first, and it is their birthright. Both occupants, the old ones and the new, have been lured into that bed by the same promise and the same desire – of "re-embedding", what has been "disembedded", of the release from the formidable task of individual self-construction, and from overwhelming individual responsibility for its results.

The old racism turned its back on the emancipatory chance entailed in the modern project. I propose that, true to its nature, it now turns its back on the emancipatory chance which the changed postmodern context of life holds. Only now, for the reason of curious amnesia or myopia, it is not alone in doing so. It sings in chorus with the lyrical voices of a growing number of social scientists and moral philosophers who extol the warmth of communal homes and bewail the trials and tribulations of the unencumbered, homeless self.

This is a type of critique of the emancipatory failure of modernity which itself does not hold hope for emancipation: this is a misdirected, and, I would say, retrograde critique of the modern project, as it only proposed to shift the site of disablement and subordination from the universalist state to the particularistic tribe. It only replaced one "essentialism" already discredited, by another, not yet fully unmasked in all its disempowering potential. True, communal self-determination may assist the initial stages of the long process of re-empowerment of human subjects – their resolve to resist the disciplinary pressure presently experienced as the most obnoxious and overwhelming. But there is a dangerous, and often overlooked point. This is where re-empowerment turns into a new disempowerment and emancipation into a new oppression. Once on this road, it is difficult to sense where to stop, and, as a rule, it is too late to stop once the point has been recognized after the fact. We would be all well advised to heed to the recent reminder by Richard Stevers in *The Culture of Cynicism: American Morality in Decline*:

> Martin Luther King Jr understood perfectly well that racial and ethnic relations would deteriorate markedly if the cultural value of integration declined. Indeed, this is precisely what has happened in the United States. The various gender, racial and ethnic groups have almost come to occupy mutually exclusive social spaces... The struggle for equality becomes a struggle for power – but power left to itself does not recognize equality. (Stevers, 1994, p. 119)

But there is a genuine emancipatory chance in postmodernity, the chance of laying down arms, suspending border skirmishes waged to keep the stranger away, taking apart the daily erected mini-Berlin walls meant to keep distance and to separate. This chance does not lie in the celebration of born-again ethnicity and in genuine or invented tribal tradition, but in bringing to its conclusion the "disembedding" work of modernity, through laying bare the intricate process of subject self-formation, through revealing the conditions of individual freedom which (rather than the right to consumer satisfaction) constitutes the hard core of citizenship, which in its turn transcends both national and tribal limitations through focusing on the right to choose one's identity as the sole universality of the citizen/human, on the ultimate, inalienable individual responsibility for the choice, and through laying bare the complex state – or tribe – managed mechanisms aimed at depriving the individual of that freedom of choice and that responsibility. The chance of human togetherness depends on the rights of the stranger and not on the answer to the question who is entitled – the state or the tribe – to decide who the strangers are.

Jacques Derrida, when interviewed by Robert Maggiori for *Liberation* (24 November 1994), appealed for rethinking rather than abandoning the modern idea of humanism. The "human right", as we begin to see it today, but above all as we may and ought to see it, is not the product of legislation, but precisely the opposite: it is what sets the limit "to force, declared laws, political discourses" and the "founded" rights (regardless who has, or demands, or usurps the prerogative to "found" authoritatively). "The human" of the traditional humanist philosophy, including the Kantian subject, is, Derrida suggests, "still too 'fraternal', subliminally virile, familial, ethnic, national etc". What, I suggest, follows from this, is that modern theorizing of human essence and human rights erred on the side of leaving too much, rather than too little, of the "encumbered" or "embedded" element in its idea of the human – and it is for this fault, rather than for siding too uncritically with the homogenising ambitions of the modern state and hence placing the "encumbering" or "embedding" authority on the wrong site, that it ought to be subjected to critical scrutiny and re-assessment.

That re-assessment is a philosophical task. But saving the possibility of emancipation from being stillborn, sets, besides the philosophical, a political task. We have noted that the odious "sliminess" of the stranger progresses as the freedom of the individuals faced with the duty of self-assertion declines. We have also noted that the postmodern setting does not so much increase the total volume of individual freedom, as re-distribute it in an increasingly polarised fashion: intensifies it among the joyfully and willingly seduced, while tapering it almost beyond existence among the deprived and panoptically regulated, with this polarization uncurbed, one can expect the present duality of the socially produced status of strangers to continue unabated. On one pole, strangerhood (and difference in general) will go on being constructed as the source of pleasurable experience and aesthetic satisfaction; on the other, as the terrifying incarnation of the unstoppable rising sliminess of the human condition, as the effigy for all future ritual burning of its horrors. And power politics will offer its usual share of opportunities for short-circuiting the poles: to protect their own emancipation-through-seduction, those close to the first pole would seek domination-through-fear over those close to the second pole, and so would aid and abet their cottage industry of horrors. Sliminess of strangers and the politics of exclusion stem from the logic of polarization – from the increasingly Two Nations, Mark Two condition indicated in my *Legislators and Interpreters*, and this is the case because the polarization arrests the process of individualization, or genuine and radical "disembedding" for the "other nation", for the oppressed who have been denied the resources for identity-building and so also (for all practical intents and purposes) the tools of citizenship. It is not merely income and wealth, life expectation and life conditions, but also – and perhaps most seminally – the right to individuality that is being increasingly polarised. And as long as it stays this way, there is little chance for the de-sliming of strangers.

References

Bauman, Zygmunt (1995) "A Catalogue of Postmodern Fears," in *Life in Fragments: Essays in Postmodern Morality*. Oxford: Blackwell.

Bennett, David (1994) "Hollywood's Indeterminacy Machine". *Arena 3*.

de Benoist, Alain (1977) *Dix ans de combat culturel pour une Renaissance*. Paris: Greece.

Douglas, Mary (1970) *Purity and Danger*. Harmondsworth: Penguin.

Evola, Julius (1985) *Eléments pour une éducation raciale*. Paris: Puiseaux.

Hebdidge, Dick (1988) *Hiding in the Light*. London: Routledge.

Sartre, Jean-Paul (1969) *Being and Nothingness: An Essay on Phenomenological Ontology*, trans. H. E. Barres. London: Methuen.

Stevers, R (1994) *The Culture of Cynicism: American Morality in Decline*. Oxford: Blackwell Publishers.

7.2   Parvenu and Pariah: The Heroes and Victims of Modernity (1997)

Socially, modernity is about standards, hope and guilt. Standards –
beckoning, alluring, or prodding; but always stretching, always a step
or two ahead of the pursuers, always forging onward just a little bit
quicker than their chasers. And always promising that the morrow
will be better than the now. And always keeping the promise fresh and
unsullied, since the morrow will forever be a day after. And always
mixing the hope of reaching the promised land with the guilt of not
walking fast enough. The guilt protects the hope from frustration; the
hope sees to it that the guilt never dries up. 'L'homme est coupable',
observed Camus, that uniquely perspicacious correspondent from the
land of modernity, 'mais il l'est de n'avoir su tirer de lui-même'
(Camus, 1964, p. 111).

Psychically, modernity is about identity: about the truth of existence
being not-yet-here, being a task, a mission, a responsibility. Like the
rest of standards, identity stays stubbornly ahead: one needs to run
breathlessly to reach it. And so one runs, pulled by hope and pushed
by guilt, though the running, however fast, feels eerily like crawling.
Surging ahead towards perpetually enticing and perpetually unfulfilled identity looks uncannily like recoiling from the flawed, illegitimate reality of the present.

Both socially and psychically, modernity is incurably self-critical:
an endless, and in the end prospectless, exercise in self-cancelling
and self-invalidating. Truly modern is not the *readiness* to delay
gratification, but the *impossibility* of being gratified. All achievement is but a pale copy of its paragon. 'Today' is but an inchoate
premonition of tomorrow; or, rather, its inferior, marred reflection.
What is is cancelled in advance by *what is to come*. But it draws
its significance and its meaning – its only meaning – from that can-
cellation.

In other words, modernity is the impossibility of staying put. To be
modern means to be on the move. One does not necessarily choose to
be on the move – as one does not choose to be modern. One is set on
the move by being cast in the kind of world torn between the beauty
of the vision and the ugliness of reality – reality having been made
ugly by the beauty of the vision. In such a world, all residents are
nomads; but nomads who wander in order to settle. Round the corner
there is, there should be, there must be, a hospitable land in which to
settle; but behind every corner new corners appear, with new frustra-
tions and new, yet undashed hopes.

The habitat of nomads is the desert – that place-no-place of which Edmond Jabès wrote that in it 'there are no avenues, no boulevards, no blind alleys and no streets. Only – here and there – fragmentary imprints of steps, quickly effaced and denied' (Jabès, 1989, p. 34). Effacing yesterday's footprints is all there is to the chimeric home-liness of the overnight stay; it makes the arrival feel, comfortingly, like being at home – that is, until it also turns into an imprint to be denied and effaced. The sight of tents pitched yesterday on the site of the overnight stay is reassuring: it fences off a plot of the desert so that it may feel like an oasis and give a sense of purpose to yesterday's wanderings. These tents pitched yesterday, being but tents, call, how-ever, the bluff of self-congratulation. They prove, were proof needed, the self-deception of existence which wants to forget its nomadic past; it shows home to be but a point of arrival, and an arrival pregnant with new departure.

Wherever they come and dearly wish to stay, the nomads find themselves to be parvenus. Parvenu, *arriviste*; someone already *in*, but not quite *of*, the place; an aspiring resident without a residence permit. Someone reminding the older tenants of the past which they want to forget and the future they would rather wish away; someone who makes the older tenants run for shelter in hastily erected permit-issuing offices. The parvenu is told to carry the 'just arrived' label, so that all the others may trust their tents to be cut in rock. The parvenu's stay must be declared temporary, so that the stay of all the others may feel eternal.

The older tenants hate the parvenus for awaking the memories and premonitions they struggle hard to put to sleep. But they can hardly do without parvenus, without some of them being branded parvenu, set apart, charged with carrying the bacillus of restlessness in their bodies; it is thanks to such a branded part, and them only, that the whole may think that the bad dreams and the morbid premonitions are other people's tales and do not quite apply to themselves. The parvenu needs a parvenu in order not to feel a parvenu. And so nomads fight other nomads for the right to issue residence permits to each other. It is the only way they can make their own residence feel secure. The only way in which they can fix time which refuses to stay still is to mark the space and protect the marks against being effaced or moved. At least, such is their desperate hope.

In Robert Musil's incisive description, the train of events is a train unrolling its rails ahead of itself. The river of time is a river sweeping its banks along with it. (Musil, 1965, p. 174). It was the modern 'melting of solids and profaning the sacreds' that brought about such trains and such rivers. Premodern trains ran predictably and boringly in circles, much like children's toy trains do. And premodern rivers stayed in their beds for a time long enough to feel immemorial. As Wylie Sypher observed, 'in any society where the class structure is so closed that everyone has the place and knows it – and keeps it', there is no place for a parvenu nor is there a purpose a parvenu could conceivably serve: 'but the nineteenth century produced a horde of parvenus' (Sypher, 1960, p. 104). Not that inordinately many people began to challenge their class-bound or otherwise-bound definitions and refused to heed their place; but the contours of places had been themselves washed up – the river banks having been swept along with the rivers, and uncertainty called *the new*, or *the better*, or *progress*, having become the only official destination of trains. Places and their names were now to be *made* (and, inevitably, re-made) 'as one goes'. In Hannah Arendt's memorable phrase, *man's autonomy turned into the tyranny of possibilities*. The small print of the great modern Act of Emancipation carried an injunction against the restfulness of certainty.

Definitions are *born with*; identities are *made*. Definitions tell you who you are, identities allure you by what you are not yet but may yet become. Parvenus were people in frantic search of identities. They chased identities because, from the start, they *had been denied* definitions. It was only too easy to conclude that it was their restlessness that put paid to definitions, and charge them with the criminal act of breaking the border-signposts. Once hurled in the vast expanse of unlimited possibilities, the parvenus were an easy prey: there were no fortified places in which to hide, no trusty definitions to wear as an armour. And from all places still protected by old ramparts, and from all places that strove to build new ones, poisonous arrows were showered.

Early in his life, Goethe's Wilhelm Meister found out that only young aristocrats can count on being taken for *what they are*, all others would be appraised or condemned for *what they do*. Wilhelm Meister drew the only logical conclusion to be drawn; he joined the theatre. On the stage, he took on and took off *roles*. This is what he was doomed to do in life anyway, but at least on stage – and only on stage – everyone expected roles to be but roles and to be played, and dropped, and replaced by other roles. In life, he would be expected to do the opposite or at least pretend that he was doing it: he would be expected to be *what he is*, though this is precisely what he was denied the right to.

Most parvenus cannot follow Meister's choice. *Life* is their stage, and in life, unlike in the theatre, skillful acting is called insincerity, not finesse; it is precisely to squeeze it out from the daily and the normal that acting as an honourable activity has been confined inside theatre walls. In life, roles must deny being roles and pretend to be identities, even if identities are not available in any other shape or form but that of roles. No one learns this truth better than the parvenus – living as they do under constant, relentless pressure (to quote Hannah Arendt) 'to have to adapt their taste, their lives, their desires'; who are 'denied the right to be themselves in anything and in any moment' (Arendt, 1986, p. 247).

Having learned the rules of the game does not mean being wiser, though. Even less does it mean being successful. There is little the parvenus can do to change their plight, however strongly they desire to do so. 'One cannot modify one's image: neither the thought, nor freedom, lie, nausea, or disgust can help one to get out of one's proper skin' (Arendt, 1986, p. 31). And yet getting out of one's proper skin is exactly what one is expected to do. The other-directed, other-monitored and other-evaluated parvenus are asked to prove the legality of their presence by being self-directed, self-monitored and self-evaluating, and *being seen* to be such. Wilhelm Meister has prudently *chosen* to be an actor: his modern successors are *forced* to be actors – though they risk condemnation and ridicule once they consent to their fate. A vicious circle, if there ever was one. And, as if to rub salt into the wound, there is that deafening silence, that overpowering indifference, that baffling aloofness, the 'I wash my hands' gesture of the Pontius Pilates who sit in judgement. As Kafka wrote in *The Trial*, 'The court wants nothing from you. It receives you when you come and dismisses you when you go.'

The silence of the court makes the defendant into his own judge: or rather it seems to be the case. With the prosecutor abstaining from censorious speeches and no judge to brief the jury, it is up to the defendants to prove their innocence. But innocence of what? Their guilt, after all, is nothing else but the very fact of having been charged, of standing in judgement. And this is one guilt they cannot deny, however smartly they argue their innocence, and however massive is the evidence they gather to support the argument.

By the whim of French legislature, the blacks of Martinique and Guadeloupe have been appointed Frenchmen, unlike the blacks of Sénégal or Côte d'Ivoire or the Arabs of Morocco. Whatever is said or written about the rights of Frenchmen extends to them; nothing remains to be proved and thus no court summonses have been issued or need to be issued. Yet the absence of a court does not mean innocence: it only means that no final judgement will be ever passed and that innocence will be never certified. The silence of the Law means the endlessness of trial. The blacks of Martinique and Guadeloupe

have to prove that their Frenchness requires no proof...Not unlike
Weber's Calvinists, they must live a life of virtue (a virtue which, in
their case, is called 'Frenchness') without the trust that the virtue will
be rewarded and despite the agonizing suspicion that even if it were
they would not know it anyway. All around agree that they acquit
themselves of the task admirably. They excel in schools. They are
the most loyal and dedicated civil servants. Louder still than their
co-citizens of a paler shade of skin they demand that the French
borders be closed to those alien blacks of Chad or Cameroon 'who
have no right to be here'. They even join Le Pen's National Front to
promote the purification of La Patrie from the hordes of the parvenus
bound to dilute the very Frenchhood they wish to embrace. By the
most finical of fastidious standards, the blacks of Martinique and
Guadeloupe are exemplary Frenchmen. To most exemplary Frenchmen this is exactly what they are – black Martinicans and Guadelou-
pians passing for exemplary Frenchmen. Well, it is precisely this
earnest effort to be exemplary Frenchmen that makes them the blacks
of Martinique or Guadeloupe...The more they do to turn into something else than they are, the more they are what they have been called
not to be. Or have they indeed been called?

To the many versions of Abraham's answer to God's call, considered by Kierkegaard, Franz Kafka, the great spokesman for the parvenus of this world, added his own: another Abraham – 'who really
does want to perform the sacrifice properly...but who cannot believe
that he has been chosen, the repulsive old man and his dirty son'.
'Although he was afraid of being laughed at, and even more afraid of
joining in the laughter, his greatest fear was that, if he were laughed at,
he would look even older and even more repulsive, and his son even
dirtier. An Abraham who comes uncalled!'

For the parvenus the game is unwinnable, at least as long as it goes
on being played by the set rules, while the exit from the game means
rebellion against the rules; indeed, a reversal of rules. Although, as
Max Frisch put it, *always* and *for everybody* in our restless world of
modernity 'identity means refusing to be what others want you to be',
you are refused the right to refuse; you have no such right, not in *this*
game, not as long as the umpires have their way. And so the frustrated
dedication turns into mutiny. The myth of belonging is exploded, and
the dazzling light of the explosion draws out of its exilic darkness the
truth of the incompleteness, the until-further-noticeness of the wanderer's existence. Being in the world the way one is (or imagines
oneself to be, or wants to be) at home, could be accomplished solely
in another world, a world one can reach only through the act of
redemption.

For parvenus like Lukács and Benjamin, as Ferenc Feher observed, 'the natural way of belonging, the desire for which never left either one, was blocked... neither could become assimilated or a nationalist.' The desire of belonging could only point towards the future, beyond the suffocating crampedness of the here and now. There was no belonging in sight except on the other side of redemption. And redemption 'can either come in the form of the Last Judgement, where there is one single yardstick to measure with, and the Supreme Authority sitting in court; or in the form of a conciliatory act of redeeming all those who shared in the community of endless human suffering' (Heller and Feher, 1991, p. 303). One could struggle for a new certitude to put paid to the uncomfortable pretensions of the present one; seek the as-yet-undiscredited authority hoped to proclaim and enforce new canons and new norms. Or one could part ways with certitudes old, new, and still to come – and follow Adorno's injunction, that only experiments are legitimate, when certitudes are no more. Both alternatives have been embraced and tried.

The parvenu Lukács spent his life searching for the authority bold and mighty enough to dismiss the judgements of today and proclaim its own judgement as if it were the Last – be it the aesthetically perfect form or the distant alliance of proletarian sufferings with universal truth. In this he followed a long string of other parvenus, from Karl Marx – announcing the universality of belonging imminent once universal man is stripped of humiliating and degrading parochial liveries – through Karl Mannheim, struggling to reforge the homelessness of the itinerant sophist into the patent of judgement superior to all settled opinions – to Husserl, making the truth-bearing subjectivity transcendental, and thus entitled to brush off the admittedly false pretensions of this-worldly subjectivities.

Benjamin's world, on the other hand, was a series of historical moments pregnant with premonitions yet littered with the corpses of miscarried hopes; one moment, for that reason, is not particularly different from another. The twin dangers against which the life-work of Benjamin militates are, in Pierre V. Zima's words, 'la différence absolue et la disjonction idéologique (la *position* d'un des deux termes)' and 'le dépassement (hégélien, marxien) vers l'affirmation, vers la *position* d'un troisième terme sur un plan plus élevé' (Zima, 1981, p. 137). Under Benjamin's pen, ambivalence turns into the crow's nest from which the archipelago of strangled chances can be sighted; instead of a malady to be cured, ambivalence is now the value to be cherished and protected. The angels – Benjamin noted in his *Agesilaus Santander* (the anagram, deciphered by Scholem as *Der Angelus Satànus*) – 'new ones each moment in countless hosts, are created so that, after they have sung their hymn before God, they cease to exist and pass away into nothingness'. And Adorno commented: Benjamin was one of the first to note that the 'individual who thinks becomes problematic to the core, yet without the existence of anything supra-individual in which the isolated subject could gain spiritual transcendence without being oppressed; it is this that he expressed in defining himself as one who left his class without, however, belonging to another' (Adorno, 1988, p. 14). Well, like Lukács, Benjamin was not alone on the road he has chosen. Simmel, with his uncanny flair for decomposing any, however mighty, a structure, into a bunch of human, all-too-human thoughts and emotions, was there first; and many would follow, to mention but Lévi-Strauss debunking progressive history with a pointer as one more tribal myth, Foucault with the discourses that themselves spawn all the limits which stand to confine and channel their formation, or Derrida with realities dissembled into the texts embracing each other in the never ending quadrille of interpretations.

As in so many similar cases, the modern revolution ended in parricide – poetically intuited by Freud in his desperate effort to penetrate the mystery of culture. The most brilliant and most faithful children of modernity could not express their filial loyalty otherwise than by becoming its gravediggers. The more they were dedicated to the construction of the artifice which modernity set about to erect, having first dethroned and legally incapacitated nature – the more they sapped the foundations of the edifice. Modernity, one may say, was from the start pregnant with its own postmodern *Aufhebung*. Her children were genetically determined to be her detractors, and – ultimately – her demolition squad. Those cast as parvenus (those-who-have-arrived), yet refused the comfort of arrival, were bound sooner or later to decry the safety of *any* safe havens; in the end they were bound to question the arrival itself as a plausible or desirable end of the travel.

Hence the astonishing case of a culture engrossed in a tooth-and-nail struggle with the social reality it was supposed, as all cultures should, to reflect and serve. In this disarticulation and the ensuing enmity between culture and reified existence modernity stands perhaps alone among all known societal arrangements. One can confidently define modernity as a form of life marked by such disarticulation: as a social condition under which *culture cannot serve reality otherwise than through undermining it*.

But hence also the uniquely tragic – or is it schizophrenic? – character of modern culture, the culture that feels truly at home only in its homelessness. In that culture, desire is stained with fear, while horror bears attractions difficult to resist. That culture dreams of belonging yet fears locks and barred windows; it dreads the solitude called freedom yet still more than anything else resents oaths of loyalty. At whatever direction it turns, that culture – like the hungry rats of Miller and Dollard's maze – finds itself suspended at the point of ambivalence, where the lines of falling allurement and rising repulsion cross. Walter Benjamin reproached his friend in entrapment and adversary in the search for escape, Gershon Scholem: 'I almost believe that you desire this in-between state, yet you ought to welcome any means of ending it.' To which Scholem replied: 'You are endangered more by your drive for community... than by the horror of loneliness that speaks from so many of your writings' (Schoem, 1982, pp. 229, 234).

In the Indian caste system, the pariah was a member of the lowest caste or *of no caste*. In an untouchable order of belonging, who could be more untouchable than those who did not belong anywhere? Modernity proclaimed no order untouchable, as all untouchable orders were to be replaced with a new, artificial order where roads are built that lead from the bottom to the top and so no one belongs anywhere forever. Modernity was thus the hope of the pariah. But the pariah could stop being a pariah only by becoming – struggling to become – a parvenu. And the parvenu, having never washed out the stain of his origin, laboured under a constant threat of deportation back to the land he tried to escape. Deportation in case he failed; deportation in case he succeeded too spectacularly for the comfort of those around. Not for a moment did the hero stop being a potential victim. Hero today, victim tomorrow – the dividing wall between the two conditions was but paper-thin. Being on the move meant belonging nowhere. And belonging nowhere meant not to count on anybody's protection: indeed, the quintessence of the pariah existence was not to be able to count on protection. The quicker you run, the faster you stay put. The greater the frenzy with which you struggle to cut yourself off from the caste of the pariah, the more you expose yourself as the pariah of non-belonging.

It was the alluring image of a majestic artifice shimmering at the end of the tunnel that set the pariah on his journey and transformed him into the parvenu. It was the agony of the endless travel that dimmed the shine of the artifice and dented its attraction: looking back on the road travelled, the seekers of homes would dismiss their past hopes as a mirage – and they would call their new frustrated sobriety the end of utopia, the end of ideology, the end of modernity, or the advent of the postmodern age.

And so they would say: artificial homelands are hallucinations at best, vicious delusions at worst. No more revolutions to end all revolutions. No more stretching oneself towards the sweet future that turns bitter the moment it becomes the present. No more philosopher kings. No more salvation by society. No more dreams about identities that are not – dreams that spoil the enjoyment of the definitions that are. Travel has not brought redemption to the parvenu. Perhaps once there is nowhere to arrive, the sorry plight of the *arriviste* will be cancelled together with the travel?

With the setting of the universal sun, wrote the schoolboy Karl Marx, moths gather to the light of the domestic lamp. With the drying up of the hi-tech artificial lake of universality, yesteryear's putrescent bogs of parochiality glisten invitingly as the natural havens for all who need to swim safely. No more salvation by society – but perhaps *community* will make the salvation unnecessary? 'We should not look for skyhooks, but only for toeholds' is how Richard Rorty sums up the mood of the bereaved, and proceeds to praise the ethno-centrism and to advise us, rather than wasting our time in the vain search for objectivity and universal standpoints, to apply ourselves to the questions, 'With what communities should you identify?' and 'What should I do with my aloneness?' (Rorty, 1991, pp. 13–14). Isaiah Berlin, on the other hand, tells his interviewers that there is nationalism which is rapacious, intolerant, cruel and bad in many other ways, but that there is also nationalism which is warm, cosy, at peace with nature and itself and therefore also, hopefully, with its neighbours: 'le doux nationalisme', as conscientious Frenchmen, baffled by the spectacular successes of Le Pen, and desperately trying to steal a march on the sinister adversary, call it. The tired wanderer sentenced to the life of a parvenu agony still wants to belong. But he gave up the hope that belonging can be attained through universality. He believes no more in long round-about routes. He dreams now of shortcuts. Or, better still, of arriving without travelling; coming home without really ever moving out.

Whatever used to be a virtue turned into vice. And the vices of yore have been (and one hopes: not posthumously) rehabilitated. The verdict has been quashed, those who passed it condemned or dismissed as incompetent judges. What modernity set to destroy, has its day of sweet vengeance. Community, tradition, the joy of being *chez soi*, the love of one's own, the sticking to one's kind, the pride of being so stuck, the roots, the blood, the soil, the nationhood – they no more stand condemned; on the contrary, it is their critics and detractors, the prophets of universal humanity, who are now challenged to prove their case and of whom it is doubted that they ever will.

Perhaps we live in a postmodern age, perhaps not. But we do live in the age of tribes and tribalism. It is tribalism miraculously reborn, that injects juice and vigour into the eulogy of community, the acclaim of belonging, the passionate search for tradition. In this sense at least, the long roundabout of modernity has brought us to where our ancestors once started. Or so it may seem.

The end of modernity? Not necessarily. In another respect, after all, modernity is very much with us. It is with us in the form of the most defining of its defining traits: that of hope, the hope of making things better than they are – since they are, thus far, not good enough. Vulgar preachers of unadorned tribalism and elegant philosophers of communally based forms of life alike teach us what they do in the name of changing things to the better. Whatever good the ideas of 'objectivity' and 'transcendence' have done for our culture can be attained equally well by the idea of 'community', says Rorty – and this is precisely what makes that latter idea attractive for yesterday's seekers of the universal roads to a world fit for human habitation. Rational designs of artificial perfection, and the revolutions meant to imprint them on the shape of the world all failed abominably to deliver on their promise. Perhaps communities, warm and hospitable, will deliver what they, the cold abstractions, could not deliver. We still want the work to be done; we just let drop the tools which have been proved useless and reach for others – which, who knows?, may still do the job. One may say that we still agree that marital happiness is a good thing; only we would no longer endorse Tolstoy's opinion that all happy marriages are happy in the same way.

We know quite well why we dislike the tools we have abandoned. For two centuries or so people deserving or demanding to be listened to with attention and respect told the story of a human habitat which curiously coincided with that of the political state and the realm of its legislative powers and ambitions. The human world was, in Parsons's memorable rendering, the 'principally co-ordinated' space – the realm upheld or about to be upheld by uniform principles maintained by the joint efforts of the legislators and the armed or unarmed executors of their will. It was such an artificial space that was represented as a habitat which 'fits naturally' human needs and – most importantly – fits the need to gratify the needs. The 'principally co-ordinated', possibly rationally designed and monitored, society was to be that good society modernity set about constructing. Two centuries is a long time – enough for all of us to learn what solitary great minds of Jeremy Bentham's type intuited from the start: that rationally designed 'principal co-ordination' fits equally well a school and a hospital as it fits a prison and a workhouse; and to find out that such a universality of application makes even the school and the hospital feel like a prison or a workhouse. That period has also shown that the wall separating the 'benign' brand of rational engineering from its malignant, genocidal variety is so rickety, slippery and porous that – to paraphrase Bertrand Russell – one does not know when one should start to cry...

As for the communities – those allegedly uncontrived, naturally growing organisms, toeholds instead of skyhooks – we do not yet know all those things we know only too well about the Grand Artifice modernity promised to build. But we may guess. We know that the modern zest for designed perfection condensed the otherwise diffuse heterophobia, and time and again channelled it, Stalin- or Hitler-style, towards genocidal outlets. We may only surmise that the messy tribalism suspicious of universal solutions would gravitate towards exilic, rather than genocidal, outlets for heterophobia. Separation rather than subjugation, confinement or annihilation. As Le Pen put it, 'I adore North Africans. But their place is in the Maghreb.' We know as well that the major conflict of the modern setting grew from the inherent ambivalence of the assimilatory pressures, which prodded towards effacing the differences in the name of a universal human pattern, while simultaneously recoiling before the success of the operation – but we may only hypothesize that a similarly conflict-pregnant ambivalence will be disclosed in the postmodern accolade of difference, which veers between the equally unpalatable and indefensible extremes of 'wet liberalism', that meekly surrenders the right to compare and evaluate the others, and rampant tribalism, denying the others the right to compare and evaluate.

There is no certainty – not even a high probability – that in the universe populated by communities no room will be left for the pariah. What seems more plausible, however, is that the parvenu's route of escape from the pariah status will be closed. Mixophilia may well be replaced with mixophobia; tolerance of difference may well be wedded to the flat refusal of solidarity; monologic discourse, rather than giving way to a dialogic one, will split into a series of soliloquies, with the speakers no more insisting on being heard, but refusing to listen into the bargain.

These are real prospects, real enough to give pause to the joyful chorus of sociologists welcoming the new soft world of communities.

Sociology has a long and distinguished record of sycophancy. Since its birth, it established itself as the principal poet-laureate of the state-centred and state-coordinated society, of the state bent on prohibiting everything which has not been first made obligatory. With the state no more interested in uniformity, losing interest in culture as a drilling routine and gladly leaving the job of social integration to variety-loving market forces, sociology is desperately seeking new courts where the skills and experience of pensioned courtiers could be gainfully employed. For many, the endemically fissiparous mini-courts of imagined communities, home ideologies and tribally invented traditions seem just the thing they need. Once more, though in a strikingly different way from before, one can flatter the practice with theoretical groundings by drawing elegant diagrams of messy reality. Once more one can herald a new ambivalence as a logical solution, and a definitive improvement on the old one. Courtiers' habits die hard.

References

Adorno, Theodor W. (1988) 'Introduction to Benjamin's Schriften (1955),' in Gary Smith (ed.) *On Walter Benjamin: Critical Essays and Recollections.* Cambridge, MA: MIT Press.

Arendt, Hannah (1986) *Rahel Varnhagen: la vie d'une Juive allemande à l'époque du Romantisme,* trans. Henri Plard. Paris: Tierce.

Camus, Albert (1964) *Carnets, janvier 1942 – mars 1951.* Paris: Gallimard.

Heller, Agnes and Feher, Ferenc (1991) *The Grandeur and Twilight of Radical Universalism.* New Brunswick, NJ: Transaction.

Jabès, Edmond (1989) *Un étranger avec, sous le bras, un livre de petit format.* Paris: Gallimard.

Musil, Robert (1965) *The Man without Qualities,* vol. 2, trans. Eithne Wilkins and Ernst Kaiser. New York: Capricorn.

Rorty, Richard (1991) *Objectivity, Relativity and Truth: Philosophical Papers,* vol. 1. Cambridge: Cambridge University Press.

Scholem, Gershon (1982) *Walter Benjamin: The Story of a Friendship.* London: Faber & Faber.

Sypher, Wylie (1960) *Rococo to Cubism in Art and Literature.* New York: Vintage.

Zima, Pierre V. (1981) 'L'Ambivalence dialectique: entre Benjamin et Bakhtine.' *Revue d'esthétique* 1.

8

The Century of Camps

8.1 Sociology After the Holocaust (1989)

> *Civilization now includes death camps and* Muselmänner *among its material and spiritual products*
> **Richard Rubenstein and John Roth, Approaches to Auschwitz**

There are two ways to belittle, misjudge, or shrug off the significance of the Holocaust for sociology as the theory of civilization, of modernity, of modern civilization.

One way is to present the Holocaust as something that happened to the Jews; as an event in *Jewish* history. This makes the Holocaust unique, comfortably uncharacteristic and sociologically inconsequential. The most common example of such a way is the presentation of the Holocaust as the culmination point of European-Christian antisemitism – in itself a unique phenomenon with nothing to compare it with in the large and dense inventory of ethnic or religious prejudices and aggressions. Among all other cases of collective antagonisms, antisemitism stands alone for its unprecedented systematicity, for its ideological intensity, for its supra-national and supra-territorial spread, for its unique mix of local and ecumenical sources and tributaries. In so far as it is defined as, so to speak, the continuation of antisemitism through other means, the Holocaust appears to be a 'one item set', a one-off episode, which perhaps sheds some light on the *pathology* of the society in which it occurred, but hardly adds anything to our understanding of this society's *normal* state. Less still does it call for any significant revision of the orthodox understanding of the historical tendency of modernity, of the civilizing process, of the constitutive topics of sociological inquiry.

Another way – apparently pointing in an opposite direction, yet leading in practice to the same destination – is to present the Holocaust as an extreme case of a wide and familiar category of social phenomena; a category surely loathsome and repellent, yet one we can (and must) live with. We must live with it because of its resilience and ubiquity, but above all because modern society has been all along, is and will remain, an organization designed to roll it back, and perhaps even to stamp it out altogether. Thus the Holocaust is classified as another item (however prominent) in a wide class that embraces many 'similar' cases of conflict, or prejudice, or aggression. At worst, the Holocaust is referred to a primeval and culturally inextinguishable, 'natural' predisposition of the human species – Lorenz's (1977) instinctual aggression or Arthur Koestler's (1978) failure of the neo-cortex to control the ancient, emotion-ridden part of the brain. As pre-social and immune to cultural manipulation, factors responsible for the Holocaust are effectively removed from the area of sociological interest. At best, the Holocaust is cast inside the most awesome and sinister – yet still theoretically assimilable category – of genocide; or else simply dissolved in the broad, all-too-familiar class of ethnic, cultural or racial oppression and persecution.

Whichever of the two ways is taken, the effects are very much the same. The Holocaust is shunted into the familiar stream of history:

> When viewed in this fashion, and accompanied with the proper citation of other historical horrors (the religious crusades, the slaughter of Albigensian heretics, the Turkish decimation of the Armenians, and even the British invention of concentration camps during the Boer War), it becomes all too convenient to see the Holocaust as 'unique' – but normal, after all. (Kren and Rappoport, 1980, p. 2)

Or the Holocaust is traced back to the only-too-familiar record of the hundreds of years of ghettos, legal discrimination, pogroms and persecutions of Jews in Christian Europe – and so revealed as a uniquely horrifying, yet fully logical consequence of ethnic and religious hatred. One way or the other, the bomb is defused; no major revision of our social theory is really necessary; our visions of modernity, of its unrevealed yet all-too-present potential, its historical tendency, do not require another hard look, as the methods and concepts accumulated by sociology are fully adequate to handle this challenge – to 'explain it', to 'make sense of it', to understand. The overall result is theoretical complacency. Nothing, really, happened to justify another critique of the model of modern society that has served so well as the theoretical framework and the pragmatic legitimation of sociological practice.

Thus far, significant dissent with this complacent, self-congratulating attitude has been voiced mostly by historians and theologians. Little attention has been paid to these voices by the sociologists. When compared with the awesome amount of work accomplished by the historians, and the volume of soul-searching among both Christian and Jewish theologians, the contributions of professional sociologists to Holocaust studies seems marginal and negligible. Such sociological studies as have been completed so far show beyond reasonable doubt that *the Holocaust has more to say about the state of sociology than sociology in its present shape is able to add to our knowledge of the Holocaust*. This alarming fact has not yet been faced (much less responded to) by the sociologists.

The way the sociological profession perceives its task regarding the event called 'the Holocaust' has been perhaps most pertinently expressed by one of the profession's most eminent representatives, Everett C. Hughes:

> The National Socialist Government of Germany carried out the most colossal piece of 'dirty work' in history on the Jews. The crucial problems concerning such an occurrence are (1) who are the people who actually carry out such work and (2) what are the circumstances in which other 'good' people allow them to do it? What we need is better knowledge of the signs of their rise to power and better ways of keeping them out of power.   (Hughes, 1962, pp. 3–10)

True to the well-established principles of sociological practice, Hughes defines the problem as one of disclosing the peculiar combination of psycho-social factors which could be sensibly connected (as the determinant) with peculiar behavioural tendencies displayed by the 'dirty work' perpetrators; of listing another set of factors which detract from the (expected, though not forthcoming) resistance to such tendencies on the part of other individuals; and of gaining in the result a certain amount of explanatory–predictive knowledge which in this rationally organized world of ours, ruled as it is by causal laws and statistical probabilities, will allow its holders to prevent the 'dirty' tendencies from coming into existence, from expressing themselves in actual behaviour and achieving their deleterious, 'dirty' effects. The latter task will be presumably attained through the application of the same model of action that has made our world rationally organized, manipulable and 'controllable'. What we need is a better technology for the old – and in no way discredited – activity of social engineering.

In what has been so far the most notable among the distinctly sociological contributions to the study of the Holocaust, Helen Fein (1979) has faithfully followed Hughes's advice. She defined her task as that of spelling out a number of psychological, ideological and structural variables which most strongly correlate with percentages of Jewish victims or survivors inside various state-national entities of Nazi-dominated Europe. By all orthodox standards, Fein produced a most impressive piece of research. Properties of national communities, intensity of local antisemitism, degrees of Jewish acculturation and assimilation, the resulting cross-communal solidarity have all been carefully and correctly indexed, so that correlations may be properly computed and checked for their relevance. Some hypothetical connections are shown to be non-existent or at least statistically invalid; some other regularities are statistically confirmed (like the correlation between the absence of solidarity and the likelihood that 'people would become detached from moral constraints'). It is precisely because of the impeccable sociological skills of the author, and the competence with which they are put in operation, that the weaknesses of orthodox sociology have been inadvertently exposed in Fein's book. Without revising some of the essential yet tacit assumptions of sociological discourse, one cannot do anything other than what Fein has done; conceive of the Holocaust as a unique yet fully determined product of a particular concatenation of social and psychological factors, which led to a temporary suspension of the civilizational grip in which human behaviour is normally held. On such a view (implicitly if not explicitly) one thing that emerges from the experience of the Holocaust intact and unscathed is the humanizing and/or rationalizing (the two concepts are used synonymously) impact of social organization upon inhuman drives which rule the conduct of pre- or anti-social individuals. Whatever moral instinct is to be found in human conduct is socially produced. It dissolves once society malfunctions. 'In an anomic condition – free from social regulation – people may respond without regard to the possibility of injuring others' (Fein, 1979, p. 34). By implication, the presence of effective social regulation makes such disregard unlikely. The thrust of social regulation – and thus of modern civilization, prominent as it is for pushing regulative ambitions to limits never heard of before – is the imposition of moral constraints on otherwise rampant selfishness and inborn savagery of the animal in man. Having processed the facts of the Holocaust through the mill of that methodology which defines it as a scholarly discipline, orthodox sociology can only deliver a message bound more by its presuppositions than by 'the facts of the case': the message that the Holocaust was a failure, not a product, of modernity.

In another remarkable sociological study of the Holocaust, Nechama Tec attempted to explore the opposite side of the social spectrum; the rescuers – those people who did not allow the 'dirty work' to be perpetrated, who dedicated their lives to the suffering others in the world of universal selfishness; people who, in short, remained moral under immoral conditions. Loyal to the precepts of sociological wisdom, Tec tried hard to find the social determinants of what by all standards of the time was an aberrant behaviour. One by one, she put to the test all hypotheses that any respectable and know-ledgeable sociologist would certainly include in the research project. She computed correlations between the readiness to help on the one hand, and various factors of class, educational, denominational, or political allegiance on the other – only to discover that there was none. In defiance of her own – and her sociologically trained readers' – expectations, Tec had to draw the only permissible conclusion: 'These rescuers acted in ways that were natural to them – spontan-eously they were able to strike out against the horrors of their times' (Tec, 1986, p. 193). In other words, the rescuers were willing to rescue because this was their nature. They came from all corners and sectors of 'social structure', thereby calling the bluff of there being 'social determinants' of moral behaviour. If anything, the contribution of such determinants expressed itself in their failure to extinguish the rescuers' urge to help others in their distress. Tec came closer than most sociologists to the discovery that the real point at issue is not: 'What can we, the sociologists, say about the Holocaust?', but, rather, 'What has the Holocaust to say about us, the sociologists, and our practice?'

While the necessity to ask this question seems both a most urgent and a most ignobly neglected part of the Holocaust legacy, its con-sequences must be carefully considered. It is only too easy to over-react to the apparent bankruptcy of established sociological visions. Once the hope to contain the Holocaust experience in the theoretical framework of malfunction (modernity incapable of suppressing the essentially alien factors of irrationality, civilizing pressures failing to subdue emotional and violent drives, socialization going awry and hence unable to produce the needed volume of moral motivations) has been dashed, one can be easily tempted to try the obvious exit from the theoretical impasse, to proclaim the Holocaust a 'paradigm' of modern civilization, its 'natural', 'normal' (who knows – perhaps also *common*) product, its 'historical tendency'. In this version, the

Holocaust would be promoted to the status of *truth* of modernity (rather than recognized as a *possibility* that modernity contains) – the truth only superficially concealed by the ideological formula imposed by those who benefit from the 'big lie'. In a perverse fashion, this view (we shall deal with it in more detail in the fourth chapter) having allegedly elevated the historical and theoretical significance of the Holocaust, can only belittle its importance, as the horrors of genocide will have become virtually indistinguishable from other sufferings that modern society does undoubtedly generate daily – and in abundance.

The Holocaust as the Test of Modernity

A few years ago a journalist of *Le Monde* interviewed a sample of former hijack victims. One of the most interesting things he found was an abnormally high incidence of divorce among the couples who went jointly through the agony of hostage experience. Intrigued, he probed the divorcees for the reasons for their decision. Most interviewees told him that they had never contemplated a divorce before the hijack. During the horrifying episode, however, 'their eyes opened', and 'they saw their partners in a new light'. Ordinary good husbands, 'proved to be' selfish creatures, caring only for their own stomachs; daring businessmen displayed disgusting cowardice; resourceful 'men of the world' fell to pieces and did little except bewailing their imminent perdition. The journalist asked himself a question; which of the two incarnations each of these Januses was clearly capable of was the true face, and which was the mask? He concluded that the question was wrongly put. Neither was 'truer' than the other. Both were possibilities that the character of the victims contained all along – they simply surfaced at different times and in different circumstances. The 'good' face seemed normal only because normal conditions favoured it above the other. Yet the other was always present, though normally invisible. The most fascinating aspect of this finding was, however, that were it not for the hijackers' venture, the 'other face' would probably have remained hidden forever. The partners would have continued to enjoy their marriage, unaware of the unprepossessing qualities some unexpected and extraordinary circumstances might still uncover in persons they seemed to know, liking what they knew.

The paragraph we quoted before from Nechama Tec's study ends with the following observation; 'were it not for the Holocaust, most of these helpers might have continued on their independent paths, some pursuing charitable actions, some leading simple, unobtrusive lives. They were dormant heroes, often indistinguishable from those around them.' One of the most powerfully (and convincingly) argued conclusions of the study was the impossibility of 'spotting in advance' the signs, or symptoms, or indicators, of individual readiness for sacrifice, or of cowardice in the face of adversity; that is, to decide, outside the context that calls them into being or just 'wakes them up', the probability of their later manifestation.

John R. Roth brings the same issue of potentiality versus reality (the first being a yet-undisclosed mode of the second, and the second being an already-realized – and thus empirically accessible – mode of the first) in a direct contact with our problem:

> Had Nazi Power prevailed, authority to determine what ought to be would have found that no natural laws were broken and no crimes against God and humanity were committed in the Holocaust. It would have been a question, though, whether the slave labour operations should continue, expand, or go out of business. Those decisions would have been made on rational grounds.   (Roth, 1980, p. 70)

The unspoken terror permeating our collective memory of the Holocaust (and more than contingently related to the overwhelming desire not to look the memory in its face) is the gnawing suspicion that the Holocaust could be more than an aberration, more than a deviation from an otherwise straight path of progress, more than a cancerous growth on the otherwise healthy body of the civilized society; that, in short, the Holocaust was not an antithesis of modern civilization and everything (or so we like to think) it stands for. We suspect (even if we refuse to admit it) that the Holocaust could merely have uncovered another face of the same modern society whose other, more familiar, face we so admire. And that the two faces are perfectly comfortably attached to the same body. What we perhaps fear most, is that each of the two faces can no more exist without the other than can the two sides of a coin.

Often we stop just at the threshold of the awesome truth. And so Henry Feingold insists that the episode of the Holocaust was indeed a new development in a long, and on the whole blameless, history of modern society; a development we had no way to expect and predict, like an appearance of a new malign strain of an allegedly tamed virus:

> The Final Solution marked the juncture where the European industrial system went awry; instead of enhancing life, which was the original hope of the Enlightenment, it began to consume itself. It was by dint of

that industrial system and the ethos attached to it that Europe was able to dominate the world.

As if the skills needed and deployed in the service of world domination were qualitatively different from those which secured the effectiveness of the Final Solution. And yet Feingold is staring the truth in the face:

> [Auschwitz] was also a mundane extension of the modern factory system. Rather than producing goods, the raw material was human beings and the end-product was death, so many units per day marked carefully on the manager's production charts. The chimneys, the very symbol of the modern factory system, poured forth acrid smoke produced by burning human flesh. The brilliantly organized railroad grid of modern Europe carried a new kind of raw material to the factories. It did so in the same manner as with other cargo. In the gas chambers the victims inhaled noxious gas generated by prussic acid pellets, which were produced by the advanced chemical industry of Germany. Engineers designed the crematoria; managers designed the system of bureaucracy that worked with a zest and efficiency more backward nations would envy. Even the overall plan itself was a reflection of the modern scientific spirit gone awry. What we witnessed was nothing less than a massive scheme of social engineering... (Feingold, 1983, p. 398)

The truth is that every 'ingredient' of the Holocaust – all those many things that rendered it possible – was normal; 'normal' not in the sense of the familiar, of one more specimen in a large class of phenomena long ago described in full, explained and accommodated (on the contrary, the experience of the Holocaust was new and unfamiliar), but in the sense of being fully in keeping with everything we know about our civilization, its guiding spirit, its priorities, its immanent vision of the world – and of the proper ways to pursue human happiness together with a perfect society. In the words of Stillman and Pfaff,

> There is more than a wholly fortuitous connection between the applied technology of the mass production line, with its vision of universal material abundance, and the applied technology of the concentration camp, with its vision of a profusion of death. We may wish to deny the connection, but Buchenwald was of our West as much as Detroit's River Rouge – we cannot deny Buchenwald as a casual aberration of a Western world essentially sane. (Stillman and Pfaff, 1964, pp. 30–1)

Let us also recall the conclusion Raul Hilberg has reached at the end of his unsurpassed, magisterial study of the Holocaust's accomplishment:

'The machinery of destruction, then, was structurally no different from organized German society as a whole. The machinery of destruction *was* the organized community in one of its special roles' (Hilberg, 1983, p. 994).

Richard L. Rubenstein has drawn what seems to me the ultimate lesson of the Holocaust. 'It bears,' he wrote, 'witness to the *advance of civilization*' (Rubenstein, 1978, p. 195). It was an advance, let us add, in a double sense. In the Final Solution, the industrial potential and technological know-how boasted by our civilization has scaled new heights in coping successfully with a task of unprecedented magnitude. And in the same Final Solution our society has disclosed to us its heretofore unsuspected capacity. Taught to respect and admire technical efficiency and good design, we cannot but admit that, in the praise of material progress which our civilization has brought, we have sorely underestimated its true potential.

> The world of the death camps and the society it engenders reveals the progressively intensifying night side of Judeo-Christian civilization. Civilization means slavery, wars, exploitation, and death camps. It also means medical hygiene, elevated religious ideas, beautiful art, and exquisite music. It is an error to imagine that civilization and savage cruelty are antithesis . . . In our times the cruelties, like most other aspects of our world, have become far more effectively administered than ever before. They have not and will not cease to exist. Both creation and destruction are inseparable aspects of what we call civilization.   (Rubenstein, 1978, p. 195)

Hilberg is a historian, Rubenstein is a theologian. I have keenly searched the works of sociologists for statements expressing similar awareness of the urgency of the task posited by the Holocaust; for evidence that the Holocaust presents, among other things, a challenge to sociology as a profession and a body of academic knowledge. When measured against the work done by historians or theologians, the bulk of academic sociology looks more like a collective exercise in forgetting and eye-closing. By and large, the lessons of the Holocaust have left little trace on sociological common sense, which includes among many others such articles of faith as the benefits of reason's rule over the emotions, the superiority of rationality over (what else?) irrational action, or the endemic clash between the demands of efficiency and the moral leanings with which 'personal relations' are so hopelessly infused. However loud and poignant, voices of the protest against this faith have not yet penetrated the walls of the sociological establishment.

I do not know of many occasions on which sociologists, *qua* sociologists, confronted publicly the evidence of the Holocaust. One such occasion (though on a small scale) was offered by the symposium on *Western Society after the Holocaust*, convened in 1978 by the Institute for the Study of Contemporary Social Problems (Legters, 1983). During the symposium, Richard L. Rubenstein presented an imaginative, though perhaps over-emotional attempt to re-read, in the light of the Holocaust experience, some of the best-known of Weber's diagnoses of the tendencies of modern society. Rubenstein wished to find out whether the things we know about, but of which Weber was naturally unaware, could have been anticipated (by Weber himself and his readers), at least as a possibility, from what Weber knew, perceived or theorized about. He thought he had found a positive answer to this question, or at least so he suggested: that in Weber's exposition of modern bureaucracy, rational spirit, principle of efficiency, scientific mentality, relegation of values to the realm of subjectivity etc. no mechanism was recorded that was capable of excluding the possibility of Nazi excesses; that, moreover, there was nothing in Weber's ideal types that would necessitate the description of the activities of the Nazi state as *excesses*. For example, 'no horror perpetrated by the German medical profession or German technocrats was inconsistent with the view that values are inherently subjective and that science is intrinsically instrumental and value-free'. Guenther Roth, the eminent Weberian scholar and a sociologist of high and deserved repute, did not try to hide his displeasure: 'My disagreement with Professor Rubenstein is total. There is just no sentence in his presentation that I can accept.' Probably incensed by the possible harm to Weber's memory (a harm lurking, as it were, in the very idea of 'anticipation'), Guenther Roth reminded the gathering that Weber was a liberal, loved the constitution and approved of the working class's voting rights (and thus, presumably, could not be recalled in conjunction with a thing so abominable as the Holocaust). He refrained, however, from confronting the substance of Rubenstein's suggestion. By the same token, he deprived himself of the possibility of seriously considering the 'unanticipated consequences' of the growing rule of reason which Weber identified as the central attribute of modernity and to which analysis he made a most seminal contribution. He did not use the occasion to face point-blank the 'other side' of the perceptive visions bequeathed by the classic of the sociological tradition; nor the opportunity to ponder whether our sad knowledge, unavailable to the classics, may enable us to find out in their insights things the full consequences of which they themselves could not be, except dimly, aware.

In all probability, Guenther Roth is not the only sociologist who would rally to the defence of the hallowed truths of our joint tradition at the expense of the adverse evidence; it is just that most other sociologists have not been forced to do so in such an outspoken way. By and large, we need not bother with the challenge of the Holocaust in our daily professional practice. As a profession, we have succeeded in all but forgetting it, or shelving it away into the 'specialist interests' area, from where it stands no chance of reaching the mainstream of the discipline. If at all discussed in sociological texts, the Holocaust is at best offered as a sad example of what an untamed innate human aggressiveness may do, and then used as a pretext to exhort the virtues of taming it through an increase in the civilizing pressure and another flurry of expert problem-solving. At worst, it is remembered as a private experience of the Jews, as a matter between the Jews and their haters (a 'privatization' to which many spokesmen of the State of Israel, guided by other than eschatological concerns, has contributed more than a minor share).

This state of affairs is worrying not only, and not at all primarily, for professional reasons – however detrimental it may be for the cognitive powers and societal relevance of sociology. What makes this situation much more disturbing is the awareness that if 'it could happen on such a massive scale elsewhere, then it can happen anywhere; it is all within the range of human possibility, and like it or not, Auschwitz expands the universe of consciousness no less than landing on the moon' (Kren and Rappoport, 1980, pp. 126, 143). The anxiety can hardly abate in view of the fact that none of the societal conditions that made Auschwitz possible has truly disappeared, and no effective measures have been undertaken to prevent such possibilities and principles from generating Auschwitz-like catastrophes; as Leo Kuper has recently found out, 'the sovereign territorial state claims, as an integral part of its sovereignty, the right to commit genocide, or engage in genocidal massacres, against people under its rule, and . . . the UN, for all practical purposes, defends this right' (Kuper, 1981, p. 161).

One posthumous service the Holocaust can render is to provide an insight into the otherwise unnoticed 'other aspects' of the societal principles enshrined by modern history. I propose that the experience of the Holocaust, now thoroughly researched by the historians, should be looked upon as, so to speak, a sociological 'laboratory'. The Holocaust has exposed and examined such attributes of our society as are not revealed, and hence are not empirically accessible, in 'non-laboratory' conditions. In other words, *I propose to treat the Holocaust as a rare, yet significant and reliable, test of the hidden possibilities of modern society.*

The Meaning of the Civilizing Process

The etiological myth deeply entrenched in the self-consciousness of our Western society is the morally elevating story of humanity emerging from pre-social barbarity. This myth lent stimulus and popularity to, and in turn was given a learned and sophisticated support by, quite a few influential sociological theories and historical narratives; the link most recently illustrated by the burst of prominence and overnight success of the Elias's presentation of the 'civilizing process'. Contrary opinions of contemporary social theorists (see, for instance, the thorough analyses of multifarious civilizing processes: historical and comparative by Michael Mann, synthetic and theoretical by Anthony Giddens), which emphasize the growth of military violence and untrammelled use of coercion as the most crucial attributes of the emergence and entrenchment of great civilizations, have a long way to go before they succeed in displacing the etiological myth from public consciousness, or even from the diffuse folklore of the profession. By and large, lay opinion resents all challenge to the myth. Its resistance is backed, moreover, by a broad coalition of respectable learned opinions which contains such powerful authorities as the 'Whig view' of history as the victorious struggle between reason and superstition; Weber's vision of rationalization as a movement toward achieving more for less effort; psychoanalytical promise to debunk, prise off and tame the animal in man; Marx's grand prophecy of life and history coming under full control of the human species once it is freed from the presently debilitating parochialities; Elias's portrayal of recent history as that of eliminating violence from daily life; and, above all, the chorus of experts who assure us that human problems are matters of wrong policies, and that right policies mean elimination of problems. Behind the alliance stands fast the modern 'gardening' state, viewing the society it rules as an object of designing, cultivating and weed-poisoning.

In view of this myth, long ago ossified into the common sense of our era, the Holocaust can only be understood as the failure of civilization (i.e. of human purposive, reason-guided activity) to contain the morbid natural predilections of whatever has been left of nature in man. Obviously, the Hobbesian world has not been fully chained, the Hobbesian problem has not been fully resolved. In other words, we do not have as yet enough civilization. The unfinished civilizing process is yet to be brought to its conclusion. If the lesson of mass murder does teach us anything it is that the prevention of similar hiccups of barbarism evidently requires still more civilizing efforts. There is nothing in this lesson to cast doubt on the future effectiveness of such efforts and their ultimate results. We certainly move in the right direction; perhaps we do not move fast enough.

As its full picture emerges from historical research, so does an alternative, and possibly more credible, interpretation of the Holocaust as an event which disclosed the weakness and fragility of human nature (of the abhorrence of murder, disinclination to violence, fear of guilty conscience and of responsibility for immoral behaviour) when confronted with the matter-of-fact efficiency of the most cherished among the products of civilization; its technology, its rational criteria of choice, its tendency to subordinate thought and action to the pragmatics of economy and effectiveness. The Hobbesian world of the Holocaust did not surface from its too-shallow grave, resurrected by the tumult of irrational emotions. It arrived (in a formidable shape Hobbes would certainly disown) in a factory-produced vehicle, wielding weapons only the most advanced science could supply, and following an itinerary designed by scientifically managed organization. Modern civilization was not the Holocaust's *sufficient* condition; it was, however, most certainly its *necessary* condition. Without it, the Holocaust would be unthinkable. It was the rational world of modern civilization that made the Holocaust thinkable. 'The Nazi mass murder of the European Jewry was not only the technological achievement of an industrial society, but also the organizational achievement of a bureaucratic society' (Browning, 1983, p. 148). Just consider what was needed to make the Holocaust unique among the many mass murders which marked the historical advance of the human species.

> The civil service infused the other hierarchies with its sure-footed planning and bureaucratic thoroughness. From the army the machinery of destruction acquired its military precision, discipline, and callousness. Industry's influence was felt in the great emphasis upon accounting, penny-saving and salvage, as well as in factory-like efficiency of the killing centres. Finally, the party contributed to the entire apparatus an 'idealism', a sense of 'mission', and a notion of history-making...
>
> It was indeed the organized society in one of special roles. Though engaged in mass murder on a gigantic scale, this vast bureaucratic apparatus showed concern for correct bureaucratic procedure, for the niceties of precise definition, for the minutiae of bureaucratic regulation, and the compliance with the law.   (Kuper, 1981, p. 121)

The department in the SS headquarters in charge of the destruction of European Jews was officially designated as the Section of Administration and Economy. This was only partly a lie; only in part can it be explained by reference to the notorious 'speech rules', designed to mislead both chance observers and the less resolute among the perpetrators. To a degree much too high for comfort, the designation faithfully reflected the organizational meaning of activity. Except for the moral repulsiveness of its goal (or, to be precise, the gigantic scale of the moral odium), the activity did not differ in any formal sense (the only sense that can be expressed in the language of bureaucracy) from all other organized activities designed, monitored and supervised by 'ordinary' administrative and economic sections. Like all other activities amenable to bureaucratic rationalization, it fits well the sober description of modern administration offered by Max Weber:

> Precision, speed, unambiguity, knowledge of the files, continuity, discretion, unity, strict subordination, reduction of friction and of material and personal costs – these are raised to the optimum point in the strictly bureaucratic administration... Bureaucratization offers above all the optimum possibility for carrying through the principle of specializing administrative functions according to purely objective considerations... The 'objective' discharge of business primarily means a discharge of business according to *calculable rules* and 'without regard for persons'. (Weber, 1970, pp. 214–15)

There is nothing in this description that warrants questioning the bureaucratic definition of the Holocaust as either a simple travesty of truth or a manifestation of a particularly monstrous form of cynicism.

And yet the Holocaust is so crucial to our understanding of the modern bureaucratic mode of rationalization not only, and not primarily, because it reminds us (as if we need such a reminder) just how formal and ethically blind is the bureaucratic pursuit of efficiency. Its significance is not fully expressed either once we realize to what extent mass murder on an unprecedented scale depended on the availability of well-developed and firmly entrenched skills and habits of meticulous and precise division of labour, of maintaining a smooth flow of command and information, or of impersonal, well-synchronized co-ordination of autonomous yet complementary actions: on those skills and habits, in short, which best grow and thrive in the atmosphere of the office. The light shed by the Holocaust on our knowledge of bureaucratic rationality is at its most dazzling once we realize the extent to which *the very idea of the* Endlösung *was an outcome of the bureaucratic culture.*

We owe to Karl Schleuner (1970) the concept of the twisted road to physical extermination of European Jewry: a road which was neither conceived in a single vision of a mad monster, nor was a considered choice made at the start of the 'problem-solving process' by the ideologically motivated leaders. It did, rather, emerge inch by inch, pointing at each stage to a different destination, shifting in response to ever-new crises, and pressed forward with a 'we will cross that bridge once we come to it' philosophy. Schleuner's concept summarizes best the findings of the 'functionalist' school in the historiography of the Holocaust (which in recent years rapidly gains strength at the expense of the 'intentionalists', who in turn find it increasingly difficult to defend the once dominant single-cause explanation of the Holocaust – that is, a vision that ascribes to the genocide a motivational logic and a consistency it never possessed).

According to the functionalists' findings, 'Hitler set the objective of Nazism: "to get rid of the Jews, and above all to make the territory of the Reich *judenfrei*, i.e., clear of Jews" – but without specifying how this was to be achieved' (Marrus, 1987, p. 41). Once the objective had been set, everything went on exactly as Weber, with his usual clarity, spelled out: 'The "political master" finds himself in the position of the "dilettante" who stands opposite the "expert", facing the trained official who stands within the management of administration' (Weber, 1970, p. 232). The objective had to be implemented; how this was to be done depended on the circumstances, always judged by the 'experts' from the point of view of feasibility and the costs of alternative opportunities of action. And so the emigration of German Jews was chosen first as the practical solution to Hitler's objective; it would resulted in a *judenfrei* Germany, were other countries more hospitable to Jewish refugees. When Austria was annexed, Eichmann earned his first accolade for expediting and streamlining the mass emigration of Austrian Jewry. But then the territory under Nazi rule began to swell. At first the Nazi bureaucracy saw the conquest and appropriation of quasi-colonial territories as the dreamt-of opportunity to fulfil the *Führer*'s command in full: *Generalgouvernment* seemed to provide the sought-after dumping ground for the Jewry still inhabiting lands of Germany proper, destined for racial purity. A separate reserve for the future 'Jewish principality' was designated around Nisko, in what was, before the conquest, central Poland. To this, however, German bureaucracy saddled with the management of the former Polish territories objected: it had already enough trouble with policing its own local Jewry. And so Eichmann spent a full year working on the Madagascar project: with France defeated, her far-away colony could be transformed into the Jewish principality that failed to materialize in Europe. The Madagascar project, however, proved to be similarly ill-fated, given the enormous distance, the volume of necessary ship-space, and the British navy presence on the high seas. In the meantime the size of the conquered territory, and so the number of Jews under German jurisdiction continued to grow. A Nazi-dominated Europe (rather than simply the 'reunited *Reich*') seemed a more and more tangible prospect. Gradually yet relentlessly, the thousand-year *Reich* took up, ever more distinctly, the shape of a German-ruled Europe. Under the circumstances, the goal of a *judenfrei* Germany could not but follow the process. Almost imperceptibly, step by step, it expanded into the objective of *judenfrei* Europe. Ambitions on such a scale could not be satisfied by a Madagascar, however accessible (though according to Eberhard Jäckel there is some evidence that still in July 1941, when Hitler expected the USSR to be defeated in a matter of weeks, the vast expanses of Russia beyond the Archangel–Astrakhan line were seen as the ultimate dumping ground for all Jews inhabiting Europe unified under German rule). With the downfall of Russia reluctant to materialize, and the alternative solutions unable to keep pace with the fast-growing problem, Himmler ordered on 1 October 1941 the final stop to all further Jewish emigration. The task of 'getting rid of the Jews' had been found another, more effective means of implementation: physical extermination was chosen as the most feasible and effective means to the original, and newly expanded, end. The rest was the matter of co-operation between various departments of state bureaucracy; of careful planning, designing proper technology and technical equipment, budgeting, calculating and mobilizing necessary resources: indeed, the matter of dull bureaucratic routine.

The most shattering of lessons deriving from the analysis of the 'twisted road to Auschwitz' is that – in the last resort – *the choice of physical extermination as the right means to the task of* Entfernung *was a product of routine bureaucratic procedures*: means–ends calculus, budget balancing, universal rule application. To make the point sharper still – the choice was an effect of the earnest effort to find rational solutions to successive 'problems', as they arose in the changing circumstances. It was also affected by the widely described bureaucratic tendency to goal-displacement – an affliction as normal in all bureaucracies as their routines. The very presence of functionaries charged with their specific tasks led to further initiatives and a continuous expansion of original purposes. Once again, expertise demonstrated its self-propelling capacity, its proclivity to expand and enrich the target which supplied its *raison d'être*.

> The mere existence of a corpus of Jewish experts created a certain bureaucratic momentum behind Nazi Jewish policy. Even when

deportations and mass murder were already under way, decrees appeared in 1942 prohibiting German Jews from having pets, getting their hair cut by Aryan barbers, or receiving the Reich sport badge! It did not require orders from above, merely the existence of the job itself, to ensure that the Jewish experts kept up the flow of discriminating measures. (Browning, 1983, p. 147)

At no point of its long and tortuous execution did the Holocaust come in conflict with the principles of rationality. The 'Final Solution' did not clash at any stage with the rational pursuit of efficient, optimal goal-implementation. On the contrary, *it arose out of a genuinely rational concern, and it was generated by bureaucracy true to its form and purpose*. We know of many massacres, pogroms, mass murders, indeed instances not far removed from genocide, that have been perpetrated without modern bureaucracy, the skills and technologies it commands, the scientific principles of its internal management. The Holocaust, however, was clearly unthinkable without such bureaucracy. The Holocaust was not an irrational outflow of the not-yet-fully-eradicated residues of pre-modern barbarity. It was a legitimate resident in the house of modernity; indeed, one who would not be at home in any other house.

This is not to suggest that the incidence of the Holocaust was *determined* by modern bureaucracy or the culture of instrumental rationality it epitomizes; much less still, that modern bureaucracy *must* result in Holocaust-style phenomena. I do suggest, however, that the rules of instrumental rationality are singularly incapable of preventing such phenomena; that there is nothing in those rules which disqualifies the Holocaust-style methods of 'social-engineering' as improper or, indeed, the actions they served as irrational. I suggest, further, that the bureaucratic culture which prompts us to view society as an object of administration, as a collection of so many 'problems' to be solved, as 'nature' to be 'controlled', 'mastered' and 'improved' or 'remade', as a legitimate target for 'social engineering', and in general a garden to be designed and kept in the planned shape by force (the gardening posture divides vegetation into 'cultured plants' to be taken care of, and weeds to be exterminated), was the very atmosphere in which the idea of the Holocaust could be conceived, slowly yet consistently developed, and brought to its conclusion. And I also suggest that it was the spirit of instrumental rationality, and its modern, bureaucratic form of institutionalization, which had made the Holocaust-style solutions not only possible, but eminently 'reasonable' – and increased the probability of their choice. This increase in probability is more than fortuitously related to the ability of modern bureaucracy to co-ordinate the action of great number of moral individuals in the pursuit of any, also immoral, ends.

Social Production of Moral Indifference

Dr Servatius, Eichmann's counsel in Jerusalem, pointedly summarized his line of defence: Eichmann committed acts for which one is decorated if one wins, and goes to the gallows if one loses. The obvious message of this statement – certainly one of the most poignant of the century not at all short of striking ideas – is trivial; might does make right. Yet there is also another message, not so evident, though no less cynical and much more alarming; Eichmann did nothing essentially different from things done by those on the side of the winners. Actions have no intrinsic moral value. Neither are they immanently immoral. Moral evaluation is something external to the action itself, decided by criteria other than those that guide and shape the action itself.

What is so alarming in the message of Dr Servatius is that – once detached from the circumstances under which it was uttered, and considered in depersonalized universal terms – it does not differ significantly from what sociology has been saying all along; or indeed, from the seldom-questioned, and still less frequently assailed, common sense of our modern, rational society. Dr Servatius's statement is shocking precisely for this reason. It brings home a truth that on the whole we prefer to leave unspoken: that as long as the commonsensical truth in question is accepted as evident, there is no sociologically legitimate way of excluding Eichmann's case from its application.

It is common knowledge by now that the initial attempts to interpret the Holocaust as an outrage committed by born criminals, sadists, madmen, social miscreants or otherwise morally defective individuals failed to find any confirmation in the facts of the case. Their refutation by historical research is today all but final. The present drift of historical thinking has been aptly summed up by Kren and Rappoport:

> By conventional clinical criteria no more than 10 per cent of the SS could be considered 'abnormal'. This observation fits the general trend of testimony by survivors indicating that in most of the camps, there was usually one, or at most a few, SS men known for their intense outbursts of sadistic cruelty. The others were not always decent persons, but their behaviour was at least considered comprehensible by the prisoners...

Our judgement is that the overwhelming majority of SS men, leaders as well as rank and file, would have easily passed all the psychiatric tests ordinarily given to American army recruits or Kansas City policemen. (Kren and Rappoport, 1980; p. 70).

That most of the perpetrators of the genocide were normal people, who will freely flow through any known psychiatric sieve, however dense, is morally disturbing. It is also theoretically puzzling, particularly when seen conjointly with the 'normality' of those organizational structures that co-ordinated the actions of such normal individuals into an enterprise of the genocide. We know already that the institutions responsible for the Holocaust, even if found criminal, were in no legitimate sociological sense pathological or abnormal. Now we see that the people whose actions they institutionalized did not deviate either from established standards of normality. There is little choice left, therefore, but to look again, with eyes sharpened by our new knowledge, at the allegedly fully understood, normal patterns of modern rational action. It is in these patterns that we can hope to uncover the possibility so dramatically revealed in the times of the Holocaust.

In the famous phrase of Hannah Arendt, the most difficult problem that the initiators of the *Endlösung* encountered (and solved with astounding success, as it were) was 'how to overcome...the animal pity by which all normal men are affected in the presence of physical suffering' (Arendt, 1964, p. 106). We know that people enlisted into the organizations most directly involved in the business of mass murder were neither abnormally sadistic nor abnormally fanatical. We can assume that they shared in the well-nigh instinctual human aversion to the affliction of physical suffering, and even more universal inhibition against taking life. We know even that when, for instance, members of the *Einsatzgruppen* and other units similarly close to the scene of actual killings were enlisted, special care was taken to weed out – bar or discharge – all particularly keen, emotionally charged, ideologically over-zealous individuals. We know that individual initiatives were discouraged, and much effort was made to keep the whole task in a businesslike and strictly impersonal framework. Personal gains, and personal motives in general, were censured and penalized. Killings induced by desire or pleasure, unlike those following orders and perpetrated in an organized fashion, could lead (at least in principle) to trial and conviction, like ordinary murder or manslaughter. On more than one occasion Himmler expressed deep, and in all likelihood genuine, concern with maintaining the mental sanity and upholding the moral standards of his many subordinates engaged daily in inhuman activity; he also expressed pride that, in his belief, both sanity and morality emerged unscathed from the test. To quote Arendt again, 'by its "objectivity" (*Sachlichkeit*), the SS dissociated itself from such "emotional" types as Streicher, that "unrealistic fool" and also from certain "Teutonic-Germanic Party bigwigs who behaved as though they were clad in horns and pelts"' (Arendt, 1964, p. 69). The SS leaders counted (rightly, it would appear) on organizational routine, not on individual zeal; on discipline, not ideological dedication. Loyalty to the gory task was to be – and was indeed – a derivative of loyalty to the organization.

The 'overcoming of animal pity' could not be sought and attained through release of other, base animal instincts; the latter would be in all probability dysfunctional regarding the organizational capacity to act; a multitude of vengeful and murderous individuals would not match the effectiveness of a small, yet disciplined and strictly coordinated bureaucracy. And then it was not at all clear whether the killing instincts can be relied on to surface in all those thousands of ordinary clerks and professionals, who, because of the sheer scale of the enterprise, must have been involved at various stages of the operation. In Hilberg's words,

> The German perpetrator was not a special kind of German . . . We know that the very nature of administrative planning, of the jurisdictional structure and of the budgetary system precluded the special selection and special training of personnel. Any member of the Order Police could be a guard at a ghetto or on a train. Every lawyer in the Reich Security Main Office was presumed to be suitable for leadership in the mobile killing units; every finance expert to the Economic-Administrative Main Office was considered a natural choice for service in a death camp. In other words, all necessary operations were accomplished with whatever personnel were at hand. (Hilberg, 1983, p. 1011)

And so, how were these ordinary Germans transformed into the German perpetrators of mass crime? In the opinion of Herbert C. Kelman (1973) moral inhibitions against violent atrocities tend to be eroded once three conditions are met, singly or together; the violence is *authorized* (by official orders coming from the legally entitled quarters), actions are *routinized* (by rule-governed practices and exact specification of roles), and the victims of the violence are *dehumanized* (by ideological definitions and indoctrinations). With the third condition we shall deal separately. The first two, however, sound remarkably familiar. They have been spelled out repeatedly in those principles of rational action that have been given universal application by the most representative institutions of modern society.

The first principle most obviously relevant to our query is that of organizational discipline; more precisely, the demand to obey commands of the superiors to the exclusion of all other stimuli for action, to put the devotion to the welfare of the organization, as defined in the commands of the superiors, above all other devotions and commitments. Among these other, 'external' influences, interfering with the spirit of dedication and hence marked for suppression and extinction, personal views and preferences are the most prominent. The ideal of discipline points towards total identification with the organization – which, in its turn, cannot but mean readiness to obliterate one's own separate identity and sacrifice one's own interests (by definition, such interests as do not overlap with the task of the organization). In organizational ideology, readiness for such an extreme kind of self-sacrifice is articulated as a moral virtue; indeed, as the moral virtue destined to put paid to all other moral demands. The selfless observance of that moral virtue is then represented, in Weber's famous words, as the honour of the civil servant; 'The honour of the civil servant is vested in his ability to execute conscientiously the order of superior authorities, exactly as if the order agreed with his own conviction. This holds even if the order seems wrong to him and if, despite the civil servant's remonstrances, the authority insists on the order'. This kind of behaviour means, for a civil servant, 'moral discipline and self-denial in the highest sense' (Weber, 1970, p. 95). Through honour, discipline is substituted for moral responsibility. The delegitimation of all but inner-organizational rules as the source and guarantee of propriety, and thus denial of the authority of private conscience, become now the highest moral virtue. The discomfort that the practising of such virtues may cause on occasion, is counterbalanced by the superior's insistence that he and he alone bears the responsibility for his subordinates' actions (as long, of course, as they conform to his command). Weber completed his description of the civil servant's honour by emphasizing strongly the 'exclusive personal responsibility' of the leader, 'a responsibility he cannot and must not reject or transfer'. When pressed to explain, during the Nuremberg trial, why he did not resign from the command of the *Einsatzgruppe* of whose actions he, as a person, disapproved, Ohlendorf invoked precisely this sense of responsibility: were he to expose the deeds of his unit in order to obtain release from duties he said he resented, he would have let his men be 'wrongly accused'. Obviously, Ohlendorf expected that the same paternalistic responsibility he observed towards 'his men' would be practised by his own superiors towards himself; this absolved him from worry about the moral evaluation of his actions – a worry he could safely leave to those who commanded him to act. 'I do not think I am in a position to judge whether his measures ... were moral or immoral ... I surrender my moral conscience to the fact I was a soldier, and therefore a cog in a relatively low position of a great machine' (Quoted in Wolfe, 1980, p. 64).

If Midas's touch transformed everything into gold, SS administration transformed everything which had come into its orbit – including its victims – into an integral part of the chain of command, an area subject to the strictly disciplinary rules and freed from moral judgement. The genocide was a composite process; as Hilberg observed, it included things done by the Germans, and things done – on German orders, yet often with dedication verging on self-abandonment – by their Jewish victims. This is the technical superiority of a purposefully designed, rationally organized mass murder over riotous outbursts of orgy killing. Co-operation of the victims with the perpetrators of a pogrom is inconceivable. The victims' co-operation with the bureaucrats of the SS was part of the design: indeed, it was a crucial condition of its success. 'A large component of the entire process depended on Jewish participation – the simple acts of individuals as well as organized activity in councils ... German supervisors turned to Jewish councils for information, money, labour, or police, and the councils provided them with these means every day of the week.' This astonishing effect of successfully extending the rules of bureaucratic conduct, complete with the delegitimation of alternative loyalties and moral motives in general to encompass the intended victims of bureaucracy, and thereby deploying their skills and labour in the implementation of the task of their destruction, was achieved (much as in the mundane activity of every other, sinister or benign, bureacracy) in a twofold way. First, the external setting of the ghetto life was so designed that all actions of its leaders and inhabitants could not but remain objectively 'functional' to German purposes. 'Everything that was designed to maintain its [ghetto] viability was simultaneously promoting a German goal ... Jewish efficiency in allocating space or in distributing rations was an extension of German effectiveness. Jewish rigour in taxation or labour utilization was a reinforcement of German stringency, even Jewish incorruptibility could be a tool of German administration.' Second, particular care was taken that at every stage of the road the victims should be put in a situation of choice, to which criteria or rational action apply, and in which the rational decision invariably agrees with the 'managerial design'. 'The Germans were notably successful in deporting Jews by stages, because those that remained behind would reason that it was necessary to sacrifice the few in order to serve the many' (Hilberg, 1983, pp. 1036,

1038, 1042). As a matter of fact, even those already deported were left with the opportunity to deploy their rationality to the very end. The gas chambers, temptingly dubbed 'bathrooms', presented a welcome sight after days spent in overcrowded, filthy cattle trucks. Those who already knew the truth and entertained no illusions still had a choice between a 'quick and painless' death, and one preceded by extra sufferings reserved for the insubordinate. Hence not only the external articulations of the ghetto setting, on which the victims had no control, were manipulated so as to transform the ghetto as a whole into an extension of the murdering machine; also the rational faculties of the 'functionaries' of that extension were deployed for the elicitation of behaviour motivated by loyalty and co-operation with the bureaucratically defined ends.

Social Production of Moral Invisibility

So far we have tried to reconstruct the social mechanism of 'overcoming the animal pity'; a social production of conduct contrary to innate moral inhibitions, capable of transforming individuals who are not 'moral degenerates' in any of the 'normal' senses, into murderers or conscious collaborators in the murdering process. The experience of the Holocaust brings into relief, however, another social mechanism; one with a much more sinister potential of involving in the perpetration of the genocide a much wider number of people who never in the process face consciously either difficult moral choices or the need to stifle inner resistance of conscience. The struggle over moral issues never takes place, as the moral aspects of actions are not immediately obvious or are deliberately prevented from discovery and discussion. In other words, the moral character of action is either invisible or purposefully concealed.

To quote Hilberg again, 'It must be kept in mind that most of the participants [of genocide] did not fire rifles at Jewish children or pour gas into gas chambers ... Most bureaucrats composed memoranda, drew up blueprints, talked on the telephone, and participated in conferences. They could destroy a whole people by sitting at their desk' (Hilberg, 1983, p. 1024). Were they aware of the ultimate product of their ostensibly innocuous bustle – such knowledge would stay, at best, in the remote recesses of their minds. Causal connections between their actions and the mass murder were difficult to spot. Little moral opprobrium was attached to the natural human proclivity to avoid worrying more than necessity required – and thus to abstain from examining the whole length of the causal chain up to its furthest links. To understand how that astounding moral blindness was possible, it is helpful to think of the workers of an armament plant who rejoice in the 'stay of execution' of their factory thanks to big new orders, while at the same time honestly bewailing the massacres visited upon each other by Ethiopians and Eritreans; or to think how it is possible that the 'fall in commodity prices' may be universally welcomed as good news while 'starvation of African children' is equally universally, and sincerely, lamented.

A few years ago John Lachs singled out the *mediation of action* (the phenomenon of one's action being performed for one by someone else, by an intermediate person, who 'stands between me and my action, making it impossible for me to experience it directly') as one of the most salient and seminal features of modern society. There is a great distance between intentions and practical accomplishments, with the space between the two packed with a multitude of minute acts and inconsequential actors. The 'middle man' shields off the outcomes of action from the actors' sight.

> The result is that there are many acts no one consciously appropriates. For the person on whose behalf they are done, they exist only verbally or in the imagination; he will not claim them as his own since he never lived through them. The man who has actually done them, on the other hand, will always view them as someone else's and himself as but the blameless instrument of an alien will...
>
> Without first hand acquaintance with his actions, even the best of humans moves in a moral vacuum: the abstract recognition of evil is neither a reliable guide nor an adequate motive... [W]e shall not be surprised at the immense and largely unintentional cruelty of men of good will...
>
> The remarkable thing is that we are not unable to recognize wrong acts or gross injustices when we see them. What amazes us is how they could have come about when each of us did none but harmless acts ... It is difficult to accept that often there is no person and no group that planned or caused it all. It is even more difficult to see how our own actions, through their remote effects, contributed to causing misery. (Lachs, 1981, pp. 12–13, 58)

The increase in the physical and/or psychic distance between the act and its consequences achieves more than the suspension of moral inhibition; it quashes the moral significance of the act and thereby pre-empts all conflict between personal standards of moral decency and immorality of the social consequences of the act. With most of the socially significant actions mediated by a long chain of complex causal and functional dependencies, moral dilemmas recede from sight, while the occasions for more scrutiny and conscious moral choice become increasingly rare.

A similar effect (on a still more impressive scale) is achieved by rendering the victims themselves psychologically invisible. This has been certainly one of the most decisive among the factors responsible for the escalation of human costs in modern warfare. As Philip Caputo observed, war ethos 'seems to be a matter of distance and technology. You could never go wrong if you killed people at long range with sophisticated weapons' (Caputo, 1977, p. 229). With killing 'at a distance', the link between the carnage and totally innocent acts – like pulling a trigger, or switching on the electric current, or pressing a button on a computer keyboard – is likely to remain a purely theoretical notion (the tendency enormously helped by the mere discrepancy of scale between the result and its immediate cause – an incommensurability that easily defies comprehension grounded in commonsensical experience). It is therefore possible to be a pilot delivering the bomb to Hiroshima or to Dresden, to excel in the duties assigned at a guided missile base, to design ever more devastating specimens of nuclear warheads – and all this without detracting from one's moral integrity and coming anywhere near moral collapse (invisibility of victims was, arguably, an important factor also in Milgram's infamous experiments). With this effect of the invisibility of victims in mind, it is perhaps easier to understand the successive improvements in the technology of the Holocaust. At the *Einsatzgruppen* stage, the rounded-up victims were brought in front of machine guns and killed at point-blank range. Though efforts were made to keep the weapons at the longest possible distance from the ditches into which the murdered were to fall, it was exceedingly difficult for the shooters to overlook the connection between shooting and killing. This is why the administrators of genocide found the method primitive and inefficient, as well as dangerous to the morale of the perpetrators. Other murder techniques were therefore sought – such as would optically separate the killers from their victims. The search was successful, and led to the invention of first the mobile, then the stationary gas chambers; the latter – the most perfect the Nazis had time to invent – reduced the role of the killer to that of the 'sanitation officer' asked to empty a sackful of 'disinfecting chemicals' through an aperture in the roof of a building the interior of which he was not prompted to visit.

The technical-administrative success of the Holocaust was due in part to the skilful utilization of 'moral sleeping pills' made available by modern bureaucracy and modern technology. The natural invisibility of causal connections in a complex system of interaction, and the 'distancing' of the unsightly or morally repelling outcomes of action to the point of rendering them invisible to the actor, were most prominent among them. Yet the Nazis particularly excelled in a third method, which they did not invent either, but perfected to an unprecedented degree. This was the method of making invisible the very humanity of the victims. Helen Fein's concept of the *universe of obligation* ('the circle of people with reciprocal obligations to protect each other whose bonds arise from their relation to a deity or sacred source of authority' [Fein, 1979, p. 4]) goes a long way towards illuminating the socio-psychological factors that stand behind the awesome effectiveness of this method. The 'universe of obligation' designates the outer limits of the social territory inside which moral questions may be asked at all with any sense. On the other side of the boundary, moral precepts do not bind, and moral evaluations are meaningless. To render the humanity of victims invisible, one needs merely to evict them from the universe of obligation.

Within the Nazi vision of the world, as measured by one superior and uncontested value of the rights of Germanhood, to exclude the Jews from the universe of obligation it was only necessary to deprive them of the membership in the German nation and state community. In another of Hilberg's poignant phrases, 'When in the early days of 1933 the first civil servant wrote the first definition of 'non-Aryan' into a civil service ordinance, the fate of European Jewry was sealed' (Hilberg, 1983, p. 1044). To induce the cooperation (or just inaction or indifference) of non-German Europeans, more was needed. Stripping the Jews of their Germanhood, sufficient for the German SS, was evidently not enough for nations which, even if they liked the ideas promoted by the new rulers of Europe, had reasons to fear and resent their claims to the monopoly of human virtue. Once the objective of *judenfrei* Germany turned into the goal of *judenfrei* Europe, the eviction of the Jews from the German nation had to be supplanted by their total dehumanization. Hence Frank's favourite conjunction of 'Jews and lice', the change in rhetoric expressed in the transplanting of the 'Jewish question' from the context of racial self-defence into the linguistic universe of 'self-cleansing' and 'political hygiene', the typhus-warning posters on the walls of the ghettos, and finally the commissioning of the chemicals for the last act from the Deutsche Gesellschaft für Schädlingsbekämpfung – the German Fumigation Company.

Moral Consequences of the Civilizing Process

Although other sociological images of the civilizing process are available, the most common (and widely shared) is one that entails, as its two centre points, the suppression of irrational and essentially anti-social drives, and the gradual yet relentless elimination of violence from social life (more precisely: concentration of violence under control of the state, where it is used to guard the perimeters of national community and conditions of social order). What blends the two centre points into one is the vision of the civilized society – at least in our own, Western and modern, form – as, first and foremost, a moral force; as a system of institutions that co-operate and complement each other in the imposition of a normative order and the rule of law, which in turn safeguard conditions of social peace and individual security poorly defended in pre-civilized settings.

This vision is not necessarily misleading. In the light of the Holocaust, however, it certainly looks one-sided. While it opens for scrutiny important trends of recent history, it forecloses the discussion of no less crucial tendencies. Focusing on one facet of the historical process, it draws an arbitrary dividing line between norm and abnormality. By de-legitimizing some of the resilient aspects of civilization, it falsely suggests their fortuitous and transitory nature, simultaneously concealing the striking resonance between most prominent of their attributes and the normative assumptions of modernity. In other words, it diverts attention from the permanence of the alternative, destructive potential of the civilizing process, and effectively silences and marginalizes the critics who insist on the double-sidedness of modern social arrangement.

I propose that the major lesson of the Holocaust is the necessity to treat the critique seriously and thus to expand the theoretical model of the civilizing process, so as to include the latter's tendency to demote, exprobate and delegitimize the ethical motivations of social action. We need to take stock of the evidence that *the civilizing process is, among other things, a process of divesting the use and deployment of violence from moral calculus, and of emancipating the desiderata of rationality from interference of ethical norms or moral inhibitions.* As the promotion of rationality to the exclusion of alternative criteria of action, and in particular the tendency to subordinate the use of violence to rational calculus, has been long ago acknowledged as a constitutive feature of modern civilization – the Holocaust-style phenomena must be recognized as legitimate outcomes of the civilizing tendency, and its constant potential.

Read again, with the benefit of hindsight, Weber's elucidation of the conditions and the mechanism of rationalization reveals these important, yet thus far underrated, connections. We see more clearly that the conditions of the rational conduct of business – like the notorious separation between the household and the enterprise, or between private income and the public purse – function at the same time as powerful factors in isolating the end-orientated, rational action from interchange with processes ruled by other (by definition, irrational) norms, and thus rendering it immune to the constraining impact of the postulates of mutual assistance, solidarity, reciprocal respect etc., which are sustained in the practices of non-business formations. This general accomplishment of the rationalizing tendency has been codified and institutionalized, not unexpectedly, in modern bureaucracy. Subjected to the same retrospective re-reading, it reveals the silencing of morality as its major concern; as, indeed, the fundamental condition of its success as an instrument of rational coordination of action. And it also reveals its capacity of generating the Holocaust-like solution while pursuing, in impeccably rational fashion, its daily problem-solving activity.

Any rewriting of the theory of the civilizing process along the suggested lines would involve by necessity a change in sociology itself. The nature and style of sociology has been attuned to the selfsame modern society it theorized and investigated; sociology has been engaged since its birth in a mimetic relationship with its object – or, rather, with the imagery of that object which it constructed and accepted as the frame for its own discourse. And so sociology promoted, as its own criteria of propriety, the same principles of rational action it visualized as constitutive of its object. It also promoted, as binding rules of its own discourse, the inadmissibility of ethical problematics in any other form but that of a communally-sustained ideology and thus heterogenous to sociological (scientific, rational) discourse. *Phrases like 'the sanctity of human life' or 'moral duty' sound as alien in a sociology seminar as they do in the smoke-free, sanitized rooms of a bureaucratic office.*

In observing such principles in its professional practice, sociology did no more than partake in the scientific culture. As part and parcel of the rationalizing process, that culture cannot escape a second look. The self-imposed moral silence of science has, after all, revealed some of its less advertised aspects when the issue of production and disposal of corpses in Auschwitz has been articulated as a 'medical problem'. It is not easy to dismiss Franklin M. Littell's warnings of the credibility crisis of the modern university: 'What kind of a medical school trained Mengele and his associates? What departments of anthropology prepared the staff of Strasbourg University's 'Institute of Ancestral Heredity'?' (Littell, 1980, p. 213). Not to wonder for whom this particular bell tolls, to avoid the temptation to shrug off these questions as of merely historical significance, one needs search no further than Colin Gray's analysis of the momentum behind the contemporary nuclear arms race: 'Necessarily, the scientists and technologists on each side are 'racing' to diminish their own ignorance (the enemy is not Soviet technology; it is the physical unknowns that attract scientific attention)...Highly motivated, technologically competent and adequately funded teams of research scientists will inevitably produce an endless series of brand new (or refined) weapon ideas'. (Gray, 1976, pp. 39–40)

References

Arendt, Hannah (1964) *Eichmann in Jerusalem: A Report on the Banality of Evil*. New York: Viking.

Browning, Christopher R. (1983) 'The German Bureaucracy and the Holocaust,' in Alex Grobman and Daniel Landes (eds) *Genocide: Critical Issues of the Holocaust*. Los Angeles: Simon Wiesenthal Center.

Caputo, Philip (1977) *A Rumour of War*. New York: Holt, Rinehart & Winston.

Fein, Helen (1979) *Accounting for Genocide: National Responses and Jewish Victimization During the Holocaust*. New York: Free Press.

Feingold, Henry L. (1983) 'How Unique Is the Holocaust?,' in Alex Grobman and Daniel Landes (eds) *Genocide: Critical Issues of the Holocaust*. Los Angeles: Simon Wiesenthal Center.

Gray, Colin (1976) *The Soviet-American Arms Race*. Lexington: Saxon House.

Hilberg, Raoul (1983) *The Destruction of the European Jews*, vol. III. New York: Holmes & Meier.

Hughes, Everett C. (1962) 'Good People and Dirty Work.' *Social Problems* 10, 1.

Kelman, Herbert C. (1973) 'Violence without Moral Restraint.' *Journal of Social Issues* 29, 4.

Koestler, Arthur (1978) *Janus: A Summing Up*. London: Hutchinson.

Kren, George M. and Rappoport, Leon (1980) *The Holocaust and the Crisis of Human Behaviour*. New York: Holmes & Meier.

Kuper, Leo (1981) *Genocide: Its Political Use in the Twentieth Century*. New Haven: Yale University Press.

Lachs, John (1981) *Responsibility of the Individual in Modern Society*. Brighton: Harvester.

Letgers, Lyman H. (ed.) (1983) *Western Society After the Holocaust*. Boulder: Westview Press.

Littell, Franklin M. (1980) 'Fundamentals in Holocaust Studies.' *Annals of the AAPSS* 450.

Lorenz, Konrad (1977) *On Aggression*. New York: Harcourt, Brace and World.

Marrus, Michael R. (1987) *The Holocaust in History*. London: University Press of New England.

Roth, John K. (1980) 'Holocaust Business.' *Annals of the AAPSS* 450.

Rubenstein, Richard L. (1978) *The Cunning of History*. New York: Harper.

Schleuner, Karl A. (1970) *The Twisted Road to Auschwitz*. Urbana: University of Illinois Press.

Stillman, Edmund and Pfaff, William (1964) *The Politics of Hysteria*. New York: Harper & Row.

Tec, Nechama (1986) *When Light Pierced the Darkness*. Oxford: Oxford University Press.

Weber, Max (1970) *From Max Weber*, ed. H. H. Gerth and C. Wright Mills. London: Routledge & Kegan Paul.

Wolfe, Robert (1980) 'Putative Threat to National Security at a Nuremberg Defence for Genocide.' *Annals of the AAPSS* 450.

8.2   Dictatorship Over Needs (1984)

There is one central message Feher, Heller and Markus hammer home with relentless patience and unyielding tenacity: The Soviet system is about control – an ever increasing, ideally total control. Control over bodies, control over souls. Control over the fashion in which men and women satisfy their needs. And control over what they feel there is to satisfy in the first place. It is by the drive to such a control that Feher, Heller and Markus explain the origin of the Soviet system. It is by the urge to maintain, extend or defend such a control that they account for the dynamics, or the stagnation, of the Soviet system. It is by the functional prerequisite of such a control that they define the logic or incongruity of the Soviet system.

In order to get their message through, Feher, Heller and Markus untiringly cut their way through a thicket of nostalgic hopes, inert images and culture-bound historicisms which tightly wrap the phenomenon under study, barring all insight into its uniqueness. Among the wrappings torn off and discarded are: a) lingering beliefs that the Soviet system is an unavoidable or adventitious deviation from the essentially socialist-oriented development – a distortion that in principle can be rectified – together with a whole family of kindred beliefs, all assuming the transient, incomplete, not-yet-defined character of the Soviet phenomenon, and all warranting the use of the socialist model as a frame of reference against which to plot the 'convergences' and 'divergences' of Soviet history; b) theories spawned by the tendency to subsume the new under the old, the bizarre under the familiar; the many portrayals of the Soviet system as a variation of an otherwise all-too-notorious tune, be it industrialization, modernization, or capitalism; c) theories that admit the 'horizontal' uniqueness of the Soviet system at the expense, however, of its 'vertical' singularity – in fact, another variety of the 'nothing-new-under-the-sun' syndrome, dissolving Soviet peculiarities in perpetuity of historical fate instead of the universality of modern trends.

From behind its many conceptual veils the Soviet phenomenon emerges as a system *sui generis*. A system which is not a version of something different than itself: neither a faulty socialism nor a mutant capitalism nor an emanation of the timeless Oriental mystery. A system which – remaining part and parcel of the modern world – sets for itself tasks no other system did. It is for these unorthodox tasks that this system has developed its unorthodox methods.

This is an utterly acceptable and desirable standpoint. Potentially, it puts an end to so many sterile, scholastic lines of investigation which contributed to the perpetual crisis of the theory of Soviet system: how far one can depart from equality, freedom, or equality and freedom and yet be an 'essentially' socialist society? How much irrationality can one feed into the economy and still remain an 'essentially' industrial society? How much chaos can be reconciled with an 'essentially' planning society? Which is the class who rules Soviet society? How did it disguise its ownership (surely, to rule one needs to own)?

These are gains, but not the only ones. It is precisely for the habit of searching for the historical and systemic connections where they could not be found that the genuine roots of the Soviet system dug deep in European history escaped the analyst's eye. Debunking the myths of the Soviet system as a supersession or alternative of capitalism, or a locally confined freak graft of Oriental depotism is the preliminary condition of coming to grips with the formidable issue of continuity between apparent idiosyncrasies of the Soviet system and some rather major social and cultural tendencies of modern Europe.

Socialism was born as the counter-culture of capitalism. That is, it rallied to the defense of the values that capitalism legitimized and preached against those values capitalism illegitimately practiced: it sought a more generous supply of the first and elimination of the latter. Thus, socialism took capitalism up seriously on its promise of equality and hence objected against inequalities made inevitable by rendering property the principle of distribution. Socialism took capitalism up seriously on its promise of freedom and hence refused to accept the dependence of labor on those who command the conditions of its employment. Socialism took capitalism up seriously on its promise of fraternity and hence condemned the great divide between capital and labor for breeding exploitation, cruelty and rift instead. Socialism was in its inception the utopia of the bourgeois revolution developed to its radical extremes and turned into a critique of bourgeois reality. Or, rather, socialism was a bourgeois-inspired effort to vindicate and resuscitate the historical project the bourgeois revolution failed to fulfill.

In this sense, socialism was a legitimate offspring of the bourgeois revolution eager to continue the work the latter started but failed to complete. Its *moral* critique of capitalism was conducted in the name of the values this revolution promoted; and the moral critique of capitalism was the only way to keep these values alive.

Since Condorcet, the utopia of the bourgeois revolution has been married to the myth of the Age of Reason. Indeed, the two blended into one until, in the self-awareness of liberal capitalism, they became indistinguishable. The moral utopia of the revolution came to be seen as inextricably tied to the program of the Enlightenment; liberty, equality, fraternity as naturally belonging together with rationalism – each complementing and being complemented by the other, each able to survive only in the company of the other, each deriving its meaning from such company. *Historical* continuity between the Enlightenment and Revolution glossed over the issue of their *logical* compatibility. Such logical inconsistencies as may appear to the analyst do not reveal a fundamental flaw in the project; if anything, they are a challenge. It is up to them to prove the legitimacy of a marriage that has been already consummated and whose reality cannot be questioned. Thus, from its turbulent beginnings, capitalism inherited not one, but two utopias; or, rather, one utopia made of two parts which, however ill-fitting, had been presumed to belong to each other for better or worse.

The socialist utopia, defending the bourgeois promise against the capitalist practice, could not but incorporate the axiom of unity between reason and justice. It wished to solve the (by definition illusory) contradictions of their marriage where capitalism failed to do so. Socialism, which proudly adopted the title of 'scientific,' proclaimed exactly this intention. It took over the utopia of liberty, equality, and fraternity. And it supplemented it with the utopia of Enlightenment: this of a rational society. The utopia of a rational society envisages, of course, a society built and administered according to the precepts of reason. But what does this mean? First and foremost, it means the substitution of order for chaos. Design for spontaneity. Plan for anarchy. In other words: control. Control over nature and control over natural propensities of men and women. This central thrust of the rationalist utopia manifested itself in a number of ways. Some of them Feher, Heller and Markus list under an unduly biased name of the 'negative utopia of capitalist industrialization': a tendency toward the central management of social affairs; a pressure toward total supervision of labor and subordination of labor to a comprehensive plan of social production; and a drive toward a universalistic economy, intolerant of all 'irrationality' identified with personal or group autonomy.

This is all true. The capitalist utopia blended moral precepts with the vision of an all-inclusive social order. In this utopia, order turned into a moral value, and moral perfection into an image of planned society. This is not, however, the whole truth. Perhaps, not even the most important part of the truth. The project of a rational society, of an orderly society, of an *ordered* society, meant more than anything else that the omnipotence of 'man as species' may and should be brought to fruition *against* the impotence of men and women as individuals; that this impotence of individual men and women to find the way of reason on their own is the paramount obstacle on the road to rational society; that individual men and women know not what is 'their best interest' and if shown it, would not necessarily obey it; that individual men and women must, therefore, be molded and drilled in order to fit the demands of a rational society; that this job of molding and drilling must be done by people who know the commands of reason and are therefore competent to judge what is in 'the best interest' of individual men and women.

The project of a rational society is, in other words, an idea of domination which sets itself goals no secular power dreamed of before. No secular power of the past viewed its activity as a moral crusade; none wished to interfere with or take responsibility for the way its subjects run their daily life. It is only the state legitimized by the utopia of a rational society that perceives of its task as that of a 'pastoral power' (Foucault) – a power aimed at the cultivation of moral virtues and identifying morally virtuous conduct as behavior geared to the rational order of society.

The socialist critique charged capitalism with failure to implement both sides of the composite moral-rational utopia. Like the two sides of the utopia, the two themes of the socialist critique blended into one to the point of becoming virtually indistinguishable. From the standpoint of the socialist critique, capitalist reality was both morally wanting and irrational; power of this twin charge derived in its entirety from the moral-rational utopia which capitalism proclaimed and nourished.

Thus, the moral utopia of a society of free and equal individuals had been thwarted by the private ownership of the means of production and the network of subordination it determined, while the utopia of a rational society was blighted by the market, competition, and all these *pouvoirs intermediaires* which pitted particularistic interests against interests of the society as a whole. The two charges fused into one;

and so did their object – capitalism as total phenomenon, complete with private ownership, market, liberalism. Socialism posited itself as the legitimate and loyal heir of the bourgeois utopia, engaged in a life-and-death battle with its capitalist mutant.

Socialism did not invent new values; it did not create a new social utopia. On both accounts, socialism has been and still remains in debt to the bourgeois revolution. All themes of the socialist program had been introduced into European culture and explored long before socialism identified itself as a separate movement and set itself against the reality this culture had gestated.

The socialist diagnosis of the obstacles to the implementation of the original Enlightenment hopes of a just and rational society cannot be dismissed as a mere error of judgment. Indeed, market, liberalism, ownership, autonomous articulation of society, etc., stand in the way of a centrally planned society, comprehensive etatization of 'pastoral power,' or unconditional subordination of individual motives and actions to the needs of the system (however and by whomever defined). If the capitalist practice demonstrates what happens to an Enlightenment utopia when its implementation is contained and circumscribed by unanticipated 'intermediary forces' the French Revolution wished but failed to annihilate, the socialist practice shows what happens when the constraining forces are removed or neutralized.

'Dictatorship over needs,' the omnipotent state in full and constant control of the body and the spirit of its subjects, is the ambition and the tendency of pastoral power. The Soviet state is this tendency set free and this ambition coming closer than anywhere else to its fulfillment. The latter happens when pastoral power is loosed from its 'capillary' deployment (typical of other modern societies) and undergoes etatization.

To sum up: the Soviet system, without being a sequence to capitalism or an alternative form of industrial society, is nonetheless no freak or refractory event in European history. Its claims to the legacy of the Enlightenment or to the unfulfilled promises of the bourgeois revolution are neither pretentious nor grotesque. And thus it contains important lessons for the rest of the world.

First, when returned to its proper historical context, the Soviet system can be seen as a practical test of the limits of Enlightenment utopia. This utopia conceived of *social* rationality as resulting from the suppression of *individual* irrationalities; of the rule of reason and common interest as the outcome of elimination of private passions and particular interests. The history of the Soviet state can be viewed as a consistent effort to act on this assumption: to clear the way to 'social' rationality of planned development through the destruction of autonomous civil society, paralyzing the market, prevention of articulation of group interests. This effort has not been entirely successful (as Feher, Heller and Markus abundantly show) but it did go further than any other society on record. The Soviet experience offers, therefore, important information about the limits of the tendency by no means confined to the territory of the Soviet state. A society that results from the suppression of individual autonomy and group interests is not only drab, dreary and oppressive: it is also wasteful and stagnant. In other words, the outcome of the suppression of 'irrationality' on the individual and group level is irrationality on the level of society. The Soviet experience settled the debate in favor of George Orwell and Aldous Huxley.

Second, precisely because the claims of the Soviet system to socialist legitimacy have considerable credibility, this system has turned into the main, perhaps clinching, argument against the credibility of the socialist utopia itself. Once the meaning of the Soviet experience has been interpreted in its true context, the hopes that there is some yet undisclosed mileage hidden in central planning, destruction of the market or centralization of the pastoral power, cannot be seriously entertained. As Feher, Heller and Markus demonstrate, the Soviet experience cannot be dismissed as inconclusive any longer. The present-day Soviet system is not a state on the way to something radically different: it is a complete system, in its own way reasonably equilibrated and viable, and certainly capable of perpetual self-reproduction. This realization marks the end of an era. The traditional socialist utopia, born as a counter-culture of capitalism and a revindication of the promises of the bourgeois revolution, has run its course as the 'conscience' of the Western society, its self-critique and the directing force in its efforts at self-improvement.

Third, a full assessment of the Soviet experience leaves little doubt as to where the hopes and effort to rectify the salient defects of industrial society should not be located. Indeed the lesson is not altogether negative. On the positive side, it suggests the necessity to prevent the trends which the original rationalist utopia deemed to be conditions of a 'good society.' Properly understood, the Soviet experience provides a powerful argument not just against the socialist counter-culture, but also (perhaps above all) against the much wider and much better entrenched culture of rationalism which gestated it. The final form of the Soviet system puts back on the agenda some fundamental premises and values of rationalization and industrial society in general, thus far accepted on both sides of the great political divide, as once more debatable points.

Fourth, in one respect at least the Soviet lesson seems to be quite specific. It points approvingly to the theories of Touraine, Foucault or the new (and reformed – see his *City and the Grassroots*) Castells, as well as to the practice of the Polish *Solidarity*, as focusing on the central problems around which the new battles for the shape of the future will be increasingly concentrated. These are problems of the power of the state and grassroots autonomy; the capacity of social movements to generate new historical subjects; the possibility of making audible the voice of groups unaccommodated within the corporatist arrangement; folding back of the pastoral power and surveillance prerogatives of the state; and, finally, the problem of technology which makes solution of all these problems (and, indeed, the continuing exercise of old liberal-democratic checks and balances) *technically* impossible.

Victor Zaslavsky's *The Neo-Stalinist State* can be seen first and foremost as filling just one, but a crucial, compartment of Feher, Heller and Markus' theoretical analysis with rich, novel and thoroughly researched substance. Zaslavsky's book is all about one topic: institutions operative in the self-reproduction of the Soviet system in general, and in the perpetuation of state control over individuals in particular. If Feher, Heller and Markus present the continuity and stability of the Soviet system as an accomplished fact, however puzzling and mysterious, Zaslavsky solves the mystery. His solution is original (most of the facts that back it have been unknown to the ordinary Soviet analyst), but has all the marks of being definitive. Point by point, Zaslavsky demonstrates how apparently unconnected aspects of the Soviet system share the function of 'tension management' and 'pattern maintenance,' i.e., stave off the articulation of conflicting interests and reinforce the control of the state over its subjects. Among the issues that have been given a particularly novel and revealing treatment one must name: the use of Soviet patriotism and the presentation of international relations both in and outside the socialist bloc, the socializing role of the army, the role of 'closed enterprises' and the function of restrictions imposed on residence and geographical mobility, the role of alcoholism, and the ingenious solution to the 'national question.'

A reading of Zaslavsky's book brings out a point that the other book did not make with sufficient force. Zaslavsky described native, indigenous institutions of the Soviet Union, which in most cases are unique to this one state, sometimes by definition non-transplantable. They are manifestly not the institutions of other 'socialist states.' One wonders to what extent the maturity of the system, namely a state when the system is able to reproduce itself by its own internal

mechanisms, and hence amenability of the system to 'systemic analysis,' has been reached in the Soviet Union alone; and to what extent
it is legitimate to engage in a 'comparative study' of Soviet-type states,
treating each member of the socialist bloc as a specimen of the same
category and using cumulatively information drawn liberally from all
countries in the bloc. After all, the development of the Soviet state as
an uncontrived, self-enveloping process took place in the Soviet Union
and in the Soviet Union alone. Everywhere else it was imposed in
disregard to the local institutions and needs and kept to a large extent
by an external force or its threat. It is a reasonable assumption,
therefore, that the maturation of the socialist utopia into its Soviet
form had not been set in motion nor shaped solely by the logic of the
doctrine. True, the general features of the mature Soviet system had
been validated in advance by the socialist utopia of justice-through-
rationality. But only in conjunction with very special historical circumstance could such a utopia materialize into a complete social
system.

This is to remind ourselves, if a reminder is needed, that in the last
account it is not doctrines, but people, that make history.

References

Feher, F., Heller, A. and Markus, G. (1983) *Dictatorship Over Needs*.
Oxford: Blackwell Publishers.

8.3   A Century of Camps? (1995)

By common consent, the seventeenth century figures in history books
under the name of the Age of Reason. Its immediate successor, predictably, is described as the Age of 'reason speaking' – of Enlightenment. Quite often one hears the nineteenth century being called the
Age of Revolutions, thus suggesting the word becoming flesh. We are
now in the last decade of the twentieth century and in the *fin-de-siècle*
atmosphere the temptations to draw the line and compute the balance
are rampant and overwhelming. (This is precisely why Jean Baudrillard, only half jokingly, advised us to skip the last decade, bound to be
wasted on obituary-writing, and go straight to the next century.) How
will our century go down in history? Will it be under the name of the
'Age of the Camps', of flesh turning cancerous?

This, of course, is not for us to decide – the coming generations are
not bound by our opinions, just like us feeling free to overturn the

views the ancestors held of themselves. By their fruits thou shalt know them, and we do not know, and cannot know, what the lasting legacy of our trials and tribulations will prove to be, and in what way our children and the children of our children would sort out the seminal from the freak, the durable from the episodic, the memorable from the forgettable, in that stretch of history filled and made by our biographies. We can hardly anticipate, let alone pre-empt, their verdict; after all, the contemporaries of the Inquisition, witchhunts, gory peasant rebellions and the vagrancy scare could be excused for having no inkling that long after their deaths their times would be called the Age of Reason.

We can hardly refrain from doing our own thinking nevertheless; we cannot neglect our human, all-too-human need to reflect, to 'make sense', to perceive a form in the formless, to divine order in chaos, to guess a method in what otherwise would feel like unadulterated madness. Aware as we are that all verdicts are bound to be only until-further-notice, that our present is the future's past and that the future is bound to reshuffle and reorder its past many times over, we still cannot help doing our own accounts and passing our own verdicts. And when we do this in the last decade of the twentieth century, the shadows cast by Auschwitz and the Gulag seem by far the longest and likely to dominate any picture we may paint. Many things happened in this century of ours, and all significant and truly consequential things tend to happen unannounced, without warning and audible notice. None of the things that happened in this century were, however, more unexpected than Auschwitz and the Gulag, and none could be more bewildering, shocking and traumatic to the people trained, as we all have been, to see their past as the relentless and exhilarating progression of the ages of reason, enlightenment and emancipatory, liberating revolutions.

It is not just the name of our own century that is at stake. How are we to see the progression that brought us here – when we are here already and know what that 'here' is like and what it is capable of? Coming after that progression, as its culmination and legitimate issue, our century – if it is to be recorded as the 'Age of the Camps' – must be also, cannot but be, the *age of revaluation*: revaluation of the past, of its inherent tendency and hidden potential, of the meaning of the last few centuries of our joint history, of the 'modernity' which that history spawned and left in its wake.

What we learned in this century is that modernity is not only about producing more and travelling faster, getting richer and moving around more freely. *It is also about – it has been about – fast and efficient killing, scientifically designed and administered genocide.*

As human history goes, cruelty and mass murder is not exactly news, and modernity could be exonerated for not quite succeeding, in the short time-span of a mere three hundred years, to eradicate hatred and aggression with thousands-of-years-old roots and to quell the passions precipitated by the millions of years of species' evolution. Some of us, indeed, console ourselves in precisely this way: we, the modern and the civilized, have not done *enough*, but what we have done was the *right* thing to do; we have not progressed far enough, but we have been moving all along in the right direction. What we need is more of the same, done with greater vigour and determination. There is nothing wrong with our civilization; its only temporary failure is that the snuffing out of the animal in the human, the barbarian in the civilized man, which it promised and did its best to achieve, took longer than expected. This is a pleasant, comforting thought. If only it were credible as well.

The problem, however, is that it is not all that credible. Even a massive outburst of evil instincts, always a flickering and brief event, would not sustain the long-term *institution* of the camps and all that huge network of co-ordinated activities which were necessary for their operation. Three days after *Kristallnacht*, the most spectacular of the street-violence explosions ignited by the Nazi regime in Germany, Hermann Göring gathered one hundred of the most prominent members of the German elite to proclaim: 'Meine Herren, diese Demonstrationen habe ich satt... The problem, in the nutshell, is unambiguously an economic one.' Sporadic explosions of spontaneous or contrived hatred would not suffice; only thoroughly modern instrumental reason, cool and unemotional, making the conduct of the operation *independent* from the feelings and ideals of its perpetrators, could do the trick. The camps were not just the old human cruelty escaping the dungeon to which it had been confined or returning from the exile where it was meant to stay till the end of time. The camps are a modern invention; an invention possible only thanks to the accomplishments modernity is proud of more than of anything else – to rationality, technology, science, its favourite and favoured children; an invention which derives its need and usefulness and functionality from the declared ambitions of modern society, a society that views having such ambitions as the foremost mark of its superiority.

I propose that the most bewildering, and indeed terrifying, lesson of the specifically twentieth-century kind of genocide is that it is not possible to surmise or anticipate (let alone to predict with any degree of confidence) the massive collapse of humanity by measuring the intensity of evil streaks in individual characters, the proportion of

individuals with sociopathic dispositions, or the frequency of hetero-
phobic beliefs. Even the most scrupulous scrutiny of the daily civility
of human conduct may be of little help. The most prestigious and
respectable press of the civilized world, the acknowledged voice of
enlightened opinion, was full of praise and admiration when reporting
the daily life of Germany under Nazi rule: *The Times*, the *New York
Times* and *Le Figaro* alike were waxing lyrical when they wrote of it:
of the streets shining with cleanliness and with law and order – no
strife, no mass demonstrations, no protest marches, no terrorist acts,
just peaceful, hospitable, well fed and smiling people. And a famous
American sociologist 'proved scientifically' and beyond reasonable
doubt and to wide public acclaim that under the Soviet regime the
youth was more socially minded and better behaving than in the West,
better protected against the notorious, pathology haunting Western
adolescence, less prone to addictions and delinquency. But it was these
law-abiding, peaceful people, disciplined workers, exemplary husbands and family fathers, who were about to commit jointly, or to
allow to be permitted, a crime without equal in human history. And it
was those disciplined and well behaving youngsters, who were about
to stand guard on the watch-towers of the Gulag Archipelago.

I propose that whoever asks her/himself how the camps were possible must not look into the statistics of overt or crypto-sadists,
psychopaths and perverts – but elsewhere: to that curious and terrifying socially invented modern contraption which permits the separation of action and ethics, of what people do from what people feel or
believe, of the nature of collective deed from the motives of individual
actors.

Modernizing Cruelty

Such conditions – conditions without which there would be no camps
and no genocide, conditions which turned the unthinkable into reality
– are accomplishments of our modern civilization, and in particular of
three features which underlie, simultaneously, its glory and its misery:
*the ability to act at a distance, the neutralization of the moral con-
straints of action*, and its 'gardening posture' – *the pursuit of artificial,
rationally designed order.*

That one can kill today without ever looking the victim in the face,
is a banal observation. Once sinking a knife into the body, or stran-
gling, or shooting at close distance have been replaced with moving
dots over a computer screen – just like one does in amusement arcade
games or on the screen of portable Nintendo – the killer does not need

to be pitiless; he does not have *the occasion* to feel pity. This is, however, the most obvious and trivial, even if the most dramatic, aspect of 'action at a distance'. The less dramatic and spectacular manifestations of our new, modern, skills of distant action are more consequential yet – all the more so for not being so evident. They consist in creating what may be called a *social and psychological*, rather than a merely *physical and optical*, distance between actors and the targets of their actions. Such social/psychological distance is produced and reproduced daily, and ubiquitously, and on a massive scale, by the modern management of action, with its three different, yet complementary aspects.

First, in a modern organization every personally performed action is a mediated action, and every actor is cast in what Stanley Milgram called the 'agentic state': almost no actor ever has a chance to develop the 'authorship' attitude towards the final outcome of the operation, since each actor is but an executor of a command and giver of another; not a writer, but a translator of someone else's intentions. Between the idea which triggers the operation and its ultimate effect there is a long chain of performers, none of whom may be unambiguously pinpointed as a sufficient, decisive link between the design and its product.

Second, there is the horizontal, functional division of the overall task: each actor has but a specific, self-contained job to perform and produces an object with no written-in destination, no information on its future uses; no contribution seems to 'determine' the final outcome of the operation, and most retain but a tenuous logical link with the ultimate effect – a link which the participants may in good conscience claim to be visible only in retrospect.

Third, the 'targets' of the operation, the people who by design or by default are affected by it, hardly ever appear to the actors as 'total human beings', objects of moral responsibility and ethical subjects themselves. As Michael Schluter and David Lee wittily yet aptly observed, 'in order to be seen at the higher levels you have to be broken up into bits and most of you thrown away' (1993, pp. 22–3). And again, about the *Gleichschaltung* tendency that inevitably follows such fragmentation: 'the institutions of the mega community deal more readily with the capacities in which people are all the same than those marking each of them out as individual and unique.' As a result, most actors in organizations deal not with human beings, but with facets, features, statistically represented traits; while only total human persons can be bearers of moral significance.

The global impact of all these aspects of modern organization is what I have called (borrowing the term from the vocabulary of the medieval Church) – the moral *adiaphorization* of action: for all practical purposes, the moral significance of the ultimate and combined effect of individual actions is excluded from the criteria by which individual actions are measured, and so the latter are perceived and experienced as *morally neutral* (more exactly, but with the same effect, moral significance is shifted from the impact of action on its appointed targets, to motives such as loyalty to the organization, collegial solidarity, the well-being of subordinates, or procedural discipline).

The fragmentation of the objects of action is replicated by the fragmentation of actors. The vertical and horizontal division of the global operation into partial jobs makes every actor into a *role-performer*. Unlike 'the person', the role-performer is an eminently replaceable and *exchangeable* incumbent of a site in the complex network of tasks – there is always a certain impersonality, a distance, a less-than-authorship relationship between the role-performer and the role performed. In none of the roles is the role-performer a whole person, as each role's performance engages but a selection of the actor's skills and personality features, and in principle should neither engage the remaining parts nor spill over and affect the rest of the actor's personality. This again makes the role-performance ethically adiaphoric: only *total* persons, only *unique* persons ('unique' in the sense of being irreplaceable in the sense that the deed would remain undone without them) can be moral subjects, bearers of moral responsibility – but modern organization derives its strength from its uncanny capacity for splitting and fragmentation, while on the other hand providing occasions for the fragments to come together again has never been modern organization's *forte*. Modern organization is *the rule of nobody*. It is, we may say, a contraption to *float responsibility* – most conspicuously, moral responsibility.

Thanks to all these inventions, often discussed under the name of 'scientific management', modern action has been liberated from the limitations imposed by ethical sentiments. *The modern way of doing things does not call for the mobilization of sentiments and beliefs.* On the contrary, the silencing and cooling off of the sentiments is its prerequisite and the paramount condition of its astounding effectiveness. Moral impulses and constraints have not been so much extinguished, as neutralized and *made irrelevant*. Men and women have been given the opportunity to commit inhuman deeds without feeling in the least inhuman themselves. It is only when (to quote Hannah Arendt again) 'the old spontaneous bestiality gave way to an absolutely cold and systematic destruction of human bodies', that 'the average German whom the Nazis notwithstanding years of the most furious propaganda could not induce to kill a Jew on his own account (not even when they made it quite clear that such a murder would go unpunished)' served 'the machine of destruction without opposition' (Arendt, 1962). *Modernity did not make people more cruel; it only invented a way in which cruel things could be done by non-cruel people.* Under the sign of modernity, evil does not need any more evil people. Rational people, men and women well riveted into the impersonal, adiaphorized network of modern organization, will do perfectly.

Unlike so many other acts of mass cruelty which mark human history, the camps were cruelty *with a purpose*. A means to an end. Of the Jewish holocaust, Cynthia Ozick wrote that it was a gesture of an artist removing a smudge from an otherwise perfect picture. That smudge happened to be certain people who did not fit the model of a perfect universe. Their destruction was a *creative* destruction, much as the destruction of weeds is a creative act in pursuit of a designed garden beauty. In the case of Hitler, the design was a race-clean society. In the case of Lenin, the design was a class-clean society. In both cases, at stake was an aesthetically satisfying, transparent, homogeneous universe free from agonizing uncertainties, ambivalence, contingency – and therefore, from the carrier of lesser value, the backward, the unteachable and the untouchable. But this was, was it not, precisely the kind of universe dreamed up and promised by the philosophers of Enlightenment, to be pursued by the despots whom they sought to enlighten. A kingdom of reason, the ultimate exercise in human power over nature, the ultimate display of the infinite human potential....

As Götz Aly and Susanne Heim have shown in their most scrupulous and penetrating study, the murder of European Jews can be fully understood only as an integral part of an overall attempt to create a New Europe, better structured and better organized than before; this vision required a massive translocation of population, which always happened to dwell where it should not and where it was *unerwünscht* since there was no use for it ... This was, the authors point out emphatically, a thoroughly *modernizing* effort, since its ultimate purpose was 'to destroy the pre-modern diversity and to introduce the "new order"' – a task which called in equal measure for *Umsiedlung, Homogenisierung* and *Mobilisierung*. It is easy, yet unforgivable, to forget that the famous Desk IVD4 headed by Eichmann was established in December 1939 to deal not only with the 'Umsiedlung' of the Jews, but also of Poles, French, Luxemburgers, Serbs, Croats and Slovenes.

The modern spirit's dream is one of a perfect society, a society purified of extant human weaknesses – and foremost among those

weaknesses are weak humans, humans not up to scratch when measured by the standard of human potential as revealed and articulated
by Reason and its spokesmen. (The mass destruction of Jews and
gypsies followed the scientifically conceived strategy elaborated by,
as Aly and Heim describe them, 'expertocracy', including first and
foremost elites of science, and tried first on the mentally ill and other
'misfits' in the ill-famed campaign of *Gnadentodt*). And the *ambition*
is to make this dream real through the continuous, determined and
radical effort of 'problem-solving', through removing one by one all
the hurdles standing on the road to the dream – and that includes the
men and women who make problems, who *are* the problem. The
modern mind treats the human habitat as a garden, whose ideal
shape is to be predetermined by carefully blueprinted and meticulously followed-up design, and implemented through encouraging
the growth of bushes and flowers envisaged by the plan – and poisoning or uprooting all the rest, the undesirable and the unplanned, the
weeds. Eastern Europe, say Aly and Heim, appeared to the 'New
Order' builders as 'one great waste land, waiting to be cleaned up
for a new building site'.

The most extreme and well documented cases of 'social engineering' in modern history (those presided over by Hitler and Stalin), all
their attendant atrocities notwithstanding, were neither outbursts of
pre-modern barbarism not yet fully extinguished by the new rational,
civilized order, nor the price paid for utopias alien to the spirit of
modernity; nor were they even, contrary to frequently voiced opinions, another chapter in the long and not at all finished history of
'heterophobia' – that spontaneous and irrational resentment of everything strange, alien, unfamiliar and thus frightening. On the contrary,
they were legitimate offspring of the modern spirit, of that urge to
assist and speed up the progress of mankind toward perfection that
was the most prominent hallmark of the modern age; of the optimistic
view that scientific and industrial progress removes in principle all
restrictions on the possible applications of planning, education and
social reform in everyday life, of that confidence that all social problems can be finally solved and the world can be remade to the
measure of human reason. The Nazi and Communist promoters of
the orderly, accident-free and deviation-free society deemed themselves the scions and knights of modern science and the true soldiers
of progress; their breathtaking visions drew legitimacy (and – let us
never forget – an embarrassingly large degree of intellectual sympathy
among the most prominent members of the 'enlightened classes' of
Europe) from such views and beliefs already firmly entrenched in the
public mind through the century and a half of post-Enlightenment

history, filled with scientistic propaganda and the visual display of the wondrous potency of modern technology. To quote Aly and Heim again, 'in their abstraction these thought-models stood in a jarring opposition to the sergeant's ire'. They needed 'scrupulously elaborated theory, which required that entire classes, minorities and peoples be displaced and decimated' (Aly and Heim, 1991, pp. 10, 14–15).

Neither the Nazi nor the Communist vision jarred with the audacious self-confidence and hubris of modernity; they merely offered to do better, and more ruthlessly (but more speedily in its result), what other modern powers dreamed of, perhaps even tried, but failed or did not have the guts to accomplish:

> What should not be forgotten is that fascist racism provided a model for a new order in society, a new internal alignment. Its basis was the racialist elimination of all elements that deviated from the norm: refractory youth, 'idlers', the 'asocial', prostitutes, homosexuals, the disabled, people who were incompetents or failures in their work. Nazi eugenics – that is, the classification and selection of people on the basis of supposed genetic 'value' – was not confined only to sterilization and euthanasia for the 'valueless' and the encouragement of fertility for the 'valuable'; it laid down criteria of assessment, categories of classification and norms of efficiency that were applicable to the population as a whole. (Peukert, 1987, p. 208)

Indeed, one must agree not only with this observation of Detlev Peukert, but also with his conclusion: that National Socialism merely 'pushed the utopian belief in all-embracing "scientific" final solutions of social problems to the ultimate logical extreme'. The determination and the freedom to go 'all the way' and reach the ultimate was Hitler's or Stalin's, yet the logic was construed, legitimized and supplied by the spirit and practice of modernity.

The most atrocious and revolting crimes of our century have been committed in the name of human mastery over nature, and so also over *human* nature, human needs, cravings, dreams. When the task of mastery is given uncontested priority over all other considerations, human beings themselves become superfluous – and the totalitarian states which gave the task such a priority strove to *make* human beings superfluous. In this context, the camps – senseless in every other respect – had their own, sinister *rationality*. The camps were the tools in that task, the wholesome means to the fulsome end, meant to perform three vital jobs. They were laboratories where the new unheard-of volumes of domination and control were explored and tested. They were schools in which the unheard-of readiness to commit cruelty in formerly ordinary human beings was trained. And they were swords held over the heads of those remaining on the other side of the barbed-wire fence, so that they would learn not only that their dissent would not be tolerated but also that their consent was not called for, and that pretty little depends on their choice between protest and acclaim. The camps were distillations of an essence diluted elsewhere, condensations of totalitarian domination and its corollary, the superfluity of man, in a pure form difficult or impossible to achieve elsewhere. The camps were patterns and blueprints for the totalitarian society, that modern dream of total order, domination and mastery run wild, cleansed of the last vestiges of that wayward and unpredictable human freedom, spontaneity and unpredictability that held it back. The camps were testing grounds for societies run as concentration camps.

This is how Ryszard Kapuścinski, the most indefatigable and observant among the war-correspondents reporting from contemporary battlefields of oppression and freedom, described in his latest book, *Imperium* (Warsaw, 1993), his experience of entering the Soviet Union through the Trans-Siberian railway:

> Barbed wire. Barbed wire – this is what one sees first...
>
> At the first glance, this barbed, rapacious barrier looks senseless and surreal; who will try to cross it, if snowy desert spreads as far as eye can reach, no tracks, no people, snow lies two metres thick, one cannot make a step – and yet this wire wants to tell you something, give you a message. It says: take note, you are crossing the border into another world. From here, you won't escape. This is a world of deadly seriousness, command and obedience. Learn how to listen, learn humility, learn how to occupy as little room as possible. Best of all do what is for you to do. Best of all keep quiet. Best of all do not ask questions.

That particular barbed wire Kapuścinski wrote about has by now been dismantled – as has been the totalitarian state that built it. But it speaks still, it keeps sending a message to all who want to listen. And the message is: there is no orderly society without fear and humiliation, there is no human mastery over the world without trampling on human dignity and exterminating human freedom, there is no fight against the obstreperous contingency of the human condition that does not in the end make humans superfluous. In the camps, it was not just human endurability that had been put to the test. It was also the feasibility of the great modern project of ultimate human order, which the test has shown to be, inevitably, an *inhuman* order. In the camps, that project found its *reductio ad absurdum*, but also its *experimentum crucis*.

To be sure, the transparent, orderly, controlled world cleansed of surprises and contingency was but one of modern dreams. Another was the dream of human freedom – not the freedom of the human species, which permits scoffing at nature with its constraints and individual humans with their wants, but the freedom of men and women as they are and desire to be and would become if given the chance. What many have *suspected* all along but most of us *know* today is that there is no way to make both dreams come true together. And today there are not many enthusiasts around impressed by the dream of engineered, State-administered order. We seem to be reconciled to the incurable messiness of the world; or are too busy chasing the seductive baits of the consumer society and thus have no time to ponder its dangers; or would have no guts or stamina to fight it, were we willing or able to pay attention.

This does not mean necessarily that the age of the camps and of genocide has drawn to its close. In 1975 the Indonesian army occupied the neighbouring territory of East Timor. Since then, 'a third of the population has been slaughtered. Whole villages have been massacred by troops given to raping, torturing and mutilating indiscriminately.' The response of the Western, civilized world? *Our* response?

> The US condoned the invasion, asking only that it should wait until after President Ford's official visit, Australia has signed trade deals with the Jakarta regime to exploit East Timor's oilfields, and Britain has supplied Indonesia's military dictatorship with large quantities of arms, including planes needed to bomb civilian communities. Asked about the British position, former Defence Minister Alan Clark replies: 'I do not really fill my mind much with what one set of foreigners is doing to another.'

This much we can read in *The Guardian* of 22 February 1994 – twenty years after the genocide of the East Timor population started. We do not know whether the troops who tortured and mutilated and killed did what they did out of a deep hatred they felt for the conquered people, or just because that was what the commanders' command and the soldiers' soldiering was about. What we do know is that the minister of the country which sold the troops the planes to do the job of extermination felt no emotions of any kind, except, perhaps, the satisfaction of a business deal well done. And since the minister in question belonged to a party which British electors voted back into power three times since the planes had been delivered and used, we may surmise that the voters, much like the minister they voted for, did not fill their minds much with what one set of foreigner did to another. We may also safely bet that it is true that the East Timorese were exterminated because the world the rulers of Indonesia wished to build had no room for them, and thus it could be created only if East Timorese were destroyed; we may say that the destruction of East Timorese was – for Indonesian rulers – an act of creation.

'Between 1960 and 1979', says Helen Fein in her comprehensive study of contemporary genocide, 'there were probably at least a dozen genocides and genocidal massacres – cases include the Kurds in Iraq, southerners in the Sudan, Tutsi in Rwanda, Hutus in Burundi, Chinese ... in Indonesia, Hindus and other Bengalis in East Pakistan, the Ache in Paraguay, many peoples in Uganda ... ' (Fein, 1993, p. 6). Some of us heard of some of these cases, some of us never heard of any. Few of us had done anything to stop them from happening or to bring those who made them happen to court. What all of us can be pretty sure of, if we put our minds to it, is that our governments, for our sake – to keep our factories open and to save *our jobs* – supplied the guns and the bullets and the poison gas to enable the murderers to do *their jobs*.

In every genocide, the victims are killed not for what they have done, but for what they are; more precisely still, for what they, being what they are, may yet become; or for what they, being what they are, may not become. Nothing the appointed victims may or may not do would affect the sentence of death – and that includes their choice between submissiveness or militancy, surrender or resistance. Who is the victim and what the victims are is a matter for their executioners to decide. In a succinct definition by Chalk and Jonassohn (1990, p. 23) 'genocide is a form of one-sided mass killing in which a state or other authority intends to destroy a group, as that group and membership in it are defined by the perpetrators.' Before the perpetrators of genocide acquire the power over their victims' *life*, they must have acquired the power over their *definition*. It is that first, essential power that makes *a priori* irrelevant everything the victims already defined as unworthy of life may do or refrain from doing. Genocide starts with *classification* and fulfils itself as a *categorial killing*. Unlike enemies in war, the victims of genocide have no selves and so are the kind of subjects who may not be judged by their deeds. They are not selves even in the sense of being bearers of guilt or sin. Their only, and sufficient, crime is having been classified into a category defined as criminal or hopelessly diseased. In the ultimate account, they are guilty of being accused.

This stoutly monological character of genocide, this resolute preemption of all dialogue, this prefabricated asymmetry of relationship, this one-sidedness of authorship and actorship alike, is – I propose – the most decisive constitutive feature of all genocide. And, obversely, genocide can not be conceived of, let alone enacted, if the structure of relationship is in one way or another prevented from being mono-logic.

Yet states, even in our relatively small, postmodern part of the globe, where states stop well short of their past totalitarian visions and abandoned or were forced to abandon the hopes of resorting once more to a monologic stance, where the order-making and order-keep-ing efforts and the coercion that goes with them – once condensed and monopolized by the sovereign state and its appointed agents – are now increasingly deregulated, privatized, dispersed, reduced in scale 'total-itarian solutions' – so Hannah Arendt warned us – 'may well survive the fall of totalitarian regimes in the form of strong temptations which will come up whenever it seems impossible to alleviate political, social, or economic misery in a manner worthy of man.' And there is plenty of misery around, and more is to come in the ever more overpopulated and polluted world running short of resources and of demand for the hands and the minds of men and women as producers. At least every tenth adult all over the wealthy part of the world (as some observers say, every third; we live, they say, already in a 'two-third society', and given the present pattern of change, will reach a 'one-third society' in thirty years or so) is currently superfluous – neither the bearer of potentially useful labour nor a potential client of the shopping malls. If the classic nation-state used to polarize society into fully fledged members of national/political community and aliens deprived of citizen rights, the market which takes over the task of integration polarizes society into fully fledged consumers, amenable to its seductive powers, and into flawed consumers, or non-consumers, unable to respond to the bait and thus from the view point of the market totally useless and redundant. To put it bluntly, yesterday's underdogs were non-producers, while today's underdogs are non-consumers. The 'under-class' which replaced the 'reserve army of labour', the unemployed and the poor of yesterday, is not marginalized through its handicapped position among the produ-cers, but through its exile from the category of consumers. Unable to respond to market stimuli in the way such stimuli are meant to elicit, such people cannot be kept at bay through the methods deployed by market forces. To such people, the old-fashioned tested methods of coercive policing and criminalization are applied by the state in its continuing capacity as the guardian of 'law and order'.

It would be silly and irresponsible to play down, under the circum-stances, the temptations of 'totalitarian solutions', always strong

when certain humans are declared redundant or forced into a superfluous condition – though in all probability the totalitarian-style
solutions will presently hide under other, more palatable names.
And it would be naive to suppose that the democratic rule of the
majority provides, of itself, a sufficient guarantee that the temptation
of totalitarian solutions will be rejected.

In times when large majorities of men and women of the affluent
countries are integrated through seduction, public relations exercises
and advertising, rather than by enforced norms, surveillance and
drilling, the repression of the marginals who escape the net of allure-
ments or are unable to climb into it becomes an inevitable complement of seduction: as the tested way of dealing with those who cannot
be dealt with through seduction, and as a stern reminder to all those
put off by the vagaries of the consumer game that the price to be paid
for not paying the price of market-life anguish is the surrender of
personal freedom.

In a recent study significantly subtitled 'Towards Gulags, Western
Style?' (1993) the Norwegian criminologist Nils Christie has convincingly demonstrated 'the capacity for modern industrial society
to institutionalize large segments of the population', manifested,
among other ways, in the steady rise of the population of prisons.
In the USA in 1986, 26 per cent of black male school drop-outs
were in jail; the numbers have risen since then, and are still growing
fast. Obviously, the prisons of liberal-democratic societies are not
the camps of totalitarian states. But the tendency to criminalize
whatever is defined as 'social disorders' or 'social pathologies',
with its attendant separation, incarceration, political and social
incapacitation and disfranchisement of the genuine or putative carriers of pathology, is to a large extent a 'totalitarian solution without a
totalitarian state – and the style of 'problem solving' it promotes
has more to do than we would wish to admit with the 'totalitarian bent', or the totalitarian temptations apparently endemic in
modernity.

But let us repeat that it would be premature to write obituaries of
the 'classic', Hitler- and Stalin-style camps. Those camps were a
modern invention, even when used in the service of anti-modern
movements. The camps, together with electronically guided weap-
onry, petrol-guzzling cars and video cameras and recorders will in
all probability remain among the modern paraphernalia most voci-
ferously demanded and most avidly snatched by societies exposed to
the modernizing pressures – even such among them as are up in arms
against other modern inventions, like *habeas corpus*, freedom of
speech, or parliamentary rule, and deride individual liberties and the

tolerance of otherness as symptoms of godlessness and degeneration. All our postmodern retrospective wisdom notwithstanding, we live and will be living for some time yet in an essentially modern and modernizing world, whose awesome and often sinister capacities have perhaps become more visible and better understood, but have not vanished for that reason. The camps are part of that modern world. It still remains to be proved that they are not its integral and irremovable part.

Is therefore our century to be branded by historians as the 'Age of the Camps'? Time will tell what the most lasting consequence of Auschwitz and the Gulag will be. Will it be the temptation to resort to their experience whenever it is impossible to alleviate accumulated human misery, or whenever the picture of future bliss is so tempting that disregard for those living in the present seems a reasonable price to pay? Or, on the contrary, will it be the role which that experience played in our sobering up to the murky side of modern progress, in our discovery of the congenital malaise of the modern spirit, in our new readiness to reflect on the human costs of social improvement? If the first possibility prevails, then indeed the Age of the Camps will be the true and legitimate heir to the ages of Reason, of Enlightenment and of Revolutions. If the second possibility comes out on top, our century may still go down in history as the Age of Awakening. We cannot be sure that the choice is ours. But we cannot say that we did not know there was a choice.

References

Aly, Götz and Heim, Susanne (1991) *Vordenker der Vernichtung: Auschwitz und die deutschen Pläne für eine neue europäische Ordnung*. Hamburg: Hiffman & Campe.

Arendt, Hannah (1962) *The Origins of Totalitarianism*. London: Allen & Unwin.

Chalk, Frank and Jonassohn, Kurt (1990) *The History and Sociology of Genocide: Analyses and Case Studies*. New Haven: Yale University Press.

Christie, Nils (1993) *Crime Control as Industry: Towards Gulags, Western Style?* London: Routledge.

Fein, Helen (1993) *Genocide: A Sociological Perspective*. London: Sage.

Peukert, D. K. (1987) *Inside Nazi Germany*, trans. Richard Deveson. New Haven: Yale University Press.

Schluter, Michael and Lee, David (1993) *The R Factor*. London: Hodder & Stoughton.

9

Ambivalence and Order

9.1 The Quest for Order (1991)

Ambivalence, the possibility of assigning an object or an event to more than one category, is a language-specific disorder: a failure of the naming (segregating) function that language is meant to perform. The main symptom of disorder is the acute discomfort we feel when we are unable to read the situation properly and to choose between alternative actions.

It is because of the anxiety that accompanies it and the indecision which follows that we experience ambivalence as a disorder – and either blame language for lack of precision or ourselves for linguistic misuse. And yet ambivalence is not the product of the pathology of language or speech. It is, rather, a normal aspect of linguistic practice. It arises from one of the main functions of language: that of naming and classifying. Its volume grows depending on the effectivity with which that function is performed. Ambivalence is therefore the *alter ego* of language, and its permanent companion – indeed, its normal condition.

To classify means to set apart, to segregate. It means first to postulate that the world consists of discrete and distinctive entities; then to postulate that each entity has a group of similar or adjacent entities with which it belongs, and with which – together – it is opposed to some other entities; and then to make the postulated real by linking differential patterns of action to different classes of entities (the evocation of a specific behavioural pattern becoming the operative definition of the class). To classify, in other words, is to give the world a *structure*: to manipulate its probabilities; to make some events more likely than some others; to behave as if events were not random, or to limit or eliminate randomness of events.

Through its naming/classifying function, language posits itself between a solidly founded, orderly world fit for human habitation, and a contingent world of randomness, in which human survival weapons – memory, the capacity for learning – would be useless, if not downright suicidal. Language strives to sustain the order and to deny or suppress randomness and contingency. An orderly world is a world in which 'one knows how to go on' (or, what amounts to the same, one knows how to find out – and find out *for sure* – how to go on), in which one knows how to calculate the probability of an event and how to increase or decrease that probability; a world in which links between certain situations and the effectivity of certain actions remain by and large constant, so that one can rely on past successes as guides for future ones. Because of our learning/memorizing ability we have vested interests in maintaining the orderliness of the world. For the same reason, we experience ambivalence as discomfort and a threat. Ambivalence confounds calculation of events and confuses the relevance of memorized action patterns.

The situation turns ambivalent if the linguistic tools of structuration prove inadequate; either the situation belongs to none of the linguistically distinguished classes, or it falls into several classes at the same time. None of the learned patterns could be proper in an ambivalent situation – or more than one of the learned patterns could be applied; whatever is the case, the outcome is the feeling of indecision, undecidability, and hence loss of control. The consequences of action become unpredictable, while randomness, allegedly done away with by the structuring effort, seems to make an unsolicited come-back.

Ostensibly, the naming/classifying function of language has the prevention of ambivalence as its purpose. Performance is measured by the neatness of the divisions between classes, the precision of their definitional boundaries, and the unambiguity with which objects may be allocated to classes. And yet the application of such criteria, and the very activity whose progress they are to monitor, are the ultimate sources of ambivalence and the reasons why ambivalence is unlikely ever to become truly extinct, whatever the amount and the ardour of the structuring/ordering effort.

The ideal that the naming/classifying function strives to achieve is a sort of commodious filing cabinet that contains all the files that contain all the items that the world contains – but confines each file and each item within a separate place of its own (with remaining doubts solved by a cross-reference index). It is the non-viability of such a filing cabinet that makes ambivalence unavoidable. And it is the perseverance with which construction of such a cabinet is pursued that brings forth ever new supplies of ambivalence.

Classifying consists in the acts of inclusion and exclusion. Each act of naming splits the world into two: entities that answer to the name;

all the rest that do not. Certain entities may be included into a class – *made a class* – only in as far as other entities are *excluded*, left outside Invariably, such operation of inclusion/exclusion is an act of violence perpetrated upon the world, and requires the support of a certain amount of coercion. It can hold as long as the volume of applied coercion remains adequate to the task of outbalancing the extent of created discrepancy. Insufficiency of coercion shows itself in the manifest reluctance of entities postulated by the act of classification to fit into assigned classes, and in the appearance of entities under- or over-defined, with insufficient or excessive meaning – sending no readable signals for action, or sending signals that confuse the recipients for being mutually contradictory.

Ambivalence is a side-product of the labour of classification; and it calls for yet more classifying effort. Though born of the naming/classifying urge, ambivalence may be fought only with a naming that is yet more exact, and classes that are yet more precisely defined: that is, with such operations as will set still tougher (counter-factual) demands on the discreteness and transparency of the world and thus give yet more occasion for ambiguity. The struggle against ambivalence is, therefore, both self-destructive and self-propelling. It goes on with unabating strength because it creates its own problems in the course of resolving them. Its intensity, however, varies over time, depending on the availability of force adequate to the task of controlling the extant volume of ambivalence, and also on the presence or absence of awareness that the reduction of ambivalence is a problem of the discovery and application of proper *technology*: a *managerial* problem. Both factors combined to make modern times an era of particularly bitter and relentless war against ambivalence.

How old is modernity? is a contentious question. There is no agreement on dating. There is no consensus on what is to be dated. And once the effort of dating starts in earnest, the object itself begins to disappear. Modernity, like all other quasi-totalities we want to prise off from the continuous flow of being, become elusive: we discover that the concept is fraught with ambiguity, while its referent is opaque at the core and frayed at the edges. Hence the contention is unlikely to be resolved. The defining feature of modernity underlying [these essays] is part of the contention.

Among the multitude of impossible tasks that modernity set itself and that made modernity into what it is, the task of order (more precisely and most importantly, of *order as a task*) stands out – as the least possible among the impossible and the least disposable among the indispensable; indeed, as the archetype for all other tasks, one that renders all other tasks mere metaphors of itself.

Order is what is not chaos; chaos is what is not orderly. Order and chaos are *modern* twins. They had been conceived amidst the disruption and collapse of the divinely ordained world, which knew of neither necessity nor accident; one that just *was* – without ever thinking how to make itself to be. That unthinking and careless world which preceded the bifurcation into order and chaos we find difficult to describe in its own terms. We try to grasp it mostly with the help of negations: we tell ourselves what that world was not, what it did not contain, what it did not know, what it was unaware of. That world would hardly have recognized itself in our descriptions. It would not understand what we are talking about. It would not have survived such understanding. The moment of understanding would have been the sign of its approaching death. And it was. Historically, this understanding was the last sigh of the passing world; and the first sound of new-born modernity.

We can think of modernity as of a time when order – of the world, of the human habitat, of the human self, and of the connection between all three – is *reflected upon*; a matter of thought, of concern, of a practice that is aware of itself, conscious of being a conscious practice and wary of the void it would leave were it to halt or merely relent. For the sake of convenience (the exact dating of birth, let us repeat, is bound to remain contentious: the project of dating is but one of the many *foci imaginarii* that, like butterflies, do not survive the moment when a pin is pushed through their body to fix them in place) we can agree with Stephen L. Collins, who in his recent study took Hobbes's vision for the birthmark of the consciousness of order, that is – in our rendition – of modern consciousness, that is of modernity. ('Consciousness', says Collins, 'appears as the quality of perceiving order in things.')

> Hobbes understood that a world in flux was natural and that order must be created to restrain what was natural ... Society is no longer a transcendentally articulated reflection of something predefined, external, and beyond itself which orders existence hierarchically. It is now a nominal entity ordered by the sovereign state which is its own articulated representative ... [Forty years after Elizabeth's death] order was coming to be understood not as natural, but as artificial, created by man, and manifestly political and social ... Order must be designed to restrain what appeared ubiquitous [that is, flux] ... Order became a matter of power, and power a matter of will, force and calculation ... Fundamental to the entire reconceptualization of the idea of society was the belief that the commonwealth, as was order, was a human creation. (Collins, 1989, pp. 4–7, 28–32)

Collins is a scrupulous historian, wary of the dangers of project-ionism and presentism, but he can hardly avoid imputing to the pre-Hobbesian world many a feature akin to our post-Hobbesian world – if only through indicating their absence; indeed, without such a strategy of description the pre-Hobbesian world would stay numb and meaningless to us. To make that world speak to us, we must, as it were, make its silences audible: to spell out what that world was unaware of. We must commit an act of violence: force that world to take a stance on issues to which it remained oblivious, and thus dismiss or bypass that oblivion that made it that world, a world so different and so incommunicado with our own. The attempt to communicate will defy its purpose. In this process of forced con-version, we shall render the hope of communication more remote still. In the end, instead of *reconstructing* that 'other world', we shall no more than *construe* 'the other' of the world of our own.

If it is true that we know that the order of things is not natural, this does not mean that the other, pre-Hobbesian, world thought of order as the work of nature: it did not think of order at all, not in a form we would think of as 'thinking of', not in the sense we think of it now. The discovery that order was *not natural* was discovery of *order as such*. The *concept* of order appeared in consciousness only simultaneously with the *problem* of order, of order as a matter of *design* and *action*, order as an obsession. To put it yet more bluntly, order as a problem emerged in the wake of the ordering flurry, as a reflection on ordering practices. Declaration of the 'non-naturalness of order' stood for an order already coming out of hiding, out of non-existence, out of silence. 'Nature' means, after all, nothing but the silence of man.

If it is true that we, the moderns, think of order as a matter of design, this does not mean that before modernity the world was complacent about designing, and expected the order to come and stay on its own and unassisted. That world lived without such altern-ative; it would not be that world at all, were it giving its thought to it. If it is true that our world is shaped by the suspicion of the brittleness and fragility of the artificial man-designed and man-built islands of order among the sea of chaos, it does not follow that before modernity the world believed that the order stretched over the sea and the human archipelago alike; it was, rather, unaware of the distinction between land and water.

We can say that the existence is modern in as far as it forks into order and chaos. The existence is modern in as far as it contains the *alternative* of order and chaos.

Indeed: order and *chaos*, full stop. If it is aimed at at all (that is, in as far as it is thought of), order is not aimed at as a substitute for an alternative order. The struggle for order is not a fight of one definition against another, of one way of articulating reality against a competitive proposal. It is a fight of determination against ambiguity, of semantic precision against ambivalence, of transparency against obscurity, clarity against fuzziness. Order as a concept, as a vision, as a purpose could not be conceived but for the insight into the total ambivalence, the randomness of chaos. Order is continuously engaged in the war of survival. The other of order is not another order: chaos is its only alternative. The other of order is the miasma of the indeterminate and unpredictable. The other is uncertainty, that source and archetype of all fear. The tropes of 'the other of order' are: undefinability, incoherence, incongruity, incompatibility, illogicality, irrationality, ambiguity, confusion, undecidability, ambivalence.

Chaos, 'the other of order', is pure negativity. It is a denial of all that order strives to be. It is against that negativity that the positivity of order constitutes itself. But the negativity of chaos is a product of order's self-constitution: its side-effect, its waste, and yet the condition *sine qua non* of its (reflective) possibility. Without the negativity of chaos, there is no positivity of order; without chaos, no order.

We can say that existence is modern in as far as it is saturated by the 'without us, a deluge' feeling. Existence is modern in as far as it is guided by the urge of designing what otherwise would not be there: designing *of itself*.

The raw existence, the existence free of intervention, the *unordered* existence, or the fringe of ordered existence, become now *nature*: something singularly unfit for human habitat – something not to be trusted and not to be left to its own devices, something to be *mastered, subordinated, remade* so as to be readjusted to human needs. Something to be held in check, restrained and contained, lifted from the state of shapelessness and given form – by effort and by force. Even if the form has been preordained by nature itself, it will not come about unassisted and will not survive undefended. Living according to nature needs a lot of designing, organized effort and vigilant monitoring. Nothing is more artificial than naturalness; nothing less natural than throwing oneself at the mercy of the laws of nature. Power, repression and purposeful action stand between nature and that socially effected order in which artificiality is natural.

We can say that existence is modern in as far as it is effected and sustained by *design, manipulation, management, engineering*. Existence is modern in as far as it is administered by resourceful (that is, possessing knowledge, skill and technology), sovereign agencies. Agencies are sovereign in as far as they claim and successfully defend the right to manage and administer existence: the right to define order and, by implication, lay aside chaos, as that left-over that escapes the definition.

The typically modern practice, the substance of modern politics, of modern intellect, of modern life, is the effort to exterminate ambivalence: an effort to define precisely – and to suppress or eliminate everything that could not or would not be precisely defined. Modern practice is not aimed at the conquest of foreign lands, but at the filling of the blank spots in the *compleat mappa mundi*. It is the modern practice, not nature, that truly suffers no void.

Intolerance is, therefore, the natural inclination of modern practice. Construction of order sets the limits to incorporation and admission. It calls for the denial of rights, and of the grounds, of everything that cannot be assimilated – for de-legitimation of the other. As long as the urge to put paid to ambivalence guides collective and individual action, intolerance will follow – even if, ashamedly, it hides under the mask of toleration (which often means: you are abominable, but I, being generous, shall let you live).

The other of the modern state is the no-man's or contested land: the under- or over-definition, the demon of ambiguity. Since the sovereignty of the modern state is the power to define and to make the definitions stick – everything that self-defines or eludes the power-assisted definition is subversive. The other of this sovereignty is no-go areas, unrest and disobedience, collapse of law and order.

The other of modern intellect is polysemy, cognitive dissonance, polyvalent definitions, contingency; the overlapping meanings in the world of tidy classifications and filing cabinets. Since the sovereignty of the modern intellect is the power to define and to make the definitions stick – everything that eludes unequivocal allocation is an anomaly and a challenge. The other of this sovereignty is the violation of the law of the excluded middle.

In both cases, resistance to definition sets the limit to sovereignty, to power, to the transparency of the world, to its control, to order. That resistance is the stubborn and grim reminder of the flux which order wished to contain but in vain; of the limits to order; and of the necessity of ordering. Modern state and modern intellect alike need chaos – if only to go on creating order. They both thrive on the vanity of their effort.

Modern existence is both haunted and stirred into restless action by modern consciousness; and modern consciousness is the suspicion or awareness of the inconclusiveness of extant order; a consciousness prompted and moved by the premonition of inadequacy, nay non-viability, of the order-designing, ambivalence-eliminating project; of the randomness of the world and contingency of identities that constitute it. Consciousness is modern in as far as it reveals ever new layers of chaos underneath the lid of power-assisted order. Modern consciousness criticizes, warns and alerts. It makes the action unstoppable by ever anew unmasking its ineffectiveness. It perpetuates the ordering practice by disqualifying its achievements and laying bare its defeats.

Thus there is a *hate–love* relation between modern existence and modern culture (in the most advanced form of self-awareness), a symbiosis fraught with civil wars. In the modern era, culture is that obstreperous and vigilant Her Majesty's Opposition which makes the government feasible. There is no love lost, harmony, nor mirror-like similarity between the two: there is only mutual need and dependence – that *complementarity* which comes out of the opposition, which *is* opposition. However modernity resents its critique – it would not survive the armistice.

It would be futile to decide whether modern culture undermines or serves modern existence. It does both things. It can do each one only together with the other. Compulsive negation is the positivity of modern culture. Dysfunctionality of modern culture is its functionality. The modern powers' struggle for artificial order needs culture that explores the limits and the limitations of the power of artifice. The struggle for order informs that exploration and is in turn informed by its findings. In the process, the struggle sheds its initial hubris: the pugnacity born of naivety and ignorance. It learns, instead, to live with its own permanence, inconclusiveness – and prospectlessness. Hopefully, it would learn in the end the difficult skills of modesty and tolerance.

References

Collins, Stephen L. (1989) *From Divine Cosmos to Sovereign State: An Intellectual History of Consciousness and the Idea of Order in Renaissance England*. Oxford: Oxford University Press.

9.2   The Social Construction of Ambivalence (1991)

There are friends and enemies. And there are *strangers*.

Friends and enemies stand in an opposition to each other. The first are what the second are not, and vice versa. This does not, however, testify to their equal status. Like most other oppositions that order simultaneously the world in which we live and our life in the world, this one is a variation of the master-opposition between the *inside* and the *outside*. The outside is negativity to the inside's positivity. The outside is what the inside is not. The enemies are the negativity to the friends' positivity. The enemies are what the friends are not. The enemies are flawed friends; they are the *wilderness* that violates friends' *homeliness*, the *absence* which is a denial of friends' *presence*. The repugnant and frightening 'out there' of the enemies is, as Derrida would say, a *supplement* – both the addition to, and displacement of the cosy and comforting 'in here' of the friends. Only by crystallizing and solidifying what they are not (or what they do not wish to be, or what they would not say they are), into the counter-image of the enemies, may the friends assert what they are, what they want to be and what they want to be thought of as being.

Apparently, there is a symmetry: there would be no enemies were there no friends, and there would be no friends if not for the yawning abyss of enmity outside. Symmetry, however, is an illusion. It is the friends who *define* the enemies, and the appearance of symmetry is itself a testimony to their asymmetrical right to define. It is the friends who control the *classification* and the *assignment*. The opposition is an achievement and self-assertion of the friends. It is the product and the condition of the friends' narrative domination, of the friends' *narrative as the domination*. As far as they dominate the narration, set its vocabulary and fill it with meaning, friends are truly at home, among friends, at ease.

The rift between friends and enemies makes *vita contemplativa* and *vita activa* into mirror reflections of each other. More importantly, it guarantees their co-ordination. Subjected to the same principle of structuration, knowledge and action chime in, so that knowledge may inform the action and the action may confirm the truth of knowledge.

The friends/enemies opposition sets apart truth from falsity, good from evil, beauty from ugliness. It also differentiates between proper and improper, right and wrong, tasteful and unbecoming. It makes the world readable and thereby instructive. It dispels doubt. It enables the knowledgeable one to go on. It assures that one goes where one should. It makes the choice look like revealing the nature-made necessity – so that man-made necessity may be immune to the vagaries of choice.

Friends are called into being by the pragmatics of co-operation. Friends are moulded out of responsibility and moral duty. Friends are those for whose well-being I am responsible *before* they reciprocate *regardless* their reciprocation; only on this condition the co-operation, ostensibly a contractual, two-directional bond, can come into effect. Responsibility must be a gift if it is ever to become an exchange.

Enemies, on the other hand, are called into being by the pragmatics of struggle. Enemies are construed out of renunciation of responsibility and moral duty. The enemies are those who refuse responsibility for my well-being *before* I relinquish my responsibility for theirs, and *regardless* of my renunciation; only on this condition the struggle, ostensibly a two-sided enmity and reciprocated hostile action, may come into effect.

While the anticipation of friendliness is not necessary for the construction of friends, anticipation of enmity is indispensable in the construction of enemies. Thus the opposition between friends and enemies is one between *doing* and *suffering*, between being a *subject* and being an *object* of action. It is an opposition between reaching out and recoiling, between initiative and vigilance, ruling and being ruled, acting and responding.

With all the opposition between them, or – rather – *because* of that opposition, each of the two opposing modes stands for relationships. Following Simmel we may say that friendship and enmity, and only they, are forms of *sociation*; indeed, they are the archetypal forms of all sociation, and together constitute its two-pronged matrix. They make the frame within which sociation is possible; they exhaust the *possibility* of 'being *with* others'. Being a friend, and being an enemy, are the two modalities in which the *Other* may be recognized as another *subject* construed as a 'subject like the self', admitted into the self's life world, be counted, become and stay relevant. If not for the opposition between friend and enemy, none of this would be possible. Without the possibility of breaking the bond of responsibility, no responsibility would impress itself as a duty. If not for the enemies, there would be no friends. Without the possibility of difference, says Derrida, 'the desire of presence as such would not find its breathing space. That means by the same token that the desire carries in itself the destiny of its nonsatisfaction. Difference produces what it forbids, making possible the very thing that it makes impossible' (Derrida, 1974, p. 143).

Against this cosy antagonism, this conflict-torn collusion of friends and enemies, the *stranger* rebels. The threat he carries is more horrifying than that which one can fear from the enemy. The stranger threatens the sociation itself – the very *possibility* of sociation. He calls the bluff of the opposition between friends and enemies as the *compleat mappa mundi*, as the difference which consumes all differences and hence leaves nothing *outside* itself. As that opposition is the foundation on which rest all social life and all differences which patch it up and hold together, the stranger saps social life itself. And all this because the stranger is neither friend nor enemy; and because he may be both. And because we do not know, and have no way of knowing, which is the case.

The stranger is one (perhaps the main one, the archetypal one) member of the family of *undecidables* – those baffling yet ubiquitous unities that, in Derrida's words again, 'can no longer be included within philosophical (binary) opposition, resisting and disorganizing it, *without ever* constituting a third term, without ever leaving room for a solution in the form of speculative dialectics'. Here are a few examples of 'undecidables' discussed by Derrida:

The *pharmakon*: the Greek generic term which includes both remedies and poisons (the term used in Plato's *Phaedrus* as a simile for writing, and for this reason – in Derrida's view – indirectly responsible, through translations that aimed at eschewing its inherent ambiguity, for the direction taken by the post-Platonian Western metaphysics). *Pharmakon*, as it were, is 'the regular, ordered polysemy that has, through skewing, indetermination, or overdetermination, but without mistranslation, permitted the rendering of the same word by "remedy", "recipe", "poison", "drug", "filter" etc.' Because of this capacity, *pharmakon* is, first and foremost, powerful because ambivalent and ambivalent because powerful: 'It partakes of both good and ill, of the agreeable and disagreeable' (Derrida, 1981a, pp. 71, 99). *Pharmakon*, after all, 'is neither remedy nor poison, neither good nor evil, neither the inside nor the outside'. *Pharmakon* consumes and overrides opposition – the very possibility of opposition.

The *hymen*: a Greek word again, standing for both membrane and marriage, which for this reason signifies at the same time virginity – the uncompromised and uncompromising difference between the 'inside' and the 'outside' – and its violation by the fusion of the self and other. In the result, *hymen* is 'neither confusion nor distinction, neither identity nor difference, neither consummation nor virginity, neither the veil nor the unveiling, neither the inside nor the outside, etc.'

The *supplement*: in French this word stands for both an addition, and a replacement. It is, therefore, the other who 'joins in', the outside that enters the inside, the difference that turns into identity. In the result, the *supplement* 'is neither a plus nor a minus, neither an outside nor the complement of an inside, neither accident nor essence, etc.' (Derrida, 1981b, pp. 42–3).

Undecidables are all *neither/nor*; which is to say that they militate against the *either/or*. Their underdetermination is their potency: because they are nothing, they may be all. They put paid to the ordering power of the opposition, and so to the ordering power of the narrators of the opposition. Oppositions enable knowledge and action; undecidables paralyse them. Undecidables brutally expose the artifice, the fragility, the sham of the most vital of separations. They bring the outside into the inside, and poison the comfort of order with suspicion of chaos.

This is exactly what the strangers do.

The Horror of Indetermination

Cognitive (classificatory) clarity is a reflection, an intellectual equivalent of behavioural certainty. They arrive and depart together. How closely they are tied together, we learn in a flash when landing in a foreign country, listening to a foreign language, gazing at foreign conduct. The hermeneutic problems which we then confront offer a first glimpse of the awesome behavioural paralysis which follows the failure of classificatory ability. To understand, as Wittgenstein suggested, is to know how to go on. This is why hermeneutic problems (which arise when the meaning is not unreflectively evident, when we become aware that words and meaning are not the same thing, that there is a *problem* of meaning) are experienced as annoying. Unresolved hermeneutical problems mean uncertainty as to how the situation ought to be read and what response is likely to bring the desired results. At best, uncertainty is confusing and felt as discomforting. At worst, it carries a sense of danger.

Much of the social organization can be interpreted as sedimentation of the systematic effort to reduce the frequency with which hermeneutical problems are encountered and to mitigate the vexation such problems cause once faced. Probably the most common method of achieving this is that of the territorial and functional separation. Were this method applied in full and with maximum effect, hermeneutic problems would diminish as the physical distance shrinks and the scope and frequency of interaction grow. The chance of misunderstanding would not materialize, or would cause but a marginal disturbance when it occurs, if the principle of separation, the consistent 'restriction of interaction to sectors of assumed common understanding and mutual interest' (Barth, 1969, p. 15) were meticulously observed.

The method of territorial and functional separation is deployed both outwardly and inwardly. Persons who need to cross into a territory where they are bound to cause and to encounter hermeneutic problems, seek enclaves marked for the use of visitors and the services of functional mediators. Tourist countries, which expect a constant influx of large quantities of 'culturally undertrained' visitors, set aside such enclaves and train such mediators in anticipation.

Territorial and functional separation is a reflection of existing hermeneutic problems; it is, however, also a most powerful factor in their perpetuation and reproduction. As long as the segregation remains continuous and closely guarded, there is little chance that the probability of misunderstanding (or at least the anticipation of such misunderstanding) will ever diminish. Persistence and constant possibility of hermeneutic problems can be seen therefore as simultaneously the motive and the product of boundary-drawing efforts. As such, they have an in-built tendency of self-perpetuation. As boundary-drawing is never foolproof and some boundary-crossing is difficult to avoid, hermeneutic problems are likely to persist as a permanent 'grey area' surrounding the familiar world of daily life. That grey area is inhabited by *unfamiliars*; by the not-yet classified, or – rather – classified by criteria similar to ours, but as yet unknown to us.

The 'unfamiliars' come in a number of kinds, of unequal consequence. One pole of the range is occupied by those who reside in *practically* remote (that is, rarely visited) lands, and are thereby limited in their role to the setting of limits of familiar territory (the *ubi leones*, written down as danger warnings on the outer boundaries of the Roman maps). Exchange with such unfamiliars (if it takes place at all) is set aside from the daily routine and from the normal web of interaction – as a function of a *special category* of people (say, commercial travellers, diplomats or ethnographers), or a *special occasion* for the rest. Both (territorial and functional) means of institutional separation easily protect – indeed, reinforce – the unfamiliarity of the unfamiliars, together with their daily irrelevance. They also guard, though obliquely, the secure homeliness of one's own territory. Contrary to a widespread opinion, the advent of television, this huge and easily accessible peephole through which the unfamiliar ways may be routinely glimpsed, has neither eliminated the institutional separation nor diminished its effectivity. One may say that McLuhan's 'global village' has failed to materialize. The frame of a cinema or TV screen staves off the danger of spillage even more effectively than tourist hotels and fenced-off camping sites; the one-sidedness of communication firmly locks the unfamiliars on the screen as, essentially, incommunicado. The most recent invention of 'thematic' shopping malls, with Carribean villages, Indian reserves and Polynesian shrines closely packed together under one roof, has brought the old technique of institutional separation to the level of perfection reached in the past only by the zoo.

The phenomenon of *strangerhood* cannot, however, be reduced to the generation of – however vexing – hermeneutic problems.

Insolvency of the learned classification is upsetting enough, yet perceived as something less than a disaster as long as it can be referred to missing knowledge. If only I learned that language; if only I cracked the mystery of those strange customs . . . By themselves, hermeneutic problems do not undermine the trust in knowledge and attainability of behavioural certainty. If anything, they reinforce both. The way in which they define the remedy as learning another *method of classification*, another set of oppositions, the meanings of another set of symptoms, only corroborates the faith in essential orderliness of the world and particularly in the ordering capacity of knowledge. A moderate dose of puzzlement is pleasurable precisely because it resolves in the comfort of reassurance (this, as any tourist knows, is a major part of the attraction held by foreign trips, the more exotic the better). The difference is something one can live with, as long as one believes that the different world is, like ours, a 'world with a key', an orderly world like ours; just another orderly world inhabited by *either* friends *or* enemies with no hybrids to distort the picture and perplex the action, and with rules and divisions one may not know as yet, but may learn if needed.

Some strangers are not, however, the *as-yet-undecided*; they are, in principle, *undecidables*. They are the premonition of that 'third element' which should not be. These are the true hybrids, the monsters – not just *unclassified*, but *unclassifiable*. They do not question just this one opposition here and now: they question oppositions as such, the very principle of the opposition, the plausibility of dichotomy it suggests and feasibility of separation it demands. They unmask the brittle artificiality of division. They destroy the world. They stretch the temporary inconvenience of 'not knowing how to go on' into a terminal paralysis. They must be tabooed, disarmed, suppressed, exiled physically or mentally – or the world may perish.

Territorial and functional separation cease to suffice once the mere *unfamiliar* turns to be the true *stranger*, aptly described by Simmel as 'the man who comes today and stays tomorrow' (Simmel, 1971, p. 143). The stranger is, indeed, someone who refuses to remain confined to the 'far away' land or go away from our own and hence *a priori* defies the easy expedient of spatial or temporal segregation. The stranger comes into the life-world and settles here, and so – unlike the case of mere 'unfamiliars' – it becomes *relevant* whether he is a friend or a foe. He made his way into the life-world *uninvited*, thereby casting me on the receiving side of his initiative, making me into the object of action of which he is the subject: all this, as we remember, is a notorious mark of the *enemy*. Yet, unlike other, 'straightforward' enemies, he is not kept at a secure distance, nor on the other side of the battleline. Worse still, he claims a right to be an object of *responsibility* – the well-known attribute of the *friend*. If we press upon him the friend/enemy opposition, he would come out simultaneously under-and over-determined. And thus, by proxy, he would expose the failing of the opposition itself. He is a constant threat to the world's order.

Not for this reason only, though. There are more. For instance, the unforgettable and hence unforgivable original sin of the late entry: the fact that he had entered the realm of the life-world at a point of time which can be exactly pinpointed. He did not belong into the life-world 'initially', 'originally', 'from the very start', 'since time immemorial', and so he questions the extemporality of the life-world, brings into relief the 'mere historicality' of existence. The memory of the *event* of his coming makes of his very presence an event in history, rather than a fact of nature. His passage from the first to the second would infringe an important boundary on the map of existence, and thus must be resolutely resisted; such a passage would amount, after all, to the admission that nature is itself an event in history and that, therefore, the appeals to natural order or natural rights deserve no preferential treatment. Being an event in history, having a beginning, the presence of the stranger always carries the potential of an end. The stranger has a freedom to go. He may also be forced to go – or, at least, forcing him to go may be contemplated without violating the order of things. However protracted, the stay of the stranger is temporary – another infringement on the division which ought to be kept intact and preserved in the name of secure, orderly existence.

Even here, however, the treacherous incongruity of the stranger does not end. The stranger undermines the spatial ordering of the world – the fought-after co-ordination between moral and topographical closeness, the staying-together of friends and the remoteness of enemies. The stranger disturbs the resonance between physical and psychical distance: he is *physically close* while remaining *spiritually remote*. He brings into the inner circle of proximity the kind of difference and otherness that are anticipated and tolerated only at a distance – where they can be either dismissed as irrelevant or repelled as hostile. The stranger represents an incongruous and hence resented 'synthesis of nearness and remoteness' (Simmel, 1971, p. 145). His presence is a challenge to the reliability of orthodox landmarks and the universal tools of order-making. His proximity (as all proximity, according to Levinas) suggests a moral relationship, while his remoteness (as all remoteness, according to Erasmus) permits solely a contractual one: another important opposition compromised.

As always, the practical incongruity follows the conceptual one. The stranger who refuses to go away gradually transforms his temporary abode into a home territory – all the more so as his other, 'original' home recedes in the past and perhaps vanishes altogether. On the other hand, however, he retains (if only in theory), his freedom to go, and so is able to view local conditions with an equanimity the native residents can hardly afford. Hence another incongruous synthesis – this time between involvement and indifference, partisanship and neutrality, detachment and participation. The commitment the stranger declares, the loyalty he promises, the dedication he demonstrates cannot be trusted: they come complete with a safety valve of easy escape which most natives often envy but seldom possess.

The stranger's unredeemable sin is, therefore, the incompatibility between his presence and other presences, fundamental to the world order; his simultaneous assault on several crucial oppositions instrumental in the incessant effort of ordering. It is this sin which throughout modern history rebounds in the constitution of the stranger as the bearer and embodiment of *incongruity*; indeed, the stranger is a person afflicted with incurable sickness of *multiple incongruity*. The stranger is, for this reason, the bane of modernity. He may well serve as the archetypal example of Sartre's *le visquex* or Mary Douglas's *the slimy* – an entity ineradicably *ambivalent*, sitting astride an embattled barricade (or, rather, a substance spilled over the top of it so that it makes it slippery both ways), blurring a boundary line vital to the construction of a particular social order or a particular life-world.

No binary classification deployed in the construction of order can fully overlap with essentially non-discrete, continuous experience of reality. The opposition, born of the horror of ambiguity, becomes the main source of ambivalence. The enforcement of any classification inevitably means the production of anomalies (that is, phenomena which are perceived as 'anomalous' only as far as they span the categories whose staying apart is the meaning of order). Thus 'any given culture must confront events which seem to defy its assumptions. It cannot ignore the anomalies which its scheme produces, except at risk of forfeiting confidence' (Douglas, 1966, p. 33). There is hardly an anomaly more anomalous than the stranger. He stands *between* friend and enemy, order and chaos, the inside and the outside. He stands *for* the treacherousness of friends, for the cunning disguise of the enemies, for fallibility of order, vulnerability of the inside.

References

Barth, Fredrick (1969) *Ethnic Groups and Boundaries: The Social Organization of Cultural Difference*. Bergen: Universitet Ferlaget.

Derrida, Jacques (1974) *Of Grammatology*, trans. Gayatri Chakravorty Spivak. Baltimore: Johns Hopkins University Press.

Derrida, Jacques (1981a) *Disseminations*, trans. Barbara Johnson. London: Athlone.

Derrida, Jacques (1981b) *Positions*, trans. Alan Bass. Chicago: University of Chicago Press.

Douglas, Mary (1966) *Purity and Danger*. London: Routledge and Kegan Paul.

Simmel, Georg (1971) 'The Stranger.' In *On Individuality and Social Forms*. Chicago: University of Chicago Press.

10

Globalization and the New Poor

10.1 On Glocalization: Or Globalization for Some, Localization for Some Others (1998)

'Order matters most when it is lost or in the process of being lost', thus James Der Derian, who explains why this matters so much today by quoting American President George Bush's declaration, after the collapse of the Soviet empire, that the new enemy is uncertainty, unpredictability and instability (Der Derian, 1991). We may add that in our modern times order came to be identified, for all practical intents and purposes, with control and administration, which in their turn came to mean an established code of practice and ability to enforce obedience to the code. In other words, the idea of order related not so much to the things as they are, as to the ways of managing them; to the capacity of *ordering*, rather than any immanent quality of the things as they happened to be by themselves and at the moment. What George Bush must have meant was not so much the dissipation of the 'order of things', as the disappearance of means and the know-how needed to *put things in order* and keep them there.

The present-day 'New world disorder' (the apt and felicitous title of Kenneth Jowitt's book) does not refer, therefore, to the state of the world after the end of the Great Schism and the collapse of the power-block political routine. It reports, rather, our sudden awareness of the essentially elemental and contingent nature of things, which before was not so much non-existent as barred from sight by the all-energy consuming day-to-day reproduction of balance between the world powers. By dividing the world, power politics conjured up the image of totality. That world was made whole by assigning to each nook and cranny of the globe its significance in the 'global order of things' – to wit, in the two power-camps' conflict and equilibrium. The world was a totality in as far as there was nothing in that world which could escape such significance and so nothing could be indifferent from the point of view of the balance between the two powers that appropriated a considerable part of the world and cast the rest in the shadow of that appropriation. Everything in the world had a meaning, and that meaning emanated from a halved, yet single centre – from the two enormous power blocks locked up, riveted and glued to each other in all-out combat. With the Great Schism out of the way, the world does not look a totality anymore; it looks rather as a field of scattered and disparate forces, sedimenting in places difficult to predict and gathering momentum impossible to arrest.

To put it in a nutshell: *no one seems to be now in control*. Worse still, it is not clear what 'being in control' could, under the circumstances, be like. As before, all ordering is local and issue-oriented, but there is no locality that could pronounce for humankind as a whole, or an issue that could stand up for the totality of global affairs. It is this novel and uncomfortable perception which has been articulated (with little benefit to intellectual clarity) in the currently fashionable concept of *globalization*. The deepest meaning conveyed by the idea of globalization is that of the indeterminate, unruly and self-propelled character of world affairs: the absence of a centre, of a controlling desk, of a board of directors, a managerial office. Globalization is Jowitt's new world disorder under another name. In this, the term 'globalization' differs radically from another term, that of 'universalization' – once constitutive of the modern discourse of global affairs, but by now fallen into disuse and by and large forgotten.

Together with such concepts as 'civilization', 'development', 'convergence', 'consensus' and many other terms of early-and classic-modern debate, universalization conveyed the hope, the intention and the determination of order-making. Those concepts were coined on the rising tide of modern powers and the modern intellect's ambitions. They announced the will to make the world different from what it was and better than it was, and to expand the change and the improvement to global, species-wide dimensions. It also declared the intention to make the life conditions of everyone everywhere, and so everybody's life chances, equal. Nothing of all that has been left in the meaning of globalization, as shaped by the present discourse. The new term refers primarily to 'global effects', notoriously unintended and unanticipated, rather than 'global undertakings'. Yes, it says, our actions may have, and often do have, global effects; but no, we neither have nor are likely to obtain the means to plan and execute actions globally. Globalization is not about what we all or at least the most resourceful and enterprising among us wish or hope *to do*. It is about what is *happening to us all*. It explicitly refers to the foggy and slushy 'no man's land' stretching beyond the reach of the design and action capacity of anybody in particular.

How has this vast expanse of man-made wilderness (not the 'natural' wilderness that modernity set out to conquer and tame; but the postdomestication wilderness that emerged *after* the conquest and *out of it*) sprung into vision with that formidable power of obstinacy which is taken to be the defining mark of 'hard reality?' A plausible explanation is the growing experience of weakness, indeed of impotence, of the habitual, taken-for-granted ordering agencies. Among the latter, the pride of place throughout the modern era belonged to the state (one is tempted to say the *territorial* state, but the idea of the state and the 'territorial sovereignty' have become, in modern practice and theory, synonymous, and thus the phrase 'territorial state' turned pleonastic). The meaning of 'the state' has been precisely that of an agency claiming the legitimate right and the resources to set up and enforce the rules and the norms binding the run of affairs over a certain territory; the rules and the norms hoped and expected to turn contingency into determination, ambivalence into *Eindeutigkeit*, randomness into predictability – in short, chaos into order. To order a certain section of the world meant to set up a state endowed with the sovereignty to do just that. And the ambition to enforce a certain model of preferred order at the expense of other, competitive, models could be implemented solely through acquiring the vehicle of the state or occupying the driving seat of the existing one. Max Weber *defined* the state as the agency claiming the monopoly of the means of coercion and their use.

Order-making requires huge and continuous effort, which in turn calls for considerable resources. The legislative and executive sovereignty of the state was accordingly perched on the 'tripod of sovereignties': military, economic and cultural. An effective order-making capacity was unthinkable unless supported: by the ability to effectively defend the territory against challenges of other models of order, from both outside and inside the realm; by the ability to balance the books of the *Nazionalökonomie*; and by the ability to muster enough cultural resources to sustain the state's identity and distinctiveness. Only a few populations aspiring to state sovereignty of their own were large and resourceful enough to pass such a demanding test. The times when the ordering job was undertaken and performed primarily, perhaps solely, through the agency of sovereign states, were for that reason the times of relatively few states; and the establishment of any sovereign state required as a rule the suppression of state-formative ambitions of many lesser collectivities: undermining whatever they might possess of inchoate military capacity, economic self-sufficiency and cultural distinctiveness. Under the circumstances, the 'global scene' was the theatre of inter-state politics, which through armed conflicts or bargaining aimed first and foremost at the drawing and maintaining ('internationally guaranteeing') of the boundaries that set apart and enclosed the territory of each state's legislative and executive sovereignty. 'Global politics' concerned itself mostly with sustaining the principle of full and uncontested sovereignty of each state over its territory, with the effacing of the few 'blank spots' remaining on the world map, and with fighting off the danger of ambivalence arising from the overlapping of sovereignties. The meaning of the 'global order', consequently, boiled down to the sum-total of a number of local orders, each effectively maintained and efficiently policed by one, and one only, territorial state.

That parcelled-out world of sovereign states was superimposed for almost a half-century and until recently with two power blocks, each promoting a certain degree of coordination between state-managed orders within the territories of their respective 'meta-sovereignty', coupled with the assumption of each state's military, economic and cultural insufficiency. Gradually yet relentlessly a new principle was promoted – in political practice faster than in political theory – of supra-state integration, with the 'global scene' viewed increasingly as the theatre of coexistence and competition between blocks of states, rather than states themselves. The Bandung initiative to establish the incongruous 'non-block block', and the recurrent efforts to align non-aligned states, was an oblique acknowledgement of that new principle. It was, though, consistently and effectively sapped by the two super-blocks, which treated the rest of the world as the 20th-century equivalent of the 'blank spots' of the 19th-century state-building and state-enclosure race. Non-alignment, refusal to join one or another of the super-blocks, sticking to the old-fashioned and increasingly obsolete principle of supreme sovereignty vested with the state, was the equivalent of that 'no man's land' ambivalence which was fought off tooth and nail, competitively yet in unison, by modern states at their formative stage.

The political super-structure of the Great Schism era barred from sight the deeper, and – as it has now transpired – more seminal and lasting transformations in the mechanism of order-making. The change affected above all the role of the state. All three legs of the 'sovereignty tripod' have been broken beyond repair. The military, economic and cultural self-sufficiency, indeed self-sustainability, of the state – any state – ceased to be a viable prospect. In order to retain their law-and-order policing ability, the states had to seek alliances and voluntarily surrender ever-larger chunks of their sovereignty.

When the curtain eventually was torn apart, it uncovered an un-familiar scene, populated by bizarre characters: states which, far from being forced to give up their sovereign rights, actively and keenly sought surrender and clamoured for their sovereignty to be taken away and dissolved into the supra-state formations; long deceased yet born again, or never heard of but now duly invented 'ethnicities' much too small and inept to pass any of the traditional tests of sovereignty, but now demanding states of their own and the right to legislate and police order on their own territory; old nations escaping the federalist cages in which they had been incarcerated against their will, only to use their newly acquired decision-making freedom to pursue dissolution of their political, economic and military independ-ence in the European Market and NATO alliance.[1] The new chance, found in ignoring the stern and demanding conditions of statehood, had found its acknowledgement in the dozens of 'new nations' rushing to add new seats in the already overcrowded UN building, not designed to accommodate such numbers of 'equals'. Paradoxically, it is the demise of state sovereignty that made the idea of statehood so tremendously popular. In the caustic estimate of Eric Hobsbawm, once the Seychelles can have a vote in the UN as good as Japan's, 'the majority of the members of the UN is soon likely to consist of the late 20th-century (republican) equivalents to Saxe-Coburg-Gotha and Schwarzburg-Sonderhausen' (Hobsbawm, 1977).

Two books have appeared recently in France which trace the over-whelming impression of 'global chaos' to the principle of *territoriality*: one that served for the duration of the modern era as the major regulative norm in the on-going struggle for law and order, but – as their authors, Thual and Badie, indicate – which proved to be a major source of the contemporary world disorder (Badie, 1995; Thual, 1995). The authors point to the present practical impotence of the states, which, however, remain to this day the only sites and agencies for the articulation and execution of laws; devoid of all real executive power, no more self-sufficient, in fact unsustainable militarily, economically or culturally, those 'weak states', 'quasi-states', often 'imported states' (in Badie's expressions) keep nevertheless claiming territorial sovereignty, capitalizing on identity wars and invoking, or rather whipping up, dormant tribal instincts. It is easy to see that the kind of sovereignty which relies on tribal sentiments alone is a natural enemy of tolerance and civilized norms of cohabitation. But the territorial fragmentation of legislative and policing power with which it is intimately associated is also, in Thual's and Badie's view, a major obstacle to the effective control over forces that truly matter, but which are all or almost all global, extraterritorial, in their character.

Thual's and Badie's arguments carry a great deal of conviction. And yet their analysis seems to stop short of unravelling the full complexity of the present plight. Contrary to what the authors suggest, the territorial principle of political organization does not stem from the natural or contrived tribal instincts alone (not even primarily), and its relation to the processes described under the name of economic and cultural globalization is not just of the 'spoke in the wheel' kind. In fact, there seems to be an intimate kinship, mutual conditioning and reciprocal reinforcement between 'globalization' and the renewed emphasis on the 'territorial principle'. Global finance, trade and information industry depend for their liberty of movement and their unconstrained freedom to pursue their ends on the political fragmentation, the *morcellement* of the world scene. They have all, one may say, developed vested interests in 'weak states' – that is, in such states as are *weak* but nevertheless remain *states*. Deliberately or subconsciously, such inter-state institutions as there are exert coordinated pressures on all member or dependent states to destroy systematically everything that could stem or slow down the free movement of capital and limit market liberty. Throwing wide open the gates and abandoning any thought of autonomous economic policy is the preliminary, and meekly complied with, condition of eligibility for financial assistance from world banks and monetary funds. Weak states are precisely what the new world order, all too often mistaken for the world disorder, needs to sustain and reproduce itself. 'Quasi-states' can be easily reduced to the (useful) role of local police precincts, securing a modicum of order required for the conduct of business, but need not be feared as effective brakes on the global companies' freedom. As Michel Crozier pointed out many years ago, domination always consists of leaving as much leeway and freedom of manoeuvre to oneself as possible, while imposing as close as possible constraint of the decision-making of the dominated side; to rule, said Crozier, is to be close to the 'source of uncertainty'. This strategy was successfully applied once by state powers, which now find themselves on its receiving end – it is now world capital and money that are the focus and the source of uncertainty. It is not difficult to see that the replacement of territorial 'weak states' by some sort of global legislative and policing powers would be detrimental to the interests of the extraterritorial companies. And so it is easy to suspect that far from acting at cross-purposes and being at war with each other, political 'tribalization' and economic 'globalization' are close allies and fellow conspirators.

Integration and fragmentation, globalization and territorialization are mutually complementary processes; more precisely still, two sides of the same process: that of the world-wide redistribution of sovereignty, power, and freedom to act. It is for this reason that – following Roland Robertson's suggestion – it is advisable to speak of *glocalization* rather than globalization, of a process inside which the coincidence and intertwining of synthesis and dissipation, integration and decomposition are anything but accidental and even less are rectifiable.

The intimate connection between the ostensibly world-wide availability of cultural tokens and increasingly diversified, territorial uses made of them has turned by now into one of the staple topics of the present-day social-scientific study and discourse. By common agreement among the analysts of contemporary scene, 'globalization' does *not* mean cultural unification; the mass production of 'cultural material' does not lead to the emergence of anything like 'global culture'. The global scene needs to be seen rather as a matrix of possibilities, from which highly varied selections and combinations can be, and are, made; through the selection and combination, from the global yarn of cultural tokens, separate and distinct identities are woven; indeed, the local industry of self-differentiation turns into a globally determined characteristic of the late 20th century, postmodern or late modern, world. The global markets of commercial goods and information make the selectivity of absorption unavoidable – while the way the selections are made tends to be locally, or communally, selected to provide new symbolic markers for the extinct and resurrected, freshly invented or as yet postulated only, identities. Community, rediscovered by the born-again romantic admirers of *Gemeinschaft* (which they see now threatened once more by the callous, disembedding and depersonalizing forces – this time, however, rooted in the *global*, world-wide *Gesellschaft*) is not an antidote for globalization, but one of its indispensable global corollaries – simultaneously products and conditions.

But the *Gemeinschaft–Gesellschaft* opposition/connection is not the only dimension of the interplay between globalizing and localizing trends. It is not even the most important and seminal of dimensions – though the emphases common in the mainstream 'globalization' literature, which habitually present it as the main line of confrontation along which the most consequential battles are fought, would suggest just that. Glocalization is first and foremost a redistribution of privileges and deprivations, of wealth and poverty, of resources and impotence, of power and powerlessness, of freedom and constraint. It is, one may say, a process of world-wide *restratification*, in the course of which a new world-wide socio/cultural self-reproducing hierarchy is put together. That difference and communal identity, which the globalization of markets and information promotes and renders 'a must', is not a diversity of equal partners. What is free choice for some is cruel fate for some others. And since those others tend to grow unstoppably in numbers and sink ever deeper in despair born of prospectless existence, one will be right to perceive glocalization as the concentration of capital, finance and all other resources of choice and effective action – but also, and in the first place, as *concentration of freedom* to act.

Commenting on the findings of the latest UN's *Human Development Report*, that the total wealth of the top 358 'global billionaires' equals the combined incomes of 2.3 billion of the poorest people (45% of the world's population), Victor Keegan of *The Guardian* called the present reshuffling of the world resources 'a new form of highway robbery' (22 July 1996). Indeed, only 22 percent of the global wealth belongs to the so-called 'developing countries', which account for about 80 per cent of the world population. This is by no means the end of the story, as the share of current income received by the poor is smaller still: in 1991, 85 percent of the world's population received only 15 percent of its income. No wonder that in the last 30 years the abysmally meagre 2.3 percent of global wealth owned by 20 percent of poorest countries fell further still, to 1.4 percent. The global network of communication, acclaimed as the gateway to a new and unheard of freedom, is clearly very selectively used; it is a narrow cleft in the thick wall, rather than a gate. Few (and fewer) people get the passes entitling them to go through. 'All computers do for the Third World these days is to chronicle their decline more efficiently' – so says Keegan. And concludes: 'If (as one American critic observed) the 358 decided to keep $5 million or so each, to tide themselves over, and give the rest away, they could virtually double the annual incomes of nearly half the people on Earth. And pigs would fly'.

In the words of John Kavanagh of the Washington Institute of Policy Research, reported in the *Independent on Sunday*, 21 July 1996:

> Globalisation has given more opportunities for the extremely wealthy to make money more quickly. These individuals have utilised the latest technology to move large sums of money around the globe extremely quickly and speculate ever more efficiently. Unfortunately, the technology makes no impact on the lives of the world poor. In fact, globalisation is a paradox; while it is very beneficial to a very few, it leaves out or marginalises two-thirds of the world's population.

As the folklore of the generation of 'enlightened classes', gestated in the new, brave and monetarist world of Reagan and Thatcher, this opening up of sluices and dynamiting all dams will make the world a free place for everybody. Freedom (of trade and of capital mobility, first and foremost) is the hothouse in which wealth would grow faster than ever before; and once the wealth is multiplied, there will be more of it for everybody. The poor of the world, both old and new, the hereditary and the computer-made, would hardly recognize their plight in that folklore. The media are the message, and the media through which the establishment of the world-wide market is being perpetrated are such that they preclude the promised 'trickle-down' effect. New fortunes grow in the virtual reality, tightly isolated from the old-fashioned rough-and-ready realities of the poor. Creation of wealth is on the way to finally emancipating itself from the old, constraining and vexing connections with making things, processing materials, creating jobs and managing people. The old rich needed the poor to make and keep them rich. They do not need the poor any more. At long last, the bliss of ultimate freedom is nigh.

Since time immemorial, the conflict between rich and poor meant being locked for life in mutual dependency; and dependency meant the need to talk and seek compromise and agreement. This is less and less the case. It is not quite clear what the new 'globalized' rich and the new 'globalized' poor would talk about, why they should feel the need to compromise and what sort of agreed *modus coexistendi* they would be inclined to seek. The globalizing and the localizing trends are mutually reinforcing and inseparable, but their respective products are increasingly set apart and the distance between them keeps growing, while reciprocal communication comes to a standstill.

These worlds sedimented on the two poles, at the top and at the bottom of the emerging hierarchy, differ sharply and become increasingly *incommunicado* to each other, much as the 'no-go areas' of contemporary cities are carefully fenced off and bypassed by the traffic lines used for the mobility of the well-off residents. If for the first world, the world of the rich and the affluent, the space has lost its constraining quality and is easily traversed in both its 'real' and 'virtual' renditions, for the second world, the world of the poor, the 'structurally redundant', real space is fast closing up – the deprivation made yet more painful by the obtrusive media display of space conquest and the '*virtual* accessibility' of distances unreachable in the non-virtual reality. Shrinking of space abolishes the flow of time; the inhabitants of the first world live in a perpetual present, going through a succession of episodes hygienically insulated from both their past and their future; those people are constantly busy and perpetually 'short of time', since each moment of time is non-extensive – an experience identical to that of the time 'full to the brim'. People marooned in the opposite world are crashed and crushed under the burden of abundant, redundant and useless time they have nothing to fill with. In their time, 'nothing ever happens'. They do not 'control' time, but neither are they controlled by it, unlike their clocking-in, clocking-out ancestors, subject to the faceless rhythm of factory time. They can only kill time, as they are slowly killed by it.

Residents of the first world live in *time*, space does not matter for them, since spanning every distance is instantaneous. It is this experience that Jean Baudrillard encapsulates in his image of 'hyperreality', where the virtual and the real are no longer separable, since both share and miss in the same measure that 'objectivity', 'externality' and 'punishing power' which Emile Durkheim listed as the symptoms of 'reality'. Residents of the second world live in *space* – heavy, resilient, untouchable – which ties down time and keeps it beyond the residents' control. Their time is void; in their time, 'nothing ever happens'. Only the virtual, television time has a structure, a 'timetable'. The other time is monotonously ticking away, it comes and goes, making no demands and leaving apparently no trace. Its sediments appear all of a sudden, unannounced and uninvited. Immaterial, time has no power over that all-too-real space to which the residents of the second world are confined.

Glocalization, to sum up, polarizes mobility – that ability to use time to annul the limitation of space. That ability – or disability – divides the world into the globalized and the localized. 'Globalization' and 'localization' may be inseparable sides of the same coin, but the two parts of the world population seem to be living on different sides, facing one side only, much like the people of Earth see and scan only one hemisphere of the moon. Some inhabit the globe; others are chained to place.

Agnes Heller recalls meeting, on one of her long-distance flights, a middle-aged woman, who was an employee of an international trade firm, spoke five languages and owned three apartments in three different places.

> ...she constantly migrates, and among many places, and always to and fro. She does it alone, not as a member of community, although many people act like her... The kind of culture she participates in is not a culture of a certain place; it is the culture of a time. It is a culture of the *absolute present*. Let us accompany her on her constant trips from Singapore to Hong Kong, London, Stockholm, New Hampshire, Tokyo, Prague and so on. She stays in the same Hilton hotel, eats the same tuna sandwich for lunch, or, if she wishes, eats Chinese food in Paris and French food in Hong Kong. She uses the same type of fax, and telephones, and computers, watches the same films, and discusses the same kind of problems with the same kind of people. (Heller, 1995)

Heller finds it easy to empathize with her companion's experience. She adds, *pro domo sua*:

> Even foreign universities are not foreign. After one delivers a lecture, one can expect the same question in Singapore, Tokyo, Paris or Manchester. They are not foreign places, nor are they homes.   (Heller, 1995)

Jeremy Seabrook remembers Michelle, a girl from a neighbouring council estate:

> At fifteen her hair was one day red, the next blonde, then jet-black, then teased into Afro kinks and after that rat-tails, then plaited, and then cropped so that it glistened close to the skull...Her lips were scarlet, then purple, then black. Her face was ghost-white and then peach-coloured, then bronze as if it were cast in metal. Pursued by dreams of flight, she left home at sixteen to be with her boyfriend, who was twenty-six...At eighteen she returned to her mother, with two children...She sat in the bedroom which she had fled three years earlier; the faded photos of yesterday's pop stars still stared down from the walls. She said she felt a hundred years old. She was weary. She'd tried all that life could offer. Nothing else was left.   (Seabrook, 1985: 59)

Heller's fellow-passenger lives in an imaginary home which she does not need, and thus does not mind being imaginary. Seabrook's acquaintance performs imaginary flights from the home she resents for being stultifyingly real. Virtuality serves both, but to each offers different services with sharply different results. To Heller's travel companion, it helps to dissolve whatever constraints a real home may impose – to dematerialize space. To Seabrook's neighbour, it brings into relief the awesome and abhorring power of a home turned into prison – it decomposes time. The first experience is lived through as postmodern freedom; the second, as the postmodern version of slavery.

The first experience is, paradigmatically, that of the tourist (and it does not matter whether the purpose of tourism is business or pleasure). The tourists become wanderers and put the dreams of homesickness above the realities of home – because they want to; because they consider it the most reasonable life-strategy 'under the circumstances', or because they have been seduced by the true or imaginary pleasures of a sensation-gatherer's life. But not all wanderers are on the move because they prefer being on the move to staying put. Many would perhaps refuse to embark on a life of wandering were they asked, but they had not been asked in the first place. If they are on the move, it is because staying at home in a world made to the measure of the tourist is a humiliation and a drag. They are on the move because they have been pushed from behind, having been first spiritually uprooted from the place that holds no promise by a force of seducation too powerful, and often too mysterious, to resist. They see their plight as anything except as a manifestation of freedom. These are the *vagabonds'* dark vagrant moons reflecting the shine of bright tourist suns; the mutants of post modern evolution, the unfit rejects of the brave new species. The vagabonds are the waste of the world which has dedicated itself to tourist services.

The tourists stay or move at their heart's desire. They abandon the site when the new, untried opportunities beckon elsewhere. The vagabonds, however, know that they won't stay for long, however strongly they wish to, since nowhere that they stop are they welcome. The tourists move because they find the world within their reach irresistibly *attractive*; the vagabonds move because they find the world within their reach unbearably *inhospitable*. The tourists travel because they *want to*; the vagabonds, because they have *no other bearable choice*. The vagabonds are, one might say, involuntary tourists, but the notion of 'involuntary tourist' is a contradiction in terms. However much the tourist strategy may be a necessity in a world marked by shifting walls and mobile roads, freedom of choice is the tourist's flesh and blood. Take it away, and the attraction, the poetry and, indeed, the liveability of the tourist's life are all but gone. Globalization is geared to the tourists' dreams and desires. Its second effect – its *side*-effect – is the transformation of many others into vagabonds. The first effect breeds and inflates the second – indomitably and unstoppably. The second is the price of the first. The question is how to force that price down.

Let me repeat: once emancipated from space, capital needs no more itinerary labour (while its most emancipated avant-garde needs hardly *any* labour, mobile or immobile). And so the pressure to pull down the last remaining barriers to the free movement of money and the money-making commodities and information goes hand in hand with the pressure to dig new moats and erect new walls (variously called 'immigration' or 'nationality' laws) barring the movement of those who are uprooted, spiritually or bodily, in the result.[2] Green light for the tourists, red light for the vagabonds. Enforced localization guards the natural selectivity of the globalizing effects. The widely noted, increasingly worrying polarization of the world and its population is not an alien, disturbing influence in the process of globalization: it is its effect.

The poor will be always with us, and so will the rich, according to the age-old popular wisdom, now unearthed from the abyss of oblivion in which it was kept during the brief romance with the 'welfare state' and the process of sponsored or assisted 'development'. The rich/poor split is neither a novelty nor a temporary irritant which, with due effort, will go away tomorrow or some time later. The point is, however, that hardly ever before was this split so unambiguously, unequivocally, a *split*; a division unredeemed and unrelieved by mutual services or reciprocal dependency; a division with no more underlying unity than that between the clean typescript and the waste-paper basket. The rich, who happen to be at the same time the resourceful and the powerful among the actors of the political scene, do not need the poor either for the salvation of their souls (which they do not believe they have and which at any rate they would not consider worthy of care) or for staying rich or getting richer (which they gather would be easier if not for the calls to share some of the riches with the poor). The poor are not God's children on which to practice the redemption of charity. They are not the 'reserve army of labour' which needs to be groomed back into wealth production. They are not the consumers who must be tempted and cajoled into 'giving the lead to recovery'. Whichever way you look at them, the poor are of no use; the vagabonds are but the ugly caricatures of the tourists – and who would enjoy the sight of one's own distortions? This is a real novelty in the world undergoing the deep transformation which, sometimes due to an optical error, sometimes to placate the conscience, is dubbed 'globalization'.

The unity/dependency which underlay most historical forms of the rich/poor division used to be in all times the necessary condition of that – however residual – solidarity with the poor, which inspired the – however half-hearted and incomplete – efforts to relieve the poor's plight. It is that unity/dependency which is now missing. No wonder the pollsters of both competing camps inform their respective candidates for the US presidency that the voters want the benefits of the poor to be cut together with the taxes of the rich. No wonder both rivals do their best to overtake each other in their proposals to cut welfare assistance and to lavish the saved funds on building new prisons and employing more police.

As Pastor John Steinbruck, the minister at Luther Place Memorial Church in Washington, recently summed it up in *The Guardian*, 28 July 1996: 'This nation has as its symbol the Statue of Liberty, with the message carved at its base 'give me your poor, your homeless, your huddled masses'. But here we are now in this damn country, the richest in history, and we've forgotten all that'.

Notes

1 As could be expected, it is the ethnic minorities or, more generally, small and weak ethnic groups, incapable of running a state independently according to the standards of the 'world of the states' era, which are as a rule most unambiguously enthusiastic about the gathering might of the supra-state formations. Hence the incongruence of claims to the statehood argued in terms of allegiance to the institutions whose declared, and even more often suspected, mission is to limit it and in the end annul it altogether.

2 Saving the affluent part of Europe from the flood of war refugees was, by the Secretary of State's admission, the decisive argument in favour of US involvement in the Bosnian war.

References

Badie, B. (1995) *La Fin des territories*. Paris: Fayard.

Der Derian, J. (1991) 'S/N: International Theory, Balkanisation and the New World Order,' *Millennium* 20, 3.

Heller, A. (1995) 'Where are We at Home?' *Thesis Eleven* 41.

Hobsbawm, E. (1977) 'Some Reflections on the Breakup of Britain.' *New Left Review* 105.

Seabrook, J. (1985) *Landscapes of Poverty*. Oxford: Blackwell.

Thual, F. (1995) *Les Conflits identitaires*. Paris: Fayard.

10.2 From the Work Ethic to the Aesthetic of Consumption (1998)

Ours is a consumer society.

We all know, more or less, what it means to be a 'consumer'. A consumer is a person who consumes, and to consume means using things up: eating them, wearing them, playing with them and otherwise causing them to satisfy one's needs or desires. Since in our part of the world it is money which in most cases 'mediates' between desire and its satisfaction, being a consumer also means – normally means – *appropriating* most of the things destined to be consumed: buying them, paying for them and so making them one's exclusive property, barring everybody else from using them without one's permission.

To consume also means to destroy. In the course of consumption, the consumed things cease to exist, literally or spiritually. Either they are 'used up' physically to the point of complete annihilation, such as when things are eaten or worn out, or they are stripped of their allure, no longer arouse and attract desire, and forfeit their capacity to satisfy one's needs and wishes – for example, an overused toy or an over-played record – and so become unfit for consumption.

This is what being a consumer means, but what do we mean when we speak of a consumer society? Is there something special about being a consumer in a consumer society? And besides, is not every known society a society of consumers, to a greater or lesser extent? All the features listed in the preceding paragraph, except perhaps the need to pay money for things meant to be consumed, are surely present in any kind of society. Of course, what sort of objects we see as the potential stuff of consumption, and how we consume them, may differ from time to time and from one place to another, but no human being anywhere or any time can stay alive without consuming.

And so when we say that ours is a 'consumer society' we must have in mind something more than the trivial, ordinary and not particularly illuminating fact that all members of that society consume. Ours is a 'consumer society' in a similarly profound and fundamental sense in which the society of our predecessors (modern society in its industrial phase described in the previous chapter) used to deserve the name of a 'producer society' in spite of the fact that people have produced since the beginning of the human species and will go on producing until the species' demise. The reason for calling that older type of modern society a 'producer society' was that it engaged its members *primarily* as producers; the way in which that society shaped up its members was dictated by the need to play this role and the norm that society held up to its members was the ability and the willingness to play it. In its present late-modern, second-modern or post-modern stage, society engages its members – again *primarily* – in their capacity as consumers. The way present-day society shapes up its members is dictated first and foremost by the need to play the role of the consumer, and the norm our society holds up to its members is that of the ability and willingness to play it.

The difference between then and now is not as radical as abandoning one role and replacing it with another. Neither of the two societies could do without at least some of its members taking charge of producing things to be consumed, and all members of both societies do, of course, consume. The difference is one of emphasis, but that shift of emphasis does make an enormous difference to virtually every aspect of society, culture and individual life. The differences are so deep and ubiquitous that they fully justify speaking of our society as a society of a separate and distinct kind – a consumer society.

The passage from producer to consumer society has entailed many profound changes; arguably the most decisive among them is, however, the fashion in which people are groomed and trained to meet the demands of their social identities (that is, the fashion in which men and women are 'integrated' into the social order and given a place in it). Panoptical institutions, once crucial in that respect, have fallen progressively out of use. With mass industrial employment fast shrinking and universal military duty replaced with small, voluntary and professional armies, the bulk of the population is unlikely ever to come under their direct influence. Technological progress has reached the point where productivity grows together with the tapering of employment; factory crews get leaner and slimmer; 'downsizing' is the new principle of modernization. As the editor of the *Financial Times* Martin Wolf calculates, between 1970 and 1994 the proportion of people employed in industry fell from 30 per cent to 20 per cent in the European Union and from 28 per cent to 16 per cent in the USA, while industrial productivity progressed on average by 2.5 per cent per annum (Wolf, 1997, p. 5).

The kind of drill in which the panoptical institutions excelled is hardly suitable for the training of consumers. Those institutions were good at training people in routine, monotonous behaviour, and reached that effect through the limitation or complete elimination of choice; but it is precisely the absence of routine and the state of constant choice that are the virtues (indeed, the 'role prerequisites') of a consumer. And so, in addition to being much reduced in the post-industrial and post-conscription world, the panoptical drill is also irreconcilable with the needs of a consumer society. The qualities of temperament and life attitudes which the panoptical drill excels in cultivating are counter-productive in the production of ideal consumers.

Ideally, acquired habits should lie on the shoulders of the consumers just like the religiously/ethically inspired vocational and acquisitive passions used to lie, as Max Weber repeated after Baxter, on the shoulders of the protestant saint: 'like a light cloak, ready to be thrown aside at any moment' (Weber, 1976, p. 181). And habits are indeed continually, daily, at the first opportunity thrown aside, never given the chance to solidify into the iron bars of a cage. Ideally, nothing should be embraced by a consumer firmly, nothing should command a commitment forever, no needs should be ever seen as fully satisfied, no desires considered ultimate. There ought to be a proviso 'until further notice' attached to any oath of loyalty and any commitment. It is the volatility, the in-built temporariness of all engagement that counts; it counts more than the engagement itself, which should not outlast the time necessary for consuming the object of desire (or for the desirability of that object to wane).

That all consumption takes time is in fact the bane of a consumer society and a major worry of the merchandisers of consumer goods. Ideally, the consumer's satisfaction ought to be instant, and this in a double sense. Consumed goods should bring satisfaction immediately, requiring no delay, no protracted learning of skills and no lengthy groundwork; but the satisfaction should end the moment the time needed for their consumption is up, and that time ought to be reduced to a bare minimum. This reduction is best achieved if the consumers cannot hold their attention nor focus their desire on any object for long; if they are impatient, impetuous and restive, and above all easily excitable and equally susceptible to losing interest.

When waiting is taken out of wanting and wanting out of waiting, the consumptive capacity of consumers may be stretched far beyond the limits set by any natural or acquired needs or determined by the physical endurability of the objects of desire. The traditional relationship between needs and their satisfaction will then be reversed: the promise and hope of satisfaction will precede the need and will be always greater than the extant need, yet not too great to preclude the desire for the goods which carry that promise. As a matter of fact, the promise is all the more attractive the less the need in question is familiar; there is a lot of fun in living through an experience one did not even know existed and was available. The excitement of the new and unprecedented sensation is the name of the consumer game. As Mark C. Taylor and Esa Saarinen put it, 'desire does not desire satisfaction. To the contrary, desire desires desire' (Taylor and Saarinen, 1994, p. 11), the desire of an *ideal* consumer at any rate. The prospect of the desire fading off, dissipating and having nothing in sight to resurrect it, or the prospect of the world with nothing left in it to be desired, must be the most sinister of the ideal consumer's horrors.

To increase their capacity for consumption, consumers must never be given rest. They need to be constantly exposed to new temptations in order to be kept in a state of a constantly seething, never wilting excitation and, indeed, in a state of suspicion and disaffection. The baits commanding them to shift attention need to confirm such suspicion while offering a way out of disaffection: 'You reckon you've seen it all? You ain't seen nothing yet!'

It is often said that the consumer market seduces its customers. But in order to do so it needs customers who are ready and keen to be seduced (just as, in order to command his labourers, the factory boss needed a crew with the habits of discipline and command-following firmly entrenched). In a properly working consumer society consumers seek actively to be seduced. They live from attraction to attraction, from temptation to temptation, from swallowing one bait to fishing for another, each new attraction, temptation and bait being somewhat different and perhaps stronger than those that preceded them; just as their ancestors, the producers, lived from one turn of the conveyer belt to an identical next.

To act like that is, for the fully-fledged, mature consumer, a compulsion, a must; yet that 'must', that internalized pressure, that impossibility of living one's life in any other way, reveals itself to them in the form of a free exercise of will. The market might have already picked them up and groomed them as consumers, and so deprived them of their freedom to ignore its temptations, but on every successive visit to a market place consumers have every reason to feel in command. They are the judges, the critics and the choosers. They can, after all, refuse their allegiance to any one of the infinite choices on display – except the choice of choosing between them, that is. The roads to self-identity, to a place in society, to life lived in a form recognizable as that of meaningful living, all require daily visits to the market place.

In the industrial phase of modernity one fact was beyond all questioning: that everyone must be a producer first, before being anything else. In 'modernity mark two', the consumers' modernity, the brute unquestionable fact is that one needs to be consumer first, before one can think of becoming anything in particular.

The Making of a Consumer

In recent years we heard politicians of all political hues speaking in unison, wistfully and enticingly, of 'consumer-led recovery'. Falling output, empty order books and sluggish high-street trade all tend to be blamed on lack of consumer interest or 'consumer confidence' (which means the consumer's desire to buy on credit is strong enough to outweigh their fear of insolvency). The hopes of all these troubles being chased away, of things starting to hum anew, are pinned on the consumers doing their duty again – wishing once more to buy, to buy a lot, and to buy ever more. 'Economic growth', the main modern measure of things being normal and in good order, the main index of a society working as it should, is seen in the consumer society as dependent not so much on the 'productive strength of the nation' (healthy and plentiful labour force, full coffers and daring entrepreneurship of the capital owners and managers), as on the zest and vigour of its consumers. The role once performed by work in linking together individual motives, social integration and systemic reproduction, has now been assigned to consumer activity.

Having dismantled the 'pre-modern' – traditional, ascriptive mechanisms of social placement, which left to men and women only the relatively straightforward task of 'sticking to one's own kind', of living up to (but not above) the standards attached to the 'social category' into which they were born – modernity charged the individual with the task of 'self-construction': building one's own social identity if not fully from scratch, at least from its foundation up. Responsibility of the individual – once confined to obeying the rules that defined in no uncertain terms what it meant to be a nobleman, a tradesman, a mercenary soldier, a craftsman, a farm tenant or a farm hand – now extended to include the choice of social definition itself and having this socially recognized and approved.

Initially, work was offered as the prime tool in coping with this new, modern duty. The sought-after and diligently built social identity took working skills, the site of employment and the career scheme attached to employment as its major determinants. Identity, once selected, had to be built once and for all, for life, and so was in principle at least the employment, the vocation, the life-work. The building of identity was to be steady and consistent, proceeding through a succession of clearly defined stages (no wonder the metaphor of 'building' was picked to convey the nature of 'identity work' to be done), and so was the work-career. The fixed itinerary of work-career and the prerequisites of lifelong identity construction fit each other well.

A steady, durable and continuous, logically coherent and tightly-structured working career is however no longer a widely available option. Only in relatively rare cases can a permanent identity be defined, let alone secured, through the job performed. Permanent, well guarded and assured jobs are now a rarity. The jobs of the old, 'for life', sometimes even hereditary, character are confined to a few old industries and old professions and are rapidly shrinking in number. New vacancies tend to be fixed term, until further notice and part-time. They are often combined with other occupations, and deprived of any safeguards of continuity, let alone of permanence. The catchword is flexibility, and this increasingly fashionable notion stands for a game of hire and fire with very few rules attached, but with power to change the rules unilaterally while the game is still being played.

Nothing truly lasting could be reasonably hoped to be erected on this kind of shifting sand. Purely and simply, the prospect of constructing a lifelong identity on the foundation of work is, for the great majority of people (except, for the time being at least, the practitioners of a few highly skilled and highly privileged professions), dead and buried.

Nevertheless, this momentous departure has not been experienced as a major earthquake or an existential threat. This is because the nature of common preoccupations with identities has also changed in a way which would render the old-fashioned work-careers utterly unsuitable and indeed out of joint with the kind of tasks and worries which the new kind of identity-care entails. In the world in which, according to George Steiner's pithy aphorism, all cultural products are calculated for 'maximal impact and instant obsolescence', a lifelong construction of an a priori designed identity would indeed spell trouble. As Ricardo Petrella put it, the present global trends direct 'economies towards the production of the ephemeral and the volatile – through the massive reduction of the life-span of products and services – and of the precarious (temporary, flexible and part-time jobs)' (Petrella, 1997, p. 17).

Whatever identity one may contemplate and desire, must possess, just like today's labour market, the quality of flexibility. It must be amenable to a change at short notice or without notice and be guided by the principle of keeping all options, or at least as many options as possible, open. The future is bound to be full of surprises, and so proceeding otherwise would amount to a self-deprivation: to the cutting off of the yet unknown, only vaguely intuited benefits that the future meanderings of fate, as well as the unprecedented and unanticipated life-offers, may bring.

Cultural fashions dynamite their entry into the public vanity fair, but they also grow obsolete and turn ludicrously old-fashioned even faster than it takes to grasp public attention. It is therefore better to keep each current identity temporary, to embrace it lightly, to make sure that it will fall away once the arms are open to embrace its new, brighter, or just untested replacement. Perhaps it would be more to the point to speak of self-identity in the plural: the life-itinerary of most individuals is likely to be strewn with discarded and lost identities. Each successive identity is likely to remain incomplete and conditional, and so the snag is how to stave off the danger of its ossification. Perhaps even the very term 'identity' has lost its usefulness, since it belies more than it reveals of the most common life-experience: more and more often concerns with social placement are fed by the fear of an identification too tough and stiff to be revoked if need be. The desire of identity and horror of satisfying that desire, the attraction and the repulsion that the thought of identity evokes, mix and blend to produce a compound of lasting ambivalence and confusion.

Concerns of this kind are much better served by the volatile, infinitely inventive and erratic market of consumer goods. Whether meant for durable or momentary consumption, consumer goods are not, by definition, intended to last forever – no resemblance here to a 'lifelong work career' or 'jobs for life'. Consumer goods are meant to be used up and to disappear; the idea of temporariness and transitoriness is intrinsic to their very denomination as objects of consumption; consumer goods have *memento mori* written all over them, even if with an invisible ink.

And so there is a sort of preordained harmony or resonance between these qualities of consumer goods and the ambivalence endemic to contemporary identity concerns. Identities, just like consumer goods, are to be appropriated and possessed, but only in order to be consumed, and so to disappear again. As in the case of marketed consumer goods, consumption of an identity should not – must not – extinguish the desire for other, new and improved identities, nor preclude the ability to absorb them. This being the requirement there is not much point in looking any further for the tools than the market place. 'Aggregate identities', loosely arranged of the purchasable, not-too-lasting, easily detachable and utterly replaceable tokens currently available in the shops, seem to be exactly what one needs to meet the challenges of contemporary living.

If this is what the energy released by identity problems is expended on, then no specialized social mechanisms of 'normative regulation' or 'pattern maintenance' are necessary; neither do they seem desirable. The traditional, panoptical methods of drill would clearly go against the grain of the consumer's tasks and prove disastrous to the society organized around desire and choice. But would any alternative method of normative regulation fare any better? Is not the very idea of normative regulation, at least on a global-societal scale, a thing of the past? Once crucial to 'get people to work' in a society of working people, did it not outlive its usefulness in the society of consumers? The sole purpose of any norm is to use the human agency of free choice to limit or altogether eliminate freedom of choice; to elbow out or to cut off completely all possibilities except one – the one promoted by the norm. But the side effect of killing choice, and particularly the choice most abominable from the point of view of normative, order-instilling regulation – a volatile, whimsical and easily revokable choice – would be equal to the killing of the consumer in the human being; the most horrifying disaster that may befall the market-centred society.

Normative regulation is thus 'dysfunctional' and so undesirable for the perpetuation, smooth functioning and prosperity of a consumer market, but it also appears repulsive to its clients. The interests of consumers and market operators meet here; in a curious and unanticipated form the message conveyed by the old adage 'what is good for General Motors is good for the United States' comes true (with the proviso, that 'United States' is nothing else but an aggregate of its citizens). The 'consumer spirit', much like the merchandising companies which thrive on it, rebels against regulation. A society of consumers is resentful of all legal restrictions imposed on freedom of choice, of any delegalization of potential objects of consumption, and manifests its resentment by widespread support willingly offered to most 'deregulatory' measures.

Similar resentment is shown in the hitherto unheard-of-approval given in the US and elsewhere to the reduction of social services – centrally administered and guaranteed provisions of necessities – providing the reduction goes hand in hand with the lowering of taxes. The slogan of 'more money in the taxpayer's pocket', so popular on the left and right of the political spectrum that it is no longer seriously contested, appeals to consumers' duty to exercise choice, a duty already internalized and reforged into the life-vocation. The promise of more money left in the pocket after taxes is attractive to the electorate not so much for the promise of more consumption, as for the prospect of more choice of what is to be consumed, more pleasures of shopping and choosing; it is to that promise of more frequently exercised choice that it is believed to owe its astonishing seductive power.

For all practical intents and purposes, it is the means, not the end, that counts. Fulfilling the vocation of the consumer means more choosing, whether or not this results in more consumption. To embrace the modality of the consumer means first and foremost falling in love with choice; only in the second, and not at all indispensable place, does it mean consuming more.

Work as Judged by Aesthetics

Producers can fulfil their vocation only collectively; production is a collective endeavour, it presumes the division of tasks, cooperation of actors and coordination of their activities. Certain partial actions can be performed on occasion singly and in solitude, but even then dovetailing them with other actions which converge on the creation of the final product remains the crucial part of the task and stays high on the performer's mind. Producers are together even when they act apart. The work of each one can only gain from more inter-individual communication, harmony and integration.

Consumers are just the opposite. Consumption is a thoroughly individual, solitary, and in the end lonely activity; an activity which is fulfilled by quenching and arousing, assuaging and whipping up a desire which is always a private, and not easily communicable sensation. There is no such thing as 'collective consumption'. True, consumers may get together in the course of consumption, but even then the actual consumption remains a thoroughly lonely, individually lived-through experience. Getting together only underlies the privacy of the consuming act and enhances its pleasures.

Choosing is more satisfying when performed in the company of other choosers, preferably inside a temple dedicated to the cult of choosing and filled to the brim with worshippers of choice; this is one of the foremost pleasures of going out to dinner in a heavily booked-up restaurant, of milling around a crowded shopping mall or amusement park, of group sex. But what is jointly celebrated in all these and similar choice is the *individuality* of choice and consumption. The individuality of each choice is restated and reconfirmed through being replicated by the copy-cat actions of the crowd of choosers. Were this not so, there would be nothing to be gained by the consumer from consuming in company. The activity of consumption is a natural enemy of all coordination and integration. It is also immune to their influence, rendering all efforts of bonding impotent in overcoming the endemic loneliness of the consuming act. Consumers are alone even when they act together.

Freedom to choose sets the stratification ladder of consumer society and so also the frame in which its members, the consumers, inscribe their life aspirations – a frame that defines the direction of efforts towards self-improvement and encloses the image of a 'good life'. The more freedom of choice one has, and above all the more choice one freely exercises, the higher up one is placed in the social hierarchy, the more public deference and self-esteem one can count on and the closer one comes to the 'good life' ideal. Wealth and income do count, of course; without them, choice is limited or altogether denied. But the role of wealth and income as *capital* – that is, money which serves first and foremost to turn out more money – recedes to a second and inferior place if it does not disappear from view (and from the pool of motivations) altogether. The prime significance of wealth and income is in the stretching of the range of consumer choice.

Hoarding, saving or investing would make sense solely for the promise they hold for the future widening of consumer choice. They are not, however, the options intended for the bulk of ordinary consumers, and were they embraced by a majority of consumers, they would spell disaster. Rising savings and shrinking credit purchases are bad news; the swelling of consumer credit is welcomed as the sure sign of 'things moving in the right direction'. A consumer society would not take lightly a call to delay gratification. A consumer society is a society of credit cards, not savings books. It is a 'now' society. A wanting society, not a waiting society.

Again, there is no need for 'normative regulation' with its attendant disciplining drill and ubiquitous policing to make sure that human wants are harnessed to the market-operators' profits, or any need to reforge the 'needs of economy', the consumer-goods economy, to match the desires of consumers. Seduction, display of untested wonders, promise of sensations yet untried but dwarfing and overshadowing everything tried before, will do nicely. Providing of course, that the message falls on receptive ears and that all eyes are focused on thrill-presaging things when scanning the signals. Consumption, ever more varied and rich consumption, must appear to the consumers as a right to enjoy, not a duty to suffer. The consumers must be guided by aesthetic interests, not ethical norms.

It is aesthetics, not ethics, that is deployed to integrate the society of consumers, keep it on course, and time and again salvage it from crises. If ethics accord supreme value to duty well done, aesthetics put a premium on sublime experience. Fulfilment of duty has its inner, time-extensive logic and so it structures time, gives it a direction, makes sense of such notions as gradual accumulation or delay of fulfilment. The search for experience, however, has no good reason to be postponed, since nothing but 'waste of opportunity' may follow the delay. Opportunity of experience does not need nor justify groundwork, since it comes unannounced and vanishes if not instantly grasped (waning, to be sure, shortly after having been grasped). Opportunity of experience is something to be caught in full flight. There is no peculiar moment especially suitable for doing this. One moment does not differ in this respect from another, each moment is equally good – 'ripe' – for the purpose.

Besides, the choice of the moment is the one choice not available to those who have chosen choice-making as their mode of life. It is not for the consumer to decide when the opportunity of a mind-boggling experience may arise, and so she or he must be ever ready to open the door and welcome it. He or she must be constantly on the alert, permanently capable of appreciating the chance when it comes and doing whatever is needed to make the best of it.

If the producer society is Platonian by heart, seeking unbreakable rules and the ultimate patterns of things, the consumer society is Aristotelian – pragmatic, flexible, abiding by the principle that one worries about crossing the bridge no earlier (but no later either) than one comes to it. The sole initiative left to a sensible consumer is to be on that spot where opportunities are known to be thick on the ground, and be there at the time when they are known to be particularly dense. Such initiative can accommodate only wisdom of a 'phronesis' kind, a collection of rules of thumb, not foolproof recipes and algorithmic commands. Hence it requires a lot of trust, and above all it needs safe havens where that trust can be securely anchored. No wonder a consumer society is also a counselling and advertising paradise, as well as a fertile soil for prophets, fortune-tellers or pedlars of magic potions and distillers of philosophical stones.

To sum up: it is the aesthetics of consumption that now rules where the work ethic once ruled. For the successful alumni of consumer training the world is an immense matrix of possibilities, of intense and ever more intense sensations, of deep and deeper still experiences (in the sense conveyed by the German notion of *Erlebnis*, as distinct from *Erfahrung*; both German terms translate into English as 'experience'. Roughly speaking, *Erlebnis* is 'what I live through', while *Erfahrung* is 'what happens to me'). The world and all its fragments are judged by their capacity to occasion sensations and *Erlebnisse* – the capacity to arouse desire, the most pleasurable phase of the consumer's life pursuits, more satisfying than the satisfaction itself. It is by the varying volumes of that capacity that objects, events and people are plotted on the map; the world map in most frequent use is aesthetic, rather than cognitive or moral.

The status occupied by work, or more precisely by the job performed, could not but be profoundly affected by the present ascendancy of aesthetic criteria. As we have seen before, work has lost its privileged position – that of an axis around which all other effort at self-constitution and identity-building rotate. But work has also ceased to be the focus of particularly intense ethical attention in terms of being a chosen road to moral improvement, repentance and redemption. Like other life activities, work now comes first and foremost under aesthetic scrutiny. Its value is judged by its capacity to generate pleasurable experience. Work devoid of such capacity – that does not offer 'intrinsic satisfaction' – is also work devoid of value. Other criteria (also its supposedly morally ennobling impact) cannot withstand the competition and are not powerful enough to save work from condemnation as useless or even demeaning for the aesthetically-guided collector of sensations.

Vocation as Privilege

There is nothing particularly new about jobs differing widely in terms of their capacity to bring satisfaction. Some jobs were always sought-after as being richly satisfying and 'fulfilling', while many others were suffered as drudgery. Certain jobs were 'meaningful' and lent them-selves more easily than other kinds of work to being regarded as a vocation, a source of pride and self-esteem. However, the point was that from the ethical perspective no job could be seriously argued to be deprived of value and demeaning; all work added to human dignity and all work equally served the cause of moral propriety and spiritual redemption. From the work ethic point of view, any work – work *as such* – 'humanized', whatever immediate pleasures (or their absence) it held in store for its performers. Ethically speaking, the feeling of a duty fulfilled was the most direct, decisive and in the end sufficient satisfaction work could bring, and in this respect all kinds of work were equal. Even the engrossing, intoxicating sensation of self-fulfilment experienced by the lucky few who could live their trade or profession as a true calling, as a secular mission of sorts, tended to be ascribed to the same awareness of the 'duty well done' which was in principle open to the performers of all jobs, even the meanest and the least engaging. The work ethic conveyed a message of equality; it played down the otherwise obvious differences between jobs, their potentials for satisfaction, their status-and prestige-bestowing capacities, as well as the material benefits they offered.

Not so the aesthetic scrutiny and evaluation of work. This emphas-izes distinction, magnifies the differences and elevates certain profes-sions to the rank of engrossing, refined objects of aesthetic, indeed artistic, experience, while denying to other kinds of remunerated livelihood-securing occupations any value at all. The 'elevated' pro-fessions call for the same qualities which are demanded for the appre-ciation of art – good taste, sophistication, discernment, disinterested dedication and a lot of schooling. Other types of work are regarded as so uniformly abject and worthless that by no stretch of the imagina-tion can they become objects of willing, unforced choice. One is likely to perform jobs of that kind only out of necessity and only if one is denied access to any other means of survival.

Jobs in the first category are 'interesting'; jobs in the second cate-gory are 'boring'. These two brief verdicts encapsulate complex aes-thetic criteria which gives them substance. Their 'no justification needed', 'no appeal allowed' bluntness bear an oblique testimony to the ascendancy of aesthetics now spreading through the land of work,

previously a province of ethics. Like everything else which may reasonably hope to become the target of desire and an object of free
consumer choice, jobs must be 'interesting' – varied, exciting, allowing for adventure, containing certain (though not excessive) measures
of risk, and giving occasion to ever-new sensations. Jobs that are
monotonous, repetitive, routine, unadventurous, allowing no initiative and promising no challenge to wits nor a chance for self-testing
and self-assertion, are 'boring'. No fully-fledged consumer would
conceivably agree to undertake them on her or his own will, unless
cast in a situation of no choice (that is, unless his or her identity as a
consumer, a free chooser, has already been forfeited, withdrawn or
otherwise denied). Such jobs are devoid of aesthetic value and for that
reason stand little chance of becoming vocations in a society of
experience-collectors.

The point is, though, that in the world where aesthetic criteria rule
supreme the jobs in question have not retained their formerly assumed
ethical value either. They would be chosen willingly only by people as
yet unprocessed by the society of consumers and unconverted to
consumerism, and thus satisfied with selling their labour in exchange
for bare survival (first generation immigrants and 'guest workers'
from poor countries, or the residents of poor countries drawn into
factories set by the immigrant capital travelling in search of cheap
labour could be said to fall into this category). Others need to be
forced into accepting jobs that offer no aesthetic satisfaction. Rough
coercion once hidden under the veneer of the work ethic now appears
bare-faced and unconcealed. Seduction and arousal of desires, those
otherwise unfailingly effective integrating/motivating vehicles of a
consumer society, are in this case appallingly irrelevant and toothless.
In order to fill jobs that fail the aesthetic test with people already
converted to consumerism, a situation of no choice, enforcement and
fight for elementary survival must be artificially re-created. This time,
though, without the saving grace of moral ennoblement.

Like freedom of choice and mobility, the aesthetic value of work has
turned into a potent stratifying factor in the society of consumers. The
trick is no longer to limit work time to the bare minimum, so vacating
more space for leisure, but on the contrary to efface altogether the line
dividing vocation from avocation, job from hobby, work from recrea-
tion; to lift work itself to the rank of supreme and most satisfying
entertainment. An entertaining job is a highly coveted privilege. And
those privileged by it jump headlong into the opportunities of strong
sensations and thrilling experience which such jobs offer. 'Worka-
holics' with no fixed hours of work, preoccupied with the challenges
of their jobs twenty-four hours a day and seven days a week, may be

found today not among the slaves, but among the elite of the lucky and successful.

Work that is rich in gratifying experience, work as self-fulfilment, work as the meaning of life, work as the core or the axis of everything that counts, as the source of pride, self-esteem, honour and deference or notoriety, in short, work as *vocation*, has become the privilege of the few; a distinctive mark of the elite, a way of life the rest may watch in awe, admire and contemplate at a distance but experience only vicariously through pulp fiction and the virtual reality of televised docu-drama. That rest is given no chance of living-through their jobs in a way the vocations are lived.

The 'flexible labour market' neither offers nor permits commitment and dedication to any currently performed occupation. Getting attached to the job in hand, falling in love with what the job requires its holder to do, identifying one's place in the world with the work performed or the skills deployed, means becoming a hostage to fate; it is neither very likely nor to be recommended, given the short-lived nature of any employment and the 'until further notice' clause entailed in any contract. For the majority of people other than the chosen few, in the present-day flexible labour market, embracing one's work as a vocation carries enormous risks and is a recipe for psychological and emotional disaster.

Under these circumstances, exhortations to diligence and dedication sound insincere and hollow, and reasonable people would be well advised to perceive them as such – to see through the trappings of apparent vocation into the game their bosses play. Bosses do not really expect employees to believe that they mean what they say – they wish only that both sides *pretend* to believe that the game is for real, and behave accordingly. From the bosses' point of view, inducing the employees to treat the pretence of a vocational pattern to their employment seriously means storing trouble which will erupt whenever the next 'downsizing' exercise or another bout of 'rationalizing' occurs. A short-term success of moralizing sermons would in any case prove counter-productive in the long run, as it would divert people's attention from what ought to be their true vocation – their consumer pursuits.

All this complex intertwining of 'do's' and 'don'ts', of dreams and their costs, of enticements to surrender and warnings against falling into such traps, is offered to the vocation-hungry audience as a spectacle. We see great sportsmen or other stars who reach the peak of their professional skill, but climb to such heights of achievement and fame at the cost of emptying their lives of anything standing in the way of that achievement. They deny themselves all the pleasures that ordinary folk set great store by. Their achievement has all the symptoms of being real. There is hardly a less controversial and more convincing arena in which 'real quality' is tested than the athletics track or the tennis court. And who would doubt the singer's excellence reflected in the riotous delirium of packed theatres? In this public spectacle, there seems to be no room for pretence, confidence tricks, putting on an act, behind-the-scene plots. All this is for real, for everyone to see and pass judgment upon. The drama of vocation is played from the beginning to the end in the open, in front of the faithful crowds. (Or so it seems. The truth, the trustworthiness of the performance, in fact takes a lot of scripting and staging).

The saints of the stardom cult are, like all saints, to be admired and held as an example, but not emulated. They embody, at the same time, the ideal of life and its inachievability. The stars of the stadium and the stage are all inordinately rich. Obviously, their dedication and self-denial bring the fruits that work-lived-as-a-vocation is famed to gestate; recitation of the mind-boggling sums of prizes for the winners of tennis, golf, snooker or chess championships or the footballers' transfer fees are as vital a part of the cult as the recitation of miracles performed or the stories of the martyrdom suffered were in the cult of the saints of faith and piety.

What the saints of the stardom cult surrender in exchange is however as spine-chilling as the gains are awe-inspiring. One of the costs is the transience of their glory. The stars shoot onto the firmament from nowhere and to that nowhere they are bound, and in it they will vanish. No wonder it is the sportsmen and sportswomen who are arguably the best actors of the vocation's morality plays: it is in the nature of their achievement that it must be short-lived, as brief and doomed an episode as youth itself. As displayed by sportswomen and men, work-lived-as-a-vocation is self-destructive, a life towards a speedy end. Vocation may be many things, but what most emphatically it is not – not in this rendition at any rate – is a proposition for the life-project or a whole-life strategy. As displayed by the stars, vocation is, like any other experience in the life of post-modern sensation-gatherers, an *episode.*

Weber's 'Puritan saints' who lived their working lives as deeply ethical endeavours, as fulfilment of divine commandments, could not but see the work of others – any work – as essentially a matter of morality. Today's elite equally naturally tends to view all work as mainly a matter of aesthetic satisfaction. As far as the reality of life at the bottom of the social hierarchy is concerned, this conception, just like the one which preceded it, is a gross travesty. However, it allows one to believe that the voluntary 'flexibility' of the work condition freely and enthusiastically chosen by those at the top, and once chosen cherished and keenly protected, must be an unqualified blessing to everybody else, including those to whom 'flexibility' means not so much freedom of choice, autonomy and the right to self-assert, as lack of security, forced uprooting and an uncertain future.

Being Poor in a Consumer Society

In its halcyon days, in the society of producers, the work ethic reached well beyond the factory floor and the walls of poorhouses. Its precepts informed the vision of a right and proper society yet to be achieved, and until then served as the horizon by which the present moves were oriented and the present state of affairs critically assessed. The vision of the ultimate condition to be reached was that of full employment, of a society consisting solely of working people.

'Full employment' occupied the somewhat ambiguous position of being simultaneously a right and a duty. Depending on which side of the 'labour-hiring contract' the principle was invoked, either one or the other of its two modalities came to the fore; but as with all norms, both aspects had to be present to secure the overall hold of the principle. The idea of full employment as an indispensable feature of 'normal society' implied both a duty universally and willingly accepted and a commonly shared will lifted to the rank of a universal right.

Defining the norm defines also the abnormal. The work ethic encapsulated abnormality in the phenomenon of unemployment – 'abnormal' was not to work. Expectedly, the persistent presence of the poor tended to be explained alternatively by the shortage of work or the shortage of the will to work. The messages of the likes of Charles Booth or Seebohm Rowntree – that one can remain poor while *in* full employment, and therefore the phenomenon of poverty cannot be explained by the insufficient spread of the work ethic – came to the British enlightened opinion as a shock. The very notion of the '*working* poor' had all the markings of a blatant contradiction in terms, certainly as long as the universal acceptance of the work ethic figured most prominently in public thinking about social problems and continued to be seen as the cure-all for social ills.

As work gradually moved away from its central position of the meeting point between individual motives, social integration and systemic reproduction, the work ethic – as we have already noted – was slowly demoted from its function of supreme regulatory principle.

By now it had backed out or had been elbowed out from many areas of social and individual life it previously directly or obliquely regimented. The non-working section of the population remained perhaps its last retreat, or rather its last chance of survival. Blaming the misery of the poor on their unwillingness to work, and so charging them with moral depravity and presenting poverty as the penalty for sin, was the last service the work ethic performed in the new society of consumers.

For most of human history the condition of poverty has meant direct jeopardy to physical survival – the threat of death from hunger, medically unattended disease or the lack of shelter. It still means all those dangers in many parts of the globe. Even when the condition of the poor is lifted above the level of sheer survival, poverty always means malnutrition, inadequate protection against vagaries of climate, and homelessness – all defined in relation to what a given society perceives to be the proper standards of nourishment, dress and accommodation.

The phenomenon of poverty does not boil down, however, to material deprivation and bodily distress. Poverty is also a social and psychological condition: as the propriety of human existence is measured by the standards of decent life practised by any given society, inability to abide by such standards is itself a cause of distress, agony and self-mortification. Poverty means being excluded from whatever passes for a 'normal life'. It means being 'not up to the mark'. This results in a fall of self-esteem, feelings of shame or feelings of guilt. Poverty also means being cut off from the chances of whatever passes in a given society for a 'happy life', not taking 'what life has to offer'. This results in resentment and aggravation, which spill out in the form of violent acts, self-deprecation, or both.

In a consumer society, a 'normal life' is the life of consumers, preoccupied with making their choices among the panoply of publicly displayed opportunities for pleasurable sensations and lively experiences. A 'happy life' is defined by catching many opportunities and letting slip but few or none at all, by catching the opportunities most talked about and thus most desired, and catching them no later than others, and preferably before others. As in all other kinds of society, the poor of a consumer society are people with no access to a normal life, let alone to a happy one. In a consumer society however, having no access to a happy or merely a normal life means to be consumers *manquees* or flawed consumers. And so the poor of a consumer society are socially defined, and self-defined, first and foremost as blemished, defective, faulty and deficient – in other words, inadequate – consumers.

In a society of consumers, it is above all the inadequacy of the person as a consumer that leads to social degradation and 'internal exile'. It is this inadequacy, this inability to acquit oneself of the consumer's duties, that turns into bitterness at being left behind, disinherited or degraded, shut off or excluded from the social feast to which others gained entry. Overcoming that consumer inadequacy is likely to be seen as the only remedy – the sole exit from a humiliating plight.

As Peter Kelvin and Joanna E. Jarrett discovered in their pioneering study of the social-psychological effects of unemployment in a consumer society, one aspect of the situation is particularly painful to people out of work, a 'seemingly unending amount of free time' coupled with their 'inability to make use of it'. 'Much of one's day-to-day existence is unstructured', but the unemployed have no means to structure it in any way recognized as making sense, as satisfying or worthwhile:

> Feeling shut away at home is one of the most frequent complaints of the unemployed ... unemployed man not only sees himself as bored and frustrated [but] seeing himself like that (as well as actually being so) also makes him irritable. Irritability becomes a regular feature of the day-to-day existence of the unemployed man. (Kelvin and Jarrett, 1985, pp. 67–9)

From his respondents (young male and female unemployed) Stephen Hutchens got the following reports of their feelings about the kind of life they led: 'I was bored, I got depressed easily – most of the time I just sat at home and looked at the paper.' 'I have no money or not enough. I get really bored.' 'I lay in a lot, unless I go to see friends and go to pubs when we have money – not much to boast about.' Hutchens sums up his findings with this conclusion: 'Certainly the most popular word used to describe the experience of being unemployed is "boring" ... Boredom and problems with time; having "nothing to do" ...' (Hutchens, 1994, pp. 58, 122).

Boredom is one complaint the consumer world has no room for and the consumer culture set out to eradicate it. A happy life, as defined by consumer culture, is life insured against boredom, life in which constantly 'something happens', something new, exciting, and exciting because it is new. The consumer market, the consumer culture's faithful companion and indispensable complement, insures against spleen, ennui, over-saturation, melancholy, acidia, being fed up or blasé – all the ailments which once haunted the life of affluence and comfort. The consumer market makes sure that no one at any time may despair or feel disconsolate because of 'having tried it all' and having thus exhausted the pool of pleasures life had to offer.

As Freud pointed out before the onset of the consumer era, there is no such thing as the *state* of happiness; we are happy only for a brief moment when satisfying a vexing need, but immediately afterwards boredom sets in. The object of desire loses its allure once the reason to desire it has disappeared. The consumer market however proved to be more inventive than Freud was imaginative. It conjured up the state of happiness which Freud deemed unattainable. It did this by seeing to it that desires were aroused faster than the time it took to placate them, and that objects of desire were replaced quicker than the time it took to get bored and annoyed with their possession. Not being bored – ever – is the norm of the consumers' life, and a realistic norm, a target within reach, so that those who fail to hit it have only themselves to blame while being an easy target for other people's contempt and condemnation.

To alleviate boredom one needs money – a great deal of money if one wishes to stave off the spectre of boredom once for all, to reach the 'state of happiness'. Desiring comes free, but to desire realistically, and so experience desire as a pleasurable state, requires resources. Medicines against boredom are not available on NHS prescriptions. Money is the entry permit to places where remedies for boredom are pedalled (such as shopping malls, amusement parks or health and fitness centres); the places the presence in which is by itself the most effective of prophylactic potions to ward off the onset of the disease; the places whose principal destination is to keep desires seething, un-quenched and unquenchable, yet deeply pleasurable thanks to anticip-ated satisfaction.

And so boredom is the psychological corollary of other stratifying factors specific to the consumer society: freedom and amplitude of choice, freedom of mobility, ability to cancel space and structure time. Being the psychological dimension of stratification, it is the one likely to be most painfully felt and most irately objected to by those with low scores. The desperate desire to escape boredom or to mitigate it is also likely to be the main motive for their action.

The odds against their action achieving its objective are, however, enormous. Common remedies against boredom are not accessible to those in poverty, while all unusual, irregular or innovative counter-measures are bound to be classified as illegitimate and bring upon their users the punitive powers of the defenders of law and order. Paradoxically, or not that paradoxically after all, tempting fate by challenging the forces of law and order may itself turn into the poor man's favourite substitute for the affluent consumer's well-tempered anti-boredom adventures, in which the volume of desired and permissible risks are cautiously balanced.

If the constitutive trait of the poor's plight is that of being a defective consumer, there is very little that those in a deprived neighbourhood can do collectively to devise alternative ways of structuring their time, particularly in a fashion recognizable as making sense and being gratifying. The charge of laziness, always hovering dangerously close over the homestead of the unemployed, could be (and was, notably during the Great Depression of the 1930s) fought against with exaggerated, ostentatious and in the end ritualistic busyness around the house – scrubbing floors and windows, washing walls, curtains and children's skirts and trousers, tending to back gardens. There is nothing, though, that one can do to resist the stigma and shame of being an inadequate consumer, even within the ghetto of similarly deficient consumers. Keeping up to the standards of the people around you will not do, since the standards of propriety are set, and constantly raised, far away from the area under the neighbourhood watch, by daily papers and the televised glossy twenty-four-hours-a-day commercials for consumer bliss. None of the substitutes that the local neighbourhood's ingenuity could invent are likely to withstand the competition, warrant self-satisfaction and assuage the pain of glaring inferiority. The assessment of one's own adequacy as a consumer is remotely controlled and the verdict cannot be protested in the court of home-grown opinion.

As Jeremy Seabrook (1988) reminds his readers, the secret of present-day society lies in 'the development of an artificially created and subjective sense of insufficiency', since 'nothing could be more menacing' to its foundational principles 'than that the people should declare themselves satisfied with what they have'. What people do have is thus played down, denigrated, dwarfed by obtrusive and all too visible displays of extravagant consumption by the better-off: 'The rich become objects of universal adoration'.

Let us recall that the rich who were put on display as personal heroes for universal adoration used to be 'self-made men', whose lives epitomized the benign effects of the work ethic strictly and doggedly adhered to. This is no longer the case. The object of adoration now is wealth itself – wealth as the warrant for a most fanciful and prodigal lifestyle. It is what one *can* do that matters, not what is to be done or what has been done. Universally adored in the persons of the rich is their wondrous ability to pick and choose the contents of their lives – places to live, partners to live with – and to change these things at will and without effort. They never seem to reach points of no return, there seems to be no visible end to their reincarnations, their future is forever richer in content and more enticing than their past. Last but not least, the only thing that seems to matter to them is the vastness of the prospects which their wealth seems to throw open. These people seem, indeed, to be guided by the aesthetic of consumption; it is their mastery of this aesthetic, not obedience to the work ethic, not their financial success, but their connoisseurship, that lie at the heart of their greatness and their right to universal admiration.

'The poor do not inhabit a separate culture from the rich', Seabrook points out. 'They must live in the same world that has been contrived for the benefit of those with money. And their poverty is aggravated by economic growth, just as it is intensified by recession and non-growth.' It is 'aggravated by economic growth', let us add, in a double sense.

First, whatever is being referred to by the concept of 'economic growth' in its present phase, goes hand in hand with the replacement of jobs by 'flexible labour' and of job security by 'rolling contracts', fixed-term appointments and incidental hire of labour; with down-sizing, restructuring and 'rationalizing' – all boiling down to the cutting of the volume of employment. Nothing manifests the connection more spectacularly than the fact that post-Thatcher Britain, the pioneer and the most zealous defender of all such 'factors of growth' and the country widely acclaimed as the most astonishing 'economic success' of the Western world, has been found also the be the site of poverty most abject among the affluent countries of the globe. The latest *Human Development Report* from the UN (United Nations) Development Programme finds the British poor poorer than those in any other Western or Westernized country. Nearly a quarter of old people in Britain live in poverty, which is five times more than in 'economically troubled' Italy and three times more than in 'falling behind' Ireland. A fifth of British children live in poverty – twice as many as in Taiwan or Italy and six times as many as in Finland. All in all, 'the proportion of poor people in "income poverty" jumped by nearly 60 per cent under [Mrs Thatcher's] government' (Quoted in Lean and Gunnell, 1997).

Second, while the poor get poorer, the very rich – those paragons of consumer virtues – get richer still. While the poorest fifth in Britain, the country of the most recent 'economic miracle', are able to buy less than their equivalents in any other major Western country, the wealth-iest fifth are among the richest in Europe, enjoying purchasing power equal to that of the legendary rich Japanese elite. The poorer are the poor, the higher and more whimsical are the patterns of life set in front of their eyes to adore, covet and wish to emulate. And so the 'subjective sense of insufficiency' with all the pain of stigma and humiliation which accompany that feeling, is aggravated by a double pressure of decreasing living standards and increasing relative (comparative) deprivation, both reinforced rather than mitigated by economic growth in its present, deregulated, *laissez-faire* form.

The sky which is the limit of consumer dreams rises ever higher while the publicly-managed magnificent flying machines once designed to lift those low down to heaven, first run out of petrol and then are dumped in the scrapyards of 'phased-out' policies or recycled into police cars.

References

Hutchens, S. (1994) *Living a Predicament: Young People Surviving Unemployment*. Aldershot: Avebury.

Kelvin, P. and Jarrett, J. E. (1985) *Unemployment: Its Social Psychological Effects*. Cambridge: Cambridge University Press.

Lean, G. and Gunnell, B. (1997) 'UK poverty is worst in the West.' *Independent on Sunday* (15 June).

Petrella, R. (1997) 'Une machine infernale.' *Le Monde diplomatique* (June).

Seabrook, J. (1988) *The Race for Riches: The Human Cost of Wealth*. Basingstoke: Marshall Pickering.

Taylor, M. C. and Saarinen, E. (1994) *Imagologies: Media Philosophy*. London: Routledge.

Weber, M. (1976) *The Protestant Ethic and the Spirit of Capitalism*, trans. T. Parsons. London: Allen & Unwin.

Wolf, M. (1997) 'Mais pourquoi cette haine des marchés?' *Le Monde diplomatique* (June).

11

The Journey Never Ends: Zygmunt Bauman talks with Peter Beilharz

PB: Zygmunt Bauman, your work brings together many influences and stimulants... there is no single clue, but various presences. Earlier, before I met you, I thought that perhaps Simmel and Gramsci were special; now I wonder about a triad – Simmel, Gramsci, and your wife, Janina?

ZB: Before I try to answer your questions, which – I fear – will prod me to self-analyze and self-evaluate, let me warn you (and save my soul for the moment): I do not believe that authors (and this includes myself in the "authorial" role) are the best, or even particularly reliable, judges of the "developmental logic" of the work they have authored. It is damned difficult to separate oneself from one's work, to stand aside, to watch it disinterestedly and describe objectively. Authors never know whether the written traces of their thoughts match the original intentions, and they cannot be sure that the intentions, even if our notoriously selective memory managed to retain them in their original shape, would seem plausible to the readers of the text (and also to the author as the reader of the text). Thoughts, once they have frozen into a text and acquired a communicable form, seem often "to have thought themselves," to wander on their own ways rather than being guided by hand to a destination which the author had selected and charted before the journey started. In a nutshell: your story or interpretation is as good (if not better) than mine. Do not confuse "the *authorial*" with "the *authoritative*," treat the authorial story as it should be treated: as one more interpretation waiting to be interpreted – and also critically scrutinized and challenged...

Having said that and cleared my conscience, I should admit that the results of your detective work sound to me convincing. Yes – Gramsci, Simmel, and Janina; Gramsci told me *what*, Simmel *how*, and Janina *what for*. Gramsci immunized me once and for all against brain-paralyzing baccilli of systems, structures, functions, billiard-ball models of the agent and mirror models of the subject's mind, determined past and preordained future. Simmel took away (seldom are expropriations such a blessing) the

youthful hope/cheek that once the "surface" incongruities and contradictions are out of the way, I'll find "down there" the clockwork running
exactly to the second; he also taught me that for the pencil of every
tendency there is an eraser of another, and that to wish to dismantle that
ambivalence in order to see better how society works is like wishing to
take the walls apart to see better what supports the ceiling (my thanks to
Harold Garfinkel for this allegory). And from Janina I learned that *Wertfreiheit* is – as human silences are concerned – not just a pipe-dream, but
also an utterly inhuman delusion; that sociologizing makes sense only in as
far as it helps humanity in life, that in the ultimate account it is the human
choices that make all the difference between lives human and inhuman,
and that society is an ingenious contraption to narrow down, perhaps
eliminate altogether, those choices.

But since you asked about "influences" and "stimulants," I feel obliged
also to expand on your list of names. The "big triad" helped me to find
answers to the big existential questions of what, how, and what for – but
there were quite a few others who supplied me with working out and
reworking my agenda of "topical relevances" and with analytical tools
which I find myself using over and over again. For instance, Mary Douglas' *Purity and Danger* – her idea of the interplay of construction and
destruction, of order as a cleaning-up operation, of ambivalence as the
enemy of order (supplemented by Fredrik Barth's point about the boundary being prior to differences); or Michel Crozier's *Bureaucratic Phenomenon*, with its eye-opening insight that the game of dominance is first and
foremost the game of uncertainties and determination; or Claude Lévi-
Strauss, with his essential discovery that there is no structure but the
endless process of structuration, that culture is essentially about making
differences and coping with the incongruences that follow that
effort...The list is long; I am heavily in debt. To run the whole list
would be futile, while to pretend that it has been exhausted would be
duplicitous or naive – but before leaving the subject at least two more
names must be evoked: Adorno, with his vision of the incurably Janus-
faced Enlightenment and (alas, my quite recent discovery) Castoriadis,
with his insistence on the link between autonomy of the individual and the
autonomy of society being, for better or worse, inextricable.

PB: More on the influences. Marx is obvious – can't live with him, can't
live without him – but do I sense that somehow you perhaps blame him, in
part, for modernism? Is there a deeper affinity in your thinking with the
romantic critique of civilization, Tönnies' anxiety over *Gemeinschaft*,
Rousseau's hostility towards civilization over culture, Spengler even? Is
modernity more loss than gain?

ZB: Again you are on target: "can't live with him nor without him." And
how could I – Marx being the point of my own, personal encounter
between history and biography...I could not blame Marx for modernity
any more than I could blame the kingfisher for winter frosts or praise the

swallow for the spring sunshine. And I do not take exception to Marx's modernism – far from it. It was, if anything, the sign of his genius to see (in the 1840s!) through the consequences of impending modernity and to adumbrate the imminence, the irreversibility, of its arrival. Yes, when it came to modernity Marx took the stance that "whatever you do could be done better," and thought not that something else altogether could be done instead: yes, Marx conceived of the "good society" as an alternative to capitalist modernity, not to modernity as such. But was it Marx's fault not to be able to see beyond modernity – or rather to see the "beyond" in the likeness of the immediate future, as its somewhat "new and improved" version, sort of "modernity Mark II"? Should we accuse that prophet of not being prophetic enough? Or for not knowing what we know?

With all that, Marx's perception of history was infinitely superior to the "perhaps we would rather not have this happening" stance of Rousseau or the "how awful that this has happened" complaint of Tönnies. New forms of life are bound to come complete with their own banes which make it easy to forget and forgive the plagues of yore. Marx was quite resolute about old diseases being poor medicine for new ailments – the truth which eluded Rousseau and Tönnies as much as it eludes the present-day communitarians. Marx was ahead of his time (and in a way ahead of our own) in accepting that the sins and vices of modernity are to be met, so to speak, on their own ground, with the help of human creativity and inventiveness rather than human memory; that the faults of modernity were to be fought with modern means, and that visualizing a healthier future must start from inventory of present pathologies: *Hic Rhodos, hic salta*. How fresh and topical is Marx's reluctance to throw out the baby together with the bathwater: individual autonomy and self-assertion is a gain, not a loss – and what one needs to do is to prevent modernity from rendering it, so often and for so many, all but impossible to practice and enjoy. Any *Gemeinschaften* of the future can be only built communities, and built on that foundation. I would not speak for "our" critique of civilization; as far as my critique is concerned, it does start from the assumption with which Marx admonished it to begin.

PB: We know little about your Polish pre-history; was there something special that you learned from Hochfeld and Ossowski? We can feel the presence of Leeds in *Memories of Class*; what of the influence of London, the LSE? And the reopening of Polish borders after 1989?

ZB: You've got me here...Now you not only want me to name my teachers, but also to disentangle the influence of each from all the others – while the ingredients each one of them supplied were precious precisely for their mutual fit, for allowing themselves to be blended. I'll try to oblige, but doubt the result.

Hochfeld and Ossowski were very different persons – politically, temperamentally, in terms of past history and their current "networking"; there was little love lost between them, on some occasions they were downright hostile towards each other and on most occasions mutually wary and non-cooperative. And yet I perceived and ingested their messages as convergent rather than contradictory. What I learned from them sedimented in the course of time as one harmonious and indivisible legacy...

They both kept me from falling into the trap of the all-quantifying, all-measuring, all-calculating kind of sociology then dominant in the United States and spreading like forest fire all over Europe. They effectively vaccinated me against the inanities of Parsons-style grand theorizing – at the time the most fashionable and snobbish game in town, and they convinced me once and for all that whatever else the "science of society" might do, it ought to be conducted for the benefit of society and not for the applause and self-aggrandizement of other "scientists of society"; that it stands or falls by being, or not conducted with this precept in mind. What I owe to Hochfeld and Ossowski together is not so much this or that element of substantive knowledge as the understanding of what it means to be a sociologist. To me, they were masters. Not many of suchlikes are left in the degree-factories of our time.

London? LSE? This was, first and foremost, the astonishing library – unlike anything I knew before (my first library with the direct access to the shelves; not just bigger than any collections I had hitherto encountered, but an entirely new mode of sociating with books) – and Robert Mac-Kenzie, my mentor when working on *Between Class and Elite*. Bob showed me politics as I'd never seen it in the books; each week, he brought to the seminar another "practising politician" for (always respectful yet always merciless) teasing, molesting, and henpecking. I do not remember learning very much about their policies – but I do vividly remember the shock of seeing and watching the actors behind the actions, politics brought down to earth, history sliced into biographies, grandiose conflicts shortchanged into school-tie loyalties and animosities, global visions dissolved into sometimes noble but most often petty personal ambitions. I suppose I was never bothered thereafter with the "problem" of macro-vs. micro-sociology: I knew from then on that the gap to be bridged was but in the eye of beholder...

PB: Marx shadows your work, perhaps especially the spirit of the young Marx. Weber's presence is more opaque, closer to American Sociology than Critical Theory. Could you tell us about your Weber?

ZB: I leave aside Max Weber wearing Levis and speaking American, but were Hegel to muse on the habits of Minerva's owl a century later than he did, he would probably take the German-speaking Weber for the epitome of the World Spirit in action and the owl's latest incarnation. Weber described the "historical tendency" of modernity just when it was about to run its course. I often come back to his sociology of religion – and each time I find it impressively learned yet unpleasantly misled and misleading since formed to answer the by now anachonistically sounding queries organized around the names *Wirtschaft und Gesellschaft* – and each time I find it more dated, describing a reality in many crucial points opposite to ours. In this respect, the difference between Simmel and Weber grows deeper by the year: the first is still our contemporary, the second more and more a venerable ancestor: you hang his picture on the wall, but you would not necessarily count on learning from him much in the way of the skills of the trade or expect him to illuminate the problems you are struggling with today. It seems to me sometimes that most interest in Weber is nowadays displayed by people not particularly eager to come to grips with contemporary society, or seeking a secure island in the turbulent sea of untested and contested authorities; I sense in these "time trips" moves akin to Plato's dream of the Great Escape – from the cave and particularly from the cave-dwellers . . .

I have to admit that I have soft spot for Weber's *Protestant Ethic*. It is a beautiful story, an excitingly told fairy tale, an ingeniously composed etiological myth – and an exquisitely effective pep-talk at the same time. And it is fraught with remarkable insights and fertile images of wider application – like that of the processes developing their own momentum and needing the ideas which guided them where they are now, no more than the satellites need the rockets which put them in the orbit. But after Elias, Foucault (and Muchembled's corrections) it hardly looks as an account of *wie es ist eigentlich gewesen*, and more like the similarly beautiful and similarly fantastic Freud's story of Moses' murder or René Girard's story of the birth of human community.

PB: *Legislators and Interpreters* is a kind of turning point in your work, into the postmodern. How would you explain that and the significance therein of Foucault and more marginally – more significantly? – Rorty?

ZB: Difficult to say now . . . Self-scrutiny, the need to examine and understand the kind of work in which we all, the professional "story tellers" of human predicament, knowingly or unknowingly participate, was I guess the legacy of Hochfeld and Ossowski which I carry with me permanently – I find myself rethinking the matter virtually in every study. *Legislators and Interpreters* was an attempt to attack the issue point-blank, with a (naive) hope to settle it once for all and for my own lasting satisfaction; what I hoped particularly to achieve was to unwrap the "double bind" (power, and "people" or "masses") in which the convoluted history of the intellectuals has been entangled from the beginning, and to spell out the sociological sense of Weber's *Wertfreiheit* and Mannheim's "scientific politics." Reading Foucault and Rorty was obviously the indispensable precondition of the whole enterprise. But if I remember correctly my own train of thoughts at the time, the decline of the legislating role and ambitions came to me during the inquiry as a discovery – and an afterthought. At least the title of the book and its subtitle, together with the concept of "postmodernity," occurred to me at a fairly late stage of the writing . . .

PB: Is the postmodern, like socialism, then, just a phase?

ZB: I was uneasy with the common uses of the "postmodern" idea. I tried hard – I admit, with no more than mixed success – to keep a distance from the pronouncements of the "end of modernity," and tried even harder to manifest exception to the celebratory mood of the preachers and enthu- siasts of the "postmodern bliss." I thought and wrote of the "postmodern" as of a new perspective, a sort of "Archimedean point of support" which one may use to turn modernity around and bring into vision what otherwise would remain unseen; it was not for me a historical or systemic concept, but a shorthand from the "external observation point" which the available interpretations of modernity sorely lacked, but now made fea- sible by the changed social location, and the changing practice, of the intellectuals. As you remember, I defined postmodernity as "modernity minus its illusions" – modernity coming to terms with its own un-fulfil- ment and un-fulfillability. I used the term "postmodernity" primarily to connote that "second disenchantment."

To make that use more transparent, I should have perhaps added to that definition from the beginning that modernization is not a road leading to modernity, but modernity's mode of being; that modernity is the state of incessant, compulsive and obsessive, modernization (and so of per- petual creative destruction, production of ambivalence and ordering urge, dissipation of structures, and structuring addiction) – and "postmo- dernity" is a condition under which we come to understand that and modify our life-strategies accordingly. I should have said that the idea of the "unfinished project of modernity" is a pleonasm, since modernity can only be a project, and an unfinished one to be sure.

At the time we talk, I feel more and more inclined to opt out from the "postmodern discourse," to cut myself off from any further association with the "end of modernity" idea. I am not enthused either with the concept of "late modernity" (how do we know it is "late"?) or "reflexive modernity" (was not modernity "reflexive" from the start? How do we know it is more reflexive now than in Comte's or Marx's times? Are we indeed more, or just differently, knowledgeable in conducting our life business than our grand- fathers used to be? And is that knowledge which we have now the carrier of more power – and above all of more autonomy?) At the moment, I am inclined to describe our kind of social condition as "light," and better still "liquid," or "liquefied" modernity – as distinct from "heavy," and better still "hard" and "solid" modernity of yore: ours is not the "constructed," administered and managed, but a diffuse, all-permeating, all-penetrating, all-saturating kind of modernity. Deregulation, privatization of all func- tions meant to be performed collectively, order without management cen- tre, power without office and fixed address – in other words, modernity is melted and spilled all over the place while its institutional warehouses are "phased out." Or perhaps it would be more telling to speak of the "soft- ware" modernity replacing the "hardware" version. We are, as before, making our ways through a maze, but our labyrinth is not cut in rock or molded of concrete, but cast out of electronically conducted information.

These are all preliminary insights; it will take time to think them through, and no less time to see through the consequences.

PB: There is a common sense that Levinas, maybe Derrida, are central thinkers for you, especially after *Postmodern Ethics*. I wonder here about the romantic shadow of Heidegger's critique of modernity, across the critique of technology to the ethic of care.

ZB: I do not believe modernity will go away once wished away; I respect philosophers and sympathize with their concern with how things are, but do not believe that they will put things right once they put their thoughts in order. This is why I entertain little hope that the answers to my questions could be found in neo-romantic nostalgia, or for that matter in Heidegger (whatever else I think of his brand of *Sein* philosophy and historiosophy – and I am far from being enthusiastic about either; I do not believe the Freiburg episode to be a mishap, an accidental stumbling – I do believe that the stone on which the Herr Rektor stumbled was his own *Weltanschauung*).

Derrida? I welcomed his courage to call undecidable undecidable; I also embraced wholeheartedly his message that the foremost achievement of interpretation is keeping the job of interpretation going. There are other precious gems in his work conceived under the sign of challenge. But most of that work is too ethereal for my purpose, too remote from my concerns. Derrida helped me greatly to comprehend the capacity and the limitations of my – our – tools. But after all, we need the tools to do a job – and by profession and temperament I am job-oriented. The job of the sociologist is to interpret the experience of human condition. I owe thanks to Derrida for telling me what to be aware and wary of when doing that job. The job itself remains to be done.

Levinas (and Løgstrup; in my mind the two great ethical inspirations merged into one) is a different – substantive rather than methodological – case. I was desperately seeking a way of positing ethical issues, and more generally the ways of talking about morality, after coming to the conclusion that uncertainty, undecidability, ambivalence are here to stay; after all, most (all?) ethical philosophy, as you know, was conducted on the twin assumptions that all these aspects of the world are the bane of the moral being – yet, fortunately, they are but dragons shortly to be strangled by the joint efforts of the philosophers and the law-givers. Can one reject these assumptions and still go on speaking seriously about morality as well as keep that other dragon – of moral nihilism – in its securely locked cage? I think I found the positive answer which I sought and which I hoped could be found in Levinas and Løgstrup. What I learned from them is that far from being a hostile territory or killing field, uncertainty and ambivalence are the natural home-ground of the moral being and may even turn into the hotbed of morality. If you look at it this way, then I think the suspicion of affinity with Heidegger's pique against modernity, technology and all the rest would not arise, all similarity would appear accidental. . . .

PB: *Modernity and the Holocaust* is often imagined as nothing more than a refusal of technology. I see in that book a historical pessimism coupled with an anthropological optimism. Is that any way to characterize your stance in general?

ZB: In my view (this is, though, but my view...) neither is quite the case, though your interpretation seems to me infinitely more plausible than the one you describe as "often imagined." My intention was to understand (explain?) modernity, not the Holocaust. And once lit by the Auschwitz pyres, it was the "gardening state," not technology, which emerged as the "villain of the piece." That one cannot build crematoria without having first created modern industry; this was a commonplace when I wrote *Modernity and the Holocaust.* What was much less obvious and hardly trivial was the awareness that it was the dream of ultimate purity and ultimate order, together with the confidence that "we can do it," which led from the tractor or fertilizer plants to the *Umsiedlung, Konzlager,* and *Endlösung* – but before that to the blueprint of weed-and pest-free societal garden.

I gather that pessimism and optimism here were mixed. Though perhaps in different proportions, in the presented view of history and the "hidden anthropology." After all, it is but through history that what is, anthropologically, a gruesome potential, is made real; and it is up to history to bring out what is, anthropologically, a hope, and sometimes a sporting chance... Am I a historical pessimist? True, history is a graveyard of missed chances and a chronicle of wrong turns, but history is also the sole location where chances can be taken up and right turns made. Trust in progress was but one, historically begotten and historically confined, form of historical optimism, and not the one to be mourned – as it was, in turns, mistaken, perilous or closing-the-eyes-that-should-have-been-kept open.

PB: After all this, at the end of modernism's century, is sociology still worth defending?

ZB: Sociology is more worthy than ever. Though, frankly, I do not think it needs much defending. Hardly ever was the "social demand" for sociology as strong as these days, when the world we live in gets simultaneously more imperious and more impervious by the moment.

Sociology was conceived in the gap between what is seen within the horizons drawn by life-business and what is relevant to the conduct of life-business – and ever since its task was to bridge the gap, to make the relevant visible and what is looked at relevant (whether that task was fulfilled in all times and by all varieties of sociology, however, is a different matter). That task is unlikely to age, let alone become obsolete. Quite the contrary. If our life-business is posited as the individual's duty and responsibility, if panopticons are demolished and replaced with DIY drills, then the scrutiny of the relevant becomes an indispensable ingredient of individual know-how: as the autonomy, self-assertion and freedom of the human agent is concerned, such scrutiny becomes, literally, a matter of life and death. This situation assigns to the work of sociology an importance it hardly ever possessed (though always claimed).

Sociology always promised to serve the "common people," but for a long time, through the era of "hardware" modernity and panoptical power, it served them mostly "by proxy" – not so much by offering enlightenment as by helping to construct a world in which enlightenment would become redundant. Now there is a chance to come down to the real job of sociological enlightenment: to draw out of darkness the hidden parameters of the human condition, to chart the convoluted networks of human dependencies, to take a stand in the ongoing battle between autonomy and heteronomy, to demystify and de-demonize the difference, the variety, the ambivalence – in short, to help men and women of our times to make use of the freedom they have and to acquire the freedom they are told they have but have not.

Mapping the network of dependencies may contribute to yet another, no less imperative task: that of bringing the solidarity of fate into the open and so helping to reforge it into solidarity of action; bringing back from exile concerns with the common good and reminding that no one can be autonomous in a heteronomous society.

Well, all this is but a chance (I would say a "historical" chance, if not for the fear of sounding pompous...). Like all chances, it can be taken up or missed. If it is missed, sociologists will have no one but themselves to blame for letting people down, as they did already a few times in the past.

PB: You view American sociology as a more parlous problem than the British case; is it the continental aspect which explains the difference? Is Americanism the central problem here? Are we best to understand globalization as Americanization?

ZB: America is a great country, and generalizing about it is a risky business. In social thought, it gave birth to quite a few powerful, truly prophetic minds and works of a genuinely milestone or watershed stature. Social thought would be so much poorer if not for Thorstein Veblen, Lewis Mumford or C. Wright Mills. Personally, I learned a great deal from Peter Berger, Erving Goffman, Harold Garfinkel, and Daniel Bell; Richard Sennett is one of very few contemporary authors who has something truly original and genuinely important to say in each successive book.

My sad and sorry observations referred to the mainstream, vernacular, run of the mill American sociology, which fell, so to speak, upon bad luck: it fell victim to its own initial success. Born at the turn of the century out of the worries of ethically sensitive social reformers appalled with human depravation and destitution in fast sprawling Mid-West conurbations, it acquired that pragmatic "we must do something" and "we can do it" bent, which in later years endeared it to the rising welfare and warfare bureaucracies. The "social reform" dimension was quickly lost or abandoned – and the sole dowry the partners in marriage were eager to accept and wished to be invested for profits was the promise of the sociologists to supply the recipes on how to bridle the unbridled and manage the un-manageable – how to "resolve conflicts," "manage human resources" in all together to "get things done." The promise, as could be expected, has proved to be much in excess of the sociologists' ability to deliver, and their self-confidence unwarranted. On the other hand, the once up-and-coming and boisterous welfare and warfare bureaucracies also lost much of their confidence and in recent decades the demand for the kind of service which mainstream American sociology trained itself to supply (or at least to be seen or hoped to supply) has shrunk and is in danger of expiring comple-tely, together with the supply of funds which the conduct of that sort of "managerial sociology" or "sociology for managers" required in such huge quantities. Hence the current crisis of purpose, the feeling of losing touch with the "public agenda." I think, though, that in the long run that crisis will prove salutary. The liability of false expectations out of the way, American sociology could perhaps rediscover the arts which its main-stream practitioners, unlike its outstanding, yet marginal personalities, have forgotten or never had the chance to learn but which give meaning to the sociological vocation.

PB: You have said to me that there are only two significant coordinates in your work – the twin themes of culture and socialism. How would you like your project to be remembered?

ZB: Yes, I said that then and repeat it now, though perhaps the laconic formula needs some elaboration. "Culture" stands for the "human made" nature of the human world; for the conviction that this world is made by the selfsame humans who are made by it, even if they imagine that world to have been put together and run by superhuman beings, laws of nature or history, heroes or saints. And what is made by humans can be also undone or redone by humans... While "socialism" stands for the realiza-tion that this "world-making" capacity tends to be very unevenly endowed, that some are more "makers" than "made," while the many others are most of the time "made" and very seldom "making" – and that this state of affairs is unjust and crying for rectification. Culture and socialism, in as far as they inform my thinking, are therefore better seen as two threads twisted into a compact line (and once intertwined, insepar-able), rather than as "co-ordinates" of theory.

I would like to think that the stubborn presence of "culture" and "soci-alism" thus understood in my "cognitive frame" and in whatever I sit down to write about, is caused by certain "ethical activism": our task, the task of social thinkers and students of human affairs, is to cry at the wolves, not to run with them. Our purpose is to count human costs, alert others to them, arouse consciences to resist them, to think of alternatives, less costly, other ways of living together. And perhaps by escaping some sort of "ethical absolutism": hardly any bliss is worth being paid for in the currency of human suffering. Neither is it true that the end justifies the means, nor that making people suffer is the means to the goal of happiness.

How I expect my "project" to be remembered? As pursued by someone who hoped against hope. But then hoping against hope is a feeble reason to be remembered. And so I do not expect much.

PB: Should we take the author's word for this? How would you like your work to be changed and interpreted?

ZB: You may, but then you may not. I would wish to assure you that the hope to be remembered is the least important (certainly the least productive) among my hopes, and the concern to make myself memorable is the least important and (certainly the most counterproductive) among my concerns – but then we all tend to suspect people who say such things as capable of duplicity or at best of self-deception; who am I to claim that I am an exception? Besides, one of the best-selling authors has complained that the shelf life of books is nowadays somewhere between milk and yoghurt. If this is so, then what one should be concerned with is that what we put on the shelves is consumed before the "use by" date. And that – I would add – the content proves nourishing when ingested, and that it would not burn a hole in the pockets of those who need the nourishment most.

PB: Thank you; we will remember you.

Leeds, UK and Melbourne, Australia

February–March 1999

Index